Virginia Woolf and the "Lust of Creation"

Virginia Woolf and the "Lust of Creation"
A Psychoanalytic Exploration

Shirley Panken

State University of New York Press

We acknowledge excerpts from the following sources: MRS. DALLOWAY, TO THE LIGHTHOUSE, THE WAVES, BETWEEN THE ACTS, THE LETTERS OF VIRGINIA WOOLF, Volumes 1, 3, and 6, MOMENTS OF BEING, and THE DIARIES OF VIRGINIA WOOLF, Volumes 2, 3, and 5, copyright 1925, 1927, 1931, 1941 by Harcourt Brace Jovanovich, Inc.; renewed 1943, 1955, 1959, 1969 by Leonard Woolf; copyright © 1975, 1976, 1977, 1980, 1984 by Quentin Bell and Angelica Garnett. Reprinted by permission of the publisher.

Published by
State University of New York Press, Albany

© 1987   State University of New York

For information, address State University of New York
Press, State University Plaza, Albany, N.Y., 12246

Library of Congress Cataloging in Publication Data

Panken, Shirley.
    Virginia Woolf and the "Lust of creation".

    Bibliography: p.
    Includes index.
    1. Woolf, Virginia, 1882-1941--Biography--Psychology.
2. Woolf, Virginia, 1882–1941--Criticism and
interpretation.   3. Psychoanalysis and literature.
4. Novelists, English--20th century--Biography.
I. Title.
PR6045.072Z854   1987   823'.912   [B]   86-29991
ISBN 0-88706-200-8
ISBN 0-88706-201-6 (pbk.)

10 9 8 7 6 5 4 3 2 1

For Irving and Ted

Contents

Acknowledgements

Writing about Virginia Woolf has been an enormously absorbing and rewarding project, as well as a great deal of fun, bringing me in touch with others who have had a keen interest in Woolf and have been extending of themselves in evaluating my manuscript.

I am greatly indebted to Professor Mitchell Leaska who encouraged my manuscript from its inception. I found his literary penetration and awareness of the psychological nuances in Virginia Woolf's novels incisive and profound. Reading portions of my early manuscript, the suggestions of Professor Virginia Hyman were also immensely helpful, at times leading to new terrain.

I am grateful to Professor Barbara Quart, to Doctors Joyce Mac-Dougall, Helen Hellman, Benjamin Brody and Murray Sherman, to Leila Lerner and Mollie Parkes for their valuable comments regarding early portions or versions of my manuscript. Special thanks to Dr. Anna Burton for her thoroughgoing critique of initial chapters; and to Dr. Bernard Meyer and his interdisciplinary group for hearing me out.

To Leila Lerner, Anita Feldman, Suzanne Hoover, Charlotte Sheedy, Helen Hillman and Shernaz Mollinger for their constructive feedback and critical astuteness regarding my later work, my gratitude.

My thanks to Lola Szladits, Curator, and to Donald Anderle, Associate Director for Special Collections, both of the Henry W. and Albert A. Berg Collection; the New York Public Library, Astor, Lenox, and Tilden Foundations for their help in providing access to the unpublished manuscripts, diaries, letters and other, unpublished source material regarding Virginia Woolf.

For her kindness and hospitality as well as the permission granted to quote from unpublished letters in connection with Virginia Woolf at the University of Sussex Library, I want to thank Mrs. E. Inglis, Assistant Librarian in the Manuscripts Section. For permission to quote from Dr. Octavia Wilberforce's letters I am also grateful to The Honorable Mrs. Mabel Smith, Trustee of Backsettown.

To Quentin Bell who has permitted quotations from Virginia Woolf's unpublished writings, I am enormously indebted. This extends to his authoritative biography, his generosity, and his willingness to discourse with me about yet another book concerning Virginia Woolf during my visit to Sussex in 1983.

Finally, my thanks to Dr. Michael Hall, Modern Archivist at King's College, Cambridge; to Mr. John Lehmann, so giving of his time during an interview with him in London during 1983; and to Harcourt Brace Jovanovich, American publisher of the works of Virginia and Leonard Woolf for permission to quote from their published writings.

I   Introduction

Invited to be a discussant of Virginia Woolf's[1] autobiographical essay, *A Sketch of the Past*,[2] this as part of an interdisiplinary conference on psychoanalysis and literature in 1980,[3] I declined. I simply had not read Virginia Woolf, though her novels, essays, and *Writer's Diary* (ed. L. Woolf, 1953) were in my book collection.

I might, with reference to my previous study concerning the genesis of masochism, have discoursed on writers of the romantic period, whose life and art seemed replete with theme and metaphor of early loss or abandonment, the connection of food with love, the suggestion that love is frequently prelude to death.

Asking Virginia Hyman, a friend and literature professor who had written about Woolf's relationship with her father, to take over for me at the conference, I thereafter experienced what is known in experimental psychology as the "Zeigarnik effect," the persistence in memory, of interrupted or incompleted tasks, which haunt one, require closure.

I now read all things Woolfian: her memoirs, novels, essays, letters, diaries, and unpublished writings, as well as biographical and critical studies; related writings on or by Leonard Woolf, Leslie Stephen, Vanessa Bell, the Bloomsbury circle, and Victorian period; relevant correspondence of family and friends.

Intrigued with the critical comments on *To The Lighthouse*, the autobiographical novel Woolf hoped would modulate her obsessive preoccupation with her parents, I wrote "Working Through and the Novel," in one sense an attempt to take a new look at the archetypal Mrs. Ramsay based on Woolf's mother, inasmuch as literary and psychoanalytic critics predominantly apotheosized the fictional mother, while some viewed her as destructive. Not believing in the sheer relativity of all reactions to a text, I felt critics for the most part displayed a transferential response to this mythical mother-image, whom the author intrinsically depicted as both Machiavellian and heroic.

Discovering the work of Professor Mitchell Leaska, Woolfian scholar, teacher, and critic who had written several interpretive texts concerning Woolf's novels and offered a subtle, multi-levelled approach to her fictional characters, I attended some of his graduate literature classes at New York University.

Turning to Woolf's life, I hoped to correct the distortions concerning her "madness," its presumed link with her creativity and to demystify the aura surrounding her emotional oscillations, the belief that "deep down in her mind she was never completely sane" (3LW79).[4] My rescue needs devolved, of course, from my psychoanalytic orientation, interest in healing, aversive feelings concerning labels that are punitive, stigmatizing and assume a life of their own, in addition to my need to respond to what I discerned as Woolf's cry for help. I hoped to challenge the "official" theory that Woolf's suicide attempt after marriage, and her suicide, were engendered by anxieties concerning completion or revision of her novel.

Contrary to Leonard Woolf's notion that completing a novel inevitably led to "madness," Virginia Woolf's reactions at such junctures were multi-layered, evidencing fear of imperfectibility and exposure, postpartum problems in relinquishing an emotionally invested, self-created world, the possibily disequilibrating effects of family reminiscences.

Virginia Woolf did not evidence noticeable agitation, breakdown or suicidal ideation on completion of a good many of her novels.[5] Illness or depression that might accompany the act of writing, at any phase, were complex in motivation, involved with enmeshments of self in context of her personal relationships at a particular time. More likely than the equation of despair and suicide with finishing a book, Woolf frequently experienced a considerable sense of fertility, that "extraordinary exhilaration, that ardor and lust of creation" (D3, Feb.28'27).[6]

Probably with negative effect, Leonard held back Virginia's first novel, *The Voyage Out*, completed in 1913, until 1915, for fear publication would exacerbate her "illness". In the interim, two of Leonard's novels, *The Village in the Jungle* (1913) and *The Wise Virgins* (1914), appeared. Virginia's novel had already received an affirmative response from Edward Garnett, a reputable literary figure and reader for Gerald Duckworth, Woolf's publisher who told her of its acceptance on April 12, 1913.

Virginia's emotional difficulties in 1913, her sleeplessness, headaches and reluctance to eat, were linked to problems in consolidating her marriage, to disillusionment, frustration, and dissociated rage in feeling forced to abandon her wish to have children. In addition, her symptoms were linked to her characterological depression and its extremities.

Leonard's thinking the fabric of thought separating Virginia's "genius and madness" was "terrifyingly thin" (3LW31), is further devaluation or misunderstanding of her creative process. In illustration he cites her description of writing the final passages of *The Waves*:

> I must record the end of *The Waves*. I wrote the words O Death fifteen
> minutes ago having reeled across the last ten pages with some moments
> of such intensity and intoxication I seemed only to stumble after my
> own voice, or almost, after some sort of speaker (as when I was mad). I
> was almost afraid, remembering the voices that used to fly ahead.

Alluding here to Virginia's diary entry of February 7, 1931, to her lyrical
descriptions that "left the ground," Leonard suggests she has in this
passage lost touch with reality. Virginia continues:

> What interests me in the last stage was the freedom and boldness with
> which my imagination picked up, used and tossed aside all the images
> and symbols which I had prepared. I am sure that this is the right way of
> using them—not in set pieces, as I had tried at first, coherently but
> simply as images; never making them work out; only suggest. Thus, I
> hope to have kept the sound of the sea and the birds, dawn and garden.

In its logic and depicted complexity of intention, this is hardly an illustration of unreality.

Through the creative process of the painter, Lily Briscoe, in *To the
Lighthouse*, Virginia further clarifies the "voices that fly ahead":

> Standing transfixed by the pear tree, impressions poured in upon her.
> To follow her thought was like following a voice which speaks too
> quickly to be taken down by pencil. The voice was her own voice, saying
> without prompting, undeniable, everlasting, contradictory things, so
> that even the fissures and humps on the bark were irrevocably fixed
> there for eternity (*TTL*, 40).

Obviously, Virginia in describing Lily's "voice which speaks too
quickly" is pointing to the artist's openness to a multitude of impinging
stimuli, the associations, memories, thoughts, feelings, hunches, images,
and words inundating her, occasionally irreconcilable, the processing
phase to follow.

The notion that creativity is linked to insanity is unfortunately but-
tressed in psychoanalytic parlance by the stated closeness of both modalities to the infantile, primitive, pre-verbal strata of the mind, referred to
as "primary" process, ostensibly most accessible to psychotic and artist.[7]
Quintessentially defining the artist, however, is the power to nuance his
or her emotions in the work, to make shape out of his or her personal
maelstrom, not true for the psychotic.[8]

In Leonard's belief that Virginia could "go mad at any moment," he
was, of course, affected by the Stephen family's scapegoating: "Oh, you

know very well the goat's mad." He was also influenced by the psychiatric lore of the time, which was unsophisticated, organically based, and powerfully entrenched. Prevailing in the late nineteenth century, persisting throughout the early part of the next century, mental illness was considered a disease of the brain or, with punitive overtones, perceived as "moral insanity."

Psychoanalysis was available in London and Dr. Ernest Jones, a leading member and founder of the London Psychoanalytic Society, practiced there from 1913. Actually Leonard had written a review of Freud's *Psychopathology of Everyday Life* in the *New English Weekly* during 1914, but continued to behave as though deeper knowledge of nervous and mental illness was minimal.

No doubt, Leonard's responsibilities regarding his wife were monumental, often insoluble, and the threat of her physical illnesses, depression, or suicide could assume retaliative, blackmailing proportions. Though Virginia's symptoms can be considered unconscious manipulation via illness, her self-destructive, masochistic orientation appears to far outweigh in suffering whatever gains were present. In discussing Leonard's interactions with his wife, the intention is not one of accusation, but one of depicting the vicissitudes between the "well" one and the "sick" one. As her caretaker, he was after all, following in the footsteps of his predecessors, Vanessa Bell and Leslie Stephen.

Originally termed neurasthenia, Virginia's Woolf's physical ailments, headaches, and exhaustion are considered "psychosomatic" in current psychiatric parlance because of their unconscious, emotional core. Reflecting an era that regarded symptoms of mental illness as mysterious and inexplicable, physiological in origin, neurasthenia was attributed to "debility" or "irritability" of the nervous system. That is, as the supply of nutriment in the nerve cells became depleted, the cells presumably lost their natural charge. In this framework, Weir Mitchell, an American psychiatrist, evolved his rest treatment to cure neurasthenia or "anemia" of the brain and hoped to stabilize the "irregular brain cells" (Chrzanowski, 142).

Dispensed to the upper classes since the 1870s, especially to women, the Weir Mitchell cure, with its emphasis on isolation,[9] bedrest in a darkened room, and deliberate overfeeding, diminished with the introduction of suggestive therapies and psychotherapy. However, Woolf herself clung to it. Dr. Maurice Craig, Woolf's "mental specialist" from 1913 until his death in 1935, adhered to no definable theoretical framework but essentially believed in "right thinking", "right doing", prescribing veronal and adjusting the individual to society (Trombley, 201, 206).

Critical of institutional psychiatrists such as Dr. Craig, Dr. Jones indicated their private practices were largely limited to signing officially required certificates, ensconcing their patients in costly rest homes, occasionally visiting them. In Dr. Jones's opinion, Dr. Savage, Woolf's family physician until 1913, as well as his successor Dr. Craig, were unsophisticated in their awareness of psychiatry (Jones, 1920, 123).

Woolf never acknowledged the possibility that her neurasthenia masked emotional disturbances. Psychoanalysis she shunned because it might blunt her creativity. Physical illness she frequently welcomed, the opportunity afforded for rumination and suspension of the everyday. She extolled the "childish outspokenness in illness," where "things are said, truths blurted out, which the cautious respectability of health, conceals. . . . There is a virgin forest in each. We go alone and like it better so . . . ."[10] Here, Woolf seems to be saying her psychosomatic ailments allow her the privacy or distance necessary to think or to express her feelings more bluntly, to be more uniquely herself, avoiding conventionalization. Illness also evoked the ministrations of others.

Though Woolf claimed to have read the complete works of Freud only as late as 1939, she was, of course, conversant with psychoanalysis because Hogarth Press, which she and Leonard embarked on in 1917, published Freud beginning in 1924. Their friends, the psychoanalysts Alix and James Strachey, translated Freud's works for Hogarth. In addition, Woolf's brother Adrian Stephen and his wife, Karen Stephen were practicing psychoanalysts.

Woolf cultivated what she terms the "unconscious" in her writing, though she probably referred to the "preconscious," which is latently conscious and more accessible than the unconscious. She extolled the "leaning tower" writers for "honestly analyzing themselves with help from Dr. Freud".[11] Most typically, Woolf, probably due to her childhood hostility towards Adrian, caricatured psychoanalysis, noted in her essay "Freudian Fiction" (*CW,* 152).

With modern psychoanalysis as frame of reference, Woolf might best be described as possessing characterological traits of a "mixed" variety, that is, "depressive," "obsessive," "masochistic," "psychosomatic." She designated these and other traits, her multiple "selves."[12]

Frequently, Woolf's more acute symptomatology assumed the form of anxiety states where the diminutiveness of her self-esteem is marked. For example, she describes

a physical feeling as if I were drumming slightly in the veins; very cold; impotent; and terrified. As if I were exposed on a high ledge in full light. Very lonely. L. (Leonard) out to lunch. Nessa[13] has Quentin[14] and dont want me. Very useless. No atmosphere round me. No words. Very apprehensive. As if something cold and horrible—a roar of laughter at my expense were about to happen. And I am powerless to ward it off. I have no protection. And this anxiety and nothingness surround me with a vacuum. It affects the thighs chiefly. And I want to burst into tears but I have nothing to cry for. Then a great restlessness seizes me, and I know that I must go on doing this dance on hot bricks till I die.

Gazing at herself in the mirror, she looked "positively terrified," referred to the "dazzle of that head-lamp" on her "poor little rabbit's body which keeps it dazed in the middle of the road" (D5, Mar.1'37).[15] Recoverability follows, but the exposed moments are traumatic.

In extreme states of vulnerability and hypersensitivity to felt rejection such as this, in this extraordinarily evocative self-revelation, Woolf demonstrates her sense of exposure and danger; her need for warmth and protection. She shows feelings of powerlessness, sterility, and nothingness; of shame and humiliation. Her loneliness and isolation prompt her to feel cast off and useless. She has a lump in her throat though cannot cry, feels paralyzed yet wants desperately to mobilize herself; seems unable to nuance strong emotions, though to some degree these are channelled into physical symptoms. Seemingly unintentional slights severely jolt her as though she had no enduring inner template of self-worth, no sense of inner or outer object relatedness or permanence, possessed a minimum degree of ego strength.

Woolf's occasional bouts of agitated depression, and her suicidal bent suggest a substrate of traumatic deprivation, a lifelong, affective, or cyclothymic disposition, with emphasis on the depressive end of the continuum. Often confusing to others, Woolf interchangeably alluded to "breakdown," "madness," or feeling at the "edge of a precipice," when depressed, highly anxious, or physically ill. The essential communication of such warnings express despondency, but they are also provocative, coercive, and demanding of attention. Woolf, stating she was suicidal, did not necessarily signify she was on the verge of acting on her feelings. She was at times histrionic or indulged in poetic despair.[16]

As with all artists, Woolf's conflicts, emotions, fantasies, dreams, memories, symptoms, relationships with others, identity struggles, and sense of self, as these shifted and evolved during different developmental phases of her life, became part of her total personality, permeate her work. The poetic exegesis of her vision and experience, the many points of view brought to bear in probing situation and character; her attunement to the moment, to interior monologue; her iconoclastic experiments in form—underscore her striving for self-definition, her thrust towards mastery. The necessity for constant artistic rebirth, a recurrent motif, remains a passionate, life-affirming force. Writing additionally involved reunion with family members now dead, ensured the immortality of family and self: "nothing makes a whole unless I am writing" (D4, May31'33).

Throughout, Woolf's approach to writing is one of consciously cultivating her subterranean thoughts and emotions, seeking to probe the inner or subjective self or selves, convinced this is the most meaningful springboard for her ensuing artistic endeavors.

Though Woolf's novels include recognizable episodes in her life, some of them avowedly autobiographical, she is not a "confessional" writer. Frequently, she thought of substituting "elegy" for novel inasmuch as her fiction dealt with unresolved issues of mourning, concerning the crucial, determining relationships in her life.

II

Not all novelists offer the temptation for a "fuller disclosure of the figure behind the veil," states Meyer, who wrote a psychoanalytic biography of Joseph Conrad; Meyer, a psychoanalyst, responded to and sought to fathom Conrad's themes of betrayal, self-destructiveness and need for self-revelation. (1967,4).

Synchronizing literary biography and psychoanalysis in his study of Henry James, Edel, a literary critic, sought to probe the Jamesian "anomalies and ambiguities—the legend, the distortion, the caricature of his personality," especially that of "intellect untouched by passion"; he also hoped to explore the creative process of that "queer monster, the artist, an obstinate finality, an inexhaustible sensibility" (Edel,1, 1953,12–13).

In my book, I hope to present an inclusive, multi-levelled, psychological and psychoanalytic understanding of Woolf's life and art, viewing her fiction aside from its aesthetic aims, as a means of gaining the love of exalted, maternal figures, of mourning her losses, of grappling with her emotional dilemmas; and as evidencing, together with biographical and autobiographical data, reverberative themes, imagery, metaphor and characterization, pointing to permutations of what I perceive to be her need for rescue.

Communicating her need to be understood, Woolf invites a psychoanalytic approach as she proclaims: "every secret of a writer's soul, experience of his life and quality of his mind, is written large in his work" (*Orlando*, 209).

Responding to this challenge, eschewing the use of psychoanalytic concepts that are diagnostic or reductionistic, how differentiate between a live patient and the text, how substitute in the psychoanalytic approach to literature, for free associations, the "basic rule" in psychoanalytic technique, or for transference interactions,[17] bedrock of the psychoanalytic situation? Since the work is inevitably related to the creator's life experiences, memories, and fantasies, cannot recurrent imagery, themes, and sequential patterns take the place of the missing associations?

In regard to intense reactions to the author, do these interfere with the aesthetic experience, or are there not interdependent, "shared needs" between "implied author" and reader? Coen points to "complementarity in the reader's longing to find the author, and the author-narrator's wishes for intense, affective contact with his readers" (Coen, 1982a, 12; 1982b, 367).

Fortunately, the notion of the purity of the text uncontaminated by external evidence has been relinquished as critics acknowledge the human equation, bias, or selective perceptions of the reader.

Skura (1982) suggests that renewed vigilance to the possibilities of language and narrative in the literary work stimulates regard for levels of meaning not typically subsumed in textual interpretation. This is paralleled in the psychoanalytic attitude of "evenly hovering attention," the analyst's sensitivity to delicate changes in awareness, occurring moment by moment. Not considering art as neurosis, symptom, or dream but the "dynamic movement towards self-conscious wholeness," Skura sees the entire psychoanalytic process as providing a model for psychoanalytic literary criticism (273).

Indicating we can best approach the literary work by relying on psychoanalytic chacterology,[18] thereby remaining in touch with the total personality, Holland (1982) suggests that in so doing we can most empathically grasp the essence of writer, reader, and fictional portrayal. Schwartz indicates that the critic's response in devising an "authorizing consciousness" via the analysis of character or audience response, best represents the missing author (42).

Concerning factors of form and communication, Gilbert Rose sees form as the "dialectic between separation and fusion, control and ambiguity, tension and release; between thought and feeling, change and constancy" (211).

Believing that fictional characters possess the "conflicts, defenses and attitudes of real people," Baudry (1984) notes that one can enter the fictional world and discern motives and feelings of which the author is not conscious. In relating the literary work to the personality of the author, Baudry views the text as "modified free association," although he advises caution in employing unconscious factors to delineate the behavior of a fictional character. Citing Keats' poetry which contains images of "fusion and orality, abandonment and depression", Baudry concurrently finds multiple losses, inability to grieve and evidence of considerable sorrow in the poet's childhood, thinks therefore it may be possible to reconstruct from imagery and metaphor, Keats' attempts to grapple with his losses (571).

Providing psychological substrate in many of Woolf's novels, her evocative imagery suggests feelings of exclusion from the maternal orbit, and a yearning for maternal protection. In this framework, many of Woolf's fictional characters are portrayed as helpless, victimized, given to unexpected, eruptive expressions of hostility. A parallelism is found in Woolf's history in her mother's early emotional unavailability, in a further sense of abandonment when her mother died, and in her plummeting self-esteem and masked rage in highly emotionally-charged situations.

In her work, Woolf engaged in what I perceive as a perpetual "working through" of her basic emotional dilemmas and losses, for much of her life. "Working through" refers to processes of grief and mourning in the psychoanalytic situation, focusing on central conflicts or themes and their variations, emotionally stated, repeated and orchestrated.[19] Repetition and elaboration Woolf grappled with in her work, but the ensuing memory reconstructions and modifications in self-image intrinsic to the experience of insight in the psychoanalytic situation, she could not achieve.[20]

Numerous studies have emerged with critical or biographical perspectives, purporting to more fully grasp Virginia Woolf's life and art, but in promulgating a specific system of thought, viewpoint or diagnostic category, fall short. Many have richly studied the life without the work or the work without biographical detail.

Though Quentin Bell's biography (1972) brilliantly and perceptively informs us about Woolf's life from an intimate vantage point, he does not choose to plunge deeply into her fiction. Concerning Woolf's childhood, adolescence, and adulthood, Bell offers us the significant data with which, together with other source material, overlooked or controversial, one can shape alternate, interpretive syntheses.

Marcus (1983) continues to celebrate Woolf's "feminist ethic" and suggests she not only "formed an identity in female history but found a set of symbols, a matriarchal mythology with which to forge the collective conscience of her sex." Pointing to an "Ariadne's thread" permeating Woolf's work, with strands of the "mystic, the marxist and the mythical," Marcus claims Woolf was "revolutionary in form and

content . . . ," left us a morality that "entreats" the "present movement
to remember" their "working class brothers," because "their oppression" is shared. (2–3)

Actually, envisioning Marxist and mystic as intertwined is difficult.
Woolf belonged to the Fabian Society, Labor Party, and Women's
Cooperative Guild, which believed in the welfare state, in issues such as
low-cost housing, greater employment, national health, the dole, universal suffrage, equal rights for women, consumer cooperatives, and old-
age pensions. She thought social reform of existing institutions would
lead to evolutionary change, and did not espouse violent, class struggle.
In *Three Guineas*, Woolf attacked the patriarchy in England for its
hypocrisy in regarding itself a democracy while at the same time "enslav-
ing" women. She did not at all times clearly distinguish between fascism
at home and abroad. Though she was a pacifist, which was the position
of the Women's Cooperative Guild, and she attacked England's "subconscious Hiterlerism" in 1940, she at the same time commended and
supported Churchill's war efforts.

In a heated exchange with Marcus, Quentin Bell (1984; 1985) disclaims Woolf's interest in politics as paramount, refutes the assertion she
was "revolutionary" or "Marxist," or, that her aunt, Carolyn Stephen
and her friend Margaret L. Davies shaped Woolf's political thinking. In
her rebuttal, Marcus (1985) holds fast to her position, as delineated in an
ongoing series of articles (1977c, 1978, 1981, 1983).

Also from the vantage point of feminism, which Phyllis Rose suggests is the "core of Woolf's emotional and intellectual being," her only
"acceptable way of stating publicy" her sense of "oppression and
persecution," Rose describes Woolf's half-brother George Duckworth's
"social and sexual bullying" as an expression of "patriarchal" domination (255).

Since the present work essentially tries to come to grips with Woolf's
total personality and is a psychoanalytically-oriented exploration of both
her emotional life and her fiction, it is more to the point to distinguish
this study from others that are psychological or psychoanalytical in
emphasis.

Handelman points to Woolf's need for "demarked spaces" or
"rooms of one's own that won't be violated" (43). Referring to Woolf's
conception of reality as "carrier of a traumatic intrusion with Woolf
herself being passive," Baudry (1980) perceives this as a "re-enactment"
of the "rape-like" encounters with her half-brothers.

Jean Love's biography delves into the personalities of Woolf's
parents and extrapolates highly important aspects of Woolf's childhood
from her parents' extended correspondence.

Woolf never fully released her "reservoir" of pain, according to Edel (1979) who felt she obliterated her feelings concerning her mother's death by offering the "details of events" (87) without their emotional elaboration. Also exploring Woolf's inability to mourn her mother's death, Spilka correctly feels her grieving process was never completed.

Pointing to issues of identity and fusion, Susan M. and Edward J. Kenney (1982) believed Woolf did not wish to "move forward out of childhood" (174). Similarly, Strouse emphasized Woolf's need for "oneness" (190) with her mother. Naremore (1973) pointed to Woolf's need to "dissolve all individuality and sink into a deathlike trance" (55). Ina and Ernest Wolf describe Virginia Woolf's need to "merge" with the "self-object" (40). By contrast, Handelman and Baudry (1980) are more cognizant of Woolf's wish for both union and separation.

Both Phyllis Rose and Naremore seek to understand Woolf via Laing's concept of the "divided self" or schizoid personality. Also invoking Laing, as well as Merleau-Ponty's theory of "disembodiment," the work of Poole and that of Trombley suggest Woolf felt her body "not the center of herself, that she existed at odds with it" (Trombley, 10).

Poole indicates that Leonard Woolf's pressure on his wife to eat rich foods proved her chief problem inasmuch as she was "terrified of becoming gross," of feeling ridiculed. Rather than encompass emotional illness as expressive in her life of the interaction between situation and character, or attribute mutual responsibilities to both Leonard and Virginia, Poole, faulting Leonard, believed "food was to divide" them "until the end."

The organic, punitive orientation of Virginia Woolf's physicians constitutes the major thrust of Trombley's book. Trombley sees the question of Woolf's "madness" as conflict between Leonard's "rationalism" and Virginia's "subjective" systems of belief.

According to Richter, Woolf depicts the actual manner in which "man sees, feels, thinks, experiences time and change" (29). Richter also suggests that the ebb and flow of Woolf's "prose rhythms" generate a "dynamic pattern of feeling to which the reader responds emotionally" (216).

Fleishman considered Woolf steeped in the past, indicates that Woolf dwelt in her novels on scenes and persons of childhood, used recurrent images, phrases, and words, endowing them with mythic overtones; that she possessed the "creative force" to present these repetitions with a "new vitality" (222). Fleishman connects her "aesthetic rhythm" (221) to "constancy and change" in human experience (223).

Suggesting that Woolf's relationship to her mother was that of an "unrequited lover," Moore (1984) believes Woolf wrote to "recreate the ambience" of her earliest memories (12). Moore felt the myth of "Demeter and Persephone," in all its permutations, is of core importance to Woolf's fiction, that it reinforces the feeling "women must take care of one another."[21] She views Woolf a "closet lesbian who hid her lesbianism in marriage" (25).

Leaska focuses on Woolf's power to "make us believe in her people by investing them with a quality beyond the personal—something primary and common to us all" (1977a, 11). Turning to Woolf's characterizations, her stress on the "human element" which catalyzes "feelings that people excite in us in real life,"[22] the present study is in rapport with Leaska.

Emphasizing Woolf's unresolved problems in mourning her mother, this study in part synchronizes with Edel and Spilka. Formulating Woolf's problems as "quarrel with grieving," Spilka is not sufficiently inclusive however, since Woolf's underlying ambivalence, her earlier feelings of exclusion and abandonment concerning her mother, the ensuing attempts to repair this dilemma, are the crucial issues. Developmental considerations must also here be borne in mind, inasmuch as studies concerning children's reactions to death of a parent, indicate children are maturationally unable to fully confront issues of loss.

In contrast to those enamored of the notion of Woolf's need to fuse with others, this study is in rapport with those who underscore Woolf's need for both intimacy and separation. Though theories of fusion and oceanic dissolution are fashionable in both literary and psychoanalytic discourse, increasingly, cognitive and developmental studies suggest the individual even in infancy does not, as previously thought, so easily merge self with other.[23] This does not gainsay Woolf's real conflicts concerning issues of "separation-individuation."[24]

Differing from Love who believed Woolf regularly confused reality with fantasy and linked Woolf's creativity with her "madness," I promulgate that although Woolf's writing frequently reflects her inner conflicts, she possessed the power to impose form over chaos, as for example, the objective depiction of her early breakdown, in her novel, *Mrs. Dalloway.*

Compared to Phyllis Rose, Marcus, and others who view Woolf's political conciousness as the crux of her life and work, I see Woolf's constant exploration of the human condition, her need to come to grips with her personal identity, emotional dilemmas, and artistic conscience as most central.

Cryptically, via warning, signal, symbol or image, Woolf's writing, autobiographical and fictional, compellingly communicates the longing to be understood, protected, taken in. Without meaningfully internalizing a consistently nurturing and sustaining relationship with her mother or father, however, Woolf's ability to heal early emotional wounds, her capacity to separate, individuate and create an integrated identity, remained unresolved.

III

Woolf grappled with what I perceive as four major constellations reverberating throughout her life, which also appear in the psychological or metaphorical substrate of her autobiographical writing, in letters, diary, and memoirs, as well as in her fiction.

1. A central refrain is Woolf's incompleted grieving process regarding her mother, Julia Stephen, evidenced in Woolf's insatiable need for maternal protection, which was generally frustrated. Concomitant to the marked ambivalence shown mother-figures, Woolf depicts the mother as distant, preoccupied, depressed, favoring youngest son, and threatened by her daughter's burgeoning sexuality. Woolf frequently wrote her novels to woo or achieve closeness to a revered mother-image, important to her at the time. Essentially, Woolf's relationship with her mother lacked intimacy and closeness; "Can I remember," Woolf asks, "being alone with her for more than a few minutes. Someone was always interrupting" (*SOTP*, 83).

Woolf, unable to resolve her love-hate feelings regarding her mother, emotionally unavailable in the early months of Virginia's life because of ill health or depression, who became even more distant when Virginia's younger brother was born—views mother-figures as ultimately abandoning. Mothers endowed with negative images in Woolf's life or fiction, represent "introjects," that is, internalized or dissociated attitudes, of frightening or angry correlates of mother, stemming from preverbal or infantile eras, when feelings towards parental figures are inchoate, fantasy-ridden, and subject to distortion.

Woolf's feminine identification in relation to her mother, was problematic. She confused feminine and maternal, longed for a mother, not a feminine model, often chose masculine women as parental figures, perhaps using her maternal father as prototype. Her sister Vanessa, three years older, was to a considerable extent, particularly after marriage, Woolf's feminine and maternal model, recipient of her romantic fantasies, which Vannessa frequently repelled however.

In childhood, Virginia preferred her father, possibly felt he used her as a buffer in the parents' marriage. Deeply guilt-ridden because of her early closeness with father, Woolf might have imagined she and her father, collusively, exacerbated her mother's illness and precipitated her death. Defending against her oedipal attachment to father and his towards her, Woolf repressed her femininity, sought to establish and retain her mother's supremacy.

Inasmuch as we know very little about Woolf's relationship with her mother and Woolf basically glorified her mother after she died, the delineations of fictional mothers show greater versimilitude. In Woolf's first novel, *The Voyage Out*, the maternal figure, initially supportive, proves jealous and intrusive regarding her surrogate-daughter's nubile state, seeks to crush her sexuality and incipient sense of independence, wills her death.

In *To the Lighthouse*, the artist, Lily Briscoe desires closeness with the maternal Mrs. Ramsay, to potentiate her feminine and artistic role, initially idealizes Mrs. Ramsay, then feels love, grief, and anger when she dies, feelings Woolf could not mobilize in mourning her mother. Woolf at the time of writing her novel embraced androgyny, more specifically Vita Sackville West, a not very sustaining mother-image, soon reinstating her earlier sense of maternal rejection. In *The Years*, in which the mother is dying from the first and the family appears merely interested in getting the process over with, Woolf's hostility towards mother-images resurfaces.

2. A second constellation is noted in Woolf's complex identification with her father, Leslie Stephen, who achieved considerable stature as a literary figure. Excessively dependent on his wife's sympathy and support, he felt distanced and disparaged by her frequent absences, the attention she bestowed on her younger son and on her mother. Perhaps to deny his feelings of weakness and impotency, he became exacting and restricting towards her and the children.

Extremely attached to her father when she was a child, Woolf might have coalesced his overt preference for her with the sexual interest and attention shown her by her half-brothers, also father-figures. Towards them she at times felt helplessness, shame, inexpressible rage. Her father, he felt, in demanding his daughters' ministrations after his wife's death, claimed maturational sacrifices that led to an irretrievable loss of possibilites.

Woolf felt her father hypocritical and excessively histrionic in mourning her mother; she resented his conspicuous attachment to Stella, Woolf's older half-sister. Quite possibly via her first breakdown, Woolf sought to wrench her father from Stella or Stella from him. Although Woolf's predominant identification was with father, she frequently saw him as a castrated image, and as someone cast off by mother. Perhaps the most decisive identification with father was her role as his literary heir.

Her fictional fathers exploit their daughters by relying on them to vitalize empty marriages. Or, fathers are caricatured as rigid and overly rational. Tyrannical in domestic situations, at times strong figures, they are also self-deprecating, crippled, or require frequent support.

In *To the Lighthouse*, Mr. Ramsay depletes his wife by his inordinate need for her solicitousness and she dies prematurely; this theme, of course, was based on the ostensible circumstances surrounding the death of Woolf's mother. Here it was Vanessa's belief that their father's insatiable need for his wife's caretaking killed her. Woolf, needing to be close to her sister, identified with Vanessa in blaming their father.

Reopening her grievances concerning her father in *The Years*, Woolf perceives the patriarchal Abel Pargiter as duplicitous in his extra-marital involvement, this theme dredged from her jealousy regarding father's all too swift turn to Stella after Julia's death. Woolf also perceived Abel as incestuously interfering with his daughters' establishment of firm identity patterns and love relationships. Where there is awareness of entrapment—the themes of *Antigone* are pervasive in this novel—it is too late for reversibility.

3. Woolf's indeterminacy regarding her self-concept and her vacillation concerning sexual and personal identification, emanated from complexities in her infantile and childhood experiences as well as in her subsequent development. These issues emerge in context of the shifting dominance-subordinate patterns in her parent's marriage and personalities; her father's conflicts regarding his masculinity; her mother's subtle control of husband and children via her frequent absences; the assumption of parental roles by older siblings after the mother's death.

Though Woolf readily attributed her heterosexual inhibitions to the sexual intimidations by her half-brothers, it is most likely that the more decisive issues were her mother's wish for a male child when Woolf was born, her sense of inadequacy and deviance concerning body-image and sexual identity, not infrequent when one is distant from mother and rivalrous with a younger, preferred brother.

Concomitantly, this situation sets up the desire to possess that which the mother values; in Woolf's case this resulted in envy of her brother, later led to criticism of the shortcomings of the masculine sex. Wishing to acquire what men possess and inability to accept one's femininity suggest early narcissistic injury, conflicts regarding identity formation, and problems of aggression, in consonance with a prevailing sense of "envy, worthlessness, damage and deprivation" (Stewart and Grossman, 193-194).

Julia Stephen's depression, excessive involvement with her family of origin, preoccupation with her dead husband, favoritism of son, distancing of Leslie, at the same time envisioning him a father-figure, did not provide a consistent or firm feminine model for Virginia. Following the mother's death, Woolf's inability to mourn, to resolve her submerged anger regarding her mother, interfered with the evolution of her feminine and heterosexual identification.

Feeling she was blamed for the sexual difficulties between herself and Leonard, Virginia interpreted his not desiring children as rejection of her femininity, though he in his turn might have been distanced by her confusion about sexual role and sexual naivete or, he saw mental illness ubiquitously lurking. In addition, although the relationship between Virginia and Leonard was overtly one between dependent child and caretaker, Woolf according to Gilbert and Guber (3), had the "pen" or "metaphorical penis" which possibly intimidated Leonard.

The reciprocal difficulties between Virginia and Leonard are fictionalized in the mutually detached relationships of Woolf's fictional couples who draw together only to separate, whose friendships must be "unemotional." In her novels, marriages are generally depicted as failed or unrewarding. Woolf's heros and heroines "pass in and out of each others' minds" rather than bodies. Woolf's sexual vacillation, sexual ambivalence, and her "drive to become both sexes" (Kubie, 217) no doubt proved unsettling and highly disruptive in her life.

4. Woolf's early fragility of self, poor tolerance for frustrating or emotionally charged events, her feelings of victimization, seemed ongoing. In addition to her psychological sense of exclusion and deviance, Woolf felt herself in relation to the literary world, "fundamentally an outsider."[26] She worked best and felt most "braced, back to the wall," felt it an "odd feeling though to write against the current" (D5, Nov.22'38). In highly anxiety-provoking circumstances, Woolf's need for punishment via physical symptoms, her inner despair and submerged rage, synchronized with her depression and preoccupation with suicide.

Enmeshing with Woolf's life situation, salient imagery, symbolism, and metaphor in both fiction and autobiography emerge as intuitively evocative of central, mythic, unconscious, emotionally weighted areas of experience. Baudry (1984) suggests similarities exist in the communicative functions of metaphor in psychoanalysis and literature, although in the latter these are more influenced, he believes, by "secondary" or intellectual processes. Metaphor, according to Kris (1982) serves "not to bring poetry close to the dream but rather to the psychic processes underlying both art and fantasy; serves as an instrument for multiplying ambiguity" (258).

Arlow (1979) refers to metaphor as an attempt to master anxiety and attain "distance from content" since direct awareness of inner conflict may lead to "catastrophic panic" (371).

The sea, a major symbol in Woolf's life and fiction, represents the rhythmic nature of existence, the inexorable cycle of building up and destroying, the nonhuman life of which she feels so much a part. Equated with the imagination, states of "trance," and the fluidity of life —the watery element was never far from consciousness.

Woolf imagined she might sink to the "bottom of the sea and live alone" with her words (D4, Sept.28'30); frequently she felt on the "flood" of creativeness (D4, Jan.5'35). In a memoir written during the last year of her life, when Woolf felt "marooned," she recalled the sounds of waves, wind, and windowblind at Cornwall, evoking childhood memories of family belongingness and enclosure. With the flooding of the marshes in Rodmell, Woolf was ecstatic, saw herself as a "stake in the water," an elementary force of nature, as though losing her human identity (D5, Nov.3'40).

Woolf withdrew her last novel, *Between the Acts*, after submitting the manuscript to John Lehmann, Leonard's partner at Hogarth Press, quite possibly because of her awareness of the novel's reverberative, undercurrent of suicide, by drowning. Deeply despondent, two of the female characters with whom Woolf is closely identified, are in estranged relationships and frequently threaten suicide in a poetic though insistent vein.

Several weeks before her death, Woolf wrote Ethel Smyth "we have no future . . . ; I'm fished out of my element and lie gasping on the ground" (L6, Mar.1'41).

In taking her life by drowning, Woolf might have sought forgiveness, and hoped to resolve her ambivalence towards her mother; she ultimately sought reunion with her mother, who following her first husband's death, "sank like an exhausted swimmer, deeper and deeper into the water" (*Rem*, 39). Woolf also wished for reconciliation with her father, the "castaway," always "voyaging in ice-bound seas" (*Rem*, 37). Generational in its metaphorical implications, the sea seemed intrinsic to the Stephens' family ethos. Woolf's suicide grimly finalized her sense of despair, doomed victory and retaliatory rage.

Chapter II through Chapter V offer a new look at controversial or untrodden biographical and autobiographical data. Chapter VI through Chapter XIV present the confluence of life and fiction in a psychologically oriented reintegration, in context of the four constellations here outlined. The final chapter suggests the meaning, to Woolf, of her creative life and explores the conditions and motivations of her final suicide.

II   The "Broken Chrysalis": Need for Maternal Protection

I

In understanding Virginia Woolf, a grasp of her early moorings as they shaped her mode of experiencing the world and affected her work remains crucial, to start with her awareness of the intricacies of her origins, the knowledge that her parents, Leslie and Julia Stephen's earlier marriages ended in the premature deaths of their respective spouses. Leslie's first wife, Minny Thackeray, died during pregnancy leaving Laura, their child, motherless, her husband bereft and "plunged into appalling gloom" (Annan, 72).

The myths concerning Julia's beauty and romantic past, her morbid preoccupation with the death of her first husband, Herbert Duckworth, which lingered throughout her marriage to Leslie, might have engendered the feeling she did not sufficiently revel in or value her second family. The alignment of family forces, the hothouse enmeshments amongst the children of each marriage, Woolf's relationship with both parents, their personalities, and relationships with each other were of central importance in her life.

From a composite of autobiographical and biographical sources[1] concerning the lives of Leslie, Julia, and kin, we learn Julia was born in India in 1846, youngest of three sisters, the favorite of her mother, formerly Maria Pattle, who was herself one of seven sisters known for their beauty and connection to French nobility. Dr. John Jackson, Julia's father, was a leading medical consultant and first professor of medicine at Calcutta Medical College, although he apparently lacked status in his own family. Mrs. Jackson returned to England when Julia was two, rejoining her other daughters already there. Dr. Jackson did not rejoin the family until 1855, when Julia was nine, at which time he resumed his practice in London. (Love, 55–56).

Possibly Julia might have felt her family disrupted by the separation, might have felt abandoned by her father and clung to mother; she did not see her father for seven years. For the most part, he seemed a shadowy appendage to the family. We are told Mrs. Jackson "dominated" her husband who was presumably lacking in "loftier moods." Woolf refers to him as a "commonplace, prosaic old man" from whom Julia acquired

19

her practicality and shrewdness (*SOTP*, 88). Julia's maternal uncle, Thoby Prinsep became to all intents and purposes father-surrogate.

Thoby Prinsep, and his wife, Sarah maintained a salon for the literary and artistic elite at Little Holland House in London and at Freshwater. They were patrons of G.F. Watts, the painter who had studios in their homes.

As a child, Julia modeled for Watts as well as for a famous sculptor of the era, Marachetti, and for Burnes-Jones who asked her to pose for the figure of a madonna in one of his paintings. Well-known as a photographer, Woolf's great aunt Julia Cameron's[2] photographs of her niece, Julia, strikingly depict her beauty. Holman Hunt, the painter, and Thomas Woolner, a sculptor, fell in love with Julia and wished to marry her. (Annan, 76–77; Bell, v.1, 15). From childhood, Julia's beauty, which elicited a good deal of admiration and was perhaps exploited, informed her consciousness of self. She looked back upon Little Holland House with considerable nostalgia, basically received the rudiments of her education there.

Although she did not receive any formal schooling, Julia learned French, which she spoke effectively, and played the piano. She was a hero-worshipper according to Woolf, harbored a passion for literature, was particularly fond of DeQuincy's "Confessions of an Opium Eater," and owned all of Scott's novels. Woolf suggests her mother had an "instinctive" rather than educated mind (*SOTP*, 86).

Fostered by the early fragmentation of her family, Julia's marked attachment to her mother as well as her mother's dependence on her, assumed central force in her life. When Julia was a young child, she tended her mother throughout recurrent illnesses, perhaps obtaining the training which later prompted her to be caretaker to others as well. A great "invalid," Mrs. Jackson also considered herself medically expert. She was perpetually prone to physical or nervous complaints, exploited, and inevitably elicited Julia's attention. She wrote Julia several times a day when they were apart (Love, 58–59). Her letters show a "tender gloating over disease and death" (Bell, v.1, 17).

In 1867, Julia, now 21, married a lawyer, Herbert Duckworth, an extremely "modest and sweet tempered man" as described by her second husband, Leslie Stephen, on examining the correspondence between Julia and Duckworth, for the eulogy he wrote after Julia's death, *The Mausoleum Book*.[3] The marriage to Duckworth, a socially poised member of the landed gentry, was, all biographers attest, idyllic, and with him Julia had "perfect happiness" (*Maus.*, 37). Suggesting Julia had "surrendered" herself to Duckworth, accepting him absolutely and unreservedly, Leslie considered hers a "dangerous" dependency however, inasmuch as Julia apparently panicked whenever she and Duckworth were apart. (Love, 61–62).

Woolf's 1908 memoir conveyed that Duckworth was "inferior" to her mother, who allegedly loved Leslie more (Rem, 32). In her 1939-1940 memoir, Woolf acknowledged Duckworth was her mother's great love because he was of a heroic mold, "handsome, magnanimous," as well as ordinary and genial (*SOTP*, 89). Woolf thought her mother married her father, Leslie Stephen, out of "pity" (91) and admiration of his intellect; she thought it paradoxical her mother was linked to two such vastly different men. Although one obtains the impression Duckworth was young, dashing, romantic, he was, surprisingly, 14 years older than Julia, but one year younger than Leslie.

Married four years, pregnant with their third child, Julia was grief-stricken when Duckworth died quite suddenly: "I was only 24 when it all seemed such a shipwreck. I have been as unhappy and as happy as it is possible for a human being to be," she stated, not permitting herself to "break down" because of her children. Choosing the role of healer, extending consolation to the sick and infirm, she showed an ongoing concern for others in need, which was her method of deflecting her grief. Thereafter, she "accepted sorrow as her lifelong partner" (*Maus*, 40).

Perhaps feeling she was valued most as her mother's "good child" Julia might have obtained a sense of competency or control in becoming, after her husband's death and for the rest of her life, a professional mourner, as it were, at the service of the sick or dying. This degree of sacrifice and dedication might have proved distancing, accusing, possibly creating a sense of guilt in her children, as though they were responsible for her sadness. Did Julia feel Duckworth's death an abandonment, perhaps similar in emotional impact to the early separation from her father?

Julia had thought of entering a convent, hoped for death, became instead a practical nurse.[4] In stating "so many things happened" to her, she "never got to be anything" to herself (Love, 82), she reveals self-consciousness about her lack of education; indicates her minimal self-esteem, her tendency to live vicariously, either through others or in giving to others. In negating the "Angel in the House" who "never had a wish of her own, but preferred to sympathize always with the needs and wishes of others" and "above all she was pure"—is Woolf referring to this aspect of her mother? Woolf felt her mother might not have allowed her a "mind of her own," or would caution "be tender, flatter, deceive, use all the arts and wiles of our sex."[5]

A good deal more is known about Leslie Stephen. Leslie, born in 1832, was his mother's favorite of the five children she bore James Stephen. Leslie's father combined his law practice with an important position in the Colonial Office, the better to pursue his campaign against slavery. In this capacity, he helped to draft the Emancipation Bill. An able administrator, he worked long hours in addition to writing for the *Edinburgh Review*. Described as self-denying and pessimistic, he was a vulnerable, unhappy man who felt unappreciated. His shyness took the form of loquacity, and he frequently alienated others. Puritanical, he did not enjoy society and was prone to nervous collapse; convinced of his ugliness, he would not look into the mirror, an aversion he passed on to his granddaughter, Virginia Woolf (Annan, 11-14).

Reputedly, Leslie was extremely volatile as a child, although his mother, Jane Venn, claimed he was sensitive and affectionate. Thinking Leslie a prodigy, genius, or incipient scholar at least, his mother, who described his early achievements in her diary, gave him lessons in arithmetic when he was three. His visual memory was impressive and he loved to draw.

Taught poetry by his mother when he was eight, he recited aloud, with great intensity,[6] his entire body shaking, thereby frightening his parents, especially when he would, apparently, lose touch with his surroundings. Consulting a physician for Leslie's maladies, his parents were told Leslie had "brain fever" or "disordered circulation," apparently a catchall diagnosis in the Victorian period. The physician urged the family to move to Brighton and enroll him in a day school, implying poetry or excessive mothering was detrimental to Leslie's sense of masculinity (Love, 38; Annan, 16). Although young Leslie's aberration had been described as "incipient psychosis", the doctor's no-nonsense suggestions indicated a sensible approach, aimed at diminution of the overstimulation at home. However, this early suppression of Leslie's poetic sensibilities fostered his subsequent doubts concerning pursuit of a literary career.

Leslie's pervasive anxieties regarding his health and physical state increased upon the death at 24 of his brother, ten years older than he, whom he resembled. Another brother, Fitzjames, three years his senior, was their father's favorite; feeling outdistanced by him. Leslie envied him his masculine physique and athletic prowess, thought of him as a more approachable father-figure, though Leslie's masculine identification remained unresolved.

Leslie's illness when he was 15, apparently his "most sickly time," compounded his sense of physical inadequacy. Ashamed of his frailty, his excessive shyness and dependency, he deplored weakness his entire life, felt himself nervous and "thinskinned"[7] like his father, although he did not otherwise feel close to him. Due to his assortment of ills, Leslie thought himself "weak and feminine" (Love, 39; Annan, 29). Dayboys at Eton for four years, he and Fitzjames were bullied, flogged, and despised as outsiders, although Fitzjames regularly defended and protected Leslie.

By contrast, at Trinity Hall College, in Cambridge, Leslie formed many friendships and engaged in athletic pursuits such as rowing, walking long distances, and mountain climbing; ultimately he attained the prized status of rowing coach. Leslie subordinated many of his intellectual aspirations to ingratiate himself with others and prove himself a leader. Possibly he sacrificed his beliefs in taking Holy Orders in 1859, necessary, however, in acquiring the status of tutor (Annan, 45). Generally, Leslie seemed divided between the role of athletic, tough-minded rationalist, which he equated with manliness, and his tendency to be self-deprecating, hypersensitive, frequently in need of emotional support.

Loss of faith, change of values concerning celibacy, death of his father, and greater financial security prompted Leslie to leave his university position at age 30 although he retained his fellowship, remained rowing coach and bursar. Feeling his life futile, however, he moved from Cambridge in 1865 to rejoin mother and sister in London; he decided to emulate his brother Fitzjames and enter journalism. Both barrister and a leading journalist of the time, Fitzjames introduced Leslie to editors of the major magazines and Leslie began to write weekly articles.

In 1867, Leslie married Minny Thackeray, daughter of the novelist, William Thackeray, assumed editorship of *Cornhill*, a prestigious London magazine, and began his major study, *The History of English Thought in the Eighteenth Century*; articles written for *Cornhill* were subsequently incorporated in his book *Hours in a Library*. Bereft when both his mother and Minny died in 1875, Leslie turned for support to his sister-in-law, Anny Thackeray. Living with Leslie and Minny during their marriage, Anny, though recipient of Leslie's "rages," stayed on after her sister's death, helping care for Leslie's young daughter, Laura (Love, 76). Leaning on her friend Julia Duckworth for emotional support at this time, Anny had previously been helpful to Julia during Julia's bereavement.

In ministering to Anny's grief over the death of Minny, Julia's sympathy encompassed Leslie. Their preoccupation with mourning brought Julia and Leslie together. In the past they had briefly met at Little Holland House, but Leslie had not been comfortable in that for him too worldly milieu.

Leslie confided in Julia, presented himself as helpless—a tortured, misanthropic recluse unable to cope with plans for the future.

Disoriented and confused, he indicated life frequently had no "meaning" for him (Love, 76). He found Julia extremely sympathetic and perhaps like his mother, alerted to his health problems. In 1877, Leslie proposed marriage which at first Julia refused, although they continued to maintain their close friendship and an almost unofficial engagement. Feeling she could give Leslie no assurance of marriage in the future and not wanting to hold him off indefinitely, sensing his "restlessness," Julia considered ending their relationship. Her morbid sadness, the feeling she deserved unhappiness, the notion that Leslie would dislike the "real" Julia, and the conviction she could hurt people suggested Julia's considerable guilt, almost as though she felt she caused Duckworth's death.

When Anny Thackeray married, Leslie felt abandoned, dramatically asked Julia to serve as Laura's personal guardian if he died while she was still a minor in need of care. He continued to regale Julia with his physical complaints and his ineptness in practical matters, beseeched her help in caring for Laura, who showed both learning and behavior problems. Julia now responded to his plea, deciding to marry, although she felt "callous" and "horribly unsentimental." The couple were separated during their brief engagement since Julia was chosen to nurse her uncle Thoby who was ill. In response to a relative's query concerning Leslie, Julia indicated she did not think he would make a good husband (Love, 101). Although Julia frequently felt intimidated by and inferior to Leslie, he appealed to her need to serve and perhaps her need to organize others' lives. In addition, she was attracted to his writings on agnosticism. They married in 1878.

Leslie's love for Minny Thackeray had been according to Annan, "protective, jocular, cosseting" and in Julia he recognized a "deeper and more sensitive character than his own, one who had borne sorrow as he would have wished to bear it but could not"; Leslie idealized Julia and sought to sacrifice himself for her. In turn, Julia thought he was a great man, and felt genuine humility regarding his achievements and intellect (Annan, 82).

Initially the Stephen marriage appeared relatively compatible, although during 1882, the year Woolf was born, numerous crises emerged: Laura's learning and behavior problems required a private governess; Leslie's editorship of the *Dictionary of National Biography* proved an endless, exhausting task. Furthermore, Leslie felt an increasing sense of emotional and sexual rejection by Julia, who seemed excessively preoccupied with the ills of mother, father, and sundry relatives, frequently leaving home to nurse them (Love, 113).

Although Leslie was shrill and peremptory in his efforts to obtain sympathy, Julia appeared the more controlling and dominant, insisting on her right or need to minister to others as she chose, which occasionally resulted in absences of long duration, leaving the children with Leslie or the servants. Of course Leslie took brief vacations, in the Alps, yet his wife's departures from home propelled bitter complaints, which in turn further distanced Julia.

Possibly Leslie was threatened in appearing the more maternal parent. A considerable part of his correspondence consists of letters to his absent wife, describing the activities, development, and unique sayings of his children, an unusual reversal of roles in the Victorian period. Leslie's and Julie's power struggles and schisms concerning their personal identities and emotional interactions left their imprint on the Stephen progeny.

Differing in their conception of Leslie's achievement, numerous biographers indicate he revealed early promise but ultimately proved a failure, presumably following generational family patterns. His most recent biographer, Annan, suggests, alternately, that following Matthew Arnold's death in 1888, Leslie Stephen achieved status as the first man of letters in England and became, in short, an "eminent Victorian." He possessed a powerful range of intellectual power, was enormously productive in writing books on history, biography, and literature, received many honorary degrees and was eventually knighted. Before his death Leslie, self-deprecatingly, faulted himself for not finishing a projected opus on philosophy and ethics (ANNAN 112–113).

II

Virginia Stephen was born on January 25, 1882, a difficult year[8] as noted, for the Stephens, who now more than ever seemed preoccupied with Laura, Woolf's half-sister, 12 years her senior and a disturbing presence at home. Laura had nervous tics, speech impediments, complained of choking at mealtime, ejected food from her mouth, was prone to "howling" and "shrieking" and was generally unmanageable (Love, 162). One obtains the impression that Laura as a young child was jolted by her mother's death and by her shifting family milieu. She was undoubtedly misunderstood, pushed to achieve by her father far beyond her capacities and felt wanting in comparison to her more dazzling Duckworth and Stephen stepsiblings. Generally, Laura was kept separate from the others. It is of considerable interest that after Anny's marriage, when Leslie's sister Caroline briefly took care of Laura, she had a measure of success in teaching and managing her niece.

In 1887, Laura age 17, was sent to live in the country; she was permanently institutionalized in York in 1891. Provided for but largely forgotten by her family, she died there in 1945. Although some biographers refer to her as mentally retarded, others consider her psychotic. Her verbal fluency and ability to read—Leslie indicated she read *Aladdin* at 11, *Robinson Crusoe* at 14, and apparently read *Alice in Wonderland* to Thoby at 16—counterindicate mental deficiency. Love seems correct in asserting that Laura's early "perversity" was more likely childhood schizophrenia (Love, 162). There is no doubt her anomalous presence proved disruptive to the Stephens; Virginia was nine when Laura left their household for good.

Working on what would evolve into 26 volumes of the *Dictionary of National Biography*, a formidable and time-consuming enterprise, Leslie frequently suffered episodes of nervous excitement, collapse, and "fits of the horrors" (Love, 134), during 1888 and 1890; in 1891 he resigned as editor. Virginia later claimed the *Dictionary* "crushed" Adrian and herself in the "womb" (D2, Dec. 3'23), used this theme in her novel, *Night and Day*.

Insofar as her position in the Stephen family was concerned, Virginia was somewhat isolated. Vanessa and Thoby, respectively three years and one and one-half years older than she, were already ensconced in an extremely close sibling tie from which she frequently felt excluded. Vanessa's most intimate relationship as a child was not with her mother but with Thoby. From early on, according to Virginia's reminiscences, Vanessa assumed a maternal role towards Thoby, "gave up her bottle" to him, taught him the alphabet.

Virginia competed for Thoby's attention and, as Vanessa stated in her memoir, "Thoby was the brother both Virginia and I adored. He and I had an intimate friendship before she came on the scene. Though life was more interesting and exciting, it was also less easy." According to Vanessa, Virginia, tantrumy as a child, could create an emotionally charged, tense atmosphere. Yet Vanessa, in turn, evoked Virginia's "purple rages."[9]

Virginia was not a particularly wanted child; we learn her parents had originally decided to bring their family to a halt after Thoby was born (Bell, v.1, 18). Nevertheless, she was conceived; her mother had hoped for a boy, already naming "him" Chad.[10] Because of Julia's ill-health and possible postpartum depression, Virginia was weaned from the breast at 10 weeks. In a letter to his wife at the time, Leslie refers to apparent difficulties in the nursing situation between his wife and Virginia: "How can you think of my disapproving of your bottlefeeding Virginia? I like you to nurse her as long as it does not hurt your health but I could not really wish you to go on one moment after it became trying really" (Apr.9, 1882; Berg).

Virginia at 21 months felt additionally displaced by the arrival of Adrian, nursed by mother for more than a year and by the close bond between mother and youngest son.[11] Photographs of Adrian were at the bedside of mother who would gaze at them from her seat in the drawing room, according to Leslie who thought Julia and Adrian shared a "special affinity of temperament" (*Maus*, 85). Leslie's and Virginia's sense of exclusion proved the catalyst drawing them together from early on. Writing Julia when Adrian was born, Leslie indicated his decided pleasure in Virginia's affection and physical demonstrativeness: she sat on his knee, said "kiss" and laid her cheek against his (Oct.10, 1883; Berg).

Reconstructing Virginia's infancy from biographical data, one hazards the notion that her early months were rocky because of her mother's intermittent availability though to be sure nannies were present. Nursed by mother or mother-surrogates for approximately two months, insufficiencies in the nursing situation between Virginia and mother are indicated, as evidenced in the parents' correspondence and in view of Woolf's ongoing preoccupation in her fiction with an extraordinary range of both orally incorporative and orally aggressive imagery.

In the period before Adrian was born, her mother might have been more involved with Virginia inasmuch as we know that in *To The Lighthouse*, Mrs. Ramsay, Woolf's fictional mother based on Julia, preferred to have her children remain "forever just as they were. Why should they grow up so fast. She would have like always to have had a baby " (*TTL*, 89–90). Virginia obliged by not talking until she was three.

Concerning the lag in Virginia's speaking, one assumes Adrian's birth proved a setback to her preferential position as youngest child. Adrian's maleness was undoubtedly made much of, further demoting Virginia. Not talking or ceasing to talk until 3 suggests oppositionalness or clinging to a more infantile mode, postponement of the greater socialization and conventionalization accompanying language acquisition, competing with her brother whom her mother called her "joy". Inasmuch as the adult Virginia emphasizes the importance to her of "rhythmic" aspects of writing, she here shows her strong connection to pre-verbal, sensory-motor, kinesthetic experiences, holding onto the more spontaneous, imaginative thinking of childhood (Galenson, 1971,49).

The other Stephen children largely parentified each other. Julia was living according to Woolf, on "such an extended surface that she had not time, nor strength, to concentrate, except for a moment if one were ill or in some child's crisis, upon me, or upon anyone, unless it were Adrian" (*SOTP*, 83).

After Adrian's birth, the Stephen household consisted of eight children, seven servants, several dogs, cats, bugs, and many relations. The four younger children had two nurseries, for day and night, on an upper floor of the five-story house at 22 Hyde Park Gate where they were born. Above them, on the same floor as the servants' rooms, Leslie worked in his attic study where he sat in his rocking chair, "sucking" on a clay pipe. With their mother away, tending to the poor, sick, or needy,[12] governesses or older siblings took over. Their father also took part in their lives, drawing for them, telling them stories, reciting his favorite poems, though Love suggests he was "at his worst" with mother absent (215). Woolf recalls that her father once recovered her toy boat which sank in the pond. On this occasion, her mother made new sails and her father rigged the boat, which points to an occasional sense of harmony in Virginia's family life.

Below the children's rooms were the bedrooms of Virginia's half-siblings via Julia's first marriage, George, Stella, and Gerald Duckworth, respectively 14, 13, and 12 years older than Virginia. Underneath these rooms were her parents'

> double bedded bedroom on the first floor, the sexual centre, the birth centre; the death centre of the house . . . ; its walls must be soaked if walls take pictures and hoard up what is done and said, with all that was most intense, with all that makes the most private being of family life. In that bed four children were begotten; there they were born (*SOTP*, 1985, 118).

Vanessa remembers Virginia as an infant in her high-chair banging impatiently for breakfast. Both Virginia and Vanessa were extremely beautiful as children. Vanessa writes: "Virginia always reminded me of a sweetpea, of a special flame color." Virginia predicted Vanessa "was to have great beauty." Always Virginia admired her sister's "calm honesty, grave assumption of responsibility for the younger children, her quiet, unceasing benevolence, her practicality and good sense" (Bell, v.1, 23).

Though an "awkward" child, Thoby as a small boy "dominated us four." He was plump, "bursting through his Norfolk jacket," not an acquiescent child but someone with a will of his own whose "rages were thorough and formidable". One of their aunts called him "Napoleonic." Woolf recalls Thoby "struggling with their half-brother Gerald"; or so "truculent with the nurses that father had to be sent for" (*SOTP*, 107). Chiefly, he enjoyed Vanessa's attention.

Considered robust physically and mentally in previous biographical accounts, we learn that Thoby during a fit of delirium at school following an episode of influenza, began screaming, then tried to leap out the window; his impulse to jump out the window was, furthermore, repeated at home one month later (Annan, 117).

Thoby's instability at age 14 suggests at does other data concerning the children of Leslie and Julia, that aside from Virginia who appeared to be the family scapegoat, her siblings also suffered emotional disturbances in childhood and thereafter.[13]

In family photographs, Adrian, as a child is generally at his mother's knee or on her lap. Apparently when he left for school in the morning, he inevitably would lose gloves, books, or coat. In her diary in the twenties, Virginia points to Adrian's need for praise as well as his "disrespect" towards her. She felt guilty she had not as a child "paired" with him (D2, Dec.3'23). Apparently, she found Vanessa and Thoby more exciting.

Despite their rivalries, Virginia and Vanessa were companionable and attached to each other. Vanessa's fondness for her sister increased after Thoby left for school, and they were thrust together a good deal. Virginia tried always to be close to Vanessa's orbit, which she exalted. Vanessa was mother-surrogate, ego-ideal, and someone Virginia could closely model herself after, although Virginia conceived herself as falling short. Frequently, Virgnia's novels incorporated aspects of Vanessa's life and art.

Considered incalculable, eccentric, and prone to accidents, Virginia was dubbed "The Goat." She in turn nicknamed Vanessa because of her ruthless honesty, "The Saint." When quite young, Virginia decided she would be a writer while Vanessa wished to be a painter.[14]

Leslie wrote his wife that Virginia at five entertained the family with stories each night, mounted the window-sill and orated until her audience "coughed" her down (Apr.17, 1887; Berg).

At nine, Virginia asked Vanessa which parent she loved most. Vanessa answered she preferred her mother, while Virginia favored her father.

Preferring for the most part to educate the children themselves, Julia and Leslie decided the boys would have elementary teaching and then go to public schools, whereas the girls' entire schooling would be at home. Although foreign governesses were occasionally employed, Julia for the most part undertook Latin and French while Leslie taught them mathematics.

Virginia Woolf claimed that because she never attended school and did not compete with children her age, she could never compare her "gifts" and "defects" with others. She was inordinately bitter about not attending a university,[15] and she resented the education privileges accorded her brothers. Actually, Leslie told Julia before their marriage that women, in his opinion, should be as well-educated as men: "I hate to see women's lives wasted simply because they have not been trained well enough to take an independent interest in any study or to be able to work efficiently at any profession" (Annan, 121).

Although he helped Vanessa obtain a sound art education, he did not send Virginia to a university possibly because of her emotional difficulties or because he thought the English education system brutalizing. Perhaps he maintained a double standard regarding money spent on his daughter's schooling, or thought he would be Virginia's best teacher.

Julia had a quick temper, and was not particularly effective as a teacher. Leslie's most valuable teaching occurred outside of his lessons, as he read to the children and asked them to discuss what they had heard, enjoining them to identify with all points of view, not necessarily with the hero or heroine of the story they were reading.

Virginia and Thoby embarked on a family newspaper, the *Hyde Park Gate News*, which she, imitating the "grandest journalistic style" (Bell, v.1, 28), took over after Thoby left for school. The first issue appeared in 1891, when she was nine, and continued weekly until 1895. Virginia's first attempt at fiction, a short story, "The Midnight Ride," was printed in the paper; she complained she had difficulty making up plots. At 10, Virginia tried writing stories in the style of Nathaniel Hawthorne. Vanessa studied drawing with Ebenezer Cook, a leading art educator at the time.

Crucial in Virginia's development, her father from early on favored his younger daughter who resembled him physically. He took great pride in her verbal facility, offered her the "tools" she needed to write and enjoyed her obvious attachment to him (Hill, 351–352). Acutely aware she was the child most responsive to and identified with his literary bent, Leslie encouraged her writing skills, and provided a solid grounding in history and biography, which he thought necessary in understanding literature. He assigned and then discussed specific areas of study with her: "She takes in a great deal and will really be an author in time" he wrote his wife, "though I cannot make up my mind in what line" (Jul.29, 1893; Berg). Actually, he hoped she would become an historian. The mutual interest in literature and the pedagogical link with her father became emotionally highly charged for Virginia. Inasmuch as Julia felt "inept with words," there is reason to think she was threatened by the closeness between father and daughter.

Though fathers customarily propel the oldest son to follow their profesfessional orientation, Leslie chose Virginia instead, as evidenced in a letter to Julia when Virginia was 11 and Thoby 13, telling his wife that

Thoby had "just the good sound brains that tell at Cambridge; some day he might be Lord Chancellor but I don't want him to be an author. That is a thing for ladies, and Ginia will do well in that line" (Aug.3, 1893; Berg). Leslie's comment implies sexual confusion as well as uncertainty concerning his own literary career.

With Thoby home from school, Virginia was enthralled with his stories of the Greeks. Envying Thoby his formal education, she decided she, too, would learn Greek. For the most part at this time, she and Vanessa were taught dancing, drawing, music, and graceful deportment —to not much avail.

Gerald and George Duckworth, Virginia's half-brothers, attended Eton and Cambridge. Born some months after his father died, Gerald was delicate as a child, and his mother gave him special attention. When Gerald was seven, he apparently "assaulted" Leslie for "playfully" pulling Julia down a low slope (Love, 171). "Georgie" was variously chaperone, big brother, and escort. Virginia considered him "strong, handsome and just: he taught us to hold our bats straight and to tell the truth, and we blushed with delight if he praised" (*Rem*, 57). The children believed that George resembled his father, Herbert Duckworth and indeed he was frequently considered father-surrogate. Virginia also depicts George as good natured, voluble, and profuse in his affections, which in his mother's lifetime he kept in check.

Virginia suggests her mother was severe with Stella, suppressed her as a child, and that Stella in turn considered her mother someone with divine power and intellect. When Stella was grown, she and mother had a closer relationship, although Stella always appeared subservient. Chaperone to the children, Stella in Virginia's view was beautiful, feminine, gentle, and sympathetic. However she was not well-educated, not fond of reading. In playing the violin, she exaggerated her inadequacy and was utterly devoid of personal ambition. Woolf further describes her as sensitive to "real things" and capable of "penetrating deeply into people" (*Rem*, 41). Her beauty attracted many suitors, the most persistent Jack Hills, who proposed in 1894, although Stella rejected him at first.

Most sharply imprinted on the lives of the children were summers spent at Talland House in Cornwall, where Virginia and Vanessa were tomboys and where "us four" (Vanessa, Thoby, Adrian, and Virginia) swam, boated, climbed, bowled, played cricket on the lawn, engaged in botanical quests and butterfly hunting. Vanessa asked her father whether St. Ives and London were two different worlds, each with its own, separate sky. The richness of Woolf's early experiences at Cornwall are attested to in the evocative nature writing in sections of *To The Lighthouse, Jacob's Room,* and *The Waves.*

Woolf's autobiographical essay, *A Sketch of the Past*, remarkable in its recall of nuclear childhood memories, spans transports of joy and rapture as well as nightmare and psychic numbness.[16] Visualizing herself in a dream-like setting, suggesting loneliness, diminutiveness, and vulnerability, Woolf recalls that as a small child she felt surrounded by "vast space," compares it to a "great hall . . . , with windows letting in strange lights; and murmurs and spaces of deep silence". This coexists with the "sense of movement, change," and instability—suggesting a feeling of "everything approaching and then disappearing, getting large, getting small, passing at different rates of speed past the little creature . . . , driven as a plant is driven up out of the earth until the stalk grows, the leaf grows, buds swell . . . " (*SOTP*, 79).

Referring to her first memory, Woolf recalls sitting on her mother's lap on the train to St. Ives. Contemplating the pattern of the anemones against her mother's black dress, she reported on the "scratch of some beads . . . as I pressed my cheek against it" (81), suggesting a sense of abrasiveness accompanying the tactile closeness, as well as awareness of her mother's depression: "She [mother] had her own sorrow waiting behind her to dip into privately" (82).

Indicating "life has a base that it stands on . . . , a bowl that one fills and fills and fills," again evoking her mother, Woolf recalls lying half-asleep in the nursery, "hearing the waves sending a splash of water over the beach, then breaking behind a yellow blind . . . , the acorn drawn across the floor as the wind blew the blind out." Exclaiming "it is almost impossible" that she had actually been there, she then felt the "purest ecstasy"[17] she could imagine (64–65).

Here there is a break in the continuity, as Woolf digresses, in effect questioning her identity: "who was I, then—was I clever, stupid, good looking, ugly, passionate, cold?" Woolf both acknowledges and suppresses her sexual feelings, of which she is exceedingly frightened, and the only area about which she claims she cannot write. The intensity of her early memories she links to the feeling of "lying in a grape, seeing through a film of semi-transparent yellow," attributed to the change from London to Cornwall (65). She then recalls the nursery and the partition connecting the balcony with her parents' bedroom. Her mother would emerge "in her white dressing gown. There were passion flowers growing on the wall. They were great starry blossoms with purple streaks and large green buds, part empty, part full" (66).

In this early memory of soothing, womb-like enclosure, experienced at the Stephens's summer house where the nursery was next door to the parents' room, the famly then a more cohesive force, her mother a more available presence, Woof's poeticized reminiscences suggest her romantic attachment to her mother and the communication her "buds" had not reached fruition.[18] Associating to these first impressions in painterly terms, she perceives extremely feminine images; that is, "globular" forms, "curved petals showing the light through," but large, unclear, and dim (66). These shapes are, she imagines, both seen and heard.

Her images are more sensual in her next memory: Describing the "buzz, the croon, the smell" in the garden, all "pressing voluptuously against some membrane," she claims she is the "container of the feeling of ecstasy, of the rapture," feels without guilt so long as these are non-sexual, "disconnected with my own body" (67–68).

Other memories concerning her childhood are frightening or nightmarish. Attributing her "Puritan" streak to her paternal grandmother's connection with the Clapham sect, Woolf alludes to her father's spartan, ascetic qualities, and she associates these with her fear of being caught looking at herself in the hall mirror, claiming she is "ashamed or afraid" of her body; this has persisted her entire life.

Next, she records her sensations when she was 6 or 7 at the time Gerald touched her genitals; he was then 18. Woolf describes the "slab" Gerald placed her on, recalls feeling his hand under her clothes, "going firmly and steadily lower and lower," remembers "resenting, disliking it . . . ; what is the word for so dumb and mixed a feeling?" In this context, she alludes to her childhood dream of looking into a mirror and seeing a "horrible face, the face of an animal, over my shoulder" (69). Woolf's sequential memory of Gerald's sexual molestation juxtaposed to her mirror dream in which she saw the face of a frightening animal, suggests she equates sexuality with primitivity of male response.

Woolf's feelings of sexual abuse and desire for revenge regarding Gerald are transformed in *The Years*, in the depicted street enounter of young Rose Pargiter with an older man who exposed himself, which Rose guiltily kept secret. The central point Woolf wishes to establish is that both she and her fictional character felt unloved, insufficiently cared for, and felt there was no parental force who could understand, clarify, or instruct, or with whom one could communicate; furthermore, their lives were considerably warped as a result of sexual fears. Threatened by heterosexual relationships, Rose presumably becomes "more like a man than a woman" (*TY*, 170). Woolf's sense of sexual interference was compounded by the amatory advances persisting over many years, of her other half-brother, George. Fear, ignorance, shame, or rage prevented Woolf from confronting him or confiding her fears to anyone. As with others who have had precocious sexual experiences that were unsought, she might have wished to protect her half-brothers or might have been conflictedly pleased at the attention shown her.

In another childhood framework, Woolf recalls a feeling of being dragged down into a "pit of absolute despair she could not escape, her body paralyzed" on learning of the suicide of a family friend. She also remembered an "idiot boy who sprang up with hand outstretched, mewing, slit-eyed, eyes red-rimmed" (*SOTP*, 78). Wordless, but with a sense of horror, she gave him some candy. Here one wonders whether the idiot boy personified her half-sister Laura, whose unmet needs, omniverous, unfulfillable, Virginia might have felt identified with and frightened by.

That night she felt sadness, collapse, as though she were passive under "some sledgehammer blow, exposed to a whole avalanche of meaning that had . . . discharged itself upon me, unprotected with nothing to ward it off." An early episode involving a physical flareup with Thoby and its sudden cessation on her part is similarly reacted to with a sense of intense hopelessness and self-derogation. At another time, trying to cross a puddle in her path, she became immobilized.[19]

Woolf referred to these childhood situations that encompassed traumatic reactions to aggressive or self-injuring behavior concerning herself or others, as "moments of being" or "scaffolding" in the background. Though she often felt unable to cope with the awareness that people hurt one another or themselves, as a writer she considered her receptivity to "shock" welcome, infinitely valuable, leading to revelations of the reality behind appearances. Here she might refer to the boundary-defining impact of pain. Her anxieties are alleviated by putting them into words; in short, she achieves an active mastery. Shocks are then no longer imbued with the power to hurt her, but afford her infinite pleasure, the "rapture" she gets when writing, in "discovering what belongs to what, making a scene come right, making a character come together" (72–73).

As Virginia turned 13, her writing in the *Hyde Park Gate News* appeared, according to Quentin Bell, more mature though not as "amusing." She attempted a "novel of manners" as well as an article concerning a "dream in which she was God" (Bell, v.1, 37). Her father continued to influence Virginia's education. In his "eye for truth, his vigilance in its defence, his sensitivity as a reader" (Gordon, 71–72), he was Virginia's "first intellectual model" (77).

Although Julia on one occasion sent Virginia's short stories to Madge Vaughan, a literary friend, for her evaluation, Woolf generally felt her father the more consistently involved, her mother's attention more divided. Her father had in the past written Julia that Virginia's beauty was "greater"; that is, "she did not have a nose like someone else in the family" (Jan.25; 1891; Berg), referring to Julia although his wife was, of course, a woman of consummate beauty. This was intended to pique Julia, but it was at Virginia's expense.

Is it possible that Julia's love for Virginia was attenuated because of her jealousy regarding Leslie's emotional attachment and intellectual rapport regarding his youngest daughter? Was his involvement with Virginia a disservice, in some sense an oedipally weighted situation where the parent, not the child, creates fairly intense filial expectations, which he inevitably disappoints?

The hostile interplay between Virginia's parents, her father's demanding dependency, her mother's alternate pattern of nurturance and withdrawal, is clearly noted in their correspondence. Her mother's frequent departures from home (was she avoiding the possibility of future pregnancies?) prompted strong remonstrances on Leslie's part, imprinting in Virginia a sense of her parents' shaky rapport.

Although the relationship between Virginia's parents is generally perceived as one in which Julia sacrificially submitted to Leslie's pleas for sympathy and his incessant demands for attention, it is also apparent that Leslie felt abandoned by his wife's absences and thereafter became querulous and accusing.

In thus depicting Julia, I risk being termed judgmental, a reproach I anticipate from those who have apotheosized Julia, based on transference reactions towards Mrs. Ramsay, Woolf's idealized portrait of her mother in *To the Lighthouse*; or based on an adherence to the Demeter-Persephone myth. Both Julia and Leslie impinged on Virginia's development in benign and negative interactions. I have tried to view Julia in terms of the adverse effects on her of the disruption of her family when she was a child, the seeming abandonment by her father although her mother left him and the endless claims made on her by her mother which may not have permitted Julia her selfhood. Marrying twice in quest of a father, Julia's prolonged grief regarding her first husband's death may have replaced the omitted mourning for loss of her childhood father. Anger and disappointment regarding her father was probably displaced onto Leslie.

Julia's problems in mothering had nothing to do, as claimed, with Victorian restrictions on women; she was a practical nurse, extremely mobile and liberated for a woman in her socioeconomic class, visited workhouses, hospitals, and left home for extended periods.

III

Woolf described her mother as increasingly worn and harassed, always in a hurry, sparing others, exhausting herself; as someone who, though still young in years, had depleted herself through a lifetime of altruistic work and whose physical resistance, finally, "burned out" (*Rem*, 34).

When her mother died on May 5, 1895, from a combination of influenza and rheumatic fever, Virginia, now 13, was in the throes of adolescence. A critical developmental phase, adolescence is frequently considered a period of "mourning"[20] that necessitates relinquishment of childhood patterns and subsumes the need for firmer identity formation, emancipation from one's family, and pull towards new relationships (A. Freud, 1958; Blos, 1967). Interference with the maturational need at this age for positive identification with one's mother as a female model, experiencing instead the severance and breakup of the family's cohesiveness, increased Virginia's sense of emotional precariousness.

Hoping to rescue and comfort her father, Virginia held out her arms to him when he staggered from the mother's sickroom, but he apparently did not respond. Stella, who now became mother-surrogate and in a sense wife-surrogate, assumed many of Julia's former activities.

Woolf deplored the pretense and hypocrisy of the mourning rituals in which her father engaged. Leslie's "oriental gloom" (*Rem*, 40), his failure at this juncture to assume an assertive, paternal role, and his piteous and collapsed demeanor were distressing to his children, provided little leadership or structure to their lives. At first painfully divided in her allegiance, Virginia subsequently linked herself with Vanessa who felt their mother's death due to Julia's submission to Leslie's domestic tyranny.

Predominantly, Virginia felt dissociation of feelings and, not untypical for this stage of development, showed for the most part, a lack of emotional readiness for the work of mourning or involvement with grief and loss. Viewing the child's inability to mourn as a "defensive measure" which emerges when emotions exceed threshold limits, Deutsch (1937) points to a continual mourning process, evidenced in later "unmotivated" depressions (228).

Virginia's sense of unlovability, her vast, unmet need for maternal support, the channelling of her guilt, grief, and anger into physical symptoms, emerged at this time. Most crucially the pattern of the mourning process is, in psychoanalytic terms, linked to the degree of ambivalence originally felt towards the dead parent; the more ambivalent the relationship, the more difficult to resolve. Virginia's negative feelings regarding her mother, largely submerged or split-off, were considerable, augmented by her sense of abandonment. Her hostile feelings were displaced onto her father, her mother now glorified, a not untypical pattern in children responding to a parent's death (Wolfenstein, 1966; Jacobson, 1965; J.B.N. Miller, 1971).

Her mother's death led to Virginia's fear of collapse of the psychic structure so far attained, created havoc in her already conflicted identification process, and established an ongoing sense of incapacity in repairing or clarifying her confusion concerning sexual identity.

Her fictional alter-ego, Lily Briscoe, resonates Virgina's feelings as Lily imagines that in the "chambers of the mind and heart" of Mrs. Ramsay were "treasures as in the tombs of kings, tablets bearing sacred inscriptions which if you could spell them out, teach one everything" (*TTL*, 79). Similarly, Virginia felt had her mother lived, she would in an ongoing sense, have been able to incorporate her wisdom, more closely identify with her feminine and maternal roles, possibly resolve her anger.

During Virginia's first breakdown in 1895, her "pulse raced . . . so fast as to be almost unbearable. She became painfully excitable, nervous, then intolerably depressed." Apparently "terrified of people" at this point, she "blushed scarlet" when approached. Self-critical, she severely derogated herself for being "vain and egotistical," found herself deficient in comparison to Vanessa, remained quite "highstrung" although she read "feverishly and continually." Dr. Seton, one of the Stephens' family physicians advised a "simple life and outdoor exercise." Woolf thereupon accompanied Stella on her many daily routines and took endless walks with father and siblings (Bell v.1, 45).

Regarding her breakdown, Woolf barely alludes to the "commotions of her mind," although afterward she referred to "those horrible voices." Perhaps we can demystify the "voices." Here Woolf indicates her obsession with her mother: "I could hear her voice, see her, imagine what she would do or say as I went about my day's doings. She was one of the invisible presences who after all play so important a part in every life." Her mother is held responsible for the feeling of being "tugged this way and that, being kept in position" (*SOTP*, 80).

On one occasion, her mother told Virginia she looked affected and therefore could not attend some anticipated event: "If you put your head to one side you won't go to the party." Her mothers mark is seemingly "branded by the naked steel, the sharp, the pure . . . ," (*Rem*, 39), which suggests her disciplinary directedness and her unyielding disposition.

On her deathbed, Julia's last communication to her daughter, who felt herself unduly tall, ungainly, and overgrown for her age, was to "hold yourself straight, goat," somewhat critical and admonishing. In Virginia's final good-byes, she found her mother's face forbidding, "immeasurably distant, hollow and stern," reminding her of "iron, cold and granulated" (*SOTP*, 92).

After the death, Virginia's sense of loss joined her feeling of liberation, so that meeting her brother Thoby returning home from school for the funeral, she felt "exalted" by the train gliding into the station and by the "blaze" of magnificent light and color, contrasting it with the shrouded rooms at home (*Rem*, 39). Possibly she felt she must atone for her excitement: the voices might have then condemned and accused, accentuating her self-loathing.

Virginia might also have suspected that Julia, always preoccupied with dying and an early, lost love, in effect threw away her life—this with the collusion of Leslie. Imagining a man sitting on her mother's deathbed, Virginia's feeling of abandonment by her mother might have been exacerbated by the fantasy Julia was rejoining her first husband.

Stella, another source of Virginia's unease was catapulted to the head of the household. Now age 26, Stella assumed a role involving the "utmost intimacy with a man who was her stepfather and an elderly man of letters she had previously regarded only with respect and formal affection" (*Rem*, 41). Virginia felt displaced, inordinately jealous regarding Stella's new status and authority. When her father so swiftly substituted Stella for Julia, Virginia hitherto thinking she was his favorite, was undoubtedly confused and angry, felt shunted aside, distanced, and estranged, felt loss of support from the parent to whom she had always been closest.

Had she seen some of Leslie's letters to Stella,[21] written as though to a lover, she might have thought him lecherous. Cautious in her acceptance of Stella's new role, Virginia submitted when ill, to her half-sister's caretaking. Isolated via her mother's death and her father's frenzied idealization of Julia, his self-encapsulation and her own state of ambivalent mourning—it is quite likely Virginia's breakdown also encompassed attention-getting components aimed to divert father from his predominant involvement with Stella.

Basically, Virginia felt the unique ambience of the Stephen's family life over, her home shattered. Her mother had been the "whole thing," keeping the "panoply of life, that which we all lived together, in motion." With her death, the "family life" that the mother brought together ceased and was replaced by a "dark cloud" settling over them. They sat "cooped up, sad, solemn, under a haze of heavy emotion, impossible to break through. The tragedy of her death was that it made her unreal" (*SOTP*, 93).

Gone was the grown-up world, those "snatched moments" that were both "soothing" and "exciting" when Virginia would run "downstairs to dinner arm in arm with her mother"; or said something to amuse her mother, or that her mother thought "very remarkable" (94-95).

With Virginia's first breakdown following the mother's death, the labelling of her symptoms as "madness" began, as well as the dual involvement with caretakers, relating to them in both child-like and rebellious attitudes. Possibly, physical symptomatology was unconsciously resorted

to in hope of restoring or appeasing her mother whose greater mobilization when the children were ill, imprinted for Virginia her future role as
patient. The focus on her body became a template for future involvement
with physical illness, in hope of enlisting that aspect of her mother, attuned to ministering to others.

Showalter links Virginia's breakdown to the advent of menstruation.[22]
Did Woolf believe her mother was threatened by, died, or abandoned her
because of her incipient sexuality? Her closeness with father?

In *To the Lighthouse*, Woolf depicts Mrs. Ramsay, a bit of a match-
maker, as jealous and disappointed once a young couple she introduced
are engaged, seeing in their love the "seeds of death." Feeling they embrace "illusion glittering eyed," Mrs. Ramsay suggests the lovers "must
be danced round with mockery, decorated with garlands" (*TTL*, 151).

Despite the disapproval of her stepfather, Stella married in 1897, two
years after her mother's death. Vanessa was now promoted to Stella's
large bedroom and Virginia given for her bed-sitting room the children's
old night nursery, which became her "cocoon," where she lived her
"confused private life." Remembering Stella's happiness, comparing
this to her fantasy of her mother's first marriage, Woolf recalled saying
to Stella: "There's never been anything like it in the world" (*SOTP*,
105).

During Virginia's adolescence, Stella's husband, Jack Hills, a forth-
right, masculine influence, spoke to Virginia quite candidly about sex.
The couple offered her the first glimmer of "love between man and
woman—so intense, so exciting, so rapturous, it was to me like a ruby,
glowing, red, clear, intense," (104) affording a standard of love.

In *The Waves*, Woolf's identification with Rhoda's sexual awakening[23] and Rhoda's wish to give "all that now flows" through her receptive
body, illuminate this phase of development insofar as Woolf too might
have fantasized. Rhoda exclaims: "Now my body unthaws. I am un-
sealed. Now the stream pours in a deep tide, fertilizing, opening the shut,
forcing the tight folded, flooding free" (*TW*, 213-214).

Retrospective delight in Stella's marriage notwithstanding, Virginia's 1897 diary reflects considerable ambivalence concerning Stella,
especially in feeling pressured to chaperone Stella and Jack on a
proposed holiday trip to Bognor prior to their marriage. Virginia
decided to go only when Vanessa agreed to accompany her. Impatient
with the rituals surrounding the marriage ceremony which took place on
April 10, 1897, Virginia also showed great irritation towards her family
in the sojourn to Brighton during the weeks following the wedding.
Possibly she was angry at father for disapproving the match for so long or
she was upset by the loss of Stella. Her father, as noted in her 1897 diary,

continued, nevertheless, to supervise Virginia's reading. Virginia at this time consumed nineteenth century biographies, novels, and histories and took instruction in the classics (Bell, v.1, 50–51).

With Stella ill of peritonitis on return from her honeymoon, Virginia found onerous the expectation she was required to spend a good deal of her time with Stella. When Stella seemed to be recovering, she felt reluctant to accompany Stella on her "carriage exercises," and she became terrified[24] of the simplest journey through the London streets though some of her observations of accidents have been validated (Bell, v.1,55).

Virginia now learned Stella was pregnant. Despite the doctor's assurances to the contrary, Stella was not getting well; Virginia's health similarly worsened. Finding Virginia quite ill at Stella's home, Dr. Seton sent her to bed, with Stella stroking and ministering to her. Virginia returned home three nights later and, without Virginia's knowledge, Stella was operated on the following evening and by the next morning, July 19, 1897, was dead either from an appendectomy, complications surrounding pregnancy, the earlier peritonitis, or a combination of these.

According to Love (193), Stella's friend, Violet Dickinson, informed Vanessa in 1942 that Stella was "injured" by Jack on their honeymoon. Apparently, Stella had an "inner malformation," rendering intercourse painful; their difficulties were exacerbated by Stella's exhaustion during the wedding and honeymoon. Years later Vanessa described the extreme "muddle and mismanagement," the "hopeless fighting against the stupidity of those in power" (Bell, v.1, 57).

Virginia might also have felt guilty lest Stella's concern towards her added to Stella's exhaustion. Or Virginia might have worried that Stella became pregnant during the trip to Bognor, and she felt additionally responsible for her death (DeSalvo, 1983, 102). Certainly Stella's death three months after marriage clearly coalesced for Virginia the morbid connection of marriage and sexuality with injury, suffering and death.

III "Passionate affection for my father alternating with passionate hatred"

I

Because Leslie seemed to Virginia and Vanessa minimally grief-stricken regarding Stella's death, they thought him a "tyrant of inconceivable selfishness who replaced the beauty and merriment of the dead with ugliness and gloom." Woolf later acknowledged she and Vanessa were exaggeratedly critical, "bitter, harsh and to a great extent unjust" toward him (*Rem*, 56).

The lives of the children were tortured and "fretted" by the deaths of mother and Stella and by the "stupid damage" inflicted: "I shrink from the years 1897 to 1904, the seven unhappy years. At 15 to have that protection removed, to be tumbled out of the family shelter, to see cracks and gashes in that fabric, to be cut by them . . . , was that good"? (*SOTP*, 117–118). Hitherto submerged family schisms appeared, for example, the explosive period concerning Vanessa's romantic involvement with Jack Hills. Defending or opposing Vanessa's stance, Virginia felt damned, but basically she sided with Vanessa.

With the blow of Stella's death, Virginia experienced as though for the first time, the full impact of her mother's death, felt a sense of "betrayal," a severe interruption in her ongoing development:

> My mother's death had been a latent sorrow—at age 13 one could not master it, envisage it, deal with it. But Stella's death two years later fell on a different substance, on someone extraordinarily unprotected, unformed, unshielded, apprehensive, receptive, anticipatory (*SOTP*, 1985, 124).[1]

Virginia felt "violently cheated" by Stella's death, of the promise Stella's marriage held, for "escape from the gloom," persisting since their mother's death. She was now "brutally" reminded not to be so foolish as to "hope for things." She thought it impossible that this "second blow of death" could descend on her, "filmy eyed" as she was, with her "wings still creased, sitting there on the edge" of her "broken chrysalis," (124) barely hatched into personhood.

Woolf describes the "red chill buds," conveying the "discomfort, misery and the quarrels, the suppressed irritations, the sharp words, the insinuations," which with the resumption of family life in Hyde Park Gate concealed the fact that in 1897, with Stella's death, Virginia and Vanessa must "take up new relationships" (*SOTP*, 121). Eventually the sisters were reunited in a "close conspiracy where they saw "life as a struggle to get some kind of standing place . . . , always battling for what was being interfered with, snatched away" (*SOTP*, 124).

They felt their greatest obstacle and burden was father, who manifested an "extraordinary dramatization of self-pity, anger and despair." Regarding budgetary matters, he felt he was "ruined, dying, tortured by the wanton extravagance of Vanessa," (124) now hostess and mistress of the house. At the last, he would toss the money to Vanessa, who remained stony throughout, and then turned to Virginia for sympathy. Never had Virginia felt such "rage and such frustration" (125), which she contained. Her father's histrionics she attributed to Vanessa's refusal to assume a deferential role towards him and to his consciousness of failure as philosopher and writer. Had her father used a "whip," Virginia masochistically imagined, his brutality would seem no greater.

Feeling her father lacking in awareness of human relationships and the mutual responsibilities thereof, Woolf points to the "horror and terror of these diplays of rage . . . ,"[2] with no prospects of greater communicaton (126).

Indicating her father was not a writer for whom she has a "natural taste," Woolf describes her "tyrant father":

> It was like being shut up in the same cage with a wild beast. Suppose I at 15, was a nervous, gibbering, little monkey. He was the pacing, dangerous, morose lion; a lion who was sulky, angered and injured; and suddenly ferocious, and then very humble, and then majestic; and then lying dusty and fly-pestered in a corner of the cage (*SOTP*, 1985, 116).

Her father rationalized his erratic behavior, according to Woolf, because he believed he was a "genius," and felt he could simply apologize after erupting and all would be serene. Yet, Woolf indicates, he knew he was not a genius; he had told her he was "only a good second class mind" (110). Her father, as we know, was himself convinced he was a failure.

Virginia basically remained deeply ambivalent regarding her father. She maintained on the one hand an intense emotional attachment toward him. Had he not given her his ring on her eighteenth birthday and was she not, in effect, his literary heir and successor? She would later write Vita Sackville West she had a "great devotion for him—what a disinterested man; how high minded, how tender to me and fierce and intolerable" (L4, Feb.19'29). In a similar vein, she described for Ethel Smyth her father's extreme sincerity, indicating she thought him "beautiful in the distinguished way a racehorse is beautiful. And he had such a fling with his hands and feet. Also he was completely unworldly. Also he begot me" (L5, Sept.7'32).

Yet Virginia continued to perceive him, particularly through Vanessa's jaundiced vision, as victimizer and tyrant. Attending art classes three days a week at the Cope school in London, Vanessa, obeisant to her father's needs for many years, was home in the afternoon to serve tea, although felt this a great burden. Of course Vanessa's hatred for her father, aside from his tirades about reckless spending, might have stemmed from his decided, early preference for Virginia.

Woolf depicted her father as both comical and terrifying. She and Vanessa were "explorers, revolutionists, reformers"; he was narrowly Victorian in 1900, "50 years behind the times," and enormously dependent on the ministration of women (*SOTP*, 126–127).

Considering her father a grandfather-figure rather than father, Virginia nevertheless shared an "odd, fumbling fellowship"[3] with him, acknowledged her indebtedness to the richness of his intellect, and his commitment to the literary process: "Perhaps I was reading Johnson. For some time we would talk and then feeling soothed, stimulated, and full of love for this unworldly, very distinguished, lonely man, I would go down to the drawing room and hear George's patter" (136).

Virginia sought to avoid George's coerciveness and pressure regarding the social amenities and felt indignant about his sexual pursuit, which she felt he cloaked as brotherly concern. In her memoir, she noted the "division in our life—downstairs there was pure convention, George; upstairs pure intellect, father" (135). Here she alluded to her dual relationship with both father-figures, to the intellectual versus the sexual dimension, and their immiscibility at this time.

Summarizing the degrees of complexity in Virginia's relationship with her father: Virginia wishing to be close to Vanessa, identified with her sister's hatred of father particularly his penuriousness, and blamed him for mother's death. Originally preferred by father as a child and favoring him over mother, Virginia felt sexually rejected when he turned to Stella after Julia's death, resented her half-sister who had not previously been close to father, and was now elevated to a position of wife and mother-surrogate. This eventuated in intense annoyance toward both Stella and her father.

Her father was hypocritical, Virginia felt, in that despite his professed love for her mother, he immediately after her death, turned to Stella as though she were his wife. Virginia also faulted her father for his opposition to Stella's marriage. Her negativism toward her father was exacerbated in thinking he cast a pall over Stella's "few months of joy" and after Stella's death would probably take Vanessa for his next "victim." Virginia's lag in social and sexual development was due, she felt, to her dependence on father. She felt he was responsible for setting up expectations which he then disappointed, only to latch onto her again after Stella's death.

Underneath Virginia's placation of her half-brothers and father, she harbored an acute aversion to what she felt was their manipulation and possessiveness. Virginia might have linked her father's early interest in her with Gerald and George's sexual intrusiveness and toward all three felt a global sense of guilt, victimization, and outrage. Manifested as well in Virginia's acerbic approach to father and predominantly positive, nostalgic portrait of mother in *A Sketch of the Past*, was a fantasied reconciliation with her mother and with this an incorporation of those attitudes of mother which were condescending or contemptuous toward men.

The conception of her father from the vantage point of 1939 to 1940, the time of writing *A Sketch of the Past*, also represents a continuation of Woolf's anger regarding the patriarchal order, catalyzed by writing *The Years* and *Three Guineas*, further affected by the outbreak of World War II. Her criticalness in addition indicates the gradual awareness of her husband's "love of domination and power," linking him with her father and linking both with the male sex in general.

II

When Leslie became ill during April 1902, with a chronic gastrointestinal disorder, diagnosed abdominal cancer, Virginia was chief caretaker; her letters to Violet Dickinson indicate immense concern and emotional closeness to her father as well as her difficulties in witnessing the crises of his illness. He gradually declined in health after surviving an abdominal operation in December 1902. Despite his weakness, he continued to see visitors.

In referring to this period, Woolf later wrote, her tone waspish as compared to the anxious letters to Violet, that her father's health had been her mother's "fetish"; and that, although Julia died easily of overwork at age 49, he found it "very difficult to die of cancer, at 72" (*SOTP*, 114). Her father gradually deteriorated in health though managed to finish the autobiographical memoir his children called *The Mausoleum Book*. He died three months later, on February 2, 1904, with a photograph of his wife facing him.

Although Virginia sought to consolidate with Vanessa, she could not totally identify with her sister's sense of relief in the aftermath of their father's death. Immersed in taking care of her father for a prolonged period, Virginia now considered herself to have been insufficiently caring or attentive to him in his illness and in his loneliness, felt none of the eulogies accorded him in letter or obituary were authentic or appropriate. She was strongly at odds with her siblings who could apparently resume their lives as of old. Thoby showed good recoverability with regard to his father's death and was absorbed in future plans; Adrian, of course, had never been close to his father.

Virginia was now seriously alienated from Vanessa, who felt exuberant on obtaining her freedom after seven years of submitting to their father. Clearly launched insofar as her feminine role and heterosexual orientation were concerned, Vanessa had "entered society" under George's sponsorship, although she was reluctant and distrustful, resenting his social pressures. Ending her love affair with Jack Hills, Vanessa formed close friendships with an older, married woman of considerable wealth and social position, Kitty Maxse, and with Marjorie Snowden, an art student. At 22, Vanessa, enrolled in the Royal Academy Painting School, was deeply committed to art.

Jealous of her sister's friendship with Kitty, Virginia was far more unformed than Vanessa in her feminine identification, having been predominantly drawn to mother-child attachments, for example, her romantic crush on Madge Vaughan, an older, married cousin who encouraged Virginia's muse. Absorbed in intellectual pursuits, reading omniverously, Virginia continued her writing "exercises", pursued Latin at Kings College, studied Greek with Clara Pater and Janet Case who later enlisted Virginia's help concerning the women's suffrage movement.[4]

Beginning in 1902, Violet Dickinson, Stella's friend, provided a solid, maternal presence in Virginia's life, giving "sympathy, understanding and love with immense generosity" (Bell, v.1,83), introduced Virginia to her "aristocratic connections"; with some of Violet's friends, Virginia felt much rapport. Violet, 17 years her senior, was sole confidant and recipient of Virginia's many anxieties during her father's illness. Bantering in tone, their letters appear warm and affectionate, frequently evidencing a private code. Occasionally, Virginia referred to herself as "Sparroy," "Kangaroo," or "Wallaby," pets to be cuddled or stroked and addressed her friend as "My Violet" or "My Woman." She fantasized a husband for Violet, actually Violet's brother towards whom she pretended jealousy. An exaggeratedly tall woman, six feet two inches, with a "breezy, masculine assurance," Violet was sexually rather undifferentiated, and she had never married. Bell indicates Virginia was "in love" with Violet (83).

Continuing to work on her "literary exercises," Virginia sent her manucripts to Violet. In a spoof of Violet, she depicted her as a powerful leader in a utopian community of women; Virginia is artist and ethereal princess. Both she and Violet oppose "litle evil creatures" who threaten destruction.[5] Most probably Virginia is here referring to her younger brother, Adrian.

Many of Woolf's fictional heroines, as undefined as she regarding feminine role, were frequently motherless, lacking firm emotional moorings. In Woolf's first, fairly autobiographical novel, *The Voyage Out*, a homosexual attachment between her heroine, Rachel, and her aunt or mother-surrogate, Helen, is obliquely suggested. Helen physically attacks her niece, Rachel, when she becomes aware of Rachel's increasing interest in Terence, Rachel's lover. During Rachel's subsequent illness and in her delirium she perceives Helen looming over her, of "gigantic size" (347), with seeming intent to harm, wishing for her death, or for total stasis in her development.

Here Woolf seems on an unconscious level to be implicating Violet, the only one of her circle similarly huge. Woolf depicts Helen-Violet as assaulted by Rachel-Virginia's turn toward heterosexuality; Rachel-Virginia could not openly deal with Helen-Violet's disapproval and retaliation.

Issues concerning identity conflict show variations throughout Woolf's life. Woolf's confusion concerning personal and feminine role, based on early feelings of exclusion regarding her mother, envy of Adrian, awareness she was supposed to be a boy, and inability to fully identify with her mother at the same time desiring nurturance and feeling romantically attached to mother-figures—was concomitant to the identification with her father, the ambiguities that emerged in his occasionally assuming the role of the more maternal, available parent, and in his emotional subordination to her mother.

After the death of Mrs. Stephen, George Duckworth, Virginia's older half-brother, then 27, was to all intents and purposes head of the family; her father was "deaf, eccentric, shut off from the world." Indicating that George lived in the "thickest emotional haze, that everything was drowned in kisses," and that one felt like an "uncomfortable minnow shut up in the same tank with an unwieldy, turbulent whale" (*SOTP*, 147), Woolf adds that after her mother's death, George was "not only father, mother, brother, and sister," but lover as well (155). George's behavior, begun as affectionate demonstrativeness, glided into amatory caresses.

Virginia also describes George's ritual inspections of her party dresses, the pressure to attend some hated social function, his condemnation, as he spoke in the "voice of the enraged male," her fear, and her "knuckling under his authority" (*SOTP*, 1985, 151-152).

Distrusting Woolf's sanity even when not in the throes of breakdown, Love (207) suggests that Woolf might be distorting the interaction with George, questions her innocence, which, Love thought, might camouflage sexual desire. Yet both Vanessa and Quentin Bell support Woolf's accusations regarding George. Although in her early diaries and letters, Woolf benignly refers to "Georgie" as a "hero" to the Stephen children, this does not contradict Woolf's perception of him as sexually invasive.

With her father's death, Virginia now had to emerge from the encapsulation characterizing her previous life with him where she had, to a considerable extent, delayed resolving troublesome issues concerning self-definition. To deflect her grief and depression, the Stephens travelled to Europe, met Thoby and his Cambridge friend, Clive Bell, in Paris, where they visited art galleries and gained entry to artists' studios. Throughout the trip, Vanessa, an aspiring painter, lent herself fully and intensely to the encounter with art and artist, while Virginia, feeling ineffectual, unable to compete with her sister's exuberance and health, was fretful, complaining, and inconsolable. Seeking to resume her writing, she felt immobilized; Virginia predicted Vanessa and Clive would become engaged "the moment she [Vanessa] saw Clive" (LI, Dec.18'06).

III

Virginia's anger, competitiveness and sexual jealousy toward Vanessa; her ambivalent feelings regarding her father, her guilt and self-reproaches following his death; her fear of facing the future, her lack of clearcut identity, her inability to relinquish familial bonds or orient herself in a heterosexual direction, were prelude to her second breakdown. She became seriously disturbed on the family's return from Europe, her distrust of Vanessa now considerable, her grief for her father "maniacal" (Bell, v.1, 89). Virginia felt truly orphaned.

A rest-cure was now considered imperative; that is, isolation, remaining in bed, and consuming large quantities of rich food and milk. Perceiving three nurses attending her as "fiends," hearing "voices[6] urging her to acts of folly," the source, she thought, was "overeating"; therefore, she must starve[7] herself. Vanessa and Violet took care of her, and as she lay in bed at Violet's house in Welwyn, she heard "birds singing in Greek", imagined "King Edward VII lurked in the azaleas, using the foulest possible language" (Bell, v.1, 90); she also tried jumping out the window.[8]

Concerning Virginia's many-levelled preoccupation with matters Greek, Thoby first spoke to her about the language and literature, which she then pursued on her own with the help of her tutor, Janet Case. Virginia was highly conversant with Greek plays; permutations of the close emotional bond between father and daughter explored in Sophocles' *Antigone* and *Electra*, subtly permeate much of her fiction, resulting in a sacrifice of the heroine's maturational process in deference to the father, a submerging of the possibility of any vital heterosexual experience of her own.

Feeling emotionally latched onto by her father, Virginia felt she subordinated more autonomous interests to accommodate him. Her hallucinations reflect an imperative need to communicate her sexual anxieties, however cryptic and eluding comprehension these manifestations of her emotional illness proved to be.

Insofar as the allusions to birds is concerned, a letter from Vanessa to an old friend, describes Virginia as some "fantastic bird, abruptly throwing up her head and crowing with delighted amusement at some idea, some work, some paradox that took her fancy" (Bell v.2, 96). Their brother, Thoby, whom Virginia called "Cresty," was passionately interested in birds and bird hunting. In a letter to Violet after her father's death, Virginia wrote: "You will be glad to hear that your Sparroy feels herself a recovered bird" (Sept.22'04).

Virginia spontaneously identified with animals and the non-human realm, compared her fictional characters to birds: In her isolation, Rezia in *Mrs. Dalloway* felt like a "bird sheltering under the thin hollow of a leaf . . . , surrounded by . . . an indifferent world; exposed; tortured; and why should she suffer? Why?" (*MD*, 99). The downward sweep of rooks frequently sets the tone for her husband, Septimus' change of mood: In a depressive image, Septimus feels his wife's mind "falling from branch to branch like a bird" (*MD*, 223). He, too, hears birds singing in Greek: "there is no crime, there is no death," which connects with his homosexual panic and the denial of his war comrade's death.[9] Septimus ultimately commits suicide by leaping out the window; Virginia jumped too, but half-heartedly. In part, she might have also felt she deserved punishment because of her inability to mourn her mother and her submission to George's lovemaking as her father "lay dying."

Perhaps the early substrate of Virginia's preoccupation with birds was her father's animal stories and drawings, his mode of communicating with his children. Undoubtedly precursor to the nicknames later used by Woolf, her father, pretending the children were themselves birds or animals, referred to himself as an "old rook" or a "fairly cheerful raven" (Love, 44).

In her essay "On Not Knowing Greek," Woolf described a nightingale whose song echoes through English literature. She compared herself to Electra who refers to "that very nightingale, that bird distraught with grief," herself "betrayed and shaken like a bird complaining" (*CR*, v.1,45); ignoring death, Electra inexorably waits for her father. The nightingale may also be viewed in context of the Greek myth[10] in which Philomela is seduced by Tereus, who has her tongue removed to prevent her from speaking. Tereus's wife Procne, in revenge, killed their son, serving him as food to her husband, then ran away with her sister, Philomela. The sisters were turned into birds: Philomela into a nightingale, Procne a swallow. Does the myth evoke Woolf's guilt regarding her mother's death? Woolf's silence regarding her half-brothers' lovemaking? Her frustrated longing to find a voice to express her rage?

Indicating her fondness for Greek choruses that "sing like birds in the pause of the wind," Woolf was drawn to the Greeks because although "violent emotions" are needed to rouse one into action, when "thus stirred by death, by betrayal, Antigone . . . . and Electra behave in the way we should" (44).

Though in a sense auditory hallucinations, "birds singing in Greek" and "King Edward using the foulest possible language" stem from multidetermined syntheses of feelings, images, memories, and fantasies Virginia could not otherwise convey, temporarily mastering intense anxiety and inner conflict. Certainly "King Edward using the foulest possible language" was linked to the invasiveness of incestuous father-figures, releasing Virginia's feelings of rage and revulsion. Virginia, furthermore, might have worried lest George would be more importunate in his sexual pursuit, now that her father was dead.

In part linked with her father, Virginia's bird imagery frequently has a distinctly phallic quality, evoking Mr. Ramsey's "beak of brass, the arid scimitar of the male which smote mercilessly again and again" (*TTL*,59), perhaps causing his wife's death. Similarly, Rhoda's sense of being "pierced by a bird's beak" in *The Waves*, suggests a persistent, masculine intrusiveness.

Virginia was, in addition, attracted to the life force,[11] the indomitableness, the passionate resiliency of birds, their ability to be supremely alive; she was identified as well with their diminutiveness and intense vulnerability with regard to the capriciousness of the human realm.

In leaping out the window, perhaps linked to the "voices urging her to acts of folly," Virginia prepared the way for her fictional doubles, Septimus in *Mrs. Dalloway* and Rhoda in *The Waves*, who also jumped, albeit successfully. We know very little concerning Virginia's first suicide attempt, only that it occurred and that she jumped from a window fairly close to the ground. Was her angry, histrionic gesture directed at rest-cures, doctors, parents, parent-surrogates including Vanessa, Violet, and nurses who sought to control her existence? Does it point to her desire to break away from Violet? Her wish to rejoin her father)

Obviously this time, she wished to live, but her suicide attempt undoubtedly subsumed a constellation of anger, protest and despair; desire for punishment, attention, and rescue. Are we to assume the nurses were "fiends" because Woolf felt they forced her to eat or insisted on her isolation? Eating is highly emotionally charged, intertwined as it is with the earliest, physical and emotional interplay with mother in the nursing situation. Virginia's resistance to eating may also correspond to the dynamics of the depressive modality. Actually, Virginia showed aversion to food or "fear of becoming too fat" for most of her life (3LW163). Her anorexic response may have been a means of defeating the hated Weir Mitchell treatment, enforced whenever she showed symptoms of restlessness, headache, or depression. She was then enjoined to eat rich food, drink several glasses of milk each day, "rest" in a darkened room, have few visitors and read minimally. Feeling this humiliating and depriving, she also felt shame regarding the effects of over-eating on her already devalued body.

In refusing food during her 1904 breakdown after her father's death, she might have been expressing grief and guilt toward father,[12] responding angrily to nurses who were authoritarian, or to Vanessa and Violet, extensions of her mother. Here she found herself in a paradoxical bind, simultaneously experiencing indignation and fearing abandonment regarding those she loved.

Not strictly suffering from anorexia nervosa, a severe physiological disturbance that can lead to death, Virginia was intermittently anorectic and showed some of the same behavioral patterns such as ambivalence regarding mother, denial of femininity, and the wish to undo the biological changes of adolescence; fear of growing up and assuming an adult female role, feeling sexuality is dangerous, and envying men their power. In her 1903 diary,[13] Virginia questioned her right to read the massive number of books written by men, anticipating their laughter regarding her efforts. Her femaleness seemed to her an unjust disadvantage. Ironically, restriction of food intake causes cessation of menses that, in turn, engenders preoccupation with pregnancy, confusion regarding body-image as well as one's physical and sexual functions. Also characteristic of anorectics and shared by Virginia are paralyzing feelings of helplessness and ineffectiveness in submitting to parents or parent-surrogates (Bruch, 1979, 58). In refusing food, anorectics acquire a spurious identity, apparently feel better defined. Similarly, Virginia in her conflicts regarding food and in her power struggles with overcontrolling, unempathic mother-figures or caretakers. Leaving Welwyn, Virginia rejoined her siblings who were on holiday and in October, 1904, visited her Aunt Caroline in Cambridge for an extended period. Vanessa and Thoby were preparing for the family's move from Hyde Park Gate to their new home in Bloomsbury.

Letters to Violet point to the glimmerings of recovery: Virginia feels as though "the dead part" of her were "coming to life." The voices she used to hear urging her "to do all kinds of wild things" are gone; she thought they "came from overeating" (L1, Sept.22'04).

In this letter, Virginia attributes her breakdown to eating rich foods, which she then contradicts because, after all, she is now well, eating a good deal, and the voices have fled. Virgninia here refers to the first phase of her treatment wherein "voices" might have been instrumental in telling her to jump. In so doing she could defeat caretakers who did not understand, similar to her later fictional double, Septimus, who considered his suicide a means of retaliating against doctors.

Virginia's life is now an "exquisite joy . . . , delivered from the miseries of the past six months . . . ; sorrow for father is more natural though life is sadder" (L1,Sept.26'04). Annoyed with Dr. Savage for insisting she not return home quite yet, Virginia wrote Violet

> I never shall believe in anything any doctor says. I'm sick of all this eternal resting and fussing and being told not to do this and that. I wish I could cut my leg off at once and have done with it, rather than go through the endless bothers and delays of a nervous breakdown (L1,Oct.30'04).

An image of castration, surprising in its fantasy of self-mutilation in one who expresses horror that people hurt one another or themselves, it is similar to Virginia's suicidal preoccupations or threats, provocative, revengeful and self-hurtful in intent.

She is now reconciled with Vanessa, always central to her well-being, and felt recovered enough to begin work with a close friend of her father, Frederick Maitland, on his biography of Leslie, which involved an intense scrutiny of his life, entire correspondence, written work and whatever secrets Virginia might not already have known.

IV "Nessa has all that I should like to have"

I

Now unchaperoned, "us four" cleaved together as they resumed their lives, established an autonomous household in Bloomsbury at 46 Gordon Square. Woolf wrote Violet, "How amiable we all are like husbands and wives, yet we all go our own way" (L1, Mar.19'04). She recalled: "We were full of experiments and reforms . . . ; everything was going to be new; everything was going to be different. Everything was on trial" (*SOTP*, 163). Squier (1985) suggests theirs was not "merely a change of house, but a rebirth" (34).

Continuing to read extensively and prepare for a writing career, Woolf wrote essays and biographical pieces, using her 1903 journal for purposes of a "sketch book," documenting her feelings, not censoring her experimental, literary gropings, trying to preserve their authenticity.

After her father's death, Woolf tried to establish an enclave for herself in journalism, and to obtain an income of sorts to defray some of the expenses incurred in her illness. With Violet's help, she obtained a connection with *The Guardian*. Publishing her first article in 1904, an account of her visit to Haworth parsonage, the Brontes' home in Yorkshire, the newspaper continued to accept her writing.

Desiring further "steady work," Woolf began a lifelong connection with *The Times Literary Supplement* in 1905; also beginning in 1905, she taught English history to workingmen and women at Morley College in London. Impressions gathered on a boat trip during a visit to Spain with Adrian in 1905 offered glimmerings of a first novel, *Melymbrosia*, although no doubt it had long been germinating. Virginia had written a story in 1904 about a young couple's fear of sexuality, their vacillation between intimacy and distance, similar to the central relationship in *Melymbrosia*.

Particularly close to Thoby now, Virginia regarded him as masculine, attractive, a mentor, a window to the world. Thoby, who had entered Cambridge in 1899, metamorphosed in physique, becoming thinner and less clumsy. Generally Thoby had an "amused, surprised, questioning" attitude towards Virginia on finding her reading Greek: "a shell-less creature I think he thought me; a simple, eager recipient of his school stories." Yet, she felt she too was "bubbling, inquisitive, restless," carrying on her own contradicting and questioning. Her discussions with him differed a good deal from those with her father; she felt with Thoby a greater sense of freedom and excitement regarding intellectual matters (*SOTP*, 108-109).

In letters to her brother while he was at school, she addressed him as "milord," and "your highness"; she, his "loving Goat." One of her letters informs him she has read Sophocles: "I have read the Antigone—Edipus Coloneus—and am in the middle of the Trachiniae." (L1, Jul.'01). Six months later she thanks him for his gift, *Select Epigrams From The Greek Anthology*, reinforcing her sense of their mutual interest in matters Greek (L1, Jan.29'02). Although she is at times teasing, she idolizes Thoby: "You are an original genius," she writes (Oct./Nov.'02).

Thoby in effect became father-figure for the Stephens after Leslie died. He "came down" from Cambridge in 1904 and was reading for the Bar. His informal gatherings, "At Home on Thursday Evenings," an arena for his Cambridge friends to meet, meditate, or exchange ideas, became to some degree part of the Stephens' extended family in 1905 and later evolved into the Bloomsbury circle. Nicknamed "The Goth," which suggested "affectionate disapproval," Thoby appeared a "little more conservative, a little more conventional" than the others in his group (Bell, v.1, 69). Virginia also attended meetings of the "Friday Club," formed by Vanessa, to discuss the visual arts.

Her brother's friends, Sidney Saxon-Turner, Walter Lamb, Lytton Strachey, Clive Bell, and Leonard Woolf, published a volume of poems called *Euphrosyne*, which Virginia mercilessly mocked. When the group would meet, she made fun of their reserve:

> they sit silent . . . , occasionally creep to a corner and chuckle over a Latin joke. Perhaps they are falling in love with Nessa; who knows? It would be a silent and very learned process. However, I dont think they are robust enough to feel very much. Oh women are my line and not these inanimate creatures (L1, Oct.1'05).

When they conversed however, Virginia was filled with "wonder." She vastly preferred their worship of G.E. Moore to the empty banter of George's society friends (Bell, v.1, 94). Yet, Virginia pondered that some of Thoby's friends, the "most gifted" of people were also the most "barren"; that friendship with them was the most "deadening". This she felt due to their homosexuality, the lack of "physical attraction" between them (*SOTP*, 172).

Returning from a vacation during which all the Stephens travelled to Greece in 1906, both Vanessa and Thoby were ailing, he with typhoid fever, though at first his physician misdiagnosed his malady as malaria. Thoby gradually became seriously ill, "passed from crisis to crisis" and succumbed to death on November 20, 1906 (Bell, v.1, 100). Virginia was in complete charge of the household at this time. Her grief was deflected, in the energy deployed in comforting Violet, also ill, from whom she at first withheld the news of Thoby's death.

Ultimately, Virginia wrote two novels to rediscover her brother, as it were, as part of her mourning process, but it is unlikely her grief for this brother cut off in his prime, was ever assuaged. To Thoby whose "other world" was Shakespeare, she linked Fortinbras' speech to Hamlet, "let four captains bear Hamlet like a soldier to the stage, for he was likely had he been put on, to have proved most royal" (*SOTP*, 199–120).

Virginia recalled she and Thoby never talked about themselves: "no confidences, no compliments, no kisses, no emotional scenes." As for sex, he grew to manhood "without saying a single thing that would have shown us by word of mouth what he was feeling. Did other boys fall in love with him" she asked; "not he with them," she averred (*SOTP*, 120). Though Virginia might have felt Thoby's intense involvement with male friendships suggested lack of firm sexual identity, she avoided the issue by stressing his normality.

Beneath Thoby's silences, she felt there was depth, susceptibility, sensibility, pride, love, and all the beliefs and desires which might have made him "privately a lover, a husband, a father, and publicly a judge for sure . . . , not a typical Englishman for he was melancholy, original, not able to take the ordinary ambitions seriously" (*SOTP*, 120). When Thoby was in Cambridge, her correspondence with him was mildly chaffing and argumentative in tone, chiefly concerning books and literature.

Two days after Thoby died, Vanessa, to balance her loss, decided she would marry Clive Bell, whom she had previously refused. Experiencing this as nothing short of desertion, Virginia anticipated that the inevitable restructuring of family ties would be disruptive. After the wedding in February, 1907, she was convinced she would never see Vanessa alone again.

Virginia and Adrian[1] moved to 29 Fitzroy Square, resumed Thoby's "Thursday Evenings," asked Bloombsuryites, heterogeneous intellectuals and old friends, to meet with them. Woolf describes her sense of freedom, in that "sex permeated our conversation. We discussed copulation with the same excitement and openness that we had discussed the nature of good." Woolf's "sentimentalized" views of marriage were now "revolutionized" and old beliefs revised; "Bloomsbury was to prove that many variations can be played on the theme of sex" (*SOTP*,174).

Most central in her life was the intense absorption in writing her first novel, *Melymbrosia*. Later called *The Voyage Out*, her novel was concerned with an introverted, artistic young woman seeking to define her identity, reaching out for maternal guidance, inexperienced and fearful in heterosexual situations. Virginia describes her credo to Madge Vaughan, who questioned her approach: "My present feeling is that this . . . dream-like world without love or heart or passion or sex is the world I really care about and find interesting." She adds that although her ideas might seem vague to Madge they are "perfectly real" to her (Woolf), finding it best to write of what she herself was in touch with rather than "dabble" in unfamiliar areas (L1, Jun.19'06).

II

When Vanessa reaturned from her honeymoon, she and Virginia saw each other as of old, lived close to one another, and spent vacations together. Virginia thought Clive was not good enough for her sister, critically describing him to Violet in an obliquely sexual sense, as that "funny little creature twitching his pink skin, jerking out his little spasms of laughter. I wonder what odd freak there is in Nessa's eyesight" (L1, Dec.30'06).

Typically, a hostile evaluation of Clive alternated with her conviction he was kind, sensitive, solicitous, as well as brotherly, affirming, and clever. To Violet she confided: "It will be some time before I can separate him from her. I don't think I have spoken to him alone since they were married" (L1, Oct.15'07). The unconscious innuendo in this "slip of the tongue" suggests Virginia desires the Bells' separation and expresses a fantasy of having Clive to herself. He introduced her to French literature, had a "gift" for eliciting the best in others, and was in addition "very affectionate," she wrote Violet.

Virginia's involvement with Clive and Vanessa appeared similar to her need to separate Vanessa and Thoby when they were children. Threatened and distanced by Vanessa's seemingly excessive preoccupation with her first child, Clive and Virginia began their flirtation (Bell, v.1, 113). Although Vanessa pretended a show of humor, she was deeply hurt and angry. Clive's interest was important to Virginia in view of both the masculine affection shown her as well as the critique of her work he offered.

She writes Clive in 1908 she dreamt of her father reading *Melymbrosia*, snorting, then dropping it on the table. Unconscious of her vicarious involvement in the conjugal relationship of sister and brother-in-law, she also tells Clive she has begun a memoir concerning Vanessa and questions writing it since she cannot possess "what you have by your side this very minute." She continues: "kiss her, most passionately in all my private places—neck, arms, eyeball, and tell her—what new thing is there to tell her? How fond I am of her husband?" (L1, Apr.15'08).

Virginia's tendency was to indiscriminately identify with wife, husband or child. Identification with Clive's intimacy with her sister, expresses Virginia's confused conception of sexual role, as well as her wish to be close to Vanessa who has abandoned her, as it were, by marrying. Preceded by the dream regarding father's disapproval of her novel, Virginia's fantasy of Clive making love to Vanessa suggests that to her, Vanessa and Clive are prototypes of mother and father, and Virginia feels rebuffed by Clive, a father-figure, regarding her fictional efforts, as though unjustly. Her intellect is found wanting; more importantly, her femininity is ignored. Wishing Clive to inform Vanessa that Virginia cares for him, echoes Leslie telling Julia that "Ginia" is more beautiful. Having Clive kiss "my private places" suggests Virginia's desire for heterosexual experience, her effort to emulate and identify with Vanessa's sexual role.

In another letter, Virginia writes Clive: "Nessa has all that I should like to have, and you, besides your own charms and exquisite fine sweetnesses which I always appreciate somehow, have her." Virginia is extraneous to their lives, she relates in a victimized vein, yet hopes "we shall make out a compromise in time" (May'08). Her dilemma clearly, was her inability to know who she preferred, mother or father, perhaps thought it best to remain their child.

Writing Vanessa about waking from a "terrible dream" in which Jack Hills reported Vanessa's "fatal injury" (L1, Aug.4'08), Virginia obliterates her sister, becomes more daring in her declarations to Clive, wishing to possess him for herself: "You can't think how I look for letters and long for Saturday. I am really shy of expressing my affection for you." During her walk between the downs, she felt "crazed" with the impetuous desire to confide this to Clive but "gave up at last, and lay with tremulous wings. I wish for nothing better—unless it were a kiss to crown it all". Then Virginia reiterates her lifelong plaint that Vanessa has the good things in life; she, Virginia, is excluded (L1, Aug.9-'08).

Rather barbed towards Clive now, Virginia describes him to Vanessa as an "exquisite, fastidious, little chipmunk, no genius", who is, however, "affectionate and tender" (L1, Aug.11'08). Following this she tells Vanessa she "cannot bear" being without her (L1, Aug.14'08). With Vanessa she now assumes a supercilious tone towards Clive. Is this how Virginia might placate her mother? In the next letter to Clive, she writes: "Nessa is horribly bored and says I take too much pains when I write to you" (L1, Aug.19'08).

Vanessa found the romantic contretemps much of a strain. The original reason for Virginia's letters to Clive concerned literary issues; in effect, Clive became her literary mentor and confidant, somewhat similar to her intellectual rapport with father and Thoby. During 1908 and 1909, Clive extended detailed criticisms[2] of early drafts of *Melymbrosia*.

On the whole he was laudatory, except for thinking her overly critical of her male fictional characters. She depends on his encouragement,[3] she writes, and in answer to his query as to why she likes his letters, tells him they are affectionate and harmonious, though perhaps he might improve his style: "You are content to do things that you do very well, but I tremble as I write." Then she tells him "whisper into your wife's ear that I love her" (L1, Aug.28'08).

Imbued with Vanessa and Clive's happiness, Virginia writes Violet that she now thinks of marriage (L1, Jan.4'09). Then she confides to Violet that her friends criticize her novel writing, suggest her characters are "cold blooded like those same Herrings," despite the fact Woolf's "passion was for love and humanity." She still feels inordinately touched by Clive's praise which is "exaggerated"; he is "angelic to take such pains to give reasons and advice" (L1, Feb.7'09). Her chief support is his caring for her and the fact that they are likely to "spend many years in the same neighborhood" (L1, Apr.13'09).

III

Her preoccupation with the Bells notwithstanding, Virginia was constantly urged to marry; together she and Vanessa evaluated her suitors. In February 1909, Lytton Strachey proposed to Virginia and she, wishing to marry and admiring him intellectually, accepted, although this agreement was dissolved the next day. Lytton realized he would be repelled by conjugal intimacies, that a conventional marriage was not what he sought. Virginia helped extricate him from his dilemma, indicating she too was not in love (Bell, v.1. 143; Holroyd, v.1,434). They remained friends yet marriage was the "right thing, the only thing, the solution required of everyone she knew", proclaimed Virginia in her novel *The Voyage Out*, oscillating wildly in her conviction, however.

In 1910, Virgina, sympathetic to the work of Janet Case joined the People's Suffrage Federation (Black, 184), had for long been supportive of feminist issues. Although Margaret L. Davies who held an important position in the Federation spoke to a Miss Rosalind Nash, who in turn

suggested Virginia might wish to write a history of the franchise movement or compile abstracts on representation—Virginia chose instead to
address envelopes (Bell, v.1, 161).

Headache or what Virginia terms numbness in the head, insomnia,
nervous irritation and lack of appetite coincided with the aftermath of
the "Dreadnought Hoax.', though Virginia's symptoms might also have
been linked to Vanessa's pregnancy and Virginia's lingering involvement
in the Bell marriage. Several sojourns with the Bells did not ameliorate
her physical ills nor prove equilibrating.

Because Vanessa was expecting a second child and now considered
her sister a decided burden, Vanessa sought a consultation with their
family physician, Dr. Savage, who urged Virginia to go to a rest-home in
Twickenham, which she called a "polite madhouse for female lunatics"
(Bell, v.1, 164). Virginia wrote her sister: "though it will be damnable
and the thought of the nurses and the food and the boredom disgusting, I
also imagine the delights of being sane again" (L1, Jun. 24'10). Apparently, Virginia refers to her psychosomatic symptoms and depression
as "madness" or as not being sane—although her articles, memoirs, and
letters throughout this period show she was perfectly in command of her
thought processes.

At Twickenham she remained in bed in a darkened room; letters,
reading, and visitors were rationed. Virginia accepted this in a
"rebellious spirit," feeling "they were all in a conspiracy" behind her
back (Bell, v.1, 165), although this attitude is not evidenced in her intitial
acquiescence to stay at the nursing home. Virginia later refers to a "conspiracy" to have her stay on at Twickenham until Vanessa's confinement
was over. Quite possibly Virginia felt coerced, gotten rid of, and manipulated by Vanessa (L1, Jul.18'10). Expecting to stay one month, she felt
forced to remain almost three weeks beyond the anticipated date for
departure, actually did not leave until Vanessa's second child was born
on August 19. During this period, Virginia's unrest was clearly consonant with her ambivalent feelings concerning Vanessa's second pregnancy.

Virginia may have frequently felt Vanessa wanted her out of the way.
Perhaps Vanessa vindictively banished her sister for the involvement
with Clive and for his with her. Vanessa indicated she would have understood Virginia's role in this unsettling triangle had Virginia been more
explicitly in love with Clive. Incredibly naive not to anticipate that
the consequences of her liaison with Clive would alienate Vanessa,
Virginia was unaware of any envy or provocativeness, inasmuch as the
relationship with Clive was not only one of taking Vanessa's place
regarding Clive, but of taking Clive's place in relation to Vanessa as
well.

During April 1911, Vanessa, Clive, and a new friend, Roger Fry, travelled to Turkey in pursuit of Byzantine art. Vanessa, who became seriously ill, was apparently nursed back to health by Roger. Journeying to Broussa to fetch her sister, Virginia detected Vanessa and Roger were in love. Although Vanessa feared her "much loved but agonizingly exasperating sister" might wish Roger for herself, this did not occur (Bell, v.1, 169).

With the gradual breakup of the Bell marriage, some mitigation of the ambiguous relationship and tension between the sisters occurred. Though Virginia had numerous marriage offers, she wrote her sister she felt blocked in writing: "all the devils came out, hairy, black ones. To be 29, unmarried, a failure, childless, insane too, no writer . . . " (L1, Jun.8'11). In writing a friend, Gwen Raverat, years later that "My affair with Clive and Nessa"[5] turned more of a knife in me than anything else has ever done" (L3, Mar.22'25), Woolf fairly accurately describes her hostility and self-destructiveness.

Although Vanessa's mortification was evoked by the betrayal of both sister and husband, she must have felt particularly humiliated by her husband's withdrawal. Still corresponding with Virginia, Clive had already resumed his earlier affair with a Mrs. Raven-Hill in 1909 (Spalding, 77) and, for the rest of his life, atlhough he did not formally dissolve his marriage to Vanessa, he was sexually and/or emotionally involved with other women.

The mutual liveliness and pleasure Woolf and Clive found in each other Woolf inculcated in her portrayal of the young Clarissa and Peter in *Mrs. Dalloway*. Their relationship lacked fruition however, because of Clarissa's presumed need for more private space, her homoerotic orientation, and her obeisance to her father's expectations she remain close to him. In the novel, considerable regret is expressed that more was not made of Clarissa's and Peter's friendship. Of course, Virginia and Clive remained intimate. When Virginia married, Clive wrote her, continuing his pursuit, that his love for her far outweighed Leonard's.[6]

V "I want everything— love, children, adventure, intimacy, work"

As students at Cambridge, Leonard Woolf and Thoby Stephen had been good friends. Through Thoby, Leonard met Virginia and Vanessa Stephen in 1904. Leonard was one of the first of Thoby's friends invited to their new home prior to his departure for Ceylon that year. Described as a "man who trembled perpetually all over, an eccentric, as remarkable in his way as Bell (Clive) and Strachey in theirs," Thoby adds: "he was a Jew" (Bell, v.1, 97).

Originally, Leonard felt he was in love with Vanessa, thinking her the more beautiful. On learning that Clive Bell had proposed to Vanessa, Leonard wrote Lytton Strachey on July 30, 1905, from Ceylon: "She (Vanessa) is so superbly like the Goth (Thoby), I often used to wonder whether he (Clive) was in love with her because of the Goth."[1] Here Leonard shows confusion in sexual identification that he transfers onto Clive.

Lytton Strachey, Leonard's chief connection with his former Cambridge world, informed Leonard of his intention to marry Virginia. Leonard wrote in return during 1908, that he managed to avoid "these degradations with women"; their "lasciviousness" or "ugliness" interfered. He then asks "Do you think Virginia would have me?" (Spater and Parsons, 53). Explaining in 1909 that he both proposed to Virginia and withdrew, Lytton persuaded Leonard to externalize his (Leonard's) interest in Virginia and marry her. He encouraged Leonard to return home, indicated Virginia was "sitting waiting for you—she's the only woman in the world with sufficient brains. She's young, wild, inquisitive, discontented and longing to be in love" (SP, 56). Lytton opened up possibilities for Leonard previously deemed unattainable.

In India for seven years, Leonard ultimately decided to return to England, leaving his post as Colonial Administrator. Arriving in London in June, 1911, Leonard contacted Lytton who advised seeing Vanessa, Lytton's original confidante in his pursuit of Virginia. Leonard met Virginia at the Bell's house the following month, then visited Virginia at her cottage in Sussex in September. From that time on, they saw a good deal of each other.

Sharing their London home with Maynard Keynes and Duncan Grant, Virginia and Adrian asked Leonard to join their household. Not long after, Leonard was convinced he was in love with Virginia and proposed early in 1912, pressuring her for an answer. She desired the status quo for the time being and Vanessa, who approved of Leonard, suggested he modulate his urgency. Unclear about her feelings, Virginia rather shakily retreated to the "hateful but convenient shelter of Twickenham," referring in her self-deprecating fashion to a "touch of my usual disease in the head, you know"; here she alluded to ordinary headache, not to mental "disease." Writing to Leonard on her release, she says: "I shall tell you wonderful stories of the lunatics . . . ; they've elected me king. I now feel very calm and move slowly like one of the great big animals at the zoo" (L1, Mar.5'12).

Not deterred by Virginia's emotional problems, Leonard continued his pursuit, with thoughts of resigning his position in Ceylon—a crucial decision for him. He exulted in the happiness he felt in being with Virginia: "talking with you as I've sometimes felt it, mind to mind together and soul to soul . . . ; apart from love, I'm fond of you as I've never been of anyone or thing in the world." He reassures her: "We often laugh about your lovableness but you don't know how lovable you are. It's what really keeps me awake far more than any desire" (Apr.12'12; Bell, v.1, 184). Did Virginia detect the hidden message?

When he wrote again asking to speak to Virginia before making a final decision about returning to Ceylon, she candidly responds she was aware of causing Leonard "pain," and therefore wished to be outspoken with him concerning her feelings. On the one hand she felt they could be happy, that he could provide "companionship, children and a busy life." She refuses to view marriage as a "profession", however, and is abashed at the immensity of Leonard's desire. His Jewishness and foreignness also deter her. Then Virginia points to her own instability, going "from hot to cold in an instant, without any reason."

Despite her equivocation, she senses some "feeling which is permanent and growing." Still, she is "half afraid" of herself, of the "thing that makes you call me . . . a hill or a rock." Is she excrutiatingly honest here or unusually self-derogating? She continues, reaching out in a wide embrace:

> Again I want everything . . . , love, children, adventure, intimacy, work. So I go from being half in love with you and wanting you to be with me always and know everything about me to the extreme of wild-

ness and aloofness. I sometimes think if I married you I could have
everything—and then—is it the sexual side of it that comes between us?

Virginia is fearful concerning her lack of sexual attraction for Leonard.
Yet his feelings for her endear him: "It is so real and so strange I feel I
must give you everything and if I can't, marriage will only be second
best" (L1, May1'12).

In an imaginative essay, Leonard alluded to Virginia as Aspasia and
himself as Pericles. Though Aspasia was a courtesan Leonard was preoccupied with her mind. He compared his Aspasia to "hills against cold,
blue sky," responded to the "glow of her mind which seems to bring
things from the center of rocks, deep streams that have lain long in
primordial places beneath the earth. She generates an air of quiet and
clearness, her mind amazingly without fear" (SP, 61–62). Virginia said
plaintively on reading this essay, Leonard had not made her lovable
enough.

Leonard decided to remain in England. Did his move from India to
London point to a crisis concerning career and personal life, that he
sought to partially resolve in marrying? Originally claiming he did not
perform adequately in the "classical papers" at Cambridge, he opted for
an appointment in the Colonial Service (1LW94), relinquishing his interest in law, presumably because he lacked financial wherewithal. Initially, in despair over his decision, he became an excellent
administrator. Frequently he referred to himself as a mediocrity, a
failure and, on two occasions, discussed the possibilty of suicide in letters
to Lytton (Mar. 21'06, Apr.21'06; SP, 52).

Living and working in Ceylon might have been an evasion of sorts,
postponement of the choice of a more meaningful lifework. He felt un-
equipped to compete in the post-Cambridge world, had been deeply affected when he was a child of eleven by the death of his father; there had
been no surrogate to take his father's place. In describing his childhood,
Leonard alludes to his father's lack of "mercy" towards anyone who
made a "silly remark" and his "irascibility" when confronted with
"obstinate stupidity." To a considerable degree, he shows identification
with this aspect of his father and admits he looked forward to "these
scenes with astonishment, alarm, and at the same time a certain enjoyment" (1LW29). As Colonial Administrator, Leonard compensatorily
acquired a temporary identity and became a powerful authority figure—
a magistrate who had to make portentous decisions that might send men
to their death, a ruler who sought ever increasing responsibilities.

Why a marriage to Virginia towards whom Leonard had little
"desire"; who referred to Leonard as "that Jew," reiterated her lack of

sexual attraction and made numerous, voluntary visits to Twickenham prior to her marriage? Perhaps a composite of his love for Virginia, who when they first met, reminded him of a painting by Velasquez or Rembrandt (1LW183); his awe of her family as part of a "social class or caste of remarkable and peculiar" abilities which "established itself as a powerful section of the ruling class in Britain in the nineteenth century"[2] (1LW186); his willing enmeshment with his wife's illness, this concomitant to his need to be in control. Ozick suggests Virginia's "madness" fed Leonard's "genius for responsibility," his "uxorious temperament" (38–39).

And Virginia, why did she marry at this point in her life? Social pressure? Need to emulate her parents? To rival or surpass Vanessa now that Vanessa and Clive were emotionally apart? Need to be released from Vanessa's parental authority, to become a mother herself and no longer the child? Need to avoid conflicts regarding homosexuality? Or, was Virginia fearful of Clive's availability and guilty over her role in the breakup of the Bell marriage, now transformed into a friendship?

Virginia felt Leonard was as intellectually competent as Lytton and showed a "reliable strength" Lytton could not maintain. The communication between Virginia and Leonard was frank and open; she relied on his closeness with Lytton and his former friendship with Thoby. Vanessa encouraged her to allow the relationship a gradual evolution. Finally, Virginia told Leonard she would marry him. She wrote Violet: "By next year I must have a child" (L1, Jul.12'12). On August 10, 1912, she and Leonard were married.

The couple returned from their honeymoon "nomadic and monogamous." Letters to Virginia's women friends announcing her marriage contain a curious blend of apology and self-denigration. Virginia's letter to Ka Cox suggests, however cavalier her tone, her sexual uncertainties: "Why do some people make such a fuss about marriage and copulation? Why do some of our friends change upon losing chastity?" (L1, Sept.4'12).

When the Woolfs consulted Vanessa on the topic of Virginia's orgasms, Vanessa wrote Clive the couple were troubled concerning Virginia's "coldness." Vanessa was aware Virginia felt annoyed when told by her sister she failed to comprehend "sexual passion in men."[3] Vanessa continued: "Apparently she [Virginia] still gets no pleasure at all from the act. They were anxious to know when I first had an orgasm" (Dec.27'12; Bell, v.2, 6).

Everyone was consulted regarding Virginia's sexual and orgasmic state, and she found wanting. Not viewing sexual matters mutual, reciprocal and requiring more prolonged working through, experimentation, or recourse to alternate expression of one's love, Spater and Parsons damningly state: "Virginia was increasingly conscious of her abnormality" (67). They reflect the general consensus that she had failed sexually or was tainted. Virginina's sense of guilt and deformity concealed her outrage at the time.

Vanessa, Leonard, and Virginia were inclined to attribute Virginia's sexual difficulties to the adverse effects of George Duckworth's lovemaking. Bell suggests her sexual disposition was due to "congenital inhibition," stating that the "erotic element in her personality was faint and tenuous" (Bell, v.2, 6).

Since Virginia alludes to her "lost virginity" (L1, Oct.11'12), we can assume she had intercourse though it is apparent she did not find sex fulfilling: "I find the climax intensely exaggerated" (L1, Sept.4'12). Although she colludes in conveying that she was sexually cold, she is not pervasively so as noted in letters sent to Leonard during periods when they were temporarily apart.

Here she elaborated her feelings with considerable affection: "Would it make you very conceited if I told you that I love you more than ever and find you beautiful and indispensable?" She wishes to inform him "delicately" that her "flanks and rump are now in finest plumage" and invites him to an "exhibition" (L2, Dec.'13). Referring to herself as "old mandrill"⁴ she wants her "master so badly and last night his empty bed was so dismal, she went and kissed the pillow" (L2, Mar.8'14).

She continues in the same vein: "There's no news except I love you and miss you more than you'd expect and it's very dull without you" (L2, Mar.12'14). On March 14: "My pet, you would never doubt my caring for you if you saw me wanting to kiss you and nuzzle you in my arms"; on March 16: "I love your little ribby body."

It was not so much that Virginia was cold or "needed to be loved without herself giving love," but rather she seemed more inclined towards a tactile, parent-child relationship. Bitterness regarding Leonard's sexual rejection is fictionalized in Woolf's description of Clarissa Dalloway, ascetic and virginal, though married and a mother. Clarissa, going to her "attic room," felt like a "nun who has left the world . . . ; there was an emptiness about the heart of life, the sheets were clean, tight stretched in a broad white band from side to side. Narrower and narrower would her bed be" (*MD*, 45). Woolf's description of Clarissa's sexual response suggests confusion regarding sexual anatomy and on some level the desire for a male orgasm.

Acknowledging Violet's wedding gift, Virginia described her pleasure on receiving a crib "fit for the illegitimate son of an Empress," adding, "My baby shall sleep in the cradle" (L2, Oct.9'12). Later, she wrote,

"We aren't going to have a baby but want to have one and six months in the country is . . . necessary" (L2, Apr.11'13). Virginia fully intended to have children—after all, her mother and great-grandmother each gave birth to seven children, her mother-in-law nine, and Vanessa, her current maternal model, two so far.

Leonard was preoccupied with what he considered Virginia's "poor health" on return from their honeymoon, took careful notes of her physical state, described her as writing with "tortured intensity." Yet, at this time Vanessa wrote Roger: "Virginia cheered me up a great deal. When she chooses she can give one the most extraordinary sense of bigness and point of view. I think she has . . . amazing courage and sanity about life" (Bell, v.2, 8). Rarely recognized, Virginia, usually accused of taking rather than giving, could apparently, be of emotional support to others.

Vanessa's accolade was short-lived. She, undoubtedly in agreement with Leonard, now questioned Virginia's desire to have children. However, Dr. Savage, Virginia's physician, consulted during January 1913, encouraged her maternal proclivities. Leonard "mistrusted" Dr. Savage's opinion and proceeded to consult Doctors Craig and Hyslop[5] as well as Jean Thomas,[6] head of the nursing home at Twickenham, although Leonard knew they were institutionally oriented and had himself stated: "doctors know nothing." He ultimately decided, and then persuaded his wife, with their concurrence, that having a baby would be too "risky and dangerous" an undertaking.

Why did Virginia not combat the verdict of Leonard and her doctors? Perhaps desire to herself be the child, or fear of the dangers of pregnancy or childbirth held her back; her father's first wife Minnie Thackeray and her half-sister Stella Duckworth died of complications surrounding pregnancy.[7] A deeper substrate of Virginia's anxieties may have resided in her uncertainties about feminine identification, the feeling she was unattractive to Leonard, her conviction of sexual ineptness, her fear of further sexual rejection, and fear of gaining weight. These anxieties notwithstanding, she initially felt identified with Vanessa's maternal role and wanted to have the experience of being a mother.

Not having a child was to be a lifelong regret; Virginia never thought of "Vanessa's fruitful state without misery and envy" (Bell, v.2, 8). Aside from the rivalry with her sister and with her sister's children, there is Virginia's sense of barrenness to consider, as well as the lack of fulfillment of needs central to her feminine and maternal identity.

Biographers sound a note of alarm, horror, and even abhorrence with regard to Woolf's desire for children and its eventualities. There is no way of discerning her adequacy as a mother. Showalter suggests Woolf "surely would have had nannies" for her children; Ozick states that Vanessa had two for hers. Vanessa, of course, was Virginia's ego-ideal and Julia Stephen her earliest maternal model.[8]

Possibly, Leonard had problems regarding his masculine identification and simply did not wish to have sexual intercourse or babies with Virginia; perhaps he divided women into "sacred" and "profane." Conceivably something in their initial sexual encounters disturbed , intimidated, or dissuaded him. Most likely he was unable to encompass both marital and maternal modalities in his wife, or a paternal role for himself.

II

The Voyage Out was finished March 9, 1913. The reader of Virginia Woolf's manuscript, gave it a positive evaluation. On April 12, her half-brother, Gerald Duckworth, now her publisher, personally informed her of its acceptance. Leonard decided to postpone publication however, because he thought this would prove anxiety-provoking for his wife; biological and literary children were now tabooed.

During the following months, Virginia was accosted by "anxieties and depressions" which were channelized into headaches, sleeplessness and aversion to food, the usual neurasthenic syndrome, with the addition of guilt and danger of suicide (3LW77). Bell tended to follow Vanessa's and Leonard's view that Virginia's suicidal wish reflexly followed completion of her novel (3LW79–82; Bell, v.2, 11). Neither he nor the other biographers have explored in depth more emotionally weighted and relevant issues.

Concerning Virginia's flare-up of symptoms, Leonard consulted Dr. Savage who once again recommended the traditional rest-cure at Twickenham. Although Virginia was strongly opposed, she remained there from July 25 to August 11, 1913. Her notes to Leonard evoke the lamentations of a "child sent away by his parents to some cruel school." All was so "cold, so unreal" (Bell, v.2, 13). She remonstrated with Leonard, then felt deep remorse towards him. Still suicidal, she left the nursing home. Despite her unsteady condition, Dr. Savage encouraged adherence to Leonard's promise that they go on an extended holiday to the inn they originally visited on their honeymoon, which they did. Since Virginia's symptoms persisted, Ka Cox was summoned in early September 1913, to "relieve" Leonard.

Virginia felt people were "laughing at her and she the cause of everyone's trouble." Intensely guilt-ridden, she felt she should, at the minimum, be punished. Her body seemed "monstrous" to her, that is, her "sordid mouth and sordid belly demanding food—repulsive matter which must then be excreted in a disgusting fashion; the only course was to refuse to eat" (Bell, v.2, 15). Assuming delusional proportions, Virginia's preoccupations point to self-hatred, distortions concerning body-image, rejection of ordinary body functions and disturbances in the ability to accurately perceive body stimuli (Bruch, 1973, 252).

Virginia was now in a most vulnerable position. Two bodies were required, at least in her day, to conceive a baby and Leonard was unwilling. "Sordid mouth and sordid belly demanding food" and the "disgusting" excretions which followed, might have released archaic memories of an intense aversion to her mother nursing her younger brother, and otherwise ministering to his infantile needs, witnessed by Virginia in early childhood, thinking her brother omnivorous and insatiable; angry her mother had not accorded her such a rich suckling experience; crushed she could not assume a maternal role at this point.

Actually, Virginia's refusal to eat, her concept of "sordid mouth" and "sordid belly," and her anal preoccupations, suggest a more severe manifestation of anorexia in 1913, when her sexuality and femininity, highly emotionally charged issues for her, were in question. She may have perceived her body as "battlefield" concerning the power struggle with caretakers, not untypical in anorexia where food is considered "dirty and damaging", the body a "despicable threat" (Sours, 226). Rejection of food may defend against fear of engulfment, fear of oral surrender and invasion, the body invested with unconscious negative identifications and feelings regarding mother or caretaker. Here passive aggression masks oral rage.[9]

Leonard describes the interaction with his wife concerning food as follows: "Our arguments were rare and almost always about eating. If the argument became heated, in a mild, vague form the delusions seemed to rise again" (3LW163). He continues: "In the worst period of the depressive stage, for weeks almost, at every meal, one had to sit, often for an hour or more, trying to induce her to eat a few mouthfuls" (3LW79).

Was Virginia Woolf's anxiety about oral and gastrointestinal matters, aside from her anorectic tendencies, affected by her father's incessant obsession with digestive functions and her mother's attentiveness to them? As we know, her father died of abdominal cancer. Did Woolf confuse oral and reproductive functions? In *Between the Acts* Woolf describes a snake choking with a toad in its mouth, unable to swallow, "birth the wrong way round" (99). In the theories of children babies can be spawned by eating, are born through the bowel or a primitive cloaca. Impregnation and birth may in a regressive sense, be associated with oral, digestive, and excretory functions (Sperling, 77). Woolf's refusal to eat reflects revival of control struggles with early caretakers, counteracting an underlying sense of powerlessness.

Accompanying the anorectic pattern is cessation of menses. Closely scrutinizing Virginia's menstruation pattern, Leonard kept records, noting she had no periods from August to November 1913, when her weight was at its lowest. During this time, she was acutely disturbed, and had four nurses in attendance (SP, 68). The inner struggle with Leonard over the issue of having children was at its height at the time she was starving herself and not menstruating.

For the first time, Virginia asked to see Dr. Henry Head, world-renowned neurologist originally referred by Roger Fry, whose opinion she valued and whose wife had been mentally ill. In consonance with Leonard's arrangement, they initially consulted Dr. Wright who used a directive approach, insisting Virginia acknowledge the fact she was ill. Later that day, September 9, 1913, they saw Dr. Head who essentially concurred, recommending a nursing home, the same procedure advocated by all consultants. This was disappointing since expectations of a new approach had been raised. Virginia felt throughout that her symptoms were her own "fault" and that she required no medical assistance.

Following protocol and accompanied by Vanessa, Leonard on the same day then sought to make his excuses to Dr. Savage who had not been informed as yet about the additional consultations and the fact he had been replaced. Ka Cox telephoned them, relaying that Virginia was unconscious and that she, Ka, found the case in which Leonard kept Virginia's medication unlocked. Apparently, Virgina had taken a hundred grains of veronal, an almost lethal amount.

Recovering from her overdose, Virginia became "deeply depressed and violently excited"; she was moved to their home in the country, with several nurses in attendance, and remained there for almost nine months. Leonard also suffered disabling, severe depression and headaches and was himself near breakdown (Bell, v.2, 16).

Difficulties in the Woolf marriage at this time were engendered by Leonard's discussions with numerous doctors concerning the advisability of having children, negating any prior consultation with his wife, annihilating her wishes, despite her considerable emotional investment in becoming a mother. Disagreements among the authorities attending Virginia and the fact there were so many,[10] in addition to their cruelty in Virginia's perception, in exiling and isolating her, forcing her to overeat —intensified her helplessness and need to counterattack.

The fact Leonard neglected to conceal his wife's sleeping medication points to his distraught and ambivalent state. In attempting suicide, she retaliated for Leonard's role in banishing her to a nursing home, post-poning publication of her book, and replacing her family physician with a succession of physicians until he found those who agreed with his predilection, namely, to avoid having children.

Taking over from Vanessa, Leonard assumed an authoritative role during his wife's illness, requiring to some degree her submission and in-fantilization; her assumption of the role of sick one. The account of Rachel's illness in *The Voyage Out*, her sense of severe isolation and lack of faith in her doctors, as well as in those taking care of her, suggest Virginia's foreboding and unmooredness during this time.

In not wishing to have children, Leonard rejected her as a woman, Virginia felt, forbidding babies and sex. A profound sense of humiliation and failure regarding her sexual and maternal roles added to her disillu-sionment with Leonard for not adhering to what she thought had been spelled out in premarital exchanges. Could Vanessa's agreement with Leonard's decision that Virginia and he should not have children imply to Virginia that Vanessa was getting even for the flirtation with Clive? Virginia sought to punish them, then redeem herself by attempting to take her life.

In portraying an insane, suicidal poet in *Mrs. Dalloway* who rejects his wife's desire for a child, Virginia, weary of her role as the sick one, might be telling Leonard that not wanting children can be deviant too. In this novel, furthermore, the thrust of the power-driven, pompous, exhor-tatory specialists who did not help, their lack of psychological sophistica-tion, their push toward merely adjusting their patients to society, and their essential punitiveness are clearly riven from Virginia Woolf's own experience.

Now Woolf's physician, Dr. Craig favored the Weir Mitchell ap-proach; he ruled out intellectual excitement, ordered rest, rich food, and sedatives for sleeping. Exploring the treatment armamentarium of Virginia Woolf's doctors, Trombley faults the use of drugs by Doctors Craig and Savage in view of her suicidal propensity, especially citing hyoscyamine. Not certain this was prescribed for Woolf, Trombley notes however, that the side-effects correspond with many of her symptoms.[11]

III

Virginia's recovery was slow. At times she could not sleep, refused to eat, and was alternately depressed and excited (Bell, v.2, 17). George Duckworth offered his home in Sussex replete with staff of servants and provided every comfort. There Virginia went with two nurses and her friend Ka Cox; despite several setbacks, she improved. She and Leonard returned mid-November 1913 to their country home, Asheham House, with Virginia still in the care of several nurses.

Virginia wrote Leonard, who was in London moving their belongings, that she was "grateful" and "repentent," thinks he ought to be an "independent man, doing things instead of wasting" his life (L2, Dec.4'13). In a letter that follows, she tells him she loves him more than ever, since she "took him into service" (L2, Dec.'13). Aware of Leonard's constant vigilance, Virginia seems glad to be alive. She had resumed the routines of her former life, began writing, seeing friends, took trips with Leonard to Cornwall and Northumberland.

Responding to the recent declaration of war, Virginia in a letter to Ka Cox writes that Asheham was "practically under martial law." Military men were "marching up and down the line, and men digging trenches"; apparently Asheham barn was to be used as a "hospital." Everyone expected an invasion. Virginia quoted Clive Bell as saying "it was the end of civilization" and the remainder of their lives would be "worthless." A great battle was expected since they are merely 15 miles from the North Sea (L2, Aug.12'14).

Leonard became deeply involved in politics and was asked by the Fabian Society to write a report on international relations, later incorporated in a book, which influenced the government's role in helping to establish the League of Nations (L2, n.53). Virginia herself now joined the Fabian Society.

In an effort to avoid the overstimulation of London, yet have the city accessible, the Woolfs bought Hogarth House in Richmond, a suburb of London. They planned to purchase a printing press and embark on a publishing enterprise of their own, thereby affording Virginia a form of occupational therapy.

Abruptly, Virginia started talking to her mother one morning (D1, Jan.31'15), although this episode was shortlived. Significantly, Virginia indicated she was for the first time reading Leonard's novel, *The Wise Virgins*, which betrayed considerable hostility towards her, as well as others to whom Leonard was close. Vanessa deplored the resemblance of Leonard's fictional characters to members of their circle; Leonard's mother threatened to "break" with him, infuriated at his portrait of her (SP, 83).

Writing Margaret Llewellyn Davies to thank her for the solicitousness shown Leonard during her illness, Virginia seemed painfully aware Margaret was, after her, the "most important woman" in Leonard's life. A "born leader," Margaret had induced Leonard to work with her Woman's Cooperative Guild and later, as Leonard ventured more deeply into politics, became his guide (Bell, v.2, 25). In her letter to Margaret, Virginia sounded ingratiating, endowing Margaret with magical powers: "In all that terrible time (of Virginia's breakdown) I thought of you and wanted to look at a picture of you but was afraid to ask." Virginia felt Margaret "saved" Leonard by giving him things to do, for which Virginia blesses her: "It seems odd for I know you so little but I felt you had a grasp on me and I could not utterly sink" (L2, Feb.25'15).

Virginia's fragility and sense of exposure to the world at this time was considerable; her anxiety lest Margaret whose surname was also the hero's in *The Wise Virgins* replace her in Leonard's affections, pre-occupied her. Certainly Leonard's and Margaret's interests were inter-twined during the period of Virginia's illness, insofar as their mutual political passions were concerned.

Evidencing a condition akin to "garrulous mania" (Bell, v.2, 25), Virginia began to speak "wildly, incoherently and incessantly," was "violent and screaming and her madness culminated in virulent ani-mosity towards Leonard" and men in general. In Vanessa's view, Leonard had reached a "state where he didn't care what happened" (Bell, v.2, 26). Fully engaged with her rage against Leonard, refusing to talk to him for many months, Virginia did not at this time attempt suicide. Exhausted, she sank into a coma, then gradually began to recover.

It is highly likely that Virginia's relapse was precipitated by her sense of personal inadequacy and inability to cope, unfavorably comparing herself to Margaret who was a highly organized, extremely political person, an ac-tivist as well, tenaciously pursuing her goals, in sound health, and a com-panion to Leonard. Margaret's influence was obviously threatening to Virginia who reveals her own precarious position: "My dear Margaret, what's the use of my writing novels? You've got the whole thing at your fingers' ends—and it will be envy not boredom that alienates my affec-tions" (L2, Aug.31'15).

However, reading Leonard's autobiographical novel, *The Wise Virgins* at this time, chiefly contributed to the resumption of Virginia's illness. Undecided between Camilla, depicted as upperclass, gentile, remote, a caricature of Virginia,[12] and Gwen who hailed from his own more bourgeois background and economic strata, Leonard's hero and alter-ego, Harry Davis, chooses Gwen who is certainly more sexual and worshipful. Although Harry professes to love Camilla, he proceeds to make love to Gwen, who finds him emotionally liberating. After Gwen seduces him, he feels masculine, phallic. Now it is necessary for Harry to marry Gwen lest she give way to despair over the unconventional behavior he has set in motion. His silent protestations notwithstanding,

Harry enters a loveless marriage and will presumably have children and a family, the "romance of life." He so tremendously admired "women who have babies" (*TWV*, 41). This in particular must have enraged Virginia.

Despite the trappings of iconoclasm, Harry's longing for simple, conventional sexual fulfillment is manifest, as well as a straightforward preference for women who idolize and desire him. Regarding Camilla, Harry felt that "below the surface at any moment something might break out destructive of you or her" (84). Yet Harry, too, was considered "violent" which Camilla finds attractive, perhaps defining her need to be awakened. Katharine, a fictional surrogate for Vanessa, feels Camilla was not "made for marriage, husband and middle-aged domesticity." Camilla insists she is not cold: "I'm very affectionate. I like silk and kisses and soft things and stroking" (82).

Leonard depicts Katharine as earthy and maternal and Camilla as pure, ethereal, and virginal.[13] Regarding her dilemma concerning marriage, Camilla asks her sister: "What am I to do? You don't want me to die young, do you?" (85). Katharine answers, with breathtaking malevolence, that might indeed be best. So much for Leonard's perception of Vanessa's hostile intentions toward Virginia. Since in his way Harry discards Camilla, he is essentially in league with Katharine. Leonard's novel, which must have been based on data Virginia provided about her family as well as on his own observations and creative plan, raises interesting issues: Katharine-Vanessa wanting Camilla-Virginia out of the way; the possibility Camilla-Virginia required a "violent" or aggressive male, perhaps her masochistic need for pain or her need to be vitalized; the fact Harry-Leonard sought an aggressive female to awaken his sexuality.

In contrast to Virginia, Leonard has been depicted by biographers as "highly passionate." Yet as far as is known, his previous sexual experience is meager. In a somewhat despairing letter written to Lytton in 1905 he communicated that "women seem to me absolutely the abomination of desolation, in Ceylon at any rate" (SP, 53). In general, he finds horseback riding in the jungle more pleasurable than "copulation" which is after all but a "moment of frenzy." Writing again to Lytton he stated "I am beginning to think it is always degrading being in love; after all, 99/100ths of it is always the desire to copulate," which repels him (May19'07; SP, 53).

Although Leonard had sexual intercourse with available prostitutes in Jaffna, he and Virginia seem equally matched in terms of emotional and maturational development. Depicting his hero as finding fault with Camilla because she is capable of emotional eruptions, Leonard was aware of his own aggression, even though he felt fairly guiltless here; he resembled his father, he wrote, because both had a "violent temper" (1LW25). Leonard and Virginia were also matched in terms of their parentlessness at an early age. By virtue of his father's death, Leonard shared some of his wife's sense of crippledness and diminution of possibilities at her mother's death.

Leonard's reluctance to have children may underscore a disinclination toward prolonged intimacy and risky issues involving potency and generativity. In addition, he was third of ten children and possibly desired more exclusive attention; furthermore, he might have had enough of taking care of younger siblings. He might have wanted an aggressive wife, perhaps like his mother, but opted instead to identify with his mother and take care of Virginia.

In his family of origin, Leonard acquired a sense of unlovability, claiming his mother cared for him less than any of the others because she felt him to be "unsympathetic to her view of the family, of the universe and of the relation of one to the other" (1LW33).[14] Leonard describes his early sexual innocence and confusion: "Love and lust like the functions of the bowels and bladder were subjects which could not be discussed or even mentioned . . . , leading to a buttoning up of mind and emotion" (1LW82). After his father's death when Leonard was 11, he acquired a "carapace" to conceal his vulnerability, developed a gradual loss of individuality after puberty, and in the progress to manhood, a "fatalistic acceptance of instability" (1LW86).[15]

Woolf's breakdown one year after marriage and her subsequent, almost lethal suicide attempt were undoubtedly precipitated by her sense of personal rejection by Leonard insofar as her feminine role and maternal desires were concerned. Her feeling of betrayal by Vanessa, who discouraged the begetting of children and her feeling of abnormality and failure in giving up the idea of motherhood also contributed.

Competition with Margaret, humiliation regarding the contents of *The Wise Virgins*, and bitter disappointment concerning the delay in publishing her first novel might have prolonged and intensified her disturbance. Finished in 1913, *The Voyage Out* did not emerge until 1915, two years following its acceptance and after two of Leonard's novels were published. Publication was suspended at Leonard's instigation in consonance with his misguided view that Virginia's "pathological hypersensitiveness to criticism" (3LW149) would result in a breakdown, rather hypothetical and anticipatory since this was Woolf's first novel.

Actually, Virginia immediately obtained extremely positive feedback from both reader and publisher. Certainly at this time the meaning of her symptoms was painfully clear: they had nothing to do with finishing her novel and everything to do with her marital crisis.

Leonard's dissimulation and scotoma regarding these issues are striking. In alluding to his wife's emotional situation in the third volume of his autobiography, *Beginning Again*, which covers the period from 1911 to 1918, Leonard trots out the worn notion that "whenever she finished her book, Virginia was in a state of mental exhaustion and was in danger of a breakdown" (3LW79). Since Leonard was writing in the 1950s and 1960s from a more objective vantage point, he knew that although Virginia was frequently, physically ill, mental illness did not accompany the completion of most of her novels, though postpartum reactions might have been present. Possibly he and she were not intimate concerning deeply personal issues. When Virginia was emotionally ill, it was clearly in congruence with psychological events in her life, involving self and other.

Strangely, Leonard accuses Virginia of rewriting her manuscripts "as much as five times from beginning to end," connecting the latter with her "madness," although this degree of revision is not unusual in writers. No doubt Virginia was fearful of the degree of self-revelation she permitted herself, evidenced in the endless rewriting of the forest episode in *The Voyage Out*, which suggested her marked conflict concerning marital versus homoerotic issues.

The Voyage Out encompassed Virginia Woolf's central difficulties at this time: her fragility of self, lack of contour regarding feminine role, precariousness in personal, especially sexual relationships, anxiety regarding the acceptance, and retaliation of mother-figures if she asserted herself. Communicating these issues, artistically transformed via her novel, might have provided some alleviation of inner turmoil in 1913.

Paradoxically, Virginia Woolf's novel was finally published on March 26, 1915, while she was in the throes of the second phase of her breakdown. The favorable notices she received sustained her and assisted her recovery. She and Leonard had a child of sorts in the acquisition of the Hogarth Press, with its enveloping and widening network of intellectual and personal relationships and its publication of distinguished books.

VI "Lying unprotected, she looked like a victim dropped from the claws of a bird of prey"— *The Voyage Out*

I

Although Woolf maintains the chronological and narrative forms of more traditional fiction in *The Voyage Out*, she is also delving into subtleties of personality and relationship; into subjective and hidden mainsprings of motivation and experience.

During the novel's gestation, from approximately 1906 to 1913, Virginia Woolf's life situation was one of intense involvement with Vanessa and Vanessa's family. Virginia wrote Clive that in thinking of Vanessa with her first child, Julian, a "page of *Melymbrosia* was strangled in the birth" (L1, Aug.9'08), which suggests that Virginia felt displaced by her nephew or at that moment, thought writing not as creative as having children. Her mode of coming to terms with Vanessa's new status as mother in 1908 was to compete with her sister, comparing the writing of this, her first novel, with the "pain" of childbirth (L1, Aug.11'08).

Feeling personally ill-defined, Virginia sought to identify with Vanessa's marital and maternal roles, unaware of the antagonisms engendered by her ambiguous friendship with Clive. In addition to his amatory interest, Clive, as we know, read and critiqued *Melymbrosia*, Virginia's early version of *The Voyage Out*, which he essentially affirmed. His sole objection was the arbitrariness he thought she introduced in what he felt was her depiction of women as sensitive, delicate, or subtle whereas her men were rude, tyrannical, or vain. Indicating that her "boldness terrified" her (L1, Feb.7'09), Woolf clung to her own viewpoint and did not thereafter offer *Melymbrosia* to Clive for his perusal.

Borrowing from Gilbert and Guber who feel, along with Emily Dickinson, that women writers "tell the truth but tell it slant" (73), DeSalvo suggests *Melymbrosia* is similarly "palimpsestic:" On one level, Woolf describes a young woman's quest for self-definition;[1] on another, she indicates women cannot consummate their journey or achieve in the heroic mode men do. DeSalvo claims *Melymbrosia*, as compared to *The*

Voyage Out, "bristles" with important social issues of the day, framing her characters' movements: "it is impossible to read *Melymbrosia* and think of Virginia Woolf as an effete dreamer spinning out her private fantasies in the solitude of her study betweeen bouts of madness." (DeSalvo, 1982, xxxvi).

Summarizing *The Voyage Out* in later years, Virginia Woolf wrote Lytton: "What I wanted to do was to give the feeling of a vast tumult of life, as various and disorderly as possible." This "should be cut short . . . by the death (of her heroine), and go on again—and the whole was to have a sort of pattern and be somehow controlled" (L1, Feb.28'16). Actually, the central theme in *The Voyage Out* is far more convoluted than either DeSalvo or Woolf would have it.

The Voyage Out offers a portrait of Rachel Vinrace, 24, whose mother died when she was 11. Rachel was raised by maiden aunts, amorphous in their ministrations, and by a fairly abrasive, possessive, chiefly absent father—shipowner and sea captain of the "Euphrosyn".[2] Enamored of music, herself a pianist, Rachel is otherwise unformed[3] and drifting, incomplete in her social and emotional development, damaged by the unevenness of her early years. She gains the sympathy and counsel of her aunt, Helen Ambrose, encountered for the first time. Accompanying her aunt on a sea voyage to South America, she meets Terence Hewet, a writer, falls in love, oscillates in her commitment, becomes ill, then dies.

In a key image, the author depicts Rachel's innocence and vulnerability: "Lying unprotected she looked like a victim dropped from the claws of a bird of prey" (37). Is the "bird of prey" her father who held on too long? Or is Rachel now in a position of passive surrender regarding her aunt, from whom she seeks maternal guidance? Woolf's powerful metaphor is sweeping in its evocation of Rachel's existential situation; her sense of feeling victimized, insuffiently protected or cared for, too swiftly or abrasively thrust out of the nest.

Though the novel on a manifest level depicts the vicissitudes of the love relationship between Terence and Rachel, two tenuously committed individuals, the "bird of prey" image reminds us that the subplot concerning the ambivalent relationship between Helen and Rachel, surrogate-mother and niece, is the more pivotal.

On her father's ship, Rachel's response to a passenger, Richard Dalloway's[4] unexpected lovemaking is typically interpreted as one of repugnance and fear. Overlooked is Rachel's feeling that "something wonderful had happened" (77) and that there was "something lovable about Richard and good in their attempted friendship and strangely piteous in the way they had parted (81)." Richard confiding in Rachel at length about himself, seemed to her an experience both new and to be savored.

Vacillating here, the author then concentrates more fully on Rachel's aversion towards Richard, channelled in a dream that night, concerning a tunnel that became a vault in which she was trapped, the walls damp, dripping, cold; here she met a small, deformed man with "long nails," squatting on the floor "gibbering," his face "pitted" like an animal's. Upon awakening, she locked her door, so real was the feeling of being pursued. A voice "moaned" for her, eyes "devoured" her; "barbarian men harrassed" the ship, "scuffling down passages, snuffling at her door" (77).

In Rachel's dream, the author links the incestuous encounter between an older, married man and Rachel, with her heroine's exaggerated feelings of anxiety, entrapment, and sexual violation. Woolf seems incapable because of her inexperience and warp in development of properly sorting out these threatening emotions. In the succeeding text, Woolf expands this rather one-dimensional conception of her heroine's and her own sexual foreboding.

Rachel's aunt, learning of her niece's encounter with Mr. Dalloway and aware of her general naivete, seeks to reassure her, bluntly indicating jealousy that she, Helen, was not approached. Helen decides at this point to instruct her niece on "how to live," or "how to be a reasonable person" (83), suggesting that instead of accompanying her father to the wilds of the Amazon, Rachel sail instead with aunt and uncle to their villa in South America.

The intricacies behind Helen's decision to leave her own young children behind and adopt another grown child as it were, is not clarified, unless this represents Woolf's fantasy of being the only child, repeated in her next novel, *Night and Day*. In wresting Rachel from her father, Helen is vicariously identified with Rachel's sexual awakening. Within three months of their arrival at the Ambrose home, Helen found Rachel less shy, given to "talk about everybody, talk that was free, unguarded;" she desired Rachel to think for herself, offered books that Rachel could choose from (124).

In Rachel's room, an "enchanted place where the poets sang and things fell into their right proportions," Rachel above all wanted to know "what's the truth of it all?" To find out, she read Ibsen's plays, acting roles "for days at a time," identified with those of his heroines eschewing conventional, social attitudes. At the suggestion of her uncle, she tried Balzac, while Terence's friends, St. John Hirst, suggested she read Gibbon's *Decline and Fall* and Burke's "Speech on the American Revolution"—a decided expansion of her horizons.

Rachel exulted in her friendship with Terence and St. John: "from them, all life seemed to radiate; the very words of books were steeped in radiance" (175). As Rachel asked "what is it to be in love?" (175), the author's anxieties intrude as she describes Rachel's discovery of "this terrible possibility of life" and compares Rachel to a "soldier preparing for battle" (176). None of the books Rachel reads, whether *Wuthering Heights, Man and Superman* or Ibsen's plays could in their dissections of love, help Rachel clarify her own emotional uncertainties (223).

Generally more assertive now, Rachel opted for "seeing life" where as Helen in reverse, was for turning back. Though Rachel has, thus far, willingly accepted her aunt's protective aegis, she has been challenging Helen. Falling in love with Terence, she is subtly aware of Helen's reluctance to acknowledge her (Rachel's) sexuality.

As Rachel flourishes, Helen becomes more disaster-ridden,[5] thinks her children are in danger and might be lying dead, crushed by motor vehicles, then shifts her morbid prognostications to the lovers. In her turn, Rachel violently "rammed Helen's gloomy theories down her throat" with "laughter, chatter, ridicule and fierce bursts of anger" at what she called the "croaking of a raven in the mud" (221).

In denouncing Helen for rejecting her children, is Rachel showing displacement of her feelings concerning her own mother who abandoned her by dying? In confronting her aunt and falling in love, Rachel is conscious of "emotions and powers" hitherto unsuspected in herself and of a "depth" in the world previously unknown (224).

Rachel continues her expostulations towards Helen, repudiating all she had before implicitly believed: "Thank God I'm not like you. You don't think or care or do anything but exist. No one feels. No one does anything but hurt. The world's bad—it's an agony. You don't help. You put an end to things" (262–263).

The author is obviously describing a crisis in her heroine's life: the "steady beat of Rachel's pulse represents the hot currents of feeling beneath; beating, struggling, fretting". Rachel feels that behind appearances, she detects the "movement of a snake". Unaware she is threatened by Rachel's turmoil, Helen "pitied her profoundly for being in love" (263). Is Rachel reacting to Helen's covert sabotage of the relationship with Terence? Is Helen distanced by Rachel's exuberance?

II

Throughout Rachel and Terence's timid, fearful, fumbling yet exciting discovery of one another, Woolf interjects an often sinister sense of the primitiveness of outer landscape. Walking in the forest with Rachel, Terence, at first uncertain, is now doubtful of his direction though eventually finds his way (272). The lovers draw together, seem more intimate, then appear to be walking at the "bottom of the world" (276); they are, in short, in a dream-state only they share. Reverting, they question their relationship and feel separate. Soon the cycle resumes once again. Terence proves insufficiently resolute or resilient in countering Helen's annihilative personality or his own inner doubts. He tells Rachel he has "had other women" (280) and asks her to marry him; then claims he "ought never to have asked" her to marry.

Rachel said she had no "doubts" and was "in love" with Terence, then thought "it will be a fight". She felt Terence had "more compassion" and was "finer" than she, which he denied (282). Beset by feelings of unreality, he wondered "why did I ask you to marry me" (282), wishes to regale her with more of his faults. Relinquishing their differences, they temporarily felt less confused and embattled. Rachel thought "this is happiness, I suppose". Aloud she said "this is happiness", which Terence echoed (283).

At this point in the text, the author presents in a dream-like episode, Rachel's fantasy of a clash with Helen over Terence:

> A hand droppped abrupt as iron on Rachel's shoulder. She fell beneath it and the grass whipped across her eyes and filled her mouth and ears. Through the waving stems she saw a figure large and shapeless against the sky. Helen was upon her. Rolled this way and that . . . , she [Rachel] was speechless and almost without sense. At last she lay still, all the grasses shaken round her by her panting (283).

Terence and Helen "loomed" over her, "flushed" and "laughing," kissing as they stood above her. Rachel thought they uttered something about "love" and "marriage." Raising herself, Rachel felt "Helen's soft body, the strong and hospitable arms, happiness swelling and breaking in one vast wave" (284).

Here Rachel communicates her fear of Helen's vengeful fury, presumably regarding Rachel's sexuality and vigorous thurst towards independence. Yet Rachel still perceives Helen as meaningful in her life; the submerged eroticism between Rachel and Helen is clearly suggested. Placatingly, Rachel accords Helen and Terence the role of heterosexual adults or marital pair, relegating to herself the status of passive, acquiescent child, spectator to their lovemaking.

The forest scene reflects because of its dissociated character, the author's deep seated sexual confusion and dissimulation. Previous versions of *The Voyage Out*[6] successively show a more aggressive, assaultive Helen and rescue of Rachel by Terence (Holograph); show a murderous Helen who tried to choke Rachel on learning she plans to marry, in addition to Rachels' exclamation that she loves Terence more (Earlier Typescript); or show homosexual overtones as Helen and Rachel "rolled indiscriminately in a bundle, imparting handfuls of grass, together with gestures which under other conditions might have been described as kisses" (Later Typescript). The tumultuous homosexual emotions between Helen and Rachel are perhaps eliminated in the published version for fear of offending Leonard who Virginia married seven months before completing her novel.

In its shifting triangularity, the forest scene, in all its permutations, suggests Rachel's profound conflict and indecision concerning homosexual versus heterosexual orientations. However, this encapsulated episode directly follows Terence's confession that he is "lustful," "lazy," "moody," his desire that Rachel must "know the worst"; that furthermore, he feels futile, "incompetent," and becomes hazy about marriage.

Beset with presentiments of disaster as she kept her eyes on the lovers, Helen eerily conveys the fragility of human flesh, "which breaks so easily and lets the life escape. A falling branch, a foot that slips, and the earth has crushed them or the water drowned them" (286). Feeling "old and depressed", ensconced in an unvital marriage, begrudging Rachel her youth and sexuality, seeking to hold onto Rachel at the same time feeling Rachel has passed "beyond her guardianship" (287), Helen proves a shaky identification figure.

The lovers continue to show oscillations in their commitment, asking each other "why there was so much pain in happiness." Feeling Rachel removed and distant, Terence tells her she looked like a "bird half asleep in its nest" (289). In thinking Rachel intermittently wished to be alone, Terence felt jealous, threatened, and considered her at such moments unreachable: "There's something I can't get hold of in you" (302). Although they thought of breaking up, they "knew they could not separate . . . ; painful and terrible it might be but they were joined forever" (303).

In this novel richly informed by fantasy and metaphoric allusion, eruptions of unconscious emotion confront us, lending depth, tremendous force, and impact to relationships and events, as for example, Terence's friend, St. John's diatribe against the presumed mindlessness and omniverousness of the hotel guests. They remind him of the "silence in the lionhouse when each beast holds a lump of raw meat in its paws."

He compares them to "hippopotomuses, swine, loathsome reptiles curled around half-decayed bodies of sheep"; the sounds evoke the "lionhouse when the bones are being mauled" (177). Or, further caricaturing the guests: they had the "appearance of crocodiles so fully gorged by their last meal that the future of the world gives them no anxiety whatever" (183).

St. John's projected ferocity, textually without seeming motivation, suggests his own or the author's disclaimed oral aggressions. We obtain a glimpse of the source of his sadism when he exclaims "What I abhor most of all is the female breast. Imagine being Venning and having to get into bed with Susan. But the really repulsive thing is that they feel nothing at all" (184), ostensibly referring to the guests. What St. John or Virginia Woolf appear to be inveighing against are the oral frustrations and deprivations connected with the mother of the nursing period.

Also in violent terms, Helen describes the vicarious interest of others in Rachel and Terence's marriage as "mouths gaping for blood" (309). When the minister reads during church services: "man goeth about to devour me . . . ; all that they imagine is to do me evil . . . . Break their teeth o God in their mouths; smite the jaw bones of the lions" (227), we are accosted with still further aggressive imagery. In this context, Helen's seemingly casual allusion to her younger brother may further clarify St. John's exaggerated oral imagery since it is linked to another younger brother, Adrian Stephen, evoking oral envy and rage in his sister, Virginia Woolf.

Continuing to ponder the advisability of marriage, at times feeling women the "enemy and parasite of men," Terence thought at one point Rachel looked as though she might kill him. As the lovers' uncertainty pervades and as Rachel increasingly perceived Helen as a flawed identification figure, we learn of the onset of Rachel's illness, a mysterious, undiagnosed, tropical fever (327). Though the doctors reassure her, they are themselves baffled.

As Terence reads from Milton's poem, Rachel seemed concentrated on the lines:

> Sabrina fair,
> Listen where thou are sitting
> Under the glassy, cool, translucent wave,
> In twisted braids of lilies knitting
> The loose train of thy amber dropping hair . . . .[7]

Sabrina the "water spirit," is a "lovely death wish," come to claim Rachel (Richter, 124). Sabrina's drowning is also attributed to her "step-

dame," enraged over her rebuff by Sabrina's father, according to
Leaska, citing myth and history (1977a, 32). During Terence's reading of
the poem, Rachel's head begins to ache and she feels feverish.

As Rachel lay in bed, she observed the "movement of the blind as it
filled with air and blew slowly out, drawing the cord with a little trailing
sound along the floor." Here, her description is similar to Woolf's ecstatic
memory of the sound of waves and window-blind cord in the nursery at
Cornwall. Yet in *The Voyage Out*, Rachel's perception seemed "terrifying" to her as though the "movement of an animal in the room" (328).
Is this connected to Rachel's fear of sexuality, as well as to Virginia's
fear and confusion regarding her parents' sexuality as she lay next to
their bedroom in Cornwall.

Not unlike Woolf's previous emotional collapse, Rachel withdraws,
feels "completely cut-off, alone with her body, unable to communicate
with the rest of the world" (330). Similar to Rachel's earlier anxiety dream
of walking through a tunnel under the Thames, she now has a fantasy she
saw "little, deformed women sitting in the archways playing cards," (331)
but the women turned into Helen and the nurse tending Rachel. Here Rachel
views Helen as a damaged individual, no longer someone to emulate or
model herself after.

Hostility regarding Terence consumed Rachel. Opening her eyes
when Terence kissed her, Rachel saw "an old woman slicing a man's
head off with a knife" (339).

In a later fantasy where Rachel escaped under water from her
"tormentors", she is not dead but presumably drowned, "curled up,"
womb-like and cosily, at the bottom of the sea. She saw and heard nothing
but a "faint, booming sound which was the sound of the sea rolling over
her head" (341).

Coming out of her coma, Rachel is in the grip of size, spatial, and
body distortions. Now conscious of her surroundings, Rachel felt she
had arrived at the "surface of the dark sticky pool and a wave seemed to
bear her up and down with it;[8] she had ceased to have any will of her own
but lay on top of the wave, conscious of some pain but chiefly
weakness." Then the wave turned into the "side of a mountain" and her
body became a "drift of melting snow" (346). As the room seemed to expand, Rachel doubted her voice ever reached the person to whom she
might be talking. Thinking her voice turned into a bird that flew away,
Rachel evokes Virginia, preoccupied with "birds singing in Greek" during her 1904 breakdown following her father's death. Rachel, transform-
ing a wave into the "side of a mountain," preceiving her knees as "huge
peaked mountains of bare bone", projects Virginia's desire to resurrect
her father who was a passionate mountain climber.

Sometimes Helen took an hour or more, Rachel thought, to raise her arm. At one point, Rachel felt Helen's body tower over her, then "come down upon her like the ceiling falling" (347), indicating Rachel's fear of Helen's malevolence.

Rachel dies, the cause of her illness unknown, suggesting capitulation to insoluble inner conflicts and crushing forces in her environment, a sense of her helplessness and surrender prevailing.[9]

Rachel's heightened sensory and bodily perceptions during her delirium are not unlike Virginia's symptoms during her early breakdowns. Neither Rachel's nor Virginia's illness appears particularly florid, or shows the mental deterioration and regression of schizophrenia, but is frequently evocative of metaphoric or figurative language. Although Rachel-Virginia's associations occasionally indicate disregard for reality considerations, they are not necessarily delusional; rather, they reflect characteristics of affective disorders: acute melancholia, distortions of body image, physical dysfunction, desire to punish or blame the self for succumbing to illness, occasionally deviant thought processes. Despite the severity of symptoms, the melancholic is more in touch with external reality (Arieti, 456).

III

Critics, preoccupied with what they consider Rachel's passivity or dreaminess suggest that whenever she feels close to another (for example, her lover), she lapses into trance or sleep. Naremore cites the following passage to illustrate his point: "She [Rachel] could not raise her finger any more and sat still, listening, and looking at the same spot. It became stranger and stranger. She was overcome with awe that things could exist at all" (*TVO*, 125). According to Naremore, Rachel's "desire for love leads to a total loss of self in death." Naremore furthermore perceives all of Woolf's novels as "uneasy compromises" the characters make between the will to live in the world and the temptation to seek "absolute unity with the world, as though everything in the environment turned into water" (Naremore, 1973, 39).

In his perception, Rachel is a "young virgin who journeys out to meet a bridegroom who is death" (55) similar to McClelland's notion that "death represents the demon lover," expressed paradoxically as the thought of yielding or dying (94). Would it not be more parsimonious, however, to say Woolf is seeking to depict a state of uncertain, sometimes precarious self and social awakening in an emotionally undeveloped young woman who lags considerably behind her chronological age and that the author wishes to remain in touch with nuances of mood suggestive of the hidden and unconscious?

Borrowing from Woolf's description of Bernard, the central character in her novel, *The Waves*, Naremore delineates Rachel as a person "without a self" or as a "divided self" (248). Although the nonself seems a favorite literary metaphor, there is literally no one without a self; to be human is to be in possession of a sense of self, however tenuous, diminutive, or grandiose. In Woolf's phrase, "the world as seen without a self," she refers to the lack of ego involvement felt in some situations or to the multiplicity of self, even though she feels there is a "key" self.

When Woolf writes about Rachel's "dissolution" she is referring to the heroine's adolescent-like, philosophical contemplation of existence at this particular cross section in her life, that is, Rachel ruminating on the possiblities of life before or after her own, "overcome with awe" that she or her surroundings "should exist at all" (*TVO*, 125). Far from dissolved, Rachel is, before her illness variously depicted as introverted, assertive, and, in her way self-sufficient and contemplative. She is highly vigilant in picking up or responding to subliminal cues or the hidden feelings of others. As a musician, she is not unlike the creative artist in her sense of separateness, complexity and special vision. Similar to the plight of the artist, she is frequently misunderstood.

Aspects of Rachel's and Woolf's lives strikingly sychronize. Both were motherless at an early age and showed gaps in their maturational process as well as considerable arrest in their integrated development. Both associate heterosexuality with attack or entrapment; both are preoccupied with guilt over sexualized encounters with father figures. Prolonged attachment to father is evidenced in both. When Rachel is "adopted" by her aunt and Woolf emerges from mourning her father's death, both contemplate for the first time the possibilities and opportunities for greater self-definition in the outer world.

Rachel receives a double message from Helen who wishes to socialize her, but on Helen's own terms: Rachel must not embark on heterosexual relationships; she must remain submissive and infantile, otherwise Helen will feel diminished and ultimately retaliate. Violet, offering maternal protection, was reluctant to relinquish Virginia to her heterosexual destiny and was, in part, a prototype for Helen. Woolf's letters to Violet prior to marriage and soon thereafter were self-deprecating, apologetic, and anxious lest Violet terminate their relationship. Vanessa, a more feminine model, angry over her sister's liaison with Clive, mocked her sexual incompetence and gave her little support in her wish to have a baby.

Although we witness a cumulative sense of Rachel's increasing assertiveness in *The Voyage Out*, she avoids the conflictual choice between tenuous mother attachment and shaky heterosexuality, via her illness. Rachel thought her rebelliousness, anger, and intention to marry wounded her aunt, and perhaps she felt responsible for Helen's depression. Did Woolf feel she killed off her mother because of her sexual burgeoning and closeness to father during her childhood and early adolescence? Or in turning to men, did she feel that she threatened Violet and therefore had to punish herself?[10]

Rachel's and Terence's love relationship, characterized by the shifting commitments made to one another, is similar to the tensions concerning sexual intimacy on the part of Virginia and Leonard who married after a period of uncertainty. In externalizing the homoerotic interplay between Helen and Rachel, Woolf focused on her conflict between the presumably dependable relationship with Violet in the past and the new one with Leonard which she might have regretted, now realizing it would be childless.

Rachel's feeling of betrayal by Terence inasmuch as in Rachel's fantasy he turns to Helen in the forest episode suggests he was in Rachel's perception a parental, possibly incestuous figure. Did Woolf similarly see Vanessa and Leonard as parental figures, holding the reins, directing her life, and restraining her? During 1913 both Leonard and Vanessa considered Virginia mentally ill, thought her problems were incurable, felt that she should not have a baby, in effect attacked her femininity. At the time Virginia attempted suicide, they were indeed together in telling Dr. Savage, who had originally encouraged Virginia to have children, he would be replaced.[11]

Virginia was disillusioned with doctors who advised her and with Leonard who frustrated her deepest needs. As we know she attempted suicide[12] during 1913 taking an almost lethal dose of veronal. Though the risk was great, Virginia harbored some glimmer of hope for rescue, since her friend Ka Cox was nearby and could call husband and sister; also Geoffrey Keynes, a doctor, was in the house at the time.

Virginia unconsciously hoped for intervention but to Rachel she gave no such choice. Edel suggests that Rachel's "voyage out into the world" becomes a "voyage into death" and that Rachel's death was basically Virginia's "killing of herself"; that "marriage now came to seem that kind of voyage" (Edel, 1979, 199).

A vengeful desire to punish her husband, and an accompanying cry for help would be more accurate, which might, of course, as with many would-be suicides have been frustrated had the gears not been enmeshing; Leonard contacted emergency aid and mobilized nurses in time.

VII "He seemed like one of those lost birds fascinated by the lighthouse and held to the glass by the splendor of the blaze"—*Night and Day*

I

In mid-1915, Woolf recovered from the second phase of her breakdown, characterized by the intensely vitriolic feelings she directed at Leonard. Emboldened by the affirmative response to *The Voyage Out*, Woolf experimented with poems, short stories, resumed diary writing, and thought of "inspired and profound" phrases all day long. She sketched outlines of books she hoped to write in the future, then began *Night and Day* to prove to herself she could write a naturalistic novel.

Again seeking closeness to Vanessa, who now lived with Duncan Grant, a fellow painter and Bloomsburyite, Woolf arranged to live fairly close to her in the Sussex countryside. With Clive and Vanessa no longer living together, Woolf was less beset by feelings of rivalry, felt Vanessa more available, and frequently assumed a protective role towards her, although the construct of Vanessa as earth mother prevailed and was of central, ongoing importance.

Woolf's deep enmeshment and identification with Vanessa, the desire to share and be part of the ambience surrounding her sister, permeated her life and art. Visiting Vanessa and her family at Wissett Farm, reinforced for Woolf the thought of writing *Night and Day*. She wrote Vanessa: "I greatly envy you your brats. I am very much interested in your life which I think of writing another novel about. It's fatal staying with you. You start so many new ideas" (L2, Jul.30'16).

In a letter to Lytton, Woolf emphasizes her involvement with Vanessa: "Don't you think they have discovered the secret of life? I thought it [Wissett] wonderfully harmonious" (L2,Jul.25'16). Vanessa's household consisted of Julian and Quentin who were Vanessa's and Clive's children, in addition to a triangular arrangement including Vanessa, Duncan, and writer David Garnett.

Woolf's naivete is striking in thinking the Wissett menage congenial. Although Vanessa and Duncan were living together and shared a mutual passion for painting, Vanessa found painful the necessity to share Duncan, predominantly homosexual, with his other lover, David Garnett (Spalding, 135). Disapproving the bohemianism of Vanessa's circle, Leonard vigilantly supervised his wife's health and resented her immersion in Vanessa's children.

At this time, 1916, Woolf, an active member of the Women's Cooperative Guild, wrote Margaret Davies that her feminism increased as the war deepened; furthermore, she wondered how "this preposterous fiction [the war] keeps going a day longer without some vigorous young woman pulling us together and marching through it" (L2, Jan.23'16). Woolf organized and chaired meetings of the local Guild at her home in Richmond and was responsible for finding speakers.

Meeting Katherine Mansfield in 1917, Woolf admired her work even though she felt intense professional envy; Mansfield's story "Prelude" became the second publication of Hogarth Press. Woolf was "shocked at Mansfield's commonness at first sight: lines so hard and cheap." However, she admitted that Katherine is "so intelligent and inscrutable that she repays friendship" (D1, Oct.11'17).

A reminder of the war, the sound of artillery fire in Flanders was within earshot. Air raids occurred each month with the "full moon," propelling the inhabitants of Hogarth House into the basement. Philip and Ottoline Morrell[1] offered easy employment on their farm to pacifists and conscientious objectors (Bell,v.2, 51–53). In Woolf's circle, this included Clive Bell and Duncan Grant. Because of his tremor, Leonard did not have to serve.

Leonard formed the "17 Club" which took its name from the events of the 1917 February Revolution in Russia. He hoped the "Club" might prove a setting for exchanges of ideas among kindred spirits, especially socialist intellectuals. Instead, it became a "center for a kind of second generation Bloomsbury," not particularly political but nonconformist, hostile to Victorians and Edwardians who, the young people felt, led the nation into war. These young men and women, some of whom worked for Hogarth Press, Virginia called "Cropheads" or "Bloomsbury Bunnies." Using the term "Underworld," she referred to critics more interested in reputation than talent (Bell, V.2, 49–50).

In discussing the writing of *Night and Day* with her sister, Woolf indicates that she, Virginia, is the "principal character"; she is aware she is "priggish and severe" but then Vanessa will see what she was like at 18

(L2, Apr.14'17). As the novel evolved, Woolf attempted to encompass aspects of her sister's life in it, conveys to her:

> I've been writing about you all the morning and have made you wear a blue dress; you've got to be immensely mysterious and romantic, which of course you are; yes, but it's the combination that's so enthralling; to crack through the paving stone and be enveloped in the mist (L2, Apr. 22'18).

At this point, thinking no one appeared interested in her writing, Woolf considers herself "useless" and wonders whether having children would make a "difference," but then "it's no good making them responsible for one's unreality" (L2, Nov.13'18). Her mood might have been related to the anticipated advent of Vanessa and Duncan's baby. Born December 25, 1918, their child, Angelica, was destined to grow up and marry her father's lover, David Garnett.

Woolf, not knowing Katherine Mansfield had tuberculosis, frequently felt put off by Mansfield's postponement of intended visits, yet felt they had been "intimate, intense rather than open." Their relationship for Woolf had always been "interesting and mingled with quite enough of the agreeable personal element to make one fond as well as curious" (D1, Feb.18'19). Woolf was pleased she was asked to write for *Athenaeum* by the editor, Middleton Murry, who had for long lived with Mansfield, Finally seeing Katherine, Woolf wrote in her diary: "as usual I find in Katherine what I don't find with the other clever women, a sense of ease and interest . . . , due to her caring so genuinely if so differently from the way I care about our precious art" (D1, Mar.22'19). Woolf notes that the writing of *Night and Day* went fairly smoothly: "In my opinion *Night and Day* is a much more mature and finished and satisfactory book than *The Voyage Out*. I don't suppose I've enjoyed any writing so much as I did the last half . . . ; indeed no part of it taxed me as *The Voyage Out* did. (D1, Mar.27'19).

Dedicated to Vanessa—"looking for a phrase, I found none to stand beside your name"—the manuscript was submitted April 1, 1919, and published on October 20, 1919; no breakdown ensued. E.M. Forster liked *Night and Day* less than *The Voyage Out* and felt *Night and Day* a strictly "formal and classical work" requiring more "lovability" in the characters compared to a book such as *The Voyage Out* which is "vague and universal." To Woolf, "Morgan has the artist's mind; he writes the simple things that clever people say." She finds him the best of critics for that reason, and she is "happier and easier" with his blame than the others' praise as though one were in the "human atmosphere once again after a blissful roll among elastic clouds and cushiony downs" (D1, Oct. 30, 19; Nov.6'19).

On the subject of critics, Woolf wishes she were actually more like George Eliot who never looked at reviews because they interfered with her writing. Nor does Woolf "take praise or blame excessively to heart," since "they interrupt, cast one's eyes backwards, make one wish to explain or investigate. I had rather write in my own way of four Passionate Snails than be . . . Jane Austen over again (D1, Dec.5'19).

Woolf could now see how readers prefer *The Voyage Out* to *Night and Day*: "I don't say I admire it more but find it a more gallant and inspiring spectacle" (D2, Feb.4'20).

II

Woolf's second novel, *Night and Day*, concerned with issues of love and marriage, described the vicissitudes of two engaged couples Katharine Hilbery and William Rodney, Mary Datchet and Ralph Denham, the severance of these relationships, their subsequent realignments and uncertain growth toward maturity. *Night and Day* showed far less turbulence and access to unconscious processess than *The Voyage Out*. That Woolf might have suppressed abrasive issues seems evidenced in the letter to her former tutor, Janet Case, pointing to the "question of the things one doesn't say. How far do our feelings take their color from the dive underground?" (L2, Nov.1'19).

Katherine's is a fairly complex characterization. She is acquiescent to her mother's desire that she assist her in writing an endless biography of her grandfather. Overly attached to, making demands on Katherine, disinclined to give her up, her father is jealous of her relationship with men.

Feeling it incumbent upon herself to take care of her mother, to "sustain, counsel and help her," Katherine remains the recipient of her mother's moods and depression and shelters her from unpleasantness or interruption.

Entangled in the "vanished figures" of her grandfather's life, Katharine sometimes overlooked the issue of her grounding in the present. She had to remind herself of her autonomy, and she frequently "lost consciousness that she was a separate being with a future of her own" (115).[2] Doubts and apprehensions on her mother's part in completing her literary efforts permeated Katharine as well. Occasionally she acknowledged her irritation regarding her mother's excessive demands.

> She had suddenly become very angry with a rage which their relation-
> ship made silent, and therefore doubly powerful and critical. She felt all
> the unfairness of the claim . . . made on her time and sympathy, and
> what her mother took, Katharine thought bitterly, she wasted (117).

Obviously Katharine felt manipulated by a family that reversed the roles of parent and child, that thrust too much responsibility on her alone.

Katharine's detachment seems a facade, counteracting the sticky nature of the relationship with her parents, their immersion in the past. Her need to escape their clutching grasp is great. A passion for mathematics and astronomy, which she pursues in secret at night, shows her desire for an ordered, abstract, less emotionally charged and diffuse life work than her mother's, though the "unwomanly" aspect of science bothered her somewhat.

She longed for a heroic, masculine dimension which encompassed the navigation of a "vast ship in a hurricane, round a black promontory of rock" or the "taming of wild ponies in the American prairies" (40). Her romantic fantasies which she indulges in a good deal, expand as she describes a "magnanimous hero, riding a great horse." He and she "rode through forests together" or "galloped by the rim of the sea" (108).

Tending to fall into dream states in which the world was replete with beauty seen in "flying glimpses" (145), Katharine equated reality with "resignation" and "stoical acceptance of fact" (145). She contemplated "a perfectly loveless marriage" with William and wished to give her mother the son she wanted; the Hilbery marriage, not a very flourishing one, was a poor model.

Rebelling against the overinvolvement in her parents' activities, Katharine exclaims: "It's life that matters, nothing but life—the process of discovering, the everlasting and perpetual process" (138). This is in the context of "gnawing" the contents of a book by Dostoevski[3] that neither parent had read, exulting that she for once was not required to share her thoughts.

Katharine views her desire to marry William as the wish to leave home and escape her parents. On realizing William does not, either, allow her the privacy she requires, Katharine thinks of breaking the engagement. Then unpredictably, perceiving his loneliness, she tells William she will marry him. Though at first Mrs. Hilbery does not wish to lose her daughter, she is made aware of her "selfishness" and en-courages the marriage (146).

The novel deals at length with Katharine's continuing indecision regarding her feelings for William and her growing attraction for Ralph.

She is sensitive to the intimacy between Ralph and Mary and cannot comprehend or assimilate Ralph's initial, impetuous proposal of marriage to her, Katharine. Katharine feels extremely identified with and guilt-ridden regarding Mary, who emerges as someone who fully accepts both her intellectual and feminine proclivities. Mary gives Ralph his freedom, aware he is not in love with her. She is unwilling to accept less, though he offers to come back. Katharine perceives her friends as "lantern-bearers whose lights wove a pattern, dissolving, joining, meeting again in combinations" (332).

Fairly complicated and unpredictable, Ralph Denham is upwardly mobile and pursues an interest in heraldry, yet his sister describes him as capable of risking his entire career for some "fantastic imagination, some idea or cause" or even for a woman (127). He loved the East and could be seen "sucking contagion" from the page of an Indian travel book. In Ralph's daydreams he assumed "noble and romantic parts" and would "set flowering, waste tracts of the earth, cure many ills or raise up beauty where none existed." His was a "fierce and potent spirit who might devour the dusty books and parchments in his office with one lick of its tongue and leave him standing in nakedness if he gave way" (129).

Ralph considered himself capable of disciplined work, thought he had a good brain, and imagined himself a member of the House of Commons when he attained age 50, with adequate means, and with an "unimportant office in a Liberal government" (129). He commended himself for subduing his extravagant impulses and for maintaining his dual existence, a "life rigidly divided into the hours of work and those of dreams" (130).

Although Ralph frequently thought Katharine "far removed," he could submit "recklessly to her without thought of future pain" (151). Claiming she cannot "endure living with other people," Katharine condescendingly thinks "an occasional man with a beard is interesting; he's detached; he lets me go my way" (354). When Ralph challenged her, she thought him arbitrary, hot-tempered, and imperious. Yet she is attracted to him.

Hoping he might be acceptable to Katharine, Ralph draws up a rather antiseptic foundation for their friendship: "such a friendship must be unemotional." Should either "fall in love," it is "at his [or her] own risk. Neither is under any obligation to the other. They must be at liberty to break or alter it at any moment . . . , say whatever they wish to say" (357).

Limited as they are in their grasp of personal relationships, each deeply invested in preserving their inviolacy, an acceptable relationship between them might only be possible on Ralph's impersonal terms.

Perceiving "this astonishing precipice on one side of which the soul was active and in broad daylight, on the other side of which it was contemplative and dark as night" (358), Katharine hopes to make the transition between "night and day" and to accept Ralph's terms of friendship.

Katharine now breaks her engagement with William. William turns to Cassandra, Katharine's cousin, attracted to her "vivacity and freshness" (361). Both "adore" Katharine who is jealous of William and Cassandra's discovery of each other. Katharine heard them speak as though they were in "another world, a world antecedent to her world, the prelude to reality" as though "lately dead, she heard the living talking." Apparently, the dream-like nature of her life had never been more apparent to her. Never had "life been more certainly an affair of four walls whose objects existed only within the range of lights and fires, beyond which lay nothing, or nothing more than darkness". She "stepped beyond the region where the light of illusion still makes it desirable to possess, to love, to struggle. She was still tormented by desires" (373).⁴

To exorcise the "ghost" of Katharine and dispel the "absurd passions" which were the "cause of so much pain and waste" (394), Ralph invites her to meet his family. Surely this would be mutually disillusioning he felt. In the episode where she is plunged into the tumult of Ralph's family, Katharine, despite her initial aversion, is animated and responsive, passing his "test" of her. Although we are reminded over and over that Katharine is cold or abstract, here we are more decisively shown her capacity to be related, warm, and giving, frequently the case with Katharine's progenitor as well. Seeing Katharine's humanity and earthiness, Ralph is fearful lest his illusion be destroyed. Katharine chides him: his romantic notions, his inability to separate her from the person he imagines her to be, she feels, is "being in delusion" (404).

Katharine believes their lives can only run parallel, never converging. Ralph insists "no one knows you as I know you" and tells Katharine he loves her not caring whether she returns his love. Although he might perceive her as cold or distant, her presence by his side "transforms the world" (502).

As Ralph declared his love Katharine thought she detected a lack of "warmth" in his voice. Preferring they remain "free" (509), possibly live together without marrying, Katharine reveals her skepticism concerning personal relationships: "always to be finding the other an illusion and going off and forgetting about them, never to be certain that you cared, or that he wasn't caring for someone not you at all." She deplores the horror of vacillation, of "being happy one moment and miserable the next—that's the reason we can't possibly marry" (513). Yet she and Ralph cannot apparently live without each other.

Ralph's discovery and acceptance of Katharine's secret passion for symbols, planets, stars, and mathematics is "exquisitely painful" to her. She must accustom herself to someone sharing her loneliness (521), now accepted Ralph's "little dot with the flames around it" representing by its "circumference of smudges" around a central point, "all that encircling glow, which for him surrounded so many of the objects of life, softening their sharp outline" as though with a faint halo. Katherine, too, observed the world in this fashion (522). They enjoyed the same sense of the impending future: "vast, mysterious, infinitely stored with undeveloped shapes which each would unwrap for the other to behold . . . " (523).

The novel ends in a romantic vein. Katharine increasingly sees Ralph as a "fire burning through its smoke, a source of life" (533), and as she spoke of the dark red fire and the smoke surrounding it, Ralph felt that he had "stepped over the threshold into the faintly lit vastness of another mind stirring with shapes," then moving away again (534). We glimpse the extent both are steeped in fantasy: "she might speak to him but with that strange tremor in his voice, those eyes blindly adoring, whom did he answer? What woman did he see? And where was she walking, and who was her companion?" (537).

In "accepting the co-existence of illusion and reality, Ralph and Katharine can now individually accept the duality and the fissure—each recognizes in his own life" (Leaska, 1977a, 61). With this awareness, Katharine can give up the emotional dependency on her family and pursue both the "life of solitude and the life of society" (*ND*, 358).

As in Shakespearian festive comedies wherein the grim realities of the daytime are replaced by the imaginative life of the night, *Night and Day* may be seen as a comedy of "transformation," establishing "love's illusions" (Fleishman, 28).

III

Night and Day shows subtlety and skill in portraying the emotional swayings of two mutually detached individuals, Katharine and Ralph, who wished to share their solitude. Their flickering connectedness, frequently obliterated, requires almost emergency-like measures to fuel and sustain it. Interestingly, Woolf here delineates a reciprocal responsibility for the lovers' difficulties, perhaps a communication that the problems between herself and Leonard were mutual.

Despite Woolf's avoidance of emotionally charged situations or confrontations in *Night and Day* they emerge within the psychological substrate of the novel in a series of powerful images, indicating Woolf's identification with her characters' sense of fragility and diminutiveness, feeling the abandoned child, forever outside the magic circle.

During a frenzied, nocturnal visit where Ralph secretly observed Katharine in her room, he felt "simplified and exhausted, like one of those lost birds fascinated by the lighthouse and held to the glass by the splendor of the blaze." Ralph responds to Katharine as though she were a "shape of light, the light itself"; he thought the room she was in provided a "steady light which cast its beams like those of a lighthouse⁵ over the trackless waste" (418–419). In imagining he was "whirled senseless against the glass," he seems overwhelmed by feelings of insignificance, exclusion and longing, in relation to the goddess-like Katharine.

Here Ralph evokes Woolf exalting Vanessa, coalescing her with a beneficent, radiant mother. Of course one can be burnt, annihilated, or blinded by such a blaze of light, especially if one feels lost initially. Eternally Woolf feels the outsider, feels the mother-figure near yet far, yearns for her warmth, strength, and protectiveness but a barrier is interposed.

Frequently, the lovers see each other only "now and then, like lights in a storm . . . , in the midst of a hurricane" (450). They appear to "pass in and out of each other's minds" (409) rather than bodies. Examining the photo of a Greek statue, concealing the lower half, Ralph fantasizes the ecstasy of being in Katharine's presence, although he consistently eliminates her sexuality. Katharine senses her real self will always be secondary to a dream Ralph has of her, not unsimilar to Leonard's linking of Virginia to Aspasia.

Face to face with intense rage or self-destructiveness in herself or her characters, Woolf is often disoriented, almost dissociated. When Ralph and Katharine, after revealing their secrets seem more intimate than ever before, we are confronted with one of Woolf's karate chops, a strange eruption from her unconscious: As the lovers' discourse is interruped by the maid who announces that a woman, refusing to give her name, has come to see Mrs. Hilbery, Ralph fantasized as Katharine left to get her mother, that the anonymous woman was a "black hunchback provided with a steel knife which she would plunge into Katharine's heart" (523). Ralph's unconscious anger, occasionally treacherous, is intermittently in evidence throughout the novel. At another time he is ashamed of his "savage wish to hurt" Katharine, though we are told Katharine "likes" it. Are these subtle suggestions of sadomasochistic interactions between Katharine and Ralph?

In the oral imagery Woolf frequently employes—for example, Ralph's "sucking contagion" from travel books, "devouring" dusty

books with a "lick" of his tongue or eating with "ferocity"—is Woolf
telling us that underneath his facade of upward striving he (or she) feels
subjectively weak or dependent on others? Is Woolf communicating via
these and other oral images, such as Katharine's "gnawing" Dostoevski
that Katharine's and her own tendency to emotionally incorporate
words, images and the emotional turbulence of others—are food for
thought and sustenance?

Night and Day continues the themes of uncertainty regarding personal and sexual identity, entangling family relationships, and conflicts
regarding love and marriage present in *The Voyage Out* and in Woolf's
life. Mrs. Hilbery, writing an endless biography that will never be finished, prodding the family to respond to her every wish and whim, of course
resembles Leslie Stephen writing his *Dictionary of National Biography*.

Inasmuch as Mrs. Hilbery is emotionally unavailable to Katharine as
Woolf perceived her mother to be, it is of considerable interest that in her
"second chance" as a novelist, to create a more loving mother, Woolf
could not conjure up an unalloyingly good mother, though Mrs. Hilbery
does ultimately and uncharacteristically emerge from her ivory tower to
encourage Katharine's love affair with Ralph.

Katharine's solicitousness regarding her mother, cushioning her
bouts of dysphoria, is a buffer of sorts in the Hilbery marriage. She is
also intermediary and surrogate-wife for her father and is chosen by him
to tell her mother about the sexual exploits of a promiscuous cousin,
since her father it too inhibited to do so. This may represent an exter-
nalization of the Duckworth brothers' sexual intimidations or possibly is
an allusion to Woolf's psychotic cousin, James Stephen, who
"violently" pursued Stella. Katharine in effect instructs her parents on
the facts of life and, in a reversal of roles, takes care of them, postponing
her own development and maturation. Woolf too felt her parents were
rooted in the past and that her growth was interfered with because of the
demands of parents and parent-surrogates in her life.

In *Night and Day*, Mr. Hilbery assumes a passive, subordinate role
regarding his wife and seems particularly distant and unable to communicate with her, treating her as though she were a hothouse flower. He
comes to life, emerges from his shadowy role, when Katharine informs
him about her decision to break with William. Here Mr. Hilbery "could
not endure that his daughter's conduct should be in any way considered
irregular" (495). His faith in her stability was shaken. He felt for the first
time in many years "responsible" for her (496), especially when he heard
Cassandra and William were engaged. His house was in a state of
"revolution; his meals would be poisoned for days" (505).

When he understood Katharine's preference was for Ralph he felt pangs of jealousy:[6] "Had he loved her to see her swept away by this torrent? To have her taken from him by this uncontrollable force, to stand by helpless, ignored? Oh how he loved her" (529). She might have married William without causing him any agony, probably because he knew her feelings for William were more filial than otherwise. As he stalked out, Katharine was quite shaken underneath her appearance of calm. Obviously, the eruption of emotions here suggests the father's excessive attachment to his daughter, his wish to retain her as surrogate-wife, the damaging effects of her enmeshment with this role.

Since Ralph is penniless and fatherless, is he merely interested in Katharine's money or family background? Ralph, evoking Leonard, wishes to leave his profession, live in a little cottage, and write books though numerous sisters and brothers are dependent on him.

Sometimes wavering in his allegiance to Katharine, Ralph for the most part is unflagging in his efforts to accommodate her needs and claims to love her more than himself, a more dependable hero than Terence Hewet in *The Voyage Out*. If one wonders why Virginia chose to live with Leonard after the distinct turnoff towards him during her manic episode in 1915, her depiction of Ralph's patience and readiness to compromise might represent Woolf's conception of her husband's constancy and acceptance of her. Although Woolf does from time to time, through the years, refer gratefully or affectionately to her married relationship with Leonard, the couples in her novels are typically estranged and isolated from one another in a deeply intimate sense.

When not the excluded, abandoned child needing succor, Woolf's ego-ideal is Mary Datchet. In Mary we are presented with a decidedly modern woman seeking fulfillment in both love and work; someone who does not compromise. Her unrequited passion for Ralph is channelled into working for a cause in which she believes. Through her portrayal of Mary, the author shows considerable sophistication in the depicted ambiguities concerning customary notions of masculinity and femininity. Mary is the person Woolf might have become or emulated, had marriage not been an imperative due to family and generational pressures.

VIII Elegy to brother: "I think of death sometimes as the end of an excursion I went on when Thoby died"—*Jacob's Room*

Katherine Mansfield's review of Woolf's novel *Night and Day* in *Athenaeum* for November 26, 1919, was critical; Mansfield thought the novel lacked "actuality," was an "orthodox performance" (Bell, v.2, 69) after the promise of *The Voyage Out*. In particular she felt Woolf ignored the impact of World War I. Although Woolf felt Mansfield's review "spiteful," she claimed she did not take criticism to heart: "Isn't this 'reputation' the deepest of all masculine instincts"? (D1, Dec.28'19), she asked. Her relationship to fame, she felt, was more balanced. Quite possibly Woolf took seriously Mansfield's thrust that *Night and Day* bypassed the war, and therefore Woolf incorporated the war as background in her next novel, *Jacob's Room*.

At the time of writing *Jacob's Room*, Woolf worked on her celebrated essay, "Modern Fiction," which criticized "materialists" such as Wells, Bennett, and Galsworthy who despite their enormous skill, write of "unimportant things" dealing with the "trivial and the transitory" (210). Her message suggested that naturalistic fiction overlooks "the thing we seek, whether we call it life or spirit, truth or reality":

> Examine for a moment an ordinary mind on an ordinary day. The mind receives a myriad of impressions—trivial, fantastic, evanescent, or engraved with the sharpness of steel. From all sides they come, an incessant shower of innumerable atoms . . .

Should the writer portray what pleased him or her, not what convention dictated, the usual plot or love interest whether comedy or tragedy, would not inevitably ensue. Furthermore, life is not a series of gig lamps symmetrically arranged; but a luminous halo,[1] a semitransparent envelope surrounding us from the beginning of consciousness to the end. . . . Let us record the atoms as they fall upon the mind, in the order in which they fall; let us trace the pattern, however disconnected and incoherent in appearance, which each sight or incident scores upon the consciousness (*CR*, v.1, 211–213).

The center of modernist thinking, Woolf continues, lies in delineating the "dark places of psychology," shadowy areas of experience, hitherto incomprehensible; in this the Russian novelists excel, in their grasp of the soul and heart, their "natural reverence for the human spirit," their sense of fatality—in short, the romantic "inconclusiveness of the Russian mind" (217). She summarizes: "everything is the proper stuff of fiction, every feeling, every thought, every quality of brain and spirit" (218).

In her conception of *Jacob's Room*, she planned a "new form for a new novel," which afforded the desired "looseness and lightness." She asked: "doesn't that get closer and yet keep form and speed and enclose everything?" Yet she wondered whether this encompasses the "human heart: there will be no scaffolding, scarcely a brick to be seen; all crepuscular, but the heart, the passion, the humor, everything as bright as fire in the mist." Hoping to avoid the intrusions of the "damned egotistical self" which in her opinion narrows and constricts writers such as Joyce and Richardson (D2, Jan.26'20), Woolf did not acknowledge their influence on her work, though she later alluded in "Modern Fiction" to Joyce's spiritual qualities, his concern "at all costs to reveal the flickerings of that innermost flame" (*CR*, v.1, 214). Was she too prudish to be aware of his nonspiritual side?

Concomitant to a dense, demanding schedule of book reviewing and essay writing and related to her mood swings, her diary indicated fluctuations in writing her new novel. Apparently, the creative flow in beginning a book sometimes reaches a plateau; self-doubts and resignation take over. Determination not to give in and the sense of an "impending shape" keep one at it. There is nothing clearcut at first, but "directly one gets to work, one is like a person walking, who has seen the country stretching out before" (D2, May 11'20).

Meeting Mansfield, the "only woman with gift enough to make talk of writing interesting," Woolf at first perceived a disconcerting "formality and coldness." She thought Mansfield belonged to the "cat kind: alien, composed, always solitary and observant." They talked about "solitude" and Woolf found Katherine expressing her own feelings as she "never heard them expressed." When the topic of Mansfield's review of *Night and Day* arose, Mansfield, in an about face, referred to *Night and Day* as an "amazing achievement. She said she could pass an examination on it" (D2, May31'20). After their visit in August, before Mansfield left for southern France, Woolf notes the "blankness of not having her to talk to." She referred to the parallelism of their approach to literature and writing, the "queerest sense of echo coming back to me from her mind the second after I've spoken" (D2, Aug.25'20).

When Woolf finally hit her stride again she worked on her novel every morning "feeling each day's work like a fence which I have to ride at, my heart in my mouth till it's over, and I've cleared or knocked the bar out" (D2, Aug.5'20). Here in a strong, aggressive image she is hoping to break barriers.

During the writing of *Jacob's Room*, Woolf, intensely competitive, is preoccupied with the work of her new friend, T.S. Eliot, who on his part, is interested in Hogarth Press as a possible publisher. She agrees with Leonard that Eliot is "disappointing in brain—less powerful than expected and with little play of mind" (D2, Sept.20'20). Eliot, she felt, ignored her as a writer. Had she been "meek," she might have "gone under, felt him and his views dominant and subversive," which seems prophetic, because this is exactly what ensued.

Her writing now comes to a halt as she confesses Eliot intimidates her: "the mind when engaged upon fiction wants all its boldness and self-confidence." She suspected that Eliot felt Joyce's work superior to hers. In addition, Eliot, six years younger than she, was writing and publishing some of his greatest poetry. Feeling overshadowed by male writers, she also felt "distanced by L. [Lytton Strachey] in every respect" (D2, Sept. 26'20).

At this time, Woolf prepared a rejoinder to Arnold Bennett who had written that men were intellectually and creatively superior to women. In answer to an article by a Bennett supporter asserting that no amount of "education and liberty of action will sensibly alter the fact that women are inferior to men in intellectual power, and that women's indisputable desire to be dominated is a proof of intellectual inferiority," Woolf submitted her counterblast, "The Intellectual Status of Women." She wrote that "the degradation of being a slave is only equalled by the degradation of being a master".[2]

Attributing her inability to write or read at this point to illness, Woolf notes "it was not Eliot that broke off Jacob" (D2, Oct.1'20), but it is highly likely she protests too much. Though her writing slowly resumes, her depression is still in evidence as she asks: "Why is life so tragic, so like a little strip of pavement over an abyss." The answer according to Woolf has to do with her childlessness, living at a distance from friends, "failing to write well." She is preoccupied with growing old, with the fact that Vanessa's children are growing up and not as available to her. Though her depression lifts in jotting down her feelings, she for the most part dismisses this form of "therapy", wishes to appear a "success" even to herself. She continues to feel incompetent, a failure: "I'm out of fashion; old; shan't do any better; have no headpiece" (D2, Oct.25'20).

Despite protestations to the contrary, Woolf is decidedly interested in reputation, perhaps stimulated by her jealousy over the success of Lytton's book, *Queen Victoria*, which he dedicated to her. She wished to confront the "question of praise and fame" and agreed with Roger Fry who felt it necessary to be "kept up to the mark; that people should be interested, and watch one's work" (D2, Apr.8'21). She feared she would be "dismissed as negligible" (L2, Apr.12'21) and was reassured to some extent by the praise of Lytton Strachey and T.S. Eliot regarding her short story, "String Quartet." Eliot telling her Joyce's *Ulysses* is "prodigious" probably attenuated her pleasure in his positive comments.

Afflicted with headache, sleeplessness, other aches and pains during June and July of 1921, Woolf's work on *Jacob's Room* stopped. Her symptoms were no doubt linked to competition and rivalry with Eliot. Forbidden by her doctor to work she wrote, "No one in the whole of Sussex is so miserable as I am or so conscious of an infinite capacity of enjoyment hoarded in me could I use it" (D2, Aug.18'21). Almost 40, Woolf had published two novels, some short stories, and innumerable articles, largely anonymous, for *The Times Literary Supplement.* She was still unknown while Eliot, Joyce, and Mansfield, she felt, were forging ahead. On November 4, 1921 she finished *Jacob's Room.*

She was ill with flu, heart murmur, and high temperature during the early months of 1922; Leonard was told she might not pull through (Bell, v.2, 84). However, she was soon well enough to work with Koteliansky on translations from Dostoevski.

When Vanessa told her there was "nothing binding" in her relationship with Duncan and was jealous of the stability of Woolf's marriage, Virginia placatingly sought to prove her childlessness was "less normal" than her sister's situation (D2, Feb.4'22).

Feeling abused concerning unfavorable reviews of her short stories, Woolf "meant to write about death, only life came beating in as usual . . . ; suppose this pain over my heart suddenly wrung me out like a dish cloth and left me dead?" (D2, Feb.17'22). She has decided not to be "popular: I'm to write what I like and they're to say what they like." Her only interest as a writer lies in some "queer individuality, not in strength or passion" (D2, Feb.18'22). Woolf continued to feel others might consider *Jacob's Room* "mad, a disconnected rhapsody" (D2, Jun.23'22).

Leonard considered *Jacob's Room* a "work of genius," although one wonders what he truly felt since he also stated Virginia's characters are like "ghosts" or "puppets, moved hither and thither by fate . . . ." Woolf felt at 40 she had begun to speak in her own voice and that she could go "ahead without praise" (D2, Jul.26'22). *Jacob's Room* was published October 20, 1922. Regarding the reviews, she is ironic: "Either I'm a great writer or nincompoop. An elderly sensualist, *The Daily News* calls me" (D2, Oct.29'22).

To Jacques Reverat, a painter with whom Virginia shared soul-searching, intense exchanges, she confided her feelings regarding the writing of *Jacob's Room*:

> We are so lonely and separated in our adventures as writers and painters. Is your art as chaotic as ours? I feel that for us writers the only chance now is to go out into the desert and peer about like devoted scapegoats for some sign of a path (L2, Dec.10'22).

II

Woolf asserts in *Jacob's Room* "It is no use trying to sum people up. One must follow hints, not exactly what is said, not yet entirely what is done." Her novel follows the traditional genre in pursuing an individual's continuous interactions with his world, but is impressionistic in form, written in terms of her recently formulated view of fiction. In *Jacob's Room* Woolf introduced her method of accumulating data about a character from multiple perspectives, as well as from her character's own subjective thoughts. The title's emphasis on Jacob's "room" alludes to Jacob's interplay with friends and the outer surround. He is never totally seen because of the incompleteness of his life, and he never realizes his potentialities.

At the novel's opening, Mrs. Elizabeth Flanders, a 45 year old widow, is at the beach with her three sons; she seems oblivious towards them, especially her middle child, Jacob, who has strayed. Regarding the oldest, Archer, who kept calling for his brother, the author tells us: his "voice had an extraordinary sadness, pure from all body, pure from all passion, going out into the world, solitary, unanswered, breaking against rocks" (8). From this we acquire a sense of the children's vulnerability, helplessness, and lack of moorings, similar to the Stephen children upon loss of their mother.

As for Jacob, he is lost and starts to cry but is diverted when he finds an animal skull with teeth in it. Finally aware her son was missing, his mother finds him, greeting him with "naughty little boy." Though his mother ordered him to drop the "horrid" skull, he tenaciously held onto the sheep's jaw and, as it turned out, clung to it his entire life (9–10).

We know little about Jacob's background except that Jacob's father, Seabrook, "had broken horses, ridden to hounds, farmed a few fields and run a little wild," and afterward worked briefly in an office. His wife referred to him as a "merchant—well, she had to call him something. An example to the boys." Mrs. Flanders is throughout rather punitive and fault finding, labelling Jacob the "only one of her sons who never obeyed." Jacob's mother mistook him for a "burglar" (23) when he returned home later than usual from a butterfly hunt, which may indicate she is not quite in the same orbit as he and essentially considers him an intruder, an outsider, someone who does not belong. Yet, unpredictably, she pulls strings for Jacob; with her friend Captain Barfoot's paternalistic assistance, Jacob, at age 18, goes to Cambridge in 1906 (29).

Ensconced at Cambridge, Jacob's portrait is elaborated further. The author tells us Jacob is serious, handsome, distinguished, optimistic, and enthusiastic; at the same time he is shy, silent, unworldly, awkward, innocent, and artistic. Jacob is a prolific reader with a catholicity of taste; he is interested in the classics, Shakespeare, the Italian Renaissance, and biographies of Wellington. His belief is that anyone of substance reads "just what he likes as the mood takes him, with extravagant enthusiasm."

He saved photographs of his mother and clung to the "sheep's jaw with the yellow teeth" in it, his connection with childhood unrelinquished. Rebellious toward authority, he frequently caricatures pomposity and believes the government is run by fools. Yet he admires the military and crested, which may be connected to his indeterminate origins: his father had been a drifter, although his mother lied about his status.

Despite occasional mocking thrusts at the college hierarchy, Jacob values a sense of tradition and affiliation at Cambridge. He

> looked satisfied; indeed masterly . . . , the sound of the clock conveying a sense of old buildings and time; and himself the inheritor; and then tomorrow; and friends; at the thought of whom, in sheer confidence and pleasure, he yawned and stretched himself (45).

Describing Jacob's vacation in Cornwall with his college friend Timmy, Woolf, obviously moved by the beloved landscapes and seascapes evocative of her own childhood, especially associated with mother and the integralness of the family at that time—is lyrical and painterly in her rendering of sounds, shapes, colors. Looking at the mainland, one could see "clefts in the cliffs, white cottages, smoke going up" which conveyed an "extraordinary look of calm, of sunny peace as if wisdom and piety had descended upon the dwellers" (48). It was as if the "end of the world had come, and cabbage fields and stone walls and coast guard stations, and above all the white sand bays with the waves breaking unseen by anyone, rose to heaven in a kind of ecstasy" (49).

Without transition she switches to a depressive, elegaic mood:

> But imperceptibly the cottage smoke droops, has the look of a mourning emblem, a flag floating its caress over a grave. The Cornish hills have stark chimneys standing on them; and somehow or other, loveliness is infernally sad. Yes, the chimneys and the coast guard stations and the little bays with the waves breaking unseen by anyone makes one remember the overpowering sorrow. And what can this sorrow be? (49)

The author, remembering Jacob's presence, reflects on his "gloom," and the difficulties of penetrating his mood since he "never spoke a word" (49).

Though all those Jacob encounters—young, old, male, female—seem enamored of him, his mother's negative regard pervades. Unreasonably disapproving of Jacob's "clumsiness" at home, his mother is "romantic" about her oldest son Archer, and "tender" towards her youngest, John. Preoccupied with the favoritism shown in her own family, Woolf discourses on the arbitrariness of human behavior: "it seems that a profound, impartial and absolutely just opinion of our fellow creatures is utterly unknown" (71). "Either we are cold or we are sentimental." She adds: "life is but a procession of shadows, and God knows why we embrace them so eagerly, and see them depart with such anguish, being shadows." Alluding to both Jacob and Thoby, Woolf asks: "Why are we surprised by a sudden vision that the young man in the chair is of all things in the world the most solid, the best known to us," when "the moment after we know nothing about him . . . ; such is the manner of our seeing, such the conditions of our love" (72).

Still impelled to "hum vibrating, like the hawk moth at the mouth of the cavern of mystery," the author endows Jacob with "qualities he had not at all." Talking to Bonomy, another college friend, much of what

Jacob said was too "dull to repeat; much unintelligible [about unknown people, and Parliament]; what remains is mostly a matter of guess work. Yet over him we hang vibrating" (73). Is Woolf stating that at times Jacob is not worth hovering over? Is she not disclosing in an unguarded moment that her brother or men are not inevitably interesting, getting even with their preferntial treatment in attending university? In alluding to the "mouth of the cavern of mystery," she also endows Jacob with feminine integuments.

Seeking an independent stance after graduation from Cambridge, Jacob has taken rooms in London and works in an office. Timmy's sister, Clara, is in love with Jacob who, in turn, is erotically attracted to Florinda, a prostitute. Jacob "honored Clara of all women"; she is the "sacred" and Florinda the "profane" love in his life. Clara's notes are deposited in a "black, wooden box" along with his mother's letters—"the lid shut upon the truth" (70). An early version of *Jacob's Room* (First Holograph Notebook) indicated the black box also contained photos of young men (Leaska, 1977a, 71). Is the "truth" his love for mother, for Clara, or for his male friends? This information both Jacob and the author wish to conceal.

Does Mrs. Flanders' fantasy of writing her son—"Don't go with bad women, do be a good boy, wear your thick shirts, and come back, come back, come back to me" (90)—impinge on Jacob? Does he sense her disapproval of his sexuality? During a scene where there is the suggestion of imminent physical intimacy with Florinda and Jacob would prefer to return instead to "male society, cloistered rooms and the works of the classics" (82), he capitulates to Florinda's charms. On discovering Florinda is unfaithful, Jacob is deeply upset, more than he can acknowledge.

His subsequent relationships with women fare none too well. He recoils, frightened and distanced when a young woman, Fanny, professes open attraction. On vacation in Greece he in turn is infatuated with a married woman, Sandra Wentworth.

Concurrently, we learn his friend Bonomy loves him, and though Jacob cares for him he does not reciprocate with any depth of feeling. Bonomy "liked to play round him like an affectionate spaniel; they would end by rolling on the floor" (165). Though Jacob remained aloof and defended, he permits himself to be admired. Ultimately, Jacob thinks women "spoil things" and feels profound disillusionment with them.

Jacob is killed in World War I at age 26. The futility and arbitrariness of war is underscored though Woolf's multi-levelled approach also conveys that Jacob's death or undoing is linked to his confused, guilt-ridden

affair with Mrs. Wentworth or, in a deeper sense, to his troubled relationship with his mother who both rejects and infantilizes him.

At the novel's end, Mrs. Flanders and Bonomy are in Jacob's rooms,
contemplating his possessions. Critical to the last, Mrs. Flanders, her
curiosity hardly contained, exclaims, as she bursts open the bedroom
door: "Such confusion everywhere." Holding up a pair of her son's old
shoes, she asks his friend: "What am I to do with these?" (176)—the battered shoes connecting with the "weakly legs" of Jacob as a child.

III

Although Woolf wrote *Jacob's Room* to "convey character without
realism," she had been haunted by the arbitrariness of her brother
Thoby's death at 26, wished to resolve her lingering sense of loss and
recapture his spirit. She hoped to dip beneath Thoby's reserve, his seemingly impregnable masculinity, and in so doing, unmask areas of more
authentic emotion. Viewing him as "powerful in mind, mastering things
rather than guessing at them," she perceived Thoby as physical, robust,
volatile, and someone with inner depth (*SOTP*, 107–108).

After Thoby's death, Woolf sought to glean as much as possible
regarding her brother's personal life. His Cambridge friends whom she
thought would be informative, were reticent, and of no help. She turned
to them nevertheless in her distress and found considerable emotional
support in their genuine love for her brother. Continuous reference to
Thoby's birthdays is noted in Woolf's letters and diary: "It is just two
years since he died and I feel immensely old as though the best in us had
gone . . . it is such an odd life without him" (L1, Nov.11'08). Though a
collection of Thoby's letters was contemplated by Hogarth Press,
publication was apparently suspended.

Concomitant to Woolf's desire to elicit Thoby's love and admiration,
his early bullying also evoked masochistic emotions of submission and
surrender. Referring to the "sudden, violent shocks" of childhood,
Woolf describes an early pummeling bout with Thoby. As she readied
herself to hit back, she found she could not engage in hurting another
person, simply "let him beat me.[3] I remember the feeling . . . of
hopeless sadness. It was as if I became aware of something terrible, and
of my own powerlessness. I slunk off alone, feeling horribly depressed"
(*SOTP*, 71). Woolf seemed anxious about alienating her brother to
whom she wished to feel close, apprehensive over the degree of her own

and her brother's aggression, concerned about her passivity, but mainfested above all a need for Thoby's acceptance and forgiveness.

On the day of their mother's death, Woolf went to the station with George and Vanessa to meet Thoby, who had been at school. She conveys a striking image of the "great glass dome at the end of the station, blazing with light," with "iron girders" casting a pattern across it. Walking along the platform she gazed "with rapture," and possibly sexual excitement, as the train "so vast and fiery red slowly steamed into the station," impressing and exalting her (*SOTP*, 93); she viewed the arch of burning glass as one of the only "clear moments in the muffled dullness that then closed over us," as though Thoby represented continuity with a sentient, powerful, outside world.

Virginia felt her relationship with Thoby closer than it might have been without their mother's death. Despite the "strange, awkward silence" that occasionally prevailed, they argued and were "naturally attracted to each other." When on holiday, he regaled her with stories about his friends. Woolf notes Thoby's "blend of mastery," his "sensibility of friendliness and composure" which lent him considerable "character." He was exceedingly "reserved," did not permit "a word of feeling" to escape him: "yet under that awkward silence there would creep out a curious sympathy, a pride in us" (*SOTP*, 109).

Attracted to Thoby's exuberance and physicality, Virginia wrote Violet on April 19, 1903, that "Thoby might stand nude . . . in the Louvre. He is a Greek god but rather too massive for the drawing room." Virginia met the first adult men she could admire and respect via her brother's Cambridge friends, eventually married one.

Knowing that Mansfield in her story "Prelude" wished to write an elegy to her own brother, killed in World War I, Woolf might have felt prodded to write an elegy to her brother in *Jacob's Room*. In her novel, Woolf gives us hints of Jacob's eventual demise by alluding to events of the years preceding the war, the rumblings of guns across the channel, and the Irish Home Rule Bill's acceptance in 1912; she comments that people were plunging "tragically to destruction." Mobilization for the war coincides with accounts in *Jacob's Room* of a "procession with banners, passing down Whitehall." In addition, the "wires of the Admiralty shivered with some faraway communication" (171). The last we read of Jacob, he is leaving Hyde Park, as a "flock of wild duck flew over the Serpentine and the trees were stood against the sky, blackly, magnificently" (173)—a beautiful, though depressive and prophetic image.

Woolf alludes but once to the actual fighting in World War I:

"Like blocks of tin soldiers the army covers the cornfield, moves up the hillside, stops, reels slightly this way and that and falls flat, save that through field glasses, it can be seen that one or two pieces will agitate up and down like fragments of a broken match stick" (155).

Zwerdling (1981) refers to Woolf's "contained rage and parody of reportorial detachment"in this passage. He believes "Flanders," the family name in *Jacob's Room* was a "synonym" for "death in battle," indicates nearly one third of British soldiers killed in World War I lost their lives in Flanders, the "heaviest losses" in his opinion, among the "young officers of Jacob's class" (896).

Actually, Jacob's "class" is indeterminate. Zwerdling describes Jacob as "well-connected if not rich, his future course apparently secure, everything in his life a traditional step to establishing success." He points to Woolf's "satiric" tone and "ironic distance," due he feels, to her "bedrock pacifism." In his view, she "disliked Jacob's life pattern intensely"; Jacob's world, "created by men for men, essentially excluded her." Envying men their "guaranteed success," she, according to Zwerdling, hated the patriarchal machinery that endowed them with a "powerful position in society, though pitied them their lack of freedom in being sent to war" (904). Ruddick quoting Woolf, alludes to Jacob as an "inheritor"; he belonged to a "world governed by divisions of class and sex, a world on the verge of war, that will destroy him" (193).

Yet, human beings are not entirely creatures of social pressures or without an intrapsychic history and capacity for self-determination of their own. The tendency of Zwerdling and Ruddick to predominantly view behavior in terms of class and sex division obscures their grasp of Woolf's text. Or they confuse Jacob with his prototype. Jacob was not "well-connected"; his father was a roustabout or neer-do-well. Like his father, Jacob has no professional identity and exhibits no clear-cut career interest; he has an unrewarding office job. As described by Woolf, he is both bohemian and gentleman. He both moves in society at a high level and has artistic aspirations.

Though each of us belongs to a particular socioeconomic group, at a particular cross section of place and time, Woolf is above all intrigued by individual uniqueness. When Woolf referred to Jacob as "inheritor," she was mildly sarcastic about the Cambridge connection and tradition. Certainly she betrayed both hostility and superiority to men in stating that some of Jacob's conversation was occasionally "too dull to repeat," but she did not "intensely dislike Jacob's life pattern." Her tone was not as Zwerdling would have it, one of "condescension," but one of describing Jacob's complexity, resisting definition, or closure. Her tone was predominantly elegaic, tinged with amusement, conveying considerable tenderness.

Woolf felt her characters "shadowy" but her method was not so much at fault, she notes, as "her ignorance in using it psychologically" (L2, Nov.23'22). Jacob's portrayal was incomplete because his life was cut short, he still adrift and unformed. Perhaps Woolf was reticent in exploring issues of Jacob's or Thoby's sexual identity, hinted at in the text. She continued to probe Thoby's character in a later novel, *The Waves*.

Jacob proclaiming "I am what I am and intend to be it," elicits from his creator "there will be no form in the world unless Jacob makes one for himself." Neither Woolf nor Jacob are clear about that form. Feeling shaky in his sexual identification and sense of personal worth, Jacob chose unavailable or unrewarding women, or proved unresponsive to those in love with him. Though he preferred male society, he was fearful of intimacy here as well. Imparting how little we know others, how minimally discern what may be below the surface, the author does not choose, in her prerogative as omniscient narrator, to delve into these subterranean depths.

Some of the dilemmas confronting Jacob existed for Woolf insofar as both were without one parent at an early age, the remaining parent at times unavailable and insufficiently protective; and, as with Jacob, the favoritism shown a younger brother was also bruising to both Woolf and Thoby, middle children in their family. Though we are not directly told Jacob feels deprived, his friend Timmy notices his moodiness, sensing Jacob is "bothered" by family matters.

The dominant chord reverberating throughout the novel is Jacob's palpable sadness. We are insistently told this, with minimal exploration of Jacob's inner life or relationships with others to assist us in understanding his emotional state. We know his mother did not from the time of his early childhood view him as particularly lovable, was constantly undermining, preferring her other sons. Yet she held onto him. Jacob is doubly afflicted, dependent on the dubious affection of a mother both rejecting and clutching. Nor did Jacob have a father who might have counteracted her critical behavior. Although Captain Barfoot, his mother's friend, enabled Jacob to attend Cambridge, the captain was lame, a damaged man with two fingers missing—not a particularly robust masculine model.

Via the strong images Woolf occasionally uses in expressing her concept of the creative process, such as "knocking the bar out," one obtains the impression of a confident, aggressive approach. During the writing of *Jacob's Room*, however, Woolf felt intensely threatened by T.S. Eliot's genius,[4] as well as his adulation of Joyce. She suffered headaches and other psychosomatic symptoms, temporarily ceased writing *Jacob's Room*, and buried her envy and sense of betrayal. Competition with men was tabooed in a cultural sense and off limits in her family, evidenced in the fighting episode with Thoby during which she suddenly froze. Refocusing on her childlessness, her felt failure as a woman, her sense of "impotence" as she called it, she reiterated that writing, fame, or reputation were not important to her when just the opposite was the case.

Lending an aspect of unreality to Woolf's delineation of Jacob is omission of his assertiveness, the clash of personality. Since the novel is an elegy to her brother, is Woolf puritanically omitting the hostile dimension which she tells us in her memoir was characteristic of Thoby's personality, especially as a child? Most probably she is concealing more deep-seated aspects of Thoby's emotional disturbance because of his adolescent suicide attempt.

The metaphorical allusions in *Jacob's Room* further flesh out Jacob, Thoby, or Woolf. Pervasive reference to Greek civilization or the "Greek myth," suggesting the immortality of beauty, reflect facets of Jacob's personality and thinking. Sandra Wentworth compares Jacob to a Greek god, to the Hermes of Praxiteles which represents Hermes nude, supporting the infant Dionysus[5] on his left arm. Hermes is the most prolific and complex of any of the major gods. Protector of flocks, he is frequently shown carrying a ram.

As we know, there is a ram's head carved over the doorway in Jacob's room. This brings to mind the skull Jacob finds as a child. Sea holly we are told, would eventually "grow through its eye sockets"; Jacob's mother retrieving Jacob when he was lost, tells the story of a man whose eye was lost in an explosion—ominous prophetic images of castration and death, pervasive in this novel.

Moths clustering round a lantern in a forest, associated with butterfly collecting and a related experience in which a "volley of shots rang in the depths of the wood, and a red underwing circled round the light and was gone . . . , never to come back though Jacob waited" for it (*JR*, 21–22), evoke a sense of loss and futility that accompanies Jacob for most of his life.

This image is similar to the "lost bird" magnetized by the lighthouse in *Night and Day*, and the moth hovering round Vanessa's window, precursor to writing *The Waves*, metaphorically suggesting, despite token indications of social adaptation, that Woolf's characters feel endangered, feel life is fleeting and unlived. They are fragile, lost, insignificant, and seek rescue—an expression of Woolf's inner state as well.

Written upon finishing *Jacob's Room*, Woolf's essay, "Reading", also deals with a butterfly hunt involving father, brother, and herself wherein a "volley of shot rang out . . . , in the deep silence of the wood which had I know not what of mournful and ominous about it," leading to an examination of the creative process. Here she refers to "repeated shocks each unfelt at the time" which loosen the "fabric." Although this suggests "collapse and disintegration," she is thinking of its creative character; that is, "order has been imposed upon tumult; form upon chaos." She emerges after a complex "internal process" with a "sense of mastery" (*CDB*, 169).

The "ominous" occurrence in the wood evokes the death of her brother, someone who possessed a submerged, artistic temperament, whose death Woolf deeply mourned but did not resolve, further probing her loss in her novel *The Waves*.

IX Sane and insane truth: "Human beings hunt in packs . . . , desert the fallen" —*Mrs. Dalloway*

I

"Mrs. Dalloway in Bond Street", initially a long short story concerned with Clarissa Dalloway's obsession with death and mourning, satirized the class system of the British social hierarchy and metamorphosed into Woolf's next novel, *Mrs. Dalloway*.

Violet Dickinson's confession on visiting Woolf that she had no "wish to live," that her friends were all dead and her brother could manage without her; that she merely wished to "tidy things up and disappear: why should I want to go on living?" (D2, Feb.16'22), was in part prototype for the character of Clarissa Dalloway. Of course Violet's comments were a thrust at Woolf, aimed to produce guilt, a reminder of their former relationship.

Not liking the feeling she is writing too quickly, Woolf is "laboriously dredging" her mind, bringing up "light buckets" (D2, Aug.16'22). Momentarily blocked, Woolf zeros in on the reason: Sidney Waterlow who spent the weekend with the Woolfs, "reproduced in his heavy, lifeless voice" the barbs of Middleton Murry whose critical crossfire accosts her. She imagines Murry dismisses her writing, saying it is "merely silly— one simply doesn't read it—you're a back number." Then "slowly the cloud withdraws" and Woolf in highly sexual terms suggests she is again "washed by the flood, warm, embracing, fertilizing, of my own thoughts." She must "rock" herself back into writing. (D2, Aug.22'22). Recovering from her bruises she is hopeful she may be on the threshold of writing "something good, something rich and deep and fluent and hard as nails while bright as diamonds" (D2, Sept.6'22).

Shocked by the death of wealthy Kitty Maxse, Vanessa's former friend and mentor, Woolf questioned Kitty's falling "very mysteriously over some bannisters." She recalled Kitty's "gaiety, yet melancholy, her tears which stayed on her cheek. Now she is buried and mourned by half the grandees of London" (D2, Oct.14'22). Kitty's death undoubtedly

115

merged with the impact of Violet's death wish. In part prototype for the heroine of Woolf's novel, Violet making short shrift of her life, was linked with Kitty's suspected suicide. Of course Woolf had access to her own and her mother's predilection for death and dying. In Woolf's initial conception, Clarissa Dalloway was scheduled to kill herself at the end of her part; her double who ultimately takes his life had not as yet been spawned.[1]

Synchronizing these issues, *Mrs. Dalloway* has evolved into a book. Woolf projects here a study of "insanity and suicide," hopes nothing will deter her from her "determination to go on . . . , so whatever happens, though the surface may be agitated, the center is secure" (D2, Oct.14.22).

The search for a more sensitive, introspective rendering of experience as compared to the "fabulous fleshy monsters" of the traditional novel was her current goal. Now part of the literary landscape, the stream of consciousness or interior monologue form seemed congenial to the extensive and profound self-examination Woolf embarked upon in writing her novel.

In *Mrs. Dalloway* she returns to the vicissitudes of love and marriage, resurrects her episodes of mental and emotional illness, giving them scrupulous documentation. She hopes to reveal the "sane and insane truth side by side" in consonance with her conflict concerning the theme of submerged homosexuality. Meeting Vita Sackville West at this time, Woolf describes the "supple ease of the artistocracy. Vita is a grenadier, hard, handsome, manly" (D2, Dec.15'22).

As always, maintaining close touch with Vanessa and her family, Woolf lamented her own "childlessness: never pretend children can be replaced by other things. They make my life seem bare sometimes." Despite the uneven reviews of critics regarding her early novels, her "inveterate romanticism" evoked an image of "forging ahead alone though suffering inwardly, stoically blazing a path through to the end" (D2, Jan.2'23).

To the death of her friend, Katherine Mansfield on January 16, 1923, Woolf reacted with astringent honesty: "A shock of relief? A rival the less? Then confusion at feeling so little, gradually blankness and disappointment; then a depression" that she could not shake. Envying Katherine's writing, "the only writing I have ever been jealous of," created difficulties in relating to her. Woolf felt "middle aged" and unable to work for several days. (D2, Jan.16'23).

After an unexpected visit from Vita and her husband, Harold Nicolson, Woolf noted: "She is a pronounced Sapphist and may have an eye on me old though I am" (D2, Feb.19'23). Attending a party at Ottoline Morrell's estate revived Woolf's interest in her Dalloway manuscript, now designated *The Hours*. Emphasizing the "despicableness" of people like Ottoline and wishing to present the "slipperiness of the soul," Woolf previously "too tolerant," avers: "the truth is, people scarcely care for each other" (D2, Jun.2'23). Writing of her need to contain her "excitement as if I were pushing through a screen; or as if something beat fiercely, close to me," she is consumed by a permeating sense of the "poetry of existence." And "as usual, I want I want"² (D2, Jun.13'23).

Lingering over the death of Katherine Mansfield, Woolf took stock as it were, mentioning Mansfield's credo about "feeling things deeply." Does she? Or, does she "fabricate with words loving them as I do. No, I think not. In this book I have almost too many ideas." Hoping to cover a large canvas, wishing to attack society, she suspects she may be "posing." Are *The Hours* riven from "deep emotion?" Apparently the "mad part" is anxiety-provoking, makes her mind "squirm so badly" she finds it hard to stay with her theme. She acknowledges that she does not possess that "reality" gift: "I insubstantise distrusting reality—its cheapness." What she wants is to get to the "bones," desiring that her "force flow straight from me at its fullest." Admitting her design is "original" and interests her deeply, she would like to "write away at it quick and fierce" (D2, Jun.19'23).

Questioning her objectivity Woolf asks: "do I write essays about myself?" She thinks it most pertinent in this book to go for the "central things", does not wish to "nail my cross to the Murrys [Middleton], who work in my flesh after the manner of the jigger insect." Predicting a struggle since her plan for the novel is so highly textured, she expects in three weeks to be "dried up." (D2, Jun.19'23).

Longing to move back to London, Woolf compares her "social side" to Leonard's intellectual side," noting: "this social side is very genuine in me . . . ; nor do I think it reprehensible. It is a piece of jewelry I inherit from my mother, a joy in laughter, something that is stimulated, not selfishly or vainly, by contact with my friends." Feeling isolated, "imprisoned" in the suburbs, she longs for the diversity of London. Leonard she finds "too much of a Puritan, a disciplinarian" (D2, Jun.28'23).

The complex feeling responses sought after in her new novel resonate in her concurrent essay "The Russian Point of View." To Woolf, understanding the soul and heart is most profoundly evidenced by the Russian writers. She feels rapport with Dostoevski for whom it is not important

whether you are noble or simple, a tramp or a great lady. Whoever you are, you are the vessel of this clay, yeasty precious stuff, the soul. The soul is not restrained by barriers. It overflows, it floods, it mingles with the souls of others (*CR*, v.1, 252–253).

She also shares Tolstoy's preoccupations: "there is always at the center of all the brilliant and flashing petals of the flower, this scorpion, 'why life?' what is the meaning of it, and what should be our aims?" (*CR*, v.1, 255).

Grappling with *The Hours* which proved the "most tantalizing and refractory of books; parts are so bad, parts so good" (D2, Aug.29'23), Woolf enunciated her literary discovery: "how I dig out beautiful caves behind my characters" which give "humanity, humour, depth." These background episodes are meant to "connect and each comes to daylight at the present moment" (D2, Aug.30'23). To place the reader within the minds of her fictional characters, to present their feelings and thoughts as they emerge at the moment, to connect present, past and future, was Woolf's goal.

Describing her immersion in one of the novel's "mad scenes", she clings as "tight to fact" as she can. Woolf worries lest the character of Mrs. Dalloway is "too stiff, too glittering and tinsely" but brings "innumerable other characters to her support. Of course I've only been feeling my way into it." Often she flounders about in a "state of misery," then touches the "hidden spring" (D2, Oct.15'23).

At the beginning of the new year, Woolf is jubilant in signing a 10-year lease for a comfortable flat in London. Now she will have "music, talk, friendships, city views within reach" (D2, Jan.9'24). Leonard, who opposed the move to London, was ill with flu; Woolf enjoyed her uncustomary role of taking care of him (D2, Feb.3'24). Their move to the city was completed by May 15; they took the two top floors at 52 Tavistock Square and Hogarth Press inhabited the basement (D2, 297).

Noting the twenty-ninth anniversary of her mother's death, Woolf recalls, in intellectualized terms, that she, then Virginia Stephen, looked out the nursery window and saw the physician leaving, the "doves descending with a fall and descent of infinite peace." Apparently she "laughed behind the hand meant to hide her tears" and through her fingers saw the "nurses sobbing" (D2, May5'24).

Visiting Knole, Vita's ancestral castle, Woolf had lunch with the Nicolsons at Long Barn, their country home. Woolf liked hobnobbing with the aristocracy (D2, Jul.5'24).

Near completion of *Mrs. Dalloway*, at a low ebb with her book which bogs down with her immersion in Septimus Smith's[3] death, Hogarth Press provides ballast, "something solid to fall back on" (D2, Aug.2'24). Work on her book of essays, the *Common Reader* is also a welcome relief (D2, Aug.3'24). Returning to *Mrs. Dalloway*, she describes her many contrasting scenes as "going from one lighted room to another, such is my brain to me" (D2, Aug.15'24). She hopes in this novel to hold onto the spontaneity of a "sketch" in an otherwise "finished and composed work" (D2, Sept.7'24).

Seeing Vita again she admired her for being "mother, wife, great lady, hostess" as well as writer, compared her to an "overripe grape in features, moustached, pouting" and although "embarrassing at breakfast, has a manly good sense and simplicity about her. . . .Oh yes I like her, could tack her on to my equipage for all times" (D2, Sept.15'24).

Living entirely in her imagination, she notes her reliance upon "spurts of thought, coming as I walk, as I sit, things churning up in my mind and so making a perpetual pageant," providing her happiest moments (D2, Sept.29'24). To allow her mind to run "loose" so that "it becomes personal or egotistic," Woolf wishes at all costs to avoid. At the same time the "irregular fire must be cultivated and perhaps to loose it one must begin by being chaotic" (D2, Nov.18'24). She claims we have "many states of consciousness or second selves" referring to her use of a fictional double (D3, Apr.27'25).

Woolf's *Common Reader* was published April 23, 1925; *Mrs. Dalloway* on May 14, 1925. Although Lytton indicated he did not like the lives of the idle rich in *Mrs. Dalloway*, Woolf is content since Hardy told her he enjoyed the *Common Reader*. Both Gerald Brenan and E.M. Forster liked *Mrs. Dalloway*. Woolf feels Forster alone penetrates her inner meaning. Blame or praise is basically irrelevant; she feels "writing is the profoundest pleasure" (D3, May 14, 1925).

II

Though the novel is in its fashion a brilliant, searing commentary on British caste and class, its permutations of power and authority, Woolf also engages in an extended mourning process regarding issues of unlived life, failed marriage, and identity confusion. Offering a poetic, profound exploration via fantasy and reminiscence, of human loneliness, suffering, recourse to self-destructiveness, and occasional self-affirmation in its delineation of inner and outer self, the novel illuminates shifting levels of reality and unreality, conscious and unconscious, informing the human condition. In particular, *Mrs. Dalloway* seeks to fathom the hazy boundaries differentiating so-called normal from irrational behavior, affirms the connection between the two. The form of *Mrs. Dalloway* disdains temporal continuity but is guided rather by the characters' inner thoughts and feelings so that eruptions from the past are congruent with associations concerning the present.

In its themes and their variations. *Mrs. Dalloway* deals with the parallel, occasionally intertwined lives of Clarissa Dalloway and Septimus Smith—one a society matron and member of the upper echelons of society with regard to her position and wealth; the other a failed poet, marginal in terms of socioeconomic status, though he experienced the temporary, indeterminate glory of participating in the war as a soldier. Woolf hopes to achieve the "sane truth" as seen in Clarissa's character and the "insane truth" noted in Septimus' emotional crisis, the crescendo reached as Clarissa's party approaches.[4] Of course Woolf is identified with both Septimus and Clarissa.

The novel begins with Clarissa, age 51, showing an extraordinary degree of effluvia in approaching the day, as she emerges on the streets of London to buy flowers for her party that evening, hoping to "kindle and illuminate" her life and the lives of others. In Clarissa's girlhood she would "burst open the French windows and plunge at Bourton in the open air" (5). Savoring the present, "creating every moment afresh," seemed linked to her recent attack of influenza, regarding which her hair has turned white and her heart weakened.

Encountering an old friend from her youth evokes Peter Walsh, her early sweetheart, "impossible but adorable." This is the "reward" for caring about people: they return when one least expects them (9). Proustian wise, she though of Peter "in the most unlikely places; it would flower out, open, shed its scent, let you touch, taste, look about you, get the whole feel of it and understanding, after years of lying lost" (232).

Perceiving Peter ineffectual, unreliable, overly dependent, and a failure, Clarissa broke with him: "there must be a little independence between people living together, day in, day out" (10). This she and Richard Dalloway, the man she married, maintained. Though convinced she was correct in leaving Peter, she regretted for years their breaking up, her pain compounded when she learned that Peter had married.

Although we are reminded of Clarissa's competence and are told she "sliced like a knife through everything," the approval of others was imperative. Characteristically, she felt like an "outsider looking on . . . , a perpetual sense of being out, out, far out to sea and alone" (11). These polarities of thought and reverie come to her the morning of her party.

Mystically, she harbored the "oddest sense of being invisible, unknown, unseen." Her body with all its capacity seemed "nothing" (14). In her insistent preoccupation with death, Clarissa thinks of the line from Shakespeare: "fear no more the heat of the sun nor the furious winter's rages" (12)[5], a reverberating refrain in the novel. Claiming few fears concerning death, she feels she would survive "somehow in the streets of London, on the ebb and flow of things, here, there." Peter, too, she was sure would survive. They "lived in each other," she "part of the trees at home; of the house there; part of people she never met . . . " (12).[6]

On the day of the party, Peter arrived unexpectedly, unannounced, in on a visit from India. Clarissa is completely at ease with him. Upon learning that he was embarked on a second marriage, Clarissa felt jealous, annoyed, repelled, all at once old and "shriveled." Distanced by her withdrawal, Peter burst into tears, whereupon Clarissa kissed and comforted him, her maternality and need to succor coming to the fore. Feeling stimulated by the tumult, she thought that had she married Peter "this gaiety would have been mine all day." She had a swift, intense, momentary fantasy, as though enacting a play, of running away with Peter[7] which she quickly quashed. In any case, "it was all over for her" (70), she insisted, fearful of involvement.

"Infernally" unhappy when Clarissa rejected him, Peter at times depicted her as cold, heartless, unyielding, like "iron or flint"; felt her arrogant, unimaginative, prudish, unable to have things out. Yet she and Peter often communicated without words. Actually he observed in her a "thread of life which for toughness, endurance, power to overcome obstacles and carrying her triumphantly through," (236) he had not previously encountered.

Peter felt she had a "woman's gift of making a world of her own" wherever she happened to be. It was Clarissa he remembeed in a roomful of people: "there she was" (115). Reverencing life, she possessed no bitterness, did not judge others; yet he felt she wasted her time in social activities, submerging her personal predilections. He perceived her paradoxicalness. In short, he loved her.

Acknowledging she was intuitive about people, Clarissa was otherwise self-derogating, felt she had a "narrow, pea-stick figure, a ridiculous face, beaked like a bird's."[8] True, she held herself well, had good hands and feet, dressed with a flair, yet felt her body, with all its capacities, "nothing." She felt anomalous in her feminine identification and thought there would be "no more marrying, no more having children now, but only this astonishing and rather solemn progress up Bond Street with the rest of them" (14). No longer did she feel like Clarissa, but wore the carapace of Mrs. Richard Dalloway, wife of a member of Parliament, felt her individuality erased.

In contrast to her initial aliveness, Clarissa on arriving home, "felt like a nun" insulated from the world; she "bowed beneath the influence, felt blessed and purified" (42). Ascetic and sacrificial though this may sound, Clarissa apparently treasures these moments and feels she must "repay" husband and servants for cushioning her existence. Discovering that her husband was lunching with another woman, Clarissa's fragility and depression were clearly in evidence; she felt herself "aged, breast-less," felt an "emptiness about the heart of life" (45), thought of her homosexual "crush" on Sally Seton.

She could not dispel a "virginity preserved through childbirth," felt she lacked something "central which permeated; something warm which broke up surfaces and rippled the cold contact of man and woman or of women together" (46). Though Clarissa had a child, she did not feel ade-quate or sufficiently affirmed in either her maternal or marital role.

Rather ambiguously the author tells us that when women confided in Clarissa and she felt touched by their "beauty" or felt "pity", she "did un-doubtedly then feel what men felt" (47). Does Clarissa feel identified with a dominant or masculine role in relation to either men or women? Clarissa's preference for reading Baron Marbot's "Memoirs" shows her con-siderable interest in the pyrotechnics of masculine power and domination.

In describing "what men felt," there is decided confusion concerning sexual anatomy and sexual role. Clarissa alludes to a "sudden revelation" that lasted a moment, a "tinge like a blush which one tried to check and then as it spread, yielded to its expansion and rushed to the farthest verge⁹ and there quivered and felt the world come closer." "Yielding" might suggest the culturally defined, feminine experience, while "expansion" could be masculine. Possibly "swollen with some astonishing significance, some pressure of rapture, which split its thin skin and gushed and poured with an extraordinary alleviation over cracks and sores" points to a masculine conception because of the notion of "swollen" and the suggestion of ejaculation, though one might think "cracks" feminine as well.

Clarissa thought she had seen an "illumination; a match burning in a crocus; an inner meaning almost expressed. But the close withdrew; the hard softened. It was over, the moment". Certainly "match burning in a crocus" suggests a heterosexual orientation that could occur between two women or man and woman, while softening of the "hard" suggests a masculine experience. Noting that apropos of "such moments [with women, too] there contrasted the bed and Baron Marbot and the candle half burnt" (47), the author implies that the previous sexual allusions, which refer to the female heterosexual role could occur between two women; her conception of female heterosexual and homosexual ex-perience remains blurred, however.

Clarissa ponders her girlhood relationship with Sally Seton at Bour-ton. She valued Sally's beauty, her quality of "abandonment," their hours of talk, about life, how they were to change the world, "abolish private property" (49). Together they read Plato, Shelley, and Willam Morris. In her idealization, Clarissa spoke of the purity, the integrity of her emotions toward Sally as being completely "disinterested," unlike one's feelings for a man. This "sense of being in league together," of mutual protectiveness, presumably exists only between women, she felt. Clarissa recalled coming down in a white frock at dinner to meet Sally, felt herself in love,"going cold with excitement."[10] Unexpectedly Sally kissed Clarissa on the lips, a present akin to a "diamond, something infinitly precious" (50–52). Interrupting them, Peter seemed determined to break into their companionship.

In Peter we glimpse a "hawklike," (249) idiosyncratic man, sensitive, well-read, and civilized. Occasionally he is portrayed as an "adventurer", a "romantic buccaneer", as "daring", "reckless" and "careless of all these proprieties" (80). Yet he is jealous, moody, self-absorbed, and at times unable to concentrate. Self-defeating in expecting rejection and failure, ineffectual in both career and marriage, he knew Clarissa valued achievement and success, hated discomfort and disorder. Dependent on women for assurance and protection, Peter is currently without family, children, is in short, a "solitary traveller" (85). He has a "vision of a giant [female] figure" made up of "sky and branches risen from the troubled sea", emenating "compassion, comprehension, absolution" (86).

An inhabitant of Peter's daydreams and unconscious, she might blow him to "nothingness with the rest." Beyond the wood he also fantasizes an old woman seeking a "lost son" (87). Here the author's voice, psyche and imagery intrude, suggesting exaltation and reunion regarding the maternal figure, yet fear of her destructiveness. In her complex portrayal of Peter, Woolf perceives him at this point as a fairly isolated, rootless human being. Peter on his part felt his life in its way rich, rewarding, potential. Clarissa's impact on him was greater than anyone he had ever known. She glided into his fantasies, "cool, ladylike, and critical, or as ravishing and romantic"; for him, she evoked pastoral settings (233).

Throughout the novel Peter fondles a knife he carries with him which seems not so much menacing as masturbatory or comfort making, an expression of his anxiety about not quite "making it" on his own. Though Peter's fantasies suggest his need for a maternal haven, which Clarissa formerly provided, she preferred for the long haul, a relatively unemotional, less sticky relationship. With Peter there was too much excitement and tumultousness, essentially frightening her.

Some measure of separateness is desirable in marriage, Clarissa believed, and this her husband, Richard, is willing to provide. Sharing a mutual interest in politics, Clarissa identified with his public spiritedness and support of the British Empire; he provides structure and formality to her life. A proper, traditional man who liked "continuity" (177), Richard is not averse to flirtations with other women, but he is not without guilt toward his wife either. He brings peace offerings, but cannot tell her he loves her (179).

Clarissa's relationship with her daughter Elizabeth is overly hovering and anxious. She is inordinately fearful lest her daughter be dominated by her history tutor, Miss Kilman,[11] with whom Elizabeth is inseparable. Clarissa's repulsion toward the tutor who she perceives as hypocritical, eavesdropping, cruel, unscrupulous, and jealous, is overriding. She hated Miss Kilman's sense of victimization, embitteredness, incessant preoccupation with issues of superiority or inferiority. Feeling demeaned by the intensity of her rage and her perception of Miss Kilman as a "brutal monster grubbing at the roots" (17), guilt and the desire to placate her daughter prompted Clarissa to invite Miss Kilman to her party (191).

Engaged in a network of visiting and kindness to others, distributing flowers and presents, which elicited admiration and affirmation from her recipients, Clarissa enjoyed a sense of power and control in so doing. Her home became a center, a meeting place of sorts, where she might assume a benevolent interest in some "raw youth." Always tempering her positive interest with the pessimistic, Clarissa, fond of nautical metaphors, would say: "as we are a doomed race chained to a sinking ship . . . , let us mitigate the sufferings of our fellow prisoners" (117).

Teased by both Peter and Richard for being the "perfect hostess," Clarissa claimed her parties were her singular gift, an attempt to "combine, to create . . . , an offering for the sake of an offering" (185).

At her party that night, though Clarissa felt euphoric and her "purity, woodenness and severity were all warmed through," (264) her triumphs had a "hollowness . . . , were not "in the heart" (265). Learning from Dr. William Bradshaw, one of her guests, that his patient, Septimus Smith had killed himself, she felt severely jolted. Clarissa felt an "embrace" in his death, wondered whether he jumped "holding his treasure,"[12] his secret.

She suspected Dr. Bradshaw of blundering. That morning she felt the "terror, the overwhelming incapacity, one's parents giving it into one's hands, this life, to be lived to the end" (281). Sharing Septimus' death she felt it "her disaster—her disgrace, her punishment to see sink and disappear here a man, there a woman, in this profound darkness." Somehow she felt Septimus a kindred spirit and was "glad" he had jumped—"thrown it away." Peering out the window to see the sky, she felt something of herself in it, then glimpsed an old woman across the way, "staring straight at her . . . , quite properly going to bed" (283), prophetic of Clarissa's old age and of things to come.

Although Clarissa assumes a facade of giving to others, attempts to appear civilized to her maids, organizes her household as befits the wife of a member of Parliament, arranges parties as her gift to others, and engages in the rituals of a member of the "ruling class," she is full of contradictions. In rapport concerning politics, she and her husband are emotionally and sexually far apart. Marrying Richard because he permitted her a greater sense of independence indicates Clarissa's dissimulation. Primarily, the author is depicting the couple's separateness and distance from one another. Seeking independence in marriage, Clarissa is deeply wounded on discovering her husband's infidelities. Toward her daughter's tutor, whom she considers a rival, Clarissa harbors malevolent hatred: the violence of her emotions may warrant categorizing her Septimus' double, although she is usually highly controlled.

In attributing the breakup with Peter to the fact "everything had to be shared," Clarissa is not at all convincing. What is wrong with sharing? Or with the fact that his interests were the "state of the world, Wagner, Pope's poetry, people's characters eternally, and the defects of her own soul? How he scolded her! How they argued" (9)! Didn't Clarissa know she was describing a vivid, alive relationship? Peter appeared to relinquish Clarissa out of a profound, masochistic need to be sacrificial, excluded, the outsider. Peter's anxiety over his status which was less charismatic than Richard's or Clarissa's, and his giving her up to Richard without a struggle in effect precipitated Clarissa's rejection of Peter.

At the time Clarissa and Peter were seeing each other, she was hopeful about her possibilities; she felt passionately fond of Sally, but she was in love with Peter. Then unpredictably there was "too much talking over" with Peter, and she turned to Richard. Was her choice of Richard linked to her homosexual interest in Sally which might be better nurtured in a less demanding marital relationship? We are given no indication of this inasmuch as considerable space is devoted to the interplay between Peter and Clarissa, past and present. His visit revitalized her, whereas Sally's visit does not seem to particularly.

Clarissa's unstated, unconscious reason for breaking with Peter may have been her father's objection to any serious, emotional involvement with men (62).[13] Her father approved when she married for status or security, the conventional verities. This Richard could provide. Acquiescent to her father's implicit wish, she married someone less threatening to him. In doing so, Clarissa subordinated her more radiant, poetic self to her husband's values. Peter wonders why, with her own perfectly good mind, Clarissa forever quotes her husband.

With Peter, Clarissa was affectionate, lively, argumentative. Relinquishing him became a permanent hurt. As with the lovers in *Night and Day*, she and Peter went "in and out of each other's minds, without effort" (94), though never each other's bodies. What are we to make of the coldness shown Peter? Either Clarissa is fearful of her femininity or must save herself for her father, who the author implies "never liked anyone" she cared for (62).

What of her "failing" Richard? She was never in love with Richard; possibly he was crude or fumbling in his lovemaking. What can "remaining virginal through childbirth" mean, and later, becoming "nun-like?" Was sex or childbirth difficult, nightmarish, painful?

Could Woolf be protesting too much, denying, because she felt deprived of having children, that childbirth can be lusty, sexual, indeed a peak experience? Or, because of the fear of masculine intrusiveness or penetration and her conflict concerning homosexual feelings, does she in panic turn off her sexuality in general?

Clarissa feels her husband's interest in her withdrawn and focused on other women, an encroachment on her fragile security. She cannot control her depressive reaction and embraces an ascetic role. Her large, social network, role as hostess, and desire to help others in need cushioned her existence. While Clarissa maintains her reverence for life, one wonders whether she wishes to live as fully as she can while alive. Despite her preoccupation with death, mourning her lost love, her anger and suspiciousness toward Miss Kilman, Clarissa can encompass and live with this hostility, morbid though it frequently appears. Crucial is her engagement in the battle, deflecting the turn towards self-destructiveness.

Clarissa's "double," Septimus Smith, 31, shabby, hesitating and trailing in his walk, with his "angular, big-nosed, intelligent, sensitive profile," nondescript eyes, "educated" hands and "loose" lips, was one of those semieducated men who devour books. Somewhat breezily we are told he left home a young boy because his mother "lied," and in addition, complained that he would come to tea with unwashed hands (127). Is Woolf thumbing her nose at Freud?

Seeing no future for an aspiring poet in his hometown, Septimus came to London, which hostile and indifferent, "swallowed up" many such as he. Septimus' demeanor soon changed from "pink, innocent oval" to "lean, contracted, hostile." He was lonely, shy, stammered, and constantly sought to improve himself; he wrote poems and fell in love with Miss Pole, a lecturer on Shakespeare who inspired him, kindling a "fire that burns only once in a lifetime," though "without heat . . . , infinitely ethereal and insubstantial" (128).

Disillusioned with his marginal existence, he was among the first to volunteer on the side of the Allies in World War I. There Septimus felt more masculine, graduated in rank, and appeared close to Evans, his officer: "it was a case of two dogs playing[14] on a hearth rug. They had to be together, share, fight, quarrel" with each other (130). Congratulating himself for his lack of emotion when Evans was killed in Italy prior to the Armistice, Septimus was conflicted in acknowledging his affection for Evans; this deflected the impingement of his homosexual feelings and affirmed his manliness.

At the end of the war he met a young woman, Rezia, daughter of the innkeeper at whose house he was billeted in Milan. They became engaged when the "panic was on him that he could not feel," when he experienced "these sudden thunderclaps of fear." With Rezia he found a haven. Frequently he felt his state a precarious one, convinced "the bed was falling" or that "he was falling . . . " (130). Increasingly he felt the world "without meaning" (133); he now asked Rezia to marry him.

Returning to England with his wife, Septimus advanced in position at his former office. The events of the novel occur in 1923[15], five years following the war, and Septimus now shows the beginning of a severe emotional and thinking disturbance. Seeing Rezia trimming hats as "pale, mysterious, like a lily, drowned, underwater," suggests his hostility, perhaps the desire to get rid of her. Hidden in the beauty of Shakespeare's language, the message or caveat, Septimus thought, the "secret signal which one generation passes under disguise to the next, is loathing, hatred, despair." Identified with Shakespeare, who he thought hated "humanity, the putting on of clothes, the begetting of children, the sordidity of mouth and belly,"[16] Septimus felt "love between men and women repulsive, the business of copulation, filth"[17] (134). Could Septimus' disgust have to do with Rezia's desire for a son at this time? His profound inability to see himself in a masculine, heterosexual role?

Showing increasing alienation and paranoid suspiciousness: "one cannot perpetuate the suffering or increase the breed of these lustful animals who have no lasting emotions . . . ," Septimus felt people have "neither kindness nor faith nor charity" beyong the "pleasure of the moment." They are hypocritical, "hunt in packs . . . , desert the fallen" (135). He perceives a prevailing malevolence in the world and feels it directed at him.

Rezia's loneliness in not having children of her own, preoccupation with the children of others, and her weeping in this "profound, silent, hopeless" way, for the first time since they married, Septimus compared to a "piston thumping." Feeling "nothing," he "descended another step into the pit" (136). Capitulating, Septimus agreed to see a doctor; now others must help. Falsely reassuring, Dr. Holmes dismissed his symptoms and told him to try diversions such as attending musicals, playing golf or taking two bromides dissolved in water.

Plagued by his unfeeling response when Evans was killed, Septimus' other "crimes" confronted him as well: the fact he "seduced" Rezia, lied to her, and married her "without loving her." In addition, he felt he had antagonized Miss Pole and was, generally, repulsive to women. His guilt overpowering, he felt the "verdict of human nature" on a monster such as he, was "death" (138).

On Dr. Holmes' next visit, he dismissed Septimus' headaches, sleeplessness, fears, and dreams as "nerve symptoms"; told his patient to eat well; pursue outside interests or hobbies; and, insisted that health is within each person's voluntary control (138). Despite Septimus' cynicism and refusal to see him, Dr. Holmes came every day, vapidly reiterating nothing was wrong, seeking to imbue him with shame concerning his threat to kill himself. Septimus thought: "once you stumble, human nature is on you. Holmes is on you." His only recourse was to flee to Italy, distance himself from Holmes (139).

Rezia's fervent desire for a child to fulfill herself and consummate her marriage challenged Septimus' shaky identity, creating his first serious emotional collapse. As we know, Septimus's feelings had been anesthetized when his officer friend, Evans, died. He married in hope of normalcy, protection, oblivion.

The years have taken their toll, and Septimus is ridden with dammed-up anger and rage[18] towards others, although his inner motivation as depicted, for this extreme degree of alienation, is fairly unclear. Is it his rebelliousness toward authority which forced him to endure the war, taught him to kill, and claimed his friend? Or is it apprehension that his affection for his friend will be disclosed? Grandiosity is shown in his identification with Shakespeare whom Septimus distortedly perceives as hating humanity, sex, procreation, and gustatory experiences. Feeling disgust and repugnance regarding his marital relationship, Septimus also feels abandoned by his wife who appeared in the past to offer unconditional love, but in his jaundiced view, now wants to replace him with children.

Feeling deserted and that others do not fathom his suffering or agitation, Septimus assumed the entire world was prodding him to kill himself. Shall it be, he wondered with a "table-knife, uglily, with floods of blood or by sucking a gaspipe?" He could not manage that. Feeling "condemned as those who are about to die are alone," he thought there was a "luxury in it, an isolation full of sublimity; a freedom which the attached can never know" (140), suggesting his sense of uniqueness and martyrdom.

Holmes could not touch this "lost relic straying on the edge of the world, this outcast"[19] who gazed back at the inhabited regions. Evans' voice spoke from behind a screen,[20] this apparently the "great revelation," and Septimus in turn, called to his friend, muttering "communication is happiness, communication is health" (141). Rezia heard him talking aloud, thought him mad, and called Dr. Holmes. Holmes in turn recommended a consultation with a Harley Street specialist, Dr. Bradshaw.

The following episodes, depicting the simultaneity of loss, suffering, and alienation in Septimus's life are compelling in the impact of their tortured prose, portraying him in and out of touch with reality. Here Woolf has her own prior emotional breakdowns to which she can refer, as well as free recourse to poetic modalities vital to the fictional mode.

With the symbolic appearance of the long, gray limousine, an image of implacable power and authority, blocking traffic on the streets of London, Clarissa's response is one of standing at attention, thinking she was witnessing the Queen, whereas Septimus gazing at the drawn blinds in the car, sees a pattern suggesting a tree. As though some "horror" (21) was taking place before him, this form wavered and threatened to burst into flames, terrifying him and mobilizing his anger regarding authority. He, not the limousine, was blocking the way; he was the fulcrum of everyone's attention he felt, his messianic thinking surfacing. Grandiose, exaggerated views of his importance emerge, this enhancement or aggrandizement of self, related to his massive sense of worthlessness and incapacity.

Yet Septimus feels part of the crowd that watches an airplane skywriting "TOFFEE." He enjoys the exquisite shapes in the sky and thinks the plane was signalling to him. Is this a collective, mythic sharing in the goodness of an orally benign universe? Tears sprang to Septimus' eyes, as poetically he thought the smoke words were "languishing and melting in the sky . . . , bestowing upon him in their inexhaustible charity and laughing goodness one shape after another of unimaginable beauty." They signalled their "intention to provide him, for nothing, forever, for looking merely, with beauty, more beauty" (31).

In certain atmospheric conditions, the crescendo of sensory stimulation as he watched the trees rising and falling,[21] quickened into life by the human voice, would have "sent Septimus mad" had Rezia not placed her hand heavily on his knee, (32) modulating his excitement. Leaves he saw as alive and connected by many fibers with his own body: "When the branch stretched, he too made that statement." Sounds become songs with "premeditation." As the "spaces between" became as important as the sounds themselves, Septimus seemed to confuse figure and ground. Taken together with a child's crying (or was this his own?) and the sound of a distant horn, Septimus felt the "birth of a new religion" (33).

Rezia could no longer tolerate her husband's idiosyncracies. Although Dr. Holmes did not take Septimus's suffering seriously, Rezia could not sit next to him, as he blindly stared and seemed not to see her, which affected her equanimity: "far rather would she that he were dead!" (33). She felt isolated, ashamed, thought her husband cowardly in wishing to take his life, told others he had been overworking. Manifesting the ordeal of a close family member of an individual in mental crisis, the attempts at dissembling, Rezia does not fathom Septimus' pathology or her own crucial interaction in his difficulties. Nor is she assisted by medical authorities.

Here we learn Rezia's wedding ring slipped off her finger. Does this signify Rezia had given up: "it was she who suffered but had nobody to tell" (34). For her, the fact Septimus threatened suicide already signified he was "gone." Thinking "no one kills from hatred" (35), Septimus feels alone with his torrential thoughts and confused perceptions.

At this point he thinks he hears sparrows on a railing opposite, chirping his name, and singing in Greek[22] "there is no crime, there is no death, freshly and piercingly from trees in the meadow of life, beyond a river where the dead walk" (36). He imagined Evans behind the railing; the need to resurrect his friend is recurrent, compelling. Obviously, the "crime" he is protesting is his love for Evans whose death he is also denying. Rezia tried to divert him but now Septimus felt in communion with the "Lord" who considerd him the "greatest of mankind . . . come to renew society," he the "scapegoat," forever suffering, beset by his "eternal loneliness" (37).

Awaiting their appointment with the "well-known" Dr. Bradshaw, Rezia felt exposed, tortured; felt others were uncomprehending. In her thoughts, she reviews Septimus' distortions: he felt people were talking behind their bedroom walls and claimed he saw an old woman's head in the middle of a fern. Occasionally, he seemed his reality-oriented self but this proved a chimera, for he would suddenly exclaim "now we'll kill ourselves," as they stood by the river. He felt people were "wicked" and made up lies as they passed him on the street; he himself knew all their thoughts, "knew everything", knew the "meaning of the world." At home Rezia must pretend she holds his hand to prevent him from falling into the "flames";[23] he saw "faces laughing at him, calling him horrible, disgusting names from the walls, (100) hands pointing round the screen" (101).

Again Septimus focuses on Rezia's missing wedding ring. Perhaps covering up she tells him she has grown thin and the ring is in her purse. Their marriage was over, thought Septimus, but with a mixture of "relief and agony." He was free, "as it was decreed the lord of men should be free, alone, called forth in advance of the mass of men to hear the truth . . . , which was to be given whole to the Prime Minister" (102). Loving humanity now, he felt he could "see through bodies," see into the future (102). His body "macerated until only the nerve fibers were left, spread like a veil upon a rock, lay very high, on the back of the world" with "red flowers" growing through his flesh, "stiff leaves" rustling by his head (103).

After remaining "high on his rock like a drowned sailor,"[24] he imagined he fell into the sea while leaning over the side of a boat (104). Convinced he had been dead, he revived and turned towards life; the world welcomed and beauty seemed ubiquitous. He expressed lyrical, exquisite joy as he watched the sun dappling the leaves in "mockery," dazzling them with "soft gold in pure good temper" (105). Beauty created out of the everyday was the "truth" and was widespread. Rezia reminded him it was time for their appointment and he imagined himself singing an "immortal ode to Time." Again Evans answered, this time from behind the tree, that the dead were in Greece waiting until the war was over, and now he, Evans, would appear. Septimus cried "for God's sake, don't come," still unable to confront his feelings for his friend (105).

Now twelve o'clock, Septimus and Rezia must visit Dr. Bradshaw. Woolf's venom and barbed, satiric thrusts towards the "ghostly helper," "the priest of science," fueled by her own sense of futility in consulting doctors who knew little about psychological motivation—combine in a vitriolic mix, attacking the steamrollering, the recourse to meaningless, mechanical, diagnostic pyrotechnics that stigmatize the patient; attacking the often misleading, hypnotic charisma of the doctor who takes no heed of the patient's individuality, his psyche, hopes, fantasies, aspirations, conflicts, the quality of his relationships and experiences.

All Septimus could say at this point was to repeat he had committed a "crime," which Rezia waved aside, apparently cutting off his need to communicate, once again. Now he ceased all efforts to talk. On hearing Septimus threatening to take his life, Dr. Bradshaw recommended a private nursing home, stating it was a "question of law" that his patient rest in bed. Answering Rezia's protestations about being separated from her husband, the doctor intoned that those we are closest to should not

be in attendance when we are ill. Septimus' complexity seemed completely overlooked: "the criminal who faced the judges, the victim exposed on
the heights, the fugitive, the drowned sailor, the poet of the immortal
ode, the Lord who had gone from life to death" (146).

Clearly Dr. Bradshaw was judgmental, punitive, possibly deplored
his patient's shabbiness or envied him his cultural accomplishments.
When Septimus tried once again to communicate his anguish, Dr. Bradshaw told him to try not to think about himself; the doctor would be in
touch concerning hospitalization that evening.

Nowhere did Dr. Bradshaw take cognizance of Septimus' emotional
state; rather, he emphasized his lack of a "sense of proportion" (146).
Woolf satirizes his approach:

> [w]hen a man comes into your room, says he is Christ and threatens to
> kill himself, you invoke proportion; order rest in bed; rest in solitude;
> silence and rest; rest without friends, without books, without messages,
> six months rest; until a man who went in weighing seven stone six comes
> out weighing twelve (149-150).

Worshipping "proportion," Dr. Bradshaw not only flourished but
"made England prosper, secluded her lunatics, forbade childbirth, pena-
lized despair, made it possible for the unfit to propagate their views"
(150).

Since Septimus' world had assumed such phantasmagoric proportions, he was determined, in a clear moment, to hold onto whatever
shred of sanity was left (215). On observing his wife ecstatically playing
with a neighbor's grandchild who came to their door (219), he was accosted by nagging, insoluble issues concerning the begetting of children.
As Septimus seemed beset by the "cries of people seeking and not
finding", then becoming distant, he again withdrew. Terrified, he tried
to fixate on numerous objects in the room to affirm their reality (220),

Septimus questioned his physicians' right to dictate to him and Rezia
responded that their behavior was due to Septimus' threat to kill himself
(223). Thinking his wife a "flowering tree" (224), he saw through her
"branches" the face of a "law-giver who had reached a sanctuary where
she feared no one," neither Holmes nor Bradshaw who contradicted each
other yet "ruled" and "inflicted" (225).

Rezia reassured Septimus nothing would separate them. Hearing Dr.
Holmes on the steps she tried to intercept him. Septimus now seriously
considered killing himself with Mrs. Filmer's "nice, clean bread knife,"
but didn't wish to "spoil" it. He thought of the "gas-fire" but it was too
late for that. Holmes was clearly ascending. Septimus did not wish to die,

but when Holmes was at the door, Septimus cried "I'll give it you" and flung himself "vigorously, violently" out the window, onto the area railing below. Holmes called him "coward" (226).

Not possessing Clarissa's life force, Septimus' self-esteem is more fragile.[25] Nor is he as related to others[26] or part of any social milieu. His control is brittle and strong emotions inundate him; at the last he turns the retaliativeness and rage primarily intended for the powers that be, for their profound indifference and misunderstanding—against himself. For the most part he is presented to us in his pathological aspects. We have been told little concerning his unflorid self, only that his floundering marriage had formerly represented a haven, escape from his plaguing insecurities, sexual confusion, and loneliness. We can predict his anxieties emanated not merely from the devastating effects of soldiering, but from earlier difficulties as well.

Since Septimus' sense of victimization and preoccupation with taking his life began before he encountered Dr. Holmes, we can assume the centrality of more underlying conflicts. Noted in some detail is his initial collapse on being unable to assimilate his wife's increasing desire to have a child. Feeling their marriage no longer meaningful to Rezia, Septimus felt intense repugnance towards her.[27] Is he unable to see himself as a procreative, generative male, or does he wish to be the only child, so to speak, and feels abandoned by Rezia's wish to change the status quo?

Yet his difficulty in mourning Evans preceded his anxieties regarding Rezia. It is, of course, not clear whether the relationship between Septimus and Evans was overtly homosexual. Probably not, because the repeated, metaphoric use of screen or barrier suggests persistent denial or concealment of homoerotic feelings to himself. Septimus' need to resurrect Evans, his guilt regarding the "crime" of loving him and the "crime" of not feeling enough is recurrent and insistent. Quite possibly he takes his life to rejoin him.

III

Some have questioned the doubleness of Clarissa and Septimus. Though the disparity is, of course, apparent, the enmeshment is quite clear. As noted, the novel starts with tremendous force and buoyancy with Clarissa bursting open doors and plunging at Bourton in the "open air," to come to a full circle with Septimus plunging out the window to his death below. In juxtaposing earlier, that Clarissa had tossed a shilling into the Serpentine but Septimus had thrown his away; in the numerous quotations from Shakespeare involving one's fleeting mortality, the author points to Clarissa's incessant preoccupation with suicide and death, similar to Woolf's own.

Both Clarissa and Septimus evidence a mystical enmeshing with the universe. Clarissa felt she would survive in the purlieus of London "laid out like a mist between the people she knew best who lifted her on their branches as she had seen the trees lift the mist, but it spread ever so far, her life, herself" (12). Her essence permeated others and would be a generative force. Feeling the trees were alive and the "leaves connected by millions of fibers with his own body" (32), Septimus's conceptions show a lack of reality consideration. He thought flowers grew through his flesh; and, that he could see through the bodies of others.

Throughout the novel, when Clarissa is presumably happiest, she thinks of death.[28] After kissing Sally she sighs: "If 'twere now to die 'twere now to be most happy."[29] Is this knocking on wood? An avoidance of future pain? Or a masochistic linking of pain with pleasure? Learning Richard was lunching with another woman she thinks of self-annihilation rather than express rage. When she heard of Septimus' suicide, she felt identified with Septimus as though this were her punishment, her penance, her expiation. In viewing Septimus' death as "defiance," (280) Clarissa romanticizes his suicide. Somewhat inconsistently, she now felt privileged to be alive: "he made her feel the fun, the beauty of living," (284).

In Septimus' warped thinking, he had already died by drowning or was consumed by fire. This was punishment for his "crime" of loving and not reacting with sufficient emotion to the death of his officer friend, for marrying without love. In Woolf's enamorment with the concept of Septimus' death as "defiance," she forgets that in her novel, Septimus thought of taking his life before his encounter with doctors; they simply exacerbate his wish.

The novel is, in its totality, a brilliant metaphor concerning the overarching theme of the double, depicting the parallelism of sanity and insanity. It is evocative of layer upon layer of meaning, perhaps not so much "tunneling" as unearthing of rich, geological strata. The design of projecting one, decisive, impactful day in the resonating lives of its protagonists, the use of multiple perspective, and the impingement of the moment are compelling in scope and depth.

As in many of Woolf's novels, themes of orality, especially in their aggressive variant, are highly informing. For example, Miss Kilman who covets Elizabeth's affection, is referred to by Clarissa as vampire-like, one of those "spectres who stand astride us and suck up our life-blood, a brutal monster, dominator and tyrant" (16). Miss Kilman omniverously eating eclairs, almost feels "split asunder" (199) as she becomes aware she is losing Elizabeth.

With the appearance of the "official" car, the author tells us the spirit of "religion was abroad, with her eyes bandaged tight and her lips gaping wide" (20). Woolf adds that nobody knew the identity of the car's passenger, but since the reference is to a feminine "spirit," perhaps Queen (123) or archetypal mother-figure, a modern painting is conjured up of a female with prominent teeth and mouth gaping wide, by the abstract expressionist, DeKooning, another artist with orally sadistic maternal introjects.

Predominantly, Woolf's embodiment of official, implacable authority is masculine and medical. Dr. Bradshaw "devoured, shut people up; naked, defenseless, the exhausted, the friendless received the impress of his will . . . " (154).

Peter felt "sucked up to some roof" by his emotion, his susceptibility. Contemptuous and disdainful of Richard Dalloway's philistinism, he thought Clarissa "swallowed" Richard's notion that no decent human being ought to read Shakespeare's sonnets, likening this to "listening at keyholes." Yet Clarissa "sucked it all in" (113).

Septimus could not taste, could not feel, thought his fellow workers "oozed thick drops of vice," vanish "screaming into the wilderness," and are plastered over with "grimaces." He had a vision of lying on a cliff with gulls "screaming" over him, wondered whether to take his life by "sucking a gaspipe" (135).

Insistent oral conflicts in Woolf's developmental history, her depression, and her tendency towards anorexia during her breakdowns point to clashes with early caretakers that undoubtedly encompassed feelings of intense deprivation and rage. The allusions to "sucking" evoke a vacuum-like omniverousness or incorporativness and conversely a fear of being devoured, reinforced by the oral aggressions of people with "grimaces," "mouths gaping wide," or "screaming." The oral images in *Mrs. Dalloway* connect with the "devouring lions" of *The Voyage Out* and with the author and her characters' considerable oral ferocity, clearly reflecting early oral frustrations and power struggles with regard to maternal images. Miss Kilman eating eclairs and feeling torn apart simultaneously points to an image suggesting danger to the body's integrity, as well as an aggressive, devouring image which together with her name, suggests the desire to castrate or orally attack.

Life in *Mrs. Dalloway* generally seems to be lived on a high tension level. We are apparently dealing with a considerable degree of submerged violence. Pitying and despising Clarissa, "bitter and burning with the need to humiliate and unmask" her, Miss Kilman felt no pain. According to Phyllis Rose, an earlier draft of *Mrs. Dalloway* "Mrs. Dalloway Holograph" presents the conflict between Clarissa and Miss Kilman as occurring within Elizabeth who felt split in choosing between the two: that is, Miss Kilman's role in the novel presumably "externalizes Elizabeth's hatred of her mother," while Woolf "hates the part of herself which hates her mother too much to give it a fair hearing. She labels it Kilman—that way lies death—and dismisses it as repulsive" (Rose 150).

Clarissa as a young woman felt Peter might make too many demands on her, that she must "break" with him or they would be "destroyed," both of them "ruined"—rather calamitous, dire forebodings. When she learned he had married, for years she felt an "arrow sticking in her heart; the grief, the anguish, the horror" (10).

Clarissa felt as though she were a "rope-walker and beneath was death." Though her predominant reaction on learning of her husband's luncheon with Lady Bruton is one of nun-like withdrawal and self-flagellation, she merely pierced her pin cushion; apparently she cannot be more direct or confronting with her anger. In Clarissa's striving for control, she composed herself and felt herself "pointed, dartlike, definite," concealing "faults, vanities, jealousies, suspicions" (55).

Recalling her pleasure when Sally kissed her, Clarissa disliked Peter's intrusion, felt that Sally was being "mauled already, maltreated" (53). She sensed Peter's hostility, his determination to break into the companionship. On hearing of Septimus' suicide, Clarissa felt her body go through it first, her dress "flamed, her body burned: Up had flashed the ground; through him, bruising, went the rusty spikes. There he lay with a thud, thud, thud in his brain, and then a suffocation of blackness . . . " (280). Realizing Dr. Bradshaw was capable of blundering, she felt Septimus' death an act of aggression against the powers that be.

In its central characterizations and imagery, the novel represents deep-seated preoccupations and unresolved conflicts of the author, closely identified with the characters Septimus and Clarissa.

The theme of unlived life pertains to all three—Clarissa, Septimus, and Woolf. As with Septimus' wife, Woolf wished to have children; throughout her life she mourned her childlessness and envied Vanessa's fertility and maternality. Yet her clash with Leonard over this, her anxieties regarding body image, and her ambivalence regarding her femininity impeded her. At times Woolf felt writing novels more exciting or as fertile a process as childbirth. Or she arranged that her fictional heroines die in childbirth, or that mother and child are estranged, as in *Mrs. Dalloway.*

Also linking Clarissa, Septimus, and Woolf is the theme of failed marriage. Septimus and his wife are divided by her imperative need to have children, a source of tremendous anxiety for Septimus, since he is in the throes of illness, given to body distortions and deepening sexual confusion. Clarissa is in a distant relationship with her husband, and their marriage is at this point sexually abstinent.[30] Certainly Woolf identifies with the discords in both Septimus' and Clarissa's marriages. Although Clarissa and Peter reminisce about their earlier happiness, painful separation, and his retaliatory marriage; and though they evidence a close bond, their relationship remains unresolved.

Clarissa, Septimus, and Woolf suppress feelings, suffer. Clarissa feels it dangerous to live even one day; Woolf is preoccupied with the ephemeralness of life; Septimus feels in almost constant danger, as though in the midst of an alien environment. Actually for him, all experiences are intensified and are at feverish pitch as he loses his hold on reality. No longer contained, his catastrophic prognostications are projected onto others, his symptoms restitutionally seeking to ward off complete disintegration.

Marked anxiety over the inability to meaningfully mourn, unite Septimus and Woolf. Septimus' "crime" that condemns him to death, so to speak, was contained in his incapacity to feel or express emotion following Even's death which in Woolf's conception was also related to homosexual panic. After her mother's death, Woolf felt the servants insincere and her father histrionic and posturing in their grief. The predominance of hostile emotions towards her mother anesthetized Woolf's response to the death, representing her defense against the threatened eruption into consciousness of unassimilable feelings of abandonment and rage, so that she never succeeded in resolving her mourning process. In her more authentic moments, Clarissa mourns the loss of the most robust relationship in her life, that with Peter, though Spilka suggests Clarissa's "real grieving was blocked" (74)[31].

Metaphors of drowning, actualized by Woolf in her future choice of suicide and death, recur in all the novels. In *Mrs. Dalloway* we find allusions to Septimus' fantasy of drowning, to Clarissa's notion of being "far out to sea," or, that we are "a doomed race" chained to a sinking ship.

Septimus, Clarissa, and Woolf are enormously self-devaluating. Clarissa and Woolf caricature their bodies, feel unfeminine, aged, or asexual; Septimus loathes and distorts his body functions, which seem true for Woolf during her emotional crisis in 1913. All three are sexually ambivalent, feel isolated, and are spectators to life. Woolf shares Septimus' and Clarissa's confusion regarding sexual identification. In

Leaska's view, Clarissa in accepting her homosexuality is more in touch
with herself, more self-aware; she is "enabled to continue her existence
even if ever more inwardly" (Leaksa, 1977a, 117).

Though Clarissa is frequently depressed, given to morbid, occasionally baleful ruminations, her personality structure is relatively more
robust than Septimus'; preoccupied with death, she is ascetic or spiritual,
not suicidal. By contrast, Septimus considers his feelings for Evans utterly alien, cannot bring them to awareness. Woolf too found it hard to face
personal issues of homosexuality forthrightly, returned to them again
and again, seemed better able to confront them in her later novels.

One does not necessarily commit suicide because of guilt over homosexuality or anger towards authority. Possibly Septimus equates the
authority-images in his life with early conceptions of malevolent parental
figures. We are told only that Septimus had altercations with his mother
over unwashed hands. In simplistic psychoanalytic parlance, Septimus
might be expressing anger towards parental or other authority figures,
has internalized the conception of a depriving, ungiving mother-image,
and in committing suicide, has turned sadistically against her, and
against his by now highly devalued self. Earlier, his depression or preoccupation with self-punishment was a desperate attempt to persuade
others to give emotional nurturance; he wished to win love and forgiveness through atonement.

Generally, however, motivation is more complex. We have a paucity
of information, have no notion of the personality of Septimus' father,
who is never alluded to. Since Septimus' early love for Miss Pole was of
an ethereal sort, his first caring relationship for another adult occurred in
regard to Evans, his officer, most probably a father-figure. Septimus'
stringent requirements on himself for masculine armoring are highly brittle. He simply could not meet the demands of his marriage, had always
been marginal in his adaptation to reality, and had begun to feel
deterioration in his relationships at work. Bitterly sarcastic regarding his
supervisor who originally befriended him, he suspiciously saw him as
"all coldness and clamminess within" (135).

Emotionally charged situations jolt him. Though he initially seeks
help, he is betrayed by the limited vision of his caretakers who he felt
wanted him out of the way. Without assuming a moral stance regarding
suicide, death as revenge is not as glorified as Woolf would have it.
Similar to Woolf, Septimus' suicidal preoccupations at first represented
a cry for help unheeded, an impasse in communication. His wife, as
recalled, viewing the severity of his illness, wished him dead.[32]

Septimus had already begun to feel displaced by Rezia's hope for a child; the illusion that his wife unconditionally affirmed him was badly shattered. In those with an already damaged self-concept as with Septimus and Woolf, suicidal wishes may follow the failure of a close relationship. In addition to his sexual confusion, Septimus experiences a sense of immense chaos, helplessness, and abandonment; of beginning thought distortion, loss of boundaries, and fear of disorganization. Rezia in a difficult position, feels isolated and ashamed of him.

Most centrally, Septimus and Woolf share a sense of anarchy and meaninglessness insofar as the opinions of psychiatric specialists are concerned. Dr. Holmes dismissed Septimus' symptoms, thinking nothing was amiss. Another specialist, Dr. Bradshaw, diagnosed Septimus' difficulties as a total breakdown with "every symptom in an advanced stage." He advised bedrest in a nursing home which Septimus dreaded and repudiated. These specialists were not able to agree; yet they were the judges meting out the "verdict."

Septimus was particularly agitated by the possibilty of separation from his wife should he go to a nursing home. Woolf felt she had wasted a good many years of her life in rest cures. Except for the earlier relationship with Dr. Savage who was her family physician and encouraged her to have children, she felt misunderstood by her doctors.

In depicting Septimus' embattledness regarding medical authority and bungling, Woolf is not omitting his confusion and complexity of motivation, though just as with herself, she is obscuring or is out of touch in this novel with earlier, more salient sources of emotional disorder. Nevertheless, *Mrs. Dalloway* is a courageous foray into little-understood channels of mental illness: the recourse to messianism and sublimity; emergence of delusional mechanisms and body distortions; the sense of extreme isolation, and occasionally, of depersonalization. Though Septimus shows perculiarities in reality-testing and intermittently hallucinates, his conflicts still evidence continuity with the dissonances of everyday life.

Essentially in Woolf's perception, Septimus has been a "border" case (127), neither "one thing or the other," had no ties to family that can be discerned. As we know, he is overwhelmed by his "crime" of inappropriately mourning Evans, actually a screen for concealment of homosexual feelings, and he therefore seeks punishment.

Here Woolf's prescience is evidenced, her conception of Septimus' personality relevant to current psychoanalytic notions of the "borderline" individual, characterized as in the case of Septimus, by poor tolerance of anxiety-provoking sitautions or strong affects, by proneness to feeling insulated and injured, and by the tendency to project blame especially towards those in authority. Frequently, primitive aggression and omnipotence alternate with extreme self-devaluation. If the need for rescue goes unheeded, self-destructive acts eventuate.

Based on the desperate lives many women lead beneath a facade of altruism, Woolf, in the portrayal of Clarissa in *Mrs. Dalloway* borrowed from her mother's and mother-surrogate's depression and unresolved mourning, their preoccupation with the ephemeralness of existence, and their suicidal propensities—not a particularly nurturing legacy for living one's life.

X "It was a house full of unrelated passions" —To the Lighthouse

I

Undertaken to grapple with the impingement of unresolved feelings concerning her parents, Woolf began her novel *To the Lighthouse* with father as model for her central character through her mother's personality prevailed to a considerable degree, in a complex, predominantly idealizing portrait, just as in Woolf's life, the relationship with Vita, her "maternal protection," had taken over at this time.

An artistic projection of the author's conception of early family relationships, *To the Lighthouse* dwells on the period of cumulative summers at St. Ives and Cornwall, where the Stephens vacationed until Virginia was 13, the year her mother died, a setting and ambience which proved in the past a decidedly idyllic one. There the Stephen family seemed a more solid entity, the mother a more central presence from whom Virginia felt support and connection. Perhaps the greater proximity of her parents—their bedroom adjoined the nursery, unlike the spatial arrangement of Hyde Park Gate—evoked the feelings of pleasurable encapsulation and heightened sensitivity to sensory impressions, providing context for her novel.

Exulting in having written her previous novel, *Mrs. Dalloway* without "break from illness," exorcising the "spell" which Murry[1] and others said she was "under" after *Jacob's Room*, Woolf finds herself thinking of a short story, "The Old Man," based on her father, Leslie Stephen. She also muses about Katherine Mansfield; had Katherine lived, others would notice Woolf was the "more gifted." (D2, Oct.17'24).

Writing Jacques Raverat, a painter living in France with whom Woolf had an intimate correspondence though they had not met for 11 years, she describes her growing attraction for Vita: Vita's legs are "like slender pillars up into her trunk which is that of a breastless cuirassier, but all about her is virginal, savage, patrician." Then Woolf adds maliciously, "why she writes is a puzzle"[2] (L3, Dec.26'24). Thanking Jacques for his birthday gift of flowers, she confides: "to tell you a secret I want to incite my lady [Vita] to elope with me." Then I'll drop

141

down on you and tell you all about it. (L3, Jan. 24'25). In her next letter Woolf writes Jacques she wished she had married a "foxhunter," alluding to Clive: "It is partly the desire to share in life somehow, which is denied to us writers" (L3, Feb.5'25). Here she confides her marriage to Leonard is wanting.

Perhaps because Jacques was dying from the "disseminated sclerosis" with which he had long been afflicted and because he asked for the proofs of *Mrs. Dalloway*, Virginia sent them to him, an unusual gesture since Leonard was the sole recipient of her completed manuscripts. After Jacques' death,[3] Virginia commiserated with his wife, Gwen, telling her how much their friendship and love sustained her during her illness before the war: "one could say anything to Jacques. If there is anything I could ever give you I would give it, but perhaps the only thing to give is to be oneself with people." Then she writes "these efforts of mine to communicate with people are partly childlessness and the horror that sometimes overcomes me" (L3, Mar.11'25). In her diary for April 8, 1925, Woolf indicated she did not wish to "doff the cap to death . . . ; it's life that matters."

With her stories "welling up" inside her, writing with "rush and urgency" she finds herself unable to work fast enough to use her "oilwell," and she compares her approach to the "sweep of a brush. I fill it up afterwards" (D3, Apr. 20'25). Woolf's desire to share Vanessa's creative sphere is evidenced here. Painterly in describing her earliest memories, Woolf would color them "pale yellow, silver and green . . . , make a picture that was globular; semi-transparent." Obviously emotionally weighted, these and other childhood memories involving sound, smell, visual, tactile, and thermal modalities are also highly sensual, "make" her "feel warm as if everything were ripe, humming, gummy" (*SOTP*, 66). They provide the impetus for exploring the creative process of Lily Briscoe, a painter, one of the central characters in *To the Lighthouse*, whose credo is based of course on Vanessa's artistic endeavors, as well as those of Woolf.

Impatient with her journalistic efforts, Woolf prefers to focus on her novel: "This is going to be fairly short; to have father's character done complete in it; and mother's and St. Ives; and childhood; and all the usual things I try to put in, life and death" (D3, May14'25). She then claimed as its central theme, her father enunciating his sense of doom and abandonment, sitting in a boat muttering as he crushes a dying mackeral, "we perished each alone," a line culled from the last stanza of "The Castaway," by William Cowper.[4] Her father was fond of Cowper and of reciting aloud.

Julia Stephen, "deadened" by the loss of her first husband, also conjured up the sea when she confessed she "could have got more real life out of the wreck" if she had "broken down more" (*Maus.*, 40). In writing the novel, Woolf felt she might thereby modulate the incessant preoccupation with her mother: "Until I was in the forties . . . , the presence of my mother obsessed me" (*SOTP*, 80).

Pleased with the success of *Mrs. Dalloway*, Woolf considers her new novel "rather an elegy" with "the sea to be heard all through it" (D3, Jun.27'25). Worried lest others consider the novel too "sentimental," that is, the themes of father, mother, children, garden, sail to the lighthouse, she hopes to lend substance by her exploration of the "flight of time." She wants to "break fresh ground" (D3, Jul.20'25).

Fluctuating between a "single and intense character of father and a far wider, slower book," she worries lest the latter might risk the "flatness" of her naturalistic novel, *Night and Day*; concludes she had best "split up emotions more completely" in *To the Lighthouse*, referring here to her many-levelled approach wherein she explores her characters from multiple angles of vision (D3, Jul.30'25).

Attending a celebration for her nephew, Quentin's fifteenth birthday, Woolf inexplicably faints and is lingeringly ill for several months with headache and exhaustion (Bell, v.2, 114), though able apparently to continue her writing. Could the birthday party have catalyzed her sense of childlessness? Not infrequently, after a visit with Vanessa and her brood Woolf laments her barren state.

Is her illness also related to a resurgence of emotions regarding her mother, evoked by the novel? Here the relationship between Lily Briscoe, Woolf's alter-ego, and Mrs. Ramsay is heavily charged with Lily's longing for emotional nurturance, concomitant to her efforts to create, and toward attaining personal autonomy. Or, did Woolf's illness reflect her anxiety concerning the uncustomarily eroticizing relationship with Vita, in addition eliciting guilt regarding Leonard?

Preoccupied with the nature of her friendship with Vita, Woolf asks: "What has happened and at what state did we last meet"? They had broken off, "wedged in the midst of a terrific argument," but everything was now "obscure" (L3, Aug.24'25).

Fantasizing a gala party in London at her studio, Woolf writes Vita: "Everybody will be discharged into this room, unmixed, undressed, unpowdered. You will emerge like a lighthouse,[5] fitful, sudden, remote—now that is rather like you" (L3, Sept.22'25).

Hoping to achieve closeness to Vanessa, Woolf instead, often threatened or alienated her sister. Her feelings of sexual jealously regarding

Vanessa are clear: "Give my love to old convolvulous[6] bed [Duncan]. What a perfect image of his voluptuous creamy grace—and then the snake no thicker than a whip, but deadly" (L3, Sept.29'25). Referring to Duncan Grant's painting here, her meaning is unclear, though her metaphors are decidedly phallic, perhaps unconsciously conveying attraction and repulsion.

Inappropriately responding to Madge Vaughan's death,[7] Woolf writes: "Rustling among my emotions I found nothing better than dead leaves." Woolf's idealized image of a former mother-figure has apparently been attenuated. Rather heartlessly, she continues: "They burned a faggot of twigs at High Gate [Cemetery] as far as I am concerned" (D3, Nov.27'25). Woolf imagined she would be deeply affected however, if any of her "six intimates"—Leonard, Vanessa, Duncan, Lytton, Clive, or Morgan—died.[8]

Bemoaning the fact she was incommunicado because of her physician's and Leonard's strictures on visitors, Woolf felt deprived in missing Vita's visit. On hearing Vita would journey to Persia for many months, Woolf laments her impending absence. With Vita away, the possibilities for greater closeness will evaporate. Before Vita's departure however, Woolf visited Long Barn, Vita's home, wrote of their meeting and sexual consummation: "These Sapphists love women; friendship is never untinged with amorosity. I like her and being with her and the splendor." Apparently Vita shows a "candle-lit radiance, pink-glowing, grape-clustered." Virginia appreciated "her maturity and full breastedness" and admired her for tackling motherhood though felt she was not particularly warm with her sons. However, Vita was what Virginia has never been, "a real woman: there is some voluptuousness about her; the grapes are ripe." (D3, Dec.21'25).

Somewhat derogatory regarding Vita's intellectual capacity, Woolf finds Vita lacking "in brain and insight." On Woolf, Vita "lavishes" the maternal care she has always wanted from "everyone." She notes Vita's eccentricity: "of course mingled with this glamour there is something loose fitting. How much shall I miss her when she travels across the desert ?" (Dec.21'25).

Vita is now a "dear, old rough coated sheep dog" and Woolf, self-deprecatingly, implores her not to "snuff the stinking tallow out of your heart—poor Virginia to wit" (L3, Dec.22'25). On her return to London after the Christmas holidays, Woolf succumbed to German measles. Illness offers a safe vantage point, perhaps retreat.

Writing Vita that Clive "raved" about her (Vita), considers her a "brilliant human being" (L3, Jan.15'26), Woolf is devising a triangular unit as of old, when she experienced vicarious pleasure in fantasizing about Vanessa's and Clive's relationship. Does she procure an enraptured male for Vita, because she, Woolf, does not believe her own charms sufficient for this lush, "lustrous" Sapphist?

With Vita off to Persia for four months, Woolf, despondent that this "abundant and fruitful" being was gone, found herself vitalized in resuming her novel once again. Writing Vita, Woolf asks her to "open the top" of her dress and Vita will find "nestling inside a most lively squirrel, with the most inquisitive habits" (L3, Jan.26'26).

Telling Lytton she had chicken pox, whooping cough, influenza, and cowpox and leads the life of a "widow of 90," (L3, Jan.26'26) is Woolf conveying her need to be taken care of? A covert desire to discard her husband?

Though Woolf decidedly misses Vita, the "glow and flattery and the festival," she adds somewhat inscrutably, "not very intimately," perhaps fearful of involvement (D3, Feb.23'26). Essentiallly, she is exuberant because her novel flows freely and swiftly, and she considers herself an enthusiast for work as was her father. A bit of the "restless searcher" in her, she has a sense of her own "strangeness walking upon the earth" (D3, Feb.27'26).

Continuing to deplore the lack of "natural happiness" in her life, she envies "geniality and family love and being on the rails of human life . . . , old and young agreeing to live together," a turn towards Vanessa now that Vita is gone (D3, Apr.9'26).

On Vita's return, Woolf muses about their relationship "left so ardent in Janaury and now what? Am I in love with her? But what is love?" Vita "in love" with Woolf "excites and flatters" but Woolf has little interest in Vita's poetry (D3, May 20'26). After they meet, Woolf feels their bond solidified (D3, May25'26).

At this time, Vanessa feels her sister's preoccupation with Vita stirs up jealousy between them. Now suffering a minor "breakdown,"[9] Woolf feels all is "insipid, tasteless, colorless." She longed for rest, avoided reading, writing, felt a "blank," then gradually came back to life, shown by her power to "make images" again (D3, Jul.31'26).

With Vita as fashion mentor, Woolf learns how to "buy nightgowns, how to make one's hair stay firm after washing," and other kindred matters vital to one's feminine identification (L3, Aug.22'26).

Now that *To the Lighthouse* is coming to an end, Woolf is both relieved and disappointed, feels this is the "greatest stretch I've put my method to, dredging up more feelings and character." She finds her novel subtler and more human than *Jacob's Room* and *Mrs. Dalloway* (D3, Sept.13'26).

Confessing she has felt "intense depression," Woolf attributes this to receiving a paucity of letters and seeing few visitors, though it is more likely her emotional state was exacerbated by feelings of childlessness: "There was Nessa humming and booming and flourishing over the hill." Actually, she and Vanessa had quarrelled over Vita. Leonard had been caustic as well, and Woolf found herself feeling threatened, diminished, and inconsequential (D3, Sept.28'26).

Feeling Vita might tire of her because she, Woolf, was so much older or that Vita might seek new relationships, or revive old ones—Woolf thought of death as surcease (L3, Nov.19'26).

Finished January 14 and published May 5, 1927, Woolf felt *To the Lighthouse* "easily the best" of her books, "fuller than *Jacob's Room* and less spasmodic than *Mrs. Dalloway*, not complicated with all that desperate accompaniment of madness. It is freer and subtler I think" (D3, Nov.23'26).

II

In *To the Lighthouse*, Mrs. Ramsay is presented in all her multifacetedness as guests and members of her household view her; as she sees herself, experiences others or ruminates in private; and as the author as omniscient narrator also perceives her. Her relationship with her children emerges as concerned and caring, though she clearly shows preference for her youngest child, James. Towards her husband, who is overrational and demanding, she is both mocking and nurturing.

At the novel's opening, we are plunged into the oppositional stance of the parents towards one another, fueled by the mother's vicarious acquiescence to James' excited request to visit the lighthouse. We witness the father's refusal, as he deflects the boy's exuberance and brooks no rejoinder, catalyzing his son's sense of injustice and vengeance.

To the Lighthouse externalizes Mrs. Ramsay's favoritism towards James and his oedipal involvement with her, describes how much he "hated the twang and twitter of his father's emotions which disturbed the perfect simplicity and good sense of his relationship with his mother" (58). Camouflaging her own considerable envy of a younger brother, Woolf arranges that Lily focus in her painting, on the close bond between mother and son, though the image is probably objectified as archetypal mother and child.

Sexually undefined, virginal, Lily Briscoe, the Ramsay's guest and voice of the author, resists Mrs. Ramsay's insistent matchmaking, maintains her sexual inviolacy, and opts for fulfillment as artist, at the same time idealizing her. Viewing Mrs. Ramsay despite her frailties, her occasional abrasiveness, as a mercurial, creative force, Lily asks herself whether she was "in love" with her (32), evoking Virginia Woolf, desiring intimacy with her mother or with mother-figures.

Inasmuch as *To the Lighthouse* is an avowedly autobiographical novel by a prestigious author, centering on the emotionally weighted, mythic conception of an apotheosized mother-figure, and since the portrayal of Mrs. Ramsay is, in addition, a compelling one, critical evaluations of the novel have been both transferential and torrential.
Numerous psychoanalytic theories have been promulgated in hope of further delineating Woolf's fictional characters, particularly the mother, and from this interpolating the personality of Julia Stephen, proceeding then to the diagnosis of Virginia Woolf herself. Emanating no doubt from the desire to comprehend the motivational sources of Woolf's emotional illness and suicide, this approach has nonetheless frequently confused fictional with actual dramatis personae.
In one such study, attempting a psychoanalytic interpretation of *To the Lighthouse*, Ina and Ernest Wolf view Mrs. Ramsay as suffering from a "prestructural defect of her psychic apparatus" (38). Somewhat astringent and technical, this depiction seems ill-suited or constricting for the elucidation of a literary character. More crucially, the issue remains one of questioning any approach to psychoanalytic literary criticism that does not have more global breadth and scope, permitting full awareness of the ambiguities and psychological complexities of situation and character.
They refer to Mrs. Ramsay's relationships as "restless, fleeting involvements with others"; she remains too "shallow and inconstant to give others much narcissistic nutriment," avoiding the "solid bond of an empathic relationship." In addition, she can neither perceive "loneliness" in others nor tolerate it herself and obscures the "defect in her own self by enmeshment with others." When not admired, she displays an experience of "beginning fragmentation," seeking repair by "merging" with others (Wolf, 39–40).
The phenomenon of psychological merger as described, is nowhere evidenced in Mrs. Ramsay's relationships in the novel. Others strive to identify or achieve unity with her however, particularly Lily. Lily alludes to Mrs. Ramsay's "sacred inscriptions" which might "teach one everything" (TTL,79). Mrs. Ramsay brought things together . . . , "affecting one almost like a work of art" (240). The Wolfs' analysis avoids noting the prismatic, complicated, divided aspects of Mrs. Ramsay who is for the most part, as depicted in *To the Lighthouse*, capable of surmounting the contradictions and pulls of her personality, with reference to self and others.

The Wolfs suggest that Mrs. Ramsay and individuals similar to her "exhaust themselves in a frenzy of involvements" thus avoiding "unbearable, empty depression" (Wolf, 40).

All too swiftly the Wolfs glide from Mrs. Ramsay's, to Mrs. Stephen's, to Virginia's Woolf's emotional illnesses. Here they surmise Virginia bestowed on Mrs. Ramsay the shortcomings of Mrs. Stephen that presumably prepared the groundwork for Virginia's emotional malady, also a "narcissistic disorder" (39).

The undesirability of diagnosing or labelling fictional characters, the distortions involved in assuming they are direct replicas of human prototypes, are manifest. Regarding *To the Lighthouse*, the Wolf's observations of Mrs. Ramsay's character are at variance with Virginia Woolf's perception.

Following the unrewarding path of ascribing to one parent full responsiblity for the emotional disturbances of children, the Wolfs overlook that despite the impact of Mrs. Stephen's personality in Virginia's life, a grasp of the entire family constellation as it impinged on her psyche and as it devolved on her writing of *To the Lighthouse* remains crucial. For example, Virginia Woolf's early closeness to father, his alternate helplessness and punitiveness regarding his wife; Virginia's fear of her mother's retaliatory displeasure regarding his early preference; Virginia's later turn-off regarding him—must be encompassed.

Occasionally meddlesome, domineering, sharp, or remote, perhaps overly committed or power-oriented in her philanthropism—Mrs. Ramsay in Woolf's fictional conception remains fully alert and responsive to children, husband, and guests, and she is a vital force throughout. She is, after all, mother of a large family of eight children and is naturally preoccupied with the unending tasks of a tumultuous, demanding household. She finds quiet moments restorative, can "be herself by herself . . . , and that was what she often felt the need of—to think, to be silent. Then, the "range of experience seemed limitless" (TTL,95). There is no indication she dreads loneliness or avoids being alone. Rather, she looks forward to privacy to read or ruminate; though she rarely encounters such opportunities, she considers them, when they do occur, highly meaningful. When by herself, she found "peace, freedom, a summoning together, a resting on a platform of stability" (96).[10]

Mrs. Ramsay's relationships with her children and husband offer significant gleanings concerning her basic personality. Observing her son James' unutterable pleasure in hearing they might make the long-awaited sailing trip to the lighthouse, imagining him "all red and ermine on the bench or directing a stern and momentous enterprise in some crisis of public affairs," Mrs. Ramsay radiates pride as he works on his cutouts from an army and navy catalogue (10).

Since Mr. Ramsay is uncompromisingly opposed to the outing, citing hazardous or adverse weather conditions, simultaneously ridiculing his wife and disillusioning his son, Mrs. Ramsay in encouraging the boy has been unconsciously provocative and challenging toward her husband, initiating a rift between father and James. Woolf does not dwell on the mother's Machiavellianism here. Rather, she attempts to approach Mrs. Ramsay from many sides, as closely as human possibilities of perception and expression can succeed in doing. Here one surmises Woolf is taking a new look at her mother's role in her parents' interaction.

Woolf emphasizes Mrs. Ramsay's empathic identification with her son's aspirations and spontaneity and the father's orbit of joylessness, although he was perfectly correct concerning the weather; it rained the next day. Despite disagreement with her husband, Mrs. Ramsay preferred the children to affirm him. Yet, James thought "had there been an axe handy, or a poker or any weapon that would have gashed a hole in his father's breast and killed him," he would have dealt him that blow (10).

During a considerable portion of her presence in the novel, Mrs. Ramsay is depicted in a giving role.[11] Suggestive of her unassuming consideration of others, she muses on the tuberculous hip the lighthouse-keeper's son may be afflicted with and thinks of sending supplies as she guilt-provokingly asks her children: "How would you like to be shut up for a whole month at a time and possibly more, in stormy weather upon a rock, to have no letters or newspapers and to see nobody . . . ?" (11–12).

The children are a collectivity, a universe unto themselves. After dinner, they disappear as "stealthy as stags" seeking privacy to "debate" among themselves. Divergences of opinions, prejudices, and antagonisms permeate their being: "Oh that they should begin so early. They were so critical, her children" (16–17). Noting the children's "entrails" all over the floor, Mrs. Ramsay wonders: "What demon possessed her youngest, her cherished?" (43). Stroking James' head as he crayoned, she hoped he would become a great artist. Opposing her husband, she evidences considerable faith in James, not caring whether he obtains a scholarship or, for that matter, goes to school at all. Here she seems overly permissive but not uninvolved, preferring artists to intellectuals.

Nowhere are the Ramsay children depicted as deprived. They "came to her naturally all day long, with this and that" (51). From her vantage point at the window, seeing one of the children in a risky situation, she "ran across the lawn in her deerstalker's hat to snatch a child from mischief" (47). Concerning their everyday activities, she heard the children "stamping and crowing on the floor above her; heard the moment they woke. In they came, fresh as roses, staring wide awake;" their trooping into the dining room after breakfast was a "positive event." Preparing them for bed in the evening, she "found them netted in their cots like birds among cherries and raspberries, still making up stories" (91). Reading fairy tales[12] to her children, Mrs. Ramsay elicits from one of her guests, an exalted tribute.

Rose, the oldest daughter, loved choosing mother's "jewels" each night before dinner. Mrs. Ramsay intuited some "buried, speechless feeling that one had for one's mother at Rose's age" (123). In *A Sketch of the Past*, Woolf recalls her sense of excitement when as a child she "chose the jewels" her mother wore to dinner.

Somewhat infantilizing, Mrs. Ramsay indicated she would like her children to remain "demons of wickedness, angels of delight, never to grow up into long-legged monsters (89). Why must they grow up and lose it all? Never will they be so happy again" (91). Quite likely her maternal role reinforced her desire to be in command. Self-questioning however, she seemed aware that her impulse to give or her enjoyment of the children's dependency, might encompass a desire to be needed and admired. Genuinely valuing her children's openness and spontaneity, she is committed to their individuality: "crabs she had to allow if Andrew really wanted to dissect them; of if Jasper believed that one could make soup from seaweed, one could not prevent it; or Rose's objects—shells, reeds, stones." She felt all her children gifted but "in quite different ways" (44).

The Ramsays' marital relationship further fleshes out Mrs. Ramsay's character. The clash of personalities at the beginning resounds throughout, coexisting, however, with a depicted solidity of the marriage. Here as with her children, Mrs. Ramsay's response subsumes complexity and sensitivity rather than shallow or frenetic enmeshment.

Mrs. Ramsay appears to have the "whole of the other sex under her protection." Towards her, they felt "trustful, childlike, reverential" (13). She pitied men, as though they "lacked something" (129). Admiration alternates with condescension. Mrs. Ramsay enjoys her husband's mind, feeling she "revered" no one more. She was not "good enough to tie his shoestrings." Nor did she wish in any sense to feel "finer" than her husband (61): "A great mind like his must be different in every way from ours" (108). His utterances "would make all the difference. He went to the heart of things" (143).

Though Mrs. Ramsay never intruded on her husband's privacy, he in his peremptory fashion, frequently demanded her attention. Seeking to be assured of his "genius," he wished to be "warmed and soothed" by his wife, his "barrenness made fertile, and all the rooms of the house made full of life" (59). Flashing her needles, the mother created drawing room and kitchen, "set them all aglow." Sitting "loosely, folding her son in her arm," Mrs. Ramsay braced herself and would "pour erect into the air a rain of energy, a column of spray, looking animated and alive" as though her energies were transformed into "force burning and illuminating." Into this "delicious fecundity, this fountain and spray of life, the fatal sterility of the male plunged itself, barren and bare" (58).

James felt all his mother's strength "flaring up to be drunk and quenched by the beak of brass . . . demanding sympathy" (59). Vaunting her ability to "surround and protect," she soon felt depleted and "spent" (60). Here the author's confusion concerning sexual and physical functions is highly discernible, equating male potency as she does, with sterility and attack, exaggerating the mother's victimization, endowing her with phallic qualities. Trying to convey the healing effect on the father of the mother's warmth, Woolf instead suggests a conjugal and sexual battle, her conception of her parents' marriage.

Feeling her husband in pursuing the "truth" distances her and others, an outrage of "human decency," Mrs. Ramsay "bent her head to let the pelt of jagged hail bespatter her unrebuked." To make amends, Mr. Ramsay offered to go to the Coast Guard for a weather report. At that moment, "there was nobody she reverenced more" (*TTL*, 51).

In her directness, Mrs. Ramsay indicated her husband might have written better books had he not married. Insisting he had no complaints, Mr. Ramsay—in the novel's sole instance of physical contact between the two—kissed her hand with an "intensity that brought the tears to her eyes." With delight, she contemplated her husband's strength and agility "though he was over 60", so "untamed and optimistic" (106–107). To Mrs. Ramsay, he appeared different from others; he would often sit at table as though "in a dream" (107).

Lily saw them at certain moments as "symbols of marriage", during which they joined that "unreal, but penetrating and exciting universe which is the world seen through the eyes of love" (73). Later, Lily revises her naive perception of the marriage.

Occasionally, Mr. Ramsay felt distanced or pained by his wife's remoteness. For example, viewing her sadness,[13] he might wish to "help" her, but she remained "aloof" from him "in her beauty." He would have withdrawn had she not "given him of her own free will what she knew he would never ask, and called to him and gone to him. For he wished, she knew to protect her" (100).

Yet Mr. Ramsay could be extraordinarily patronizing toward his wife; he might question her understanding of the book she was reading, exaggerating her "ignorance, her simplicity" (182). Her need to hide domestic matters, particularly financial expenditures for fear of incurring his wrath (62), this in full view of the children, proved humilitating for her. As husband emerged restored and renewed, Mrs. Ramsay seemed to collapse. Power struggles would ensue during which Mr. Ramsay sought verbal reassurances of his wife's love. Frequently, she refused such overtures, unable to express feelings as easily as he, though eventually she proffered her love in her own way; then he "knew that she loved him" (184-185).

Mrs. Ramsay's respect for her husband is shown in her tribute to the "admirable fabric of the masculine intelligence which ran up and down, crossed this way and that, like iron girders . . . upholding the world, so that she could trust herself to it utterly" (159); she discerned that her husband's feeling of failure had to do with his inordinate need for perfection. Perhaps she could not encompass both the frailties and presumed power of men; the whole effort of creating and flowing rested on her, she felt. Quite possibly, she was repelled by her husband's aging and was attracted to younger men, such as Paul Rayley.

Her moodiness more profound than her husband's, Mrs. Ramsay frequently felt "there was no treachery too base for the world to commit. No happiness lasted." She had no illusions (98). Life was seen in a negative vein as "terrible, hostile and quick to pounce on you. There were the eternal problems: suffering, death, the poor" (92). She felt herself a "wedged-shaped core of darkness, invisible to others, spreading, unfathomably deep"; occasionally "we rise to the surface and this is what you see us by" (*TTL*, 95-96).

Despite her depressive moods, Mrs. Ramsay shows recoverability and an awareness of alternative choices. Usually revived by her compassion for others or alerted to a particular sight or sound, she manifested then a creative, life-affirming, occasionally lyrical sense of her milieu.

Though Ernest and Ina Wolf's theoretical bent is to view Mrs. Ramsay's relationship with others as elusive or narcissistic enmeshments, the stream of consciousness method as Virginia Woolf uses it, in its multiple shifts of mood and nuances of thought and feeling, emanates a sense of seeming chaos, looseness, scatteredness, or flux. In this context, we are either moving freely in time within the consciousness of a single individual or moving from person to person at a single moment in time. Virginia Woolf addresses herself to the impingements of the moment, the confluence of past and present, depicting seemingly random thoughts and images which ultimately offer conflicting, layered aspects of a situation, simultaneously. These variables might, to the Wolfs, represent fleeting, shallow or inconstant involvement.

A studied tenuousness or evanescence of expression was one of Virginia Woolf's chief stylistic characteristics. No attempt was made to preserve the firm outline of chronological events; experience is frequently broken down into a series of rapidly dissolving impressions. Because of the allusion made to an early, traumatic love experience, Mrs. Ramsay might also be preoccupied with the transience of life, and therefore, with living in the moment, true of Julia Stephen, her prototype.

A tripartite novel, the first section of *To the Lighthouse* introduces us to the Ramsays and their guests, though predominantly offers multiple perspectives of Mrs. Ramsay. The second section consists of the author's poetic conception of the falling apart of the Ramsay family, initiated by Mrs. Ramsay's sudden death, followed by the deaths of their son Andrew from explosives in World War I and daughter Prue from an illness in childbirth. Woolf refers to the latter calamities as "drench of hail," "wind and destruction" (193), "floods," "gigantic chaos streaked with lightening" (202). This section Woolf finds her "most difficult abstract" piece of writing: "I have to give an empty house, no people's characters, the passage of time, all eyeless and featureless with nothing to cling to" (D3, Apr.18'26).

In the third section, 10 years later, Cam and James Ramsay, respectively, 17 and 16 at this phase of the family's life cycle, perhaps commensurate with Virginia and Adrian in late adolescence in 1899, feel intense alienation toward their father, vow to "fight tyranny to the death", though Cam is also aware of her father's concern and lovability. Finally, at the father's instigation, all three embark on the voyage, long postponed, to the lighthouse, the children going along hostilely, with James at the tiller. They hoped their father would be thwarted and the entire trip founder. On the boat, stories were told of "sailors pitting muscle and brain against the waves and wind." Mr. Ramsay "liked men to work like that and women to keep house and sit beside sleeping children indoors," though their men might be drowned in the storm (245). Cam felt pride in her father's adventurousness, when she was not remembering the pact with James. To a degree, the children, carrying parcels to the lighthouse, felt coerced by their father, taking part in rites he desired for his own well-being, in memory of the dead, though they were indeed intoxicated with the sea.

Watching his house recede in the distance, Mr. Ramsay muttered "we perished each alone" (247) and as he thought of his isolation and aging, added, "but I beneath a rougher sea" (248). Saturated with his misery and sorrow, a widower bereft and desolate, he reenacted a "little drama" wherein he, highly evocative of Leslie Stephen, imagined the exquisite pleasure of women's sympathy bestowed on him (248). Cam was torn between compassion for her father, the "suppliant," who seeing her consternation wished to soothe her, and adherence to the pact with brother, the "lawgiver" whom she considered "god-like."

Cam wished passionately to respond to her father, for "no one attracted her more; his hands were beautiful," as were "his feet,"[14] "voice," "words," "haste," "temper," "oddity," "passion," "remoteness." Still, Cam remembered his "crass blindness . . . which poisoned her childhood" and evoked bitter quarels so that even now she awakened at night "trembling with rage and remembered some command of his; some insolence; 'do this, do that,' his dominance" (253).

Yet her father as he worked in his study "was not vain nor a tyrant and did not wish to make you pity him." Seeing Cam reading a book, he gently asked whether he could in any way help (282). Virginia similarly visited her father as he worked in his study until "slowly he realized my presence. Rising he would go to the shelves, put the book back and very kindly ask me what I had made of it" (*SOTP*, 136).

James, based on Adrian Stephen, was incensed with his father's injustice, despotism, "making people do what they didn't want to do, cutting off their right to speak" (274). Nearing the lighthouse, James saw "the whitewashed rocks, the tower stark and straight, barred with black and white; he could even see washing spread on the rocks to dry" (276). In a moment of personal revelation he felt he could encompass the lighthouse of old, as soft, hazy, flowing—"the eye opening and shutting" (277)—as well as fortress-like and somewhat prosaic. He could learn to embrace both realms of reality, a reconciliation of opposites, one of Woolf's central themes.

III

Observing the Ramsay's trip to the lighthouse, Lily on shore, sought to resume her painting, trying to absorb the unassimilable changes that have been precipitated by the death of Mrs. Ramsay and by the passage of time. In Lily, admiration then devaluation of Mr. Ramsay parallels Mrs. Ramsay's vacillation regarding her husband. Lily views him as tyrannical and demanding, then redeemingly thinks he has a "fiery unworldliness, loves dogs and and his children" (40). Later, she repeats a similar dichotomy: "he is blind, deaf, and dumb to the ordinary . . . , but with an eye like an eagle's to the extraordinary" (107). Not minding his need of flattery, she detested his narrowness and remoteness. Basically, she seemed to fear his sexuality: "That man will be down on me in a minute", demanding something she could not give. (223). Blaming him for his wife's death, Lily, evoking Vanessa, felt Mr. Ramsay "never gave," only "took." Yet, "giving, giving, giving," Mrs. Ramsay died (223).

Lily felt an implicit demand on his part that she not go ahead with her work until she acquiesced to his need for sympathy and solace. Should she "surrender herself up to him entirely . . . before it swept her down in its flood?" (226) He inflicted the "immense pressure of his concentrated woe, his age, frailty, desolation" (228). Lily felt him a figure of "infinite pathos" (230).

When Lily casually imparted she liked his boots however, his "pall, draperies, infirmities" disappeared (229). Obviously, all he required was some degree of affirmation which his wife did not readily accord him. As the children emerged, ready for their trip, Lily felt a sudden emptiness at her previous callousness. Now, he was the "leader" preparing for his expedition. Though at first she saw him as a "lion seeking whom he could devour with his desperation and exaggeration," she witnessed his "sudden recovery[15] of vitality and interest in ordinary human beings (233)." He entered "another region as though shedding ambition and worry."

Woolf's intuitive description of Lily observing the Ramsays conveys the author's conception of the meaning to her, of her own creative process. Lily taking as springboard for her painting the Ramsays' personalities, idiosyncracies, and relationships in context of their surroundings, sees "all of this dancing up and down like a company of gnats, each separate but all marvellously controlled, in an invisible elastic net, in and about the branches of the pear tree." Then her thought which had "spun quicker and quicker, exploded of its own intensity." She felt "released" (40–41].

In her painting, Lily initially grappled with the aura of Mrs. Ramsay, her son James as a small boy, the house and garden on one side, the hedge by which Mr. Ramsay measured his pacing on the other side. Lily's objective, to connect the disparate masses with the awkward white space inbetween, maintaining the unity of the whole—evokes Woolf writing her novel, trying to fathom her relationship with her parents, theirs with each other, and with the children. Conspicuously omitted is the clash of emotions regarding the tight orbit of mother and son. To Lily, painting is a question of "lights and shadows," the "relations of masses." Objects of "universal veneration," mother and child might be reduced to a "purple shadow without irreverence. A light here required a shadow there" (81–82).

In Lily's perception, the interplay of "lines cutting across, slicing down," as well as the "mass of the hedge," seemed sharply etched as she painted the scene over and over in imagination through the years. Innumerable references to the "hedge," its intricacy, its darkness, and its "green caves of blue and browns" (234) suggest barrier, undergrowth, entanglement, psychic conflict.

As Lily raised her brush, it trembled in a "painful but exciting ecstasy" in the air. Since one stroke led to "innumerable risks, to frequent and irrevocable decisions," all that seemed simple in contemplation became in the doing inordinately complex. Lily now took the plunge: "with a curious physical sensation" as though urged forward and at the same time held back, she painted her "first, quick, decisive stroke". Achieving a "dancing rhythmical movement," she synchronized pauses and strokes (235). Covering her canvas with shaky brown lines which soon enclosed a "space," she felt catapulted "into the presence of this formidable, ancient enemy of hers, this truth, this reality, which emerged stark at the back of appearances" (236). Woolf seems to be saying the artist must thrust aside preconceived ideas and penetrate beyond surface reality.

Hesitating, Lily asked "why always be drawn out and haled away? Why not be left in peace?" Seeking the form she was after eventuated in a sense of perpetual struggle wherein she felt inevitably "worsted" (236). Before she gave up the "fluidity" of life for the intense absorption of painting, Lily felt naked; felt herself an "unborn soul, a soul reft of body." Imagining herself on some "windy pinnacle, exposed without protection to all the blasts of doubt" (237), she questioned her purpose. Without explicit guidelines, the artist must forge new terrain regarding which there is no certainty or predictable goal.

Confronting her, the canvas "protruded . . . , pressing on her eyeballs." Unexpectedly, precariously, she dipped among the blues and umbers, moving her brush back and forth, slowly and rhythmically. (237) Her hand "quivered with life"; the rhythm she acquired sustained her efforts. She found herself losing consciousness of outer things, her name, her personality, her appearance, those around her. Her mind excavated from its "depths," numerous "scenes, names, sayings, memories, and ideas," past and present, similar to a "fountain spurting over that glaring, hideously difficult white space," while she worked around it with greens and blues (238).

As she worked, Lily thought Mrs. Ramsay resolved her life into supreme simplicity, by combining disparate situations, making "something which survived," which affected one like a "work of art." Ruminating on the "meaning of life," Lily discovered there was no "great revelation," only "little daily miracles, illuminations, matches struck unexpectedly in the dark." Mrs. Ramsay would say "life stand still here . . . , making of the moment something permanent-this was of the nature of a revelation". In the midst of chaos Lilly felt Mrs. Ramsay superimposed meaning and "shape;" Lily attributed her insights to Mrs. Ramsay (240–241).[16]

Tackling the problem of space which persisted, Lily decided that however beautiful the surface, "beneath, the fabric must be clamped together with bolts of iron," referring here to the crucial role of form and structure. As though opening a door and finding a "high cathedral-like place, very dark, very solemn" (255), Lily as she painted sensed Mrs. Ramsay's beneficent presence next to her.

Frequently, Lily felt she was in imminent danger, as though she walked a "narrow plank, perfectly alone, over the sea" (256). As she applied the blue paint, she "tunnelled" her way further into the past, thought of Mrs. Ramsay bringing a young couple, Minta and Paul, together and how badly that worked out. She, Lily, felt immune, avoided marriage[17] or capitulation to Mrs. Ramsay's mania for pairing people.

Lily doubted that words could express the emotions of her body or describe the "emptiness" she frequently felt (265). Mrs. Ramsay's absence filled her body with a "hardness, a hollowness, a strain. To want and not to have, how that wrung the heart." Silently chiding Mrs. Ramsay for so cavalierly "returning" after having departed, Lily saw the "drawing-room steps, the frill of the chair inside, the puppy tumbling on the terrace, the whole wave and whisper of the garden" unexpectedly evolve into "curves and arabesques flourishing round a center of complete emptiness" (266).

Should Lily demand an explanation of why life was "so short, so inexplicable?" Possibly then "the space would fill; those empty flourishes would form into shape . . . ; Mrs. Ramsay would return" (268). Her anger diminished, Lily thought of Mrs. Ramsay placing a "wreath" to her forehead and going forth with a "companion," stepping with alacrity across the fields. Wherever Lily happened to be, that vision returned and consoled (270). As with Julia Stephen, Mrs. Ramsay might have had an early love and Lily sees Mrs. Ramsay rejoining him.

Watching the Ramsay boat, Lily thought of the meanings "distance" imposes on one's feelings and perceptions (284). Then, imagining she stood "up to the lips" in a watery substance, along with the Ramsays and all "sorts of waifs and strays of things besides," she wished to "move and float and sink in it" (286); she requires both involvement and distance in the pursuit of the aesthetic.

Unable now to recover that "razor edge of balance between two opposite forces," Lily wished to grasp "that very jar on the nerves, the thing itself before it has been made anything" (287). One got nowhere by urgency or pressure. Everything impinging on her this morning, seemed, as though happening for the first time. She felt Mrs. Ramsay "infallibly turned to the human race, making her nest in its heart" (292). Mrs. Ramsay's instinct was towards action, distressing to those who did not share it. No longer simplifying the Ramsay's relationship, which was "no monotony of bliss," what with Mrs. Ramsay's impatience and quickness, Mr. Ramsay's nervousness and complaints, Lily heard "doors slamming and blinds fluttering" all through the house, scenes in which Mr. Ramsay would "whizz his plate through the window" (296). The Ramsays resorted to long, uneasy silences which Mr. Ramsay was the first to break, trying to make up, until his wife finally responded to something in his tone and they would "have it out together" (297).[18] Often Mrs. Ramsay would be concerned about the effect of these marital struggles on her young daughter, Prue.

As she painted, Lily's faculties were in a "trance,[19] frozen over superficially, but moving underneath with extreme speed" (298). Feeling the old horror return of "wanting" and "not to have," she called out to Mrs. Ramsay. Her frustration became part of "ordinary experience": to feel simply "that's a chair; that's a table," and, concurrently, with her heightened perception, feel that it was a "miracle," or "ecstasy." In Lily's view, Mrs. Ramsay sat there "quite simply in the chair, flicked her needles to and fro, knitted her stocking, cast her shadow on the step" (300).[20]

Lily sensed the Ramsays had now reached the lighthouse and felt that whatever it was she wished to extend to Mr. Ramsay that morning, she had accomplished in her painting: "There it was her picture. Yes, with all its greens and blues, its lines running up and across, its attempt at something." Looking at the steps, she no longer saw Mrs. Ramsay. Then she looked at her canvas which seemed "blurred." With a "sudden intensity, as if she saw it clear for a second, she drew a line there, in the center. It was done, it was finished. I have had my vision" (309–310). Lily's "line" subsumes the integrating force of the lighthouse, symbol of longing and unattainability, goal now achieved.

Originally inspired by Mrs. Ramsay, the lighthouse trip suggests continuity with the mother, concomitant growth and maturation on the children's part and on Lily's, as well as a restructuring of the negative image of the father. On successful completion of the voyage, in his commendation of James' efforts, James' intense pleasure in hearing this—Mr. Ramsay redeems himself as a strong, parental image.

In identifying with Mrs. Ramsay's pattern of creating a "wholeness not there in life," in reconciling with Mr. Ramsay, Lily is free to finish her painting. Not merging but freedom to create and partially individuate is evidenced, though at the same time, Woolf conveys via Lily her own sense of deep loss concerning her mother's death inasmuch as her mother, she felt, had much to teach her. Via her painting, Lily has, like Woolf, become a creator and through her vision, Mrs. Ramsay and Julia Stephen are resurrected. At the end of the lighthouse trip, Lily combines her new perception of the father with the mother's complexity, in a more realistic grasp of the Ramsay marriage, and is thereby able to finish her painting. Woolf in writing *To the Lighthouse* is similarly taking a new look at her parents.

Acknowledging her mother's contribution to her creative process, previously attributed to her father, seemed a reparative act, though this did not gainsay Woolf's early imprinting of an ongoing sense of maternal deprivation exacerbated during adolescence by her mother's abandonment by death.

Feeling at one with the Ramsays and her surroundings, Lily thought she must be "in love with them all, in love with this world" (*TTL* 37). Similarly, Greenacre (1957), addressing herself to the psychological implications of the creative process beginning with the childhood of the artist, describes the child's or artist's "love affair with the world" (490), refers to an intense richness and empathy of response to form, color, rhythm, actually to all sense modalities and body states. She points to the artist's "fantasy" of a "collective audience" (490) as recipient of the artistic product which frequently modulates the effect of "critical situations involving individual object relationships" (491).

In this context, Mahler, et al (1975) who have written at length on early developmental processes in children, also describe the child's "love affair with the world" (70). With the development of cognition, learning to walk freely with upright posture, feeling "elated" and "exhilarated" on practicing, testing and mastering new skills and abilities, making ever new forays and discoveries in the "expanding world"—the child assumes a uniquely new vantage point, which Mahler equates with the child's "psychological birth" (71). When dissonances in integrated development occur during this pivotal period, the child may remain eternally conflicted between the wish for autonomy and the fear of re-engulfment or abandonment. Resolution of object constancy, identity formation and a delineated sense of self may prove a lifelong process.

Nothing is known concerning Lily's childhood, the reason she adopted the Ramsays or they her. But smitten and intertwined with them, their children, their home, their ambience, she was; she in a sense, sought as an adult to make up for what she lacked in childhood. In the Ramsays' home, "full of unrelated passions" (212), she felt free to follow her own bent, practice her art, in short to paint, more meaningful to her than any other pursuit. Like her progenitor, "nothing pleased her more than this sublime power, this heavenly gift, this silent stare" (24). Towards Mrs. Ramsay, she felt a gamut of emotions; her lament "to want and want and not to have" (266), echoes Woolf writing in a similar vein, in her diary, at an earlier time. Lily and Woolf wanting so badly evoke a sense of unassuaged insatiability. They see life as treacherous, like "a wave, which bore one up with it and threw one down with a dash on the beach" (73).

Lily's wish for intimacy with Mrs. Ramsay alternates with her desire to be solitary. Disagreeing with Mrs. Ramsay who felt "all must marry," Lily was not "made" for marriage (77), looked forward to her "loneliness" (39). She felt love wondrous, beautiful, and necessary, yet the "stupidest and most barbaric of human passions." When Paul Rayley's presumed indifference "scorched" her, she felt she need never marry and undergo that "degradation," "horror," "cruelty," "unscrupulosity," or feel exposed to those "fangs" (154).

Woolf's emotional state is not a simple assimilation of her mother's maladies or "narcissistic defects," but an emergent of her total personality as it evolved in her family setting. Woolf's grief, confusion, and simultaneous sense of liberation and abandonment due to the death of her mother were superimposed on a substrate of each exclusion from the maternal orbit and an already imprinted vulnerability of self.

Julia Stephen's death created a severe disruption of the Stephens' family cohesiveness and interfered with Virginia's identification process during adolescence. Virginia felt loss of support and estrangement regarding her father, who she felt was extraordinarily prone to dramatizing his plight, giving little to his children at this time, though he made up for it later on as Mr. Ramsay did. Towards her father in memoir and in fiction, Virginia shows sharp oscillations of love and hate, whereas the ambivalence regarding her mother emerges indirectly, in innuendo or metaphoric elaboration. Virginia clung to her "love affair with the world" which Greenacre describes as an "obligatory condition" in the development of the "creatively gifted," one of intense empathy of response to sensations of "invigoration, inspiration and awe." Difficulties in development arose for Virginia in maintaining integrated images of self and other, in resolving separation, individuation and identity issues, leading to a constant search for romanticized, maternal surrogates.

In *To the Lighthouse*, Woolf surrounds her fictional family with the exalted island of her childhood, with the sea, in its inexorable change, rhythm, movement, and sound, promulgated as a cosmic, elemental, awesome, sexual, alternatively creative, and destructive force. Waves are anthropomorphized as "rolling, gambolling and slapping the rocks as if they were wild creatures who were perfectly free, who tossed and tumbled and sported like this forever."

At first, Mrs. Ramsay views waves as protective: "the monotonous fall of the waves on the beach for the most part beat a measured and soothing tattoo to her thoughts." She repeated, as she sat with her children the words of an old children's song: "I am guarding you, I am your support." Then unexpectedly, treacherously, the waves offered no such "kindly meaning, but like a ghostly roll of drums, remorselessly beat the measure of life, made one think of the destruction of the island and its engulfment in the sea" (27–28).

Throughout, images of navigation and sailing suggest Mr. Ramsay's self-image as mariner and commander of the voyage to the lighthouse; he fantasizes the threat of storm and shipwreck, himself a castaway.[21] His wife's perception of him, as a "stake driven into the bed of a channel upon which the gulls perch and the waves beat," seems opposed to his feeling that the "sea eats the ground" he stands on, he like a "desolate sea bird, alone" (68–69).

Diabolically, the bottom of the sea proves welcoming when one is depleted, as fantasized by Mrs. Ramsay who at the same time, suicidally identifies with a weary sailor who "thinks had the ship sunk, he would have whirled round and round and found rest on the floor of the sea" (127). When thinking of love or marriage, Lily felt a "head-long desire to throw herself off the cliff and be drowned looking for a pearl brooch on a beach" (261).

Lily's ruminations are close to Woolf's inner scenario, in which she never gives up the option of taking her life, in this way exerting control over death. This alternates with the sea's seminal effect on the creative process: "these waters were unfathomably deep. Into them had spilled so many lives, the Ramsays, the children; some common feeling held the whole" (286).

Woolf is persistently preoccupied with watery metaphors. Upset about aging and an inappropriate comment by Clive, she comments: "Time was when I should have ended the evening fast stuck in black despair, gone to bed like a diver with pursed lips shooting into oblivion" (D3, Jul.20'25). Comparing herself to Vita who is in "full sail on the high tides," Woolf is merely "coasting down back waters." Feeling a failure as a woman, regretting her childlessness, she describes a "painful wave swelling about her heart—tossing me up" (D3, Sept.15'26). She treasures her "plunge into deep waters . . . the assault of truth" (D3, Sept.28'26).

Connected with the sea, the metaphor of light and lighthouse provides a further source of imagery, giving the novel central structure. Though painfully penetrating, the light in its beneficence and radiance makes for sensory richness and gratification. Mrs. Ramsay, looking at the lighthouse sees "its steady light, the pitiless, the remorseless, which was so much her yet so little her, which had her at its beck and call" (99).

She seemed "hypnotized" as though its fingers stroked some "sealed vessel in her brain whose bursting would flood her with delight," knew "happiness" which "silvered the rough waves . . . as daylight faded, and the blue went out of the sea and it rolled in waves of pure lemon which curved and swelled and broke upon the beach"; the "ecstasy burst in her eyes, waves of pure delight raced over the floor of her mind and she felt it is enough" (99-100). Woolf permits in this lyrical passage in response to the nonhuman environment, a sensual, even sexual flow[22] otherwise missing in her characterizations.

In the celebrated scene describing the family at dinner, Woolf writes: "inside the room seemed to be order and dry land; there, outside, a reflection in which things wavered and vanished, waterily. They were all conscious of making a party together in a hollow, on an island; had their common cause in that fluidity out there" (147).

Sharply etched in graphic, symbolic images, Mrs. Ramsay is a powerful presence: sitting by the window, suggestive of the home's enclosure and its more extended scope; knitting a "reddish-brown, hairy stocking,"[23] which pointed to her compassionateness; reading fairy tales to her children or ministering to them at bedtime, linked with intimate, maternal rituals; presiding over her candlelit dinner, bringing the disparate group together. Demeter-like inasmuch as she participates in marriage and harvest ceremonies, she is also portrayed as at times "short-sighted," "malicious," "willful," or "commanding." Intertwined with the central image of "lighthouse," Mrs. Ramsay emerges as a powerful, phallic, mother-figure.

In Mrs. Ramsay's meddling in the lives of others, Lily felt she "led her victims to the altar." We are told in serving her dinner, Mrs. Ramsay "hovered like a hawk suspended" (157), a rather predatory image. In Lily's perception, Mrs. Ramsay occasionally "wore" the shape of a "dome," evoking a cathedral-like vision or a protective carapace. Like a bee, Lily "haunted the dome-shaped hives with their murmurs and stirrings" (80). Though at times distant, unattainable, interfering or sharp, Mrs. Ramsay, center of a humming, swarming universe, is crucial for Lily's socialization. Not particularly feminine, Mrs. Ramsay was decidedly maternal, and richly presided over her household.

Mrs. Ramsay emerges within the highly textured network of subjective and behavioral processes depicted in the novel[24] as a conflicted, enigmatic, somewhat abstract, mythical being. Her death enshrouded in mystery and manipulated by artistic prerogative, may have been precipitated by her sacrificial deference to her husband's repeated demands which we are told deplete her; or by her desire to rejoin a lost love. Throughout Woolf shows considerable power of conscious and unconscious psychological perception in her delineation of the ambiguities, conflicts and divisions within Mrs. Ramsay's personality.

To the Lighthouse underscores Lily-Virginia's incessant revaluation of mother- and father-images, the need despite Mrs. Ramsay's imperfections, for her embrace or example, in addition to the need to identify with aspects of her feminine role; the turn to father after mother's death, both extolling and damning him. His controlling dependency and overrational strictures notwithstanding, he is in his way a paternal force, preserving continuity with the mother's more poetic sensibilities.

Lily's irresolution regarding sexual identification is suggested in her repudiation of love and marriage, at least for herself, though she does not eschew friendship with men. For her, the role of artist is of central concern. Though probing deeply on some levels, Woolf is unwilling to fully explore the wellsprings of her own or Lily's inner being.

Evaluations of Mrs. Ramsay, an archetypal figure, have been profuse, for the most part endowing her with proportions of earth mother. Fleishman accords her "queenly stature" and "royalty of form" (124). According to Marder, the home in *To the Lighthouse* "may take on the sanctity of a shrine in which the mother-priestess celebrates a communion, uniting the members of the family circle by means of a mystical life force." He claims Mrs. Ramsay connects both the "conventions of civilized life and the primal rhythms that underlie all things" (45–46).

Skeptical of Mrs. Ramsay's idealization, other critics feel she is controlling, domineering, abrasive, austere, isolated, or remote; or that she seeks to ingratiate herself via her beneficent deeds. Leaska suggests, despite Mrs. Ramsay's prowess in bringing people together, she is unable to express "deep feelings or open herself spontaneously in anger, hurt or love" (Leaska, 1977a, 124).

Lilienfeld notes that the quality of the Ramsay "marriage compromise" limits growth, frustrates husband and wife, does not make for "mature intellectual interchange." Had Mr. Ramsay acknowledged his wife's perceptiveness, Lilienfeld believes he might have shared with her his anxieties about his work. If Mrs. Ramsay had found "self-fulfillment" outside her home, she would not have invited her husband's dependency (Lilienfeld, 162). Actually, Julia Stephen pursued interests outside her family but this alone did not make for harmony. It is of note that in *To the Lighthouse*, Woolf managed to have the mother's activities center on husband and children, much more than was the case in the Stephen household.

In *To the Lighthouse*, Mrs. Ramsay emerges as heroic but flawed. Lily felt "one wanted 50 pairs of eyes to see with" and these "not enough to get round that one woman with" (294). Woolf's view of Mrs. Ramsay depicts her awareness of the needs of each of the children though she clearly favors her youngest son. We also learn Mrs. Ramsay is not keen on having her children grow up, which might not augur well for their autonomy. Of course her depression and occasional withdrawal affect children and husband, though Woolf comments only on Mrs. Ramsay's distancing of husband. When not "bitter and black," Mrs. Ramsay plunges into life, has a gift for savoring the moment. Giving to others, helping the infirm and needy, marrying people off, preoccupy her. She admits she achieves a sense of control in so doing.

Mrs. Ramsay admired her husband, even revered his achievements, but she feels herself intellectually inadequate. Yet, since she says she "prefers boobies to clever men who wrote dissertations" (85), how does that leave room for her husband? His need for her support inordinately depletes her, though many years later after her death, when Lily briefly affirms Mr. Ramsay's need for approval, he does not intrude further, goes his own way. Mrs. Ramsay resents her husband's rational attitudes but at times seems to overreact, feeling the "drench of dirty water" (51) defiling her, suggesting her need to feel victimized.

Woolf's portrait of Mrs. Ramsay's gifts as housekeeper, mother and wife is fairly authentic of her mother, except that Julia Stephen was not as attentive to her children as Mrs. Ramsay was; of course in life this might not be possible in a household with eight children. She was a practical nurse, frequently absented herself from home; leaving husband and children, she was on a deeper level more attached to her mother and dead husband. Duckworth might have been the romantic father she never had. Perhaps Julia left home, though for shorter periods, just as her mother left her husband. Julia closely identified with her mother in her condescension toward men; because of the extended absence of her father, Julia also tended at times to be overly worshipful towards father-figures. In this vein, Woolf perceptively describes Mrs. Ramsay as finding her husband both "venerable and laughable." Though Woolf's portrayal of her father in guise of Mr. Ramsay might show evidence of caricature, she seemed more balanced in *To the Lighthouse*, where she depicts the mutual tensions of husband and wife, as compared to her predominantly negative portrayal of father in the early version of *A Sketch of the Past*.

Forty-five when *To the Lighthouse* was completed, Woolf claimed she ceased thinking about her parents, as though writing her novel was a form of self-analysis. Her father re-emerged in her thoughts as a contemporary, she claimed, presumably no longer the domestic tyrant of her adolescence. Had he lived, she surmised, she would not be a writer; "his life would have entirely ended mine" (D3, Nov.28'28). She would not feel as free to write about her family or feel as free to project her fantasies.

The ambivalence shown her parents continued, reemerging in her later novel, *The Years*, where she dealt with the theme of sacrificing one's youth in deference to the father; nor did Woolf essentially resolve her obsession with her mother. Despite the predominantly integrating impact of her writing, the immersion in artistic reconstructions of her family evoked painful anxieties, conveyed the inexorableness of personal losses. Conflicts concerning unresolved issues of mourning remained dormant. Grief stricken and enraged regarding Mrs. Ramsay's "desertion," Lily Briscoe was in touch with emotions Woolf found she could not herself directly face, concerning her mother's life and death.

XI "Now a thousand hints and mysteries became plain to her that were primarily hidden—the obscurity which divides the sexes"—*Orlando: A Biography*

I

Woolf's turmoil in 1926 emerged not so much from completing *To the Lighthouse* as alleged, but from the emotional oscillations in relation to Vita, the negative reverberations in Woolf's marriage, the competitive interactions with Vanessa. Vita's interest in others and her frequent unavailability mobilized Woolf's masculine strivings, the desire to stir up their somewhat languishing relationship, as she promulgated her next novel, *Orlando*.

Necessitating an intense scrutiny of Vita's life as well as psyche, writing *Orlando* concomitantly involved Woolf's close identification with Vita, in effect placing herself in Vita's skin, learning what it felt like to masquerade as a man.

Although Woolf enjoys her fame she also feels "more desperate . . . as the river shoots to Niagara—my new vision of death; active, positive, like all the rest, exciting; and of great importance—as an experience" (D3, Nov.23'26). Endowed with complex overtones, this death threat, relegated to her diary, has an intellectualized, poeticized as well as tantrumy quality. We learn Vita is planning another trip to Persia and Leonard is apparently finding the relationship between Vita and Virginia a "bore."

Woolf is haunted by some "semi-mystic, very profound life of a woman," eventually Orlando, where "time shall be utterly obliterated (D3, Nov.23'26). Observing Vita "stalking in her Turkish dress . . . like some tall sailing ship, a covey of noble English life: dogs walloping, children crowding and a cart bringing wood to be sawn," Woolf became aware this ritual was part of an endless cycle. Vita's ancestors too

167

tramped on the snow with their dogs running next to them so that the "centuries seemed lit up, the past experessive, articulate . . . ." (D3, Jan.23'27). After her tour of Vita's estate at Knole, Woolf is further stimulated to write her book concerning Vita's life.

Bereft by Vanessa's departure for the south of France to nurse an ailing Duncan, Woolf longs for Vita, also abroad, who is "so fruity, so rich" (L3, Feb.5'27). Voicing in her diary the excitement and surge of sexuality concerning her intended book on Vita—Woolf refers to that "extraordinary exhilaration, that ardor and lust of creation" (D3, Feb.28'27).

Upset "sentimentally and partly from vanity" in not hearing from Vita, Woolf nevertheless records her conception of a new work called "The Jessamy Brides," about two women who are poor, live at the top of a house: "Sapphism is to be suggested." Apparently "satire is to be the main note . . . and wildness. The Ladies are to have Constantinople in view. Dreams of golden domes. My own lyric vein is to be satirized. Everything mocked . . ." (D3, Mar.14'27).

Writing Vanessa how "odd" that the "flowers of female youth will die with their buds unopened" Woolf relates a dream wherein Dora Carrington[1] asked Duncan to help her conceive a child which he obligingly agreed to do (L3, Apr.14'27). Woolf's persistent desire for a child, perhaps her wish to share Vanessa's lover is contained in the dream, as well as in the regret she might never have her "buds" opened. Yet in her next letter to her sister she conveys that she distrusts the "maternal passion"; that "motherhood is more destructive and limiting than marriage" (L3, Apr.2'27), evidencing a by now predictable ebb and flow of feelings regarding childbearing and maternity, her books an alternative offering.

Writing an article, "Poetry, Fiction and the Future," to be delivered at Oxford, Woolf feels "flooded with ideas" (D3, May11'27); the positive reviews of her novel, *To the Lighthouse* also contribute to her elation at this time.

Responding to Vita's congratulatory letter regarding *To the Lighthouse*, Woolf refers to her father, prototype for Mr. Ramsay, as an "adorable man, somehow tremendous," indicating she was "more like him than her mother" (L3, May13'27). Also enthusiastic about *To the Lighthouse*, Vanessa considers it a "sublime, almost upsetting spectacle, an amazing portrait of mother," Virginia a supreme "portrait painter"; Vanessa has "lived in it, found the rising of the dead almost painful" (D3, May16'27). Responding to her sister, Woolf told Vanessa she, to a large extent, inspired Mrs. Ramsay. To Roger Fry's question concerning the symbolism of the lighthouse, Woolf indicated she meant "nothing" by it. She expected it to be a repository of her readers' emotions. Writing "remains a complete mystery" to her (L3, May27'27).

To the Lighthouse a marked success, Woolf is an established writer: "they don't laugh at me any longer." Yet jealousy regarding the presentation of the Hawthornden Prize to Vita for the best literary production of 1926 for her poem "The Land" has sparked Woolf's "sudden and very sharp" headache. Woolf considered the selection committee philistine, felt there was "no one, full-grown mind among us. In truth, it was the thick, dull middle class of letters that met; not the aristocracy" (D3, Jun.18'27).

Was Vita deflecting the attention and feedback Woolf craved at this point regarding To the Lighthouse; cramping her style? Vita's poetry was distinctly lightweight, Woolf felt, although the critics were laudatory. Woolf could not take Vita's interest in poetry seriously, feeling Vita never "breaks fresh ground." Rather, she is a "conventional writer, lacks some cutting edge . . . , some invaluable idiosyncracy, intensity, for which I would not have all the sons in the world" (D3, Jul.4'27).

This does not impede Woolf's determined sexual pursuit of Vita: "Bad, wicked beast" she writes, "to think of sporting with oysters, lethargic, glucous lipped, lewd, lascivious . . . ; your oyster has been in tears on the telephone. You only be a careful dolphin in your gambolling or you'll find Virginia's soft crevices lined with hooks" (L3, Jul.4'27). Continuing her amatory tone: "I like your energy. I love your legs. I long to see you." (L3, Aug.22'27). Provoked by Vita's affairs with others, Woolf seeks to make Vita jealous in turn, concerning the amorous letters she (Virginia) receives from Philip Morrell.

During this dense, emotional interplay, Virginia and Leonard quarrel and make up, although she is again cranky about Vita's split affections: "If Dotty's yours I'm not. It is too hot to argue and I'm too depressed" (L3, Sept.2'27).

Woolf projects her "grand historical picture," gestating for a long period, concerning the "outlines" of all her friends wherein "Vita should be Orlando,[2] a young nobleman" (D3, Sept.20'27). The book would be a "biography beginning in the year 1500 and continuing to the present day . . . , with a changeover from one sex to another" (D3, Oct.5'27). At a party at the Keynes', Woolf's main topic of conversation proved to be a newspaper story concerning a woman who changed sex (Bell, v.2, 132) which seems consonant with the theme of Orlando.

Asking Vita how she would feel should Orlando turn out "to be you and the lusts of your flesh and the lure of your mind (heart you have none)"—Woolf learned Vita would not be displeased (L3, Oct.9'27). Never had Woolf desired to see Vita more: "I want to see you in the

lamplight in your emeralds; just to sit and look at you and get you to talk
—is it true you love giving pain," she ingenuously asked Vita.

Woolf's importunate wooing of Vita also seemed stimulated by
Vita's involvement with Mary Campbell. Reproaching Vita for "muddl-
ing" her life, Woolf remonstrates a bit blackmailingly: "if you've given
yourself to Campbell, I'll have no more to do with you and so it shall be
written plainly for all the world to read in *Orlando*" (L3, Oct.13'27). A
sordid denouement ensued when Mary's husband discovered his wife's
affair with Vita and threatened to kill Mary.

Questioning Vita regarding her prolonged love affair with Violet
Trefusius with whom she disguised herself as a man, their initial attraction, their quarrels, as well as Vita's heterosexual relationships before
her marriage—Woolf now feels in the "thick of the greatest rapture"
known to her. She is writing in a "mock style very clear and plain," so it
will be properly understood, though the "balance between truth and fantasy must be careful" (D3, Oct.22'27).

At the annual holiday festivities with the Bells, Woolf thought of her
"insatiable desire" to write something before she dies: this "ravaging
sense of the shortness and feverishness of life makes me cling like a man
on a rock to my one anchor." She no longer thinks she would like the
"physicalness of having children" of her own, can instead "dramatize"
herself as a parent (D3, Dec.20'27).

Comparing herself with Vanessa's maternal state Woolf finds herself
diminished, her sister by far the "largest, most humane of the two" of
them, thinks of her now with an "admiration that has no envy in it",
with some semblance of the "old childish feeling we were in league
together against the world; and how proud I am of her triumphant winning of all our battles" . . . , as Vanessa forges ahead, "past the goal
with her children round her" (D3, Dec.22'27).

With Vanessa and her menage in southern France, Woolf writes:
"God, how I miss you—there's nobody to chatter with and I miss
Angelica who I find essential to my pleasure, and I miss Duncan who I
adore" (L3, Jan.19'28).

Torpid and in bed with headache, feeling keenly the separation from
Vita as well, Woolf is "hacking" away at the last chapter of *Orlando*:
"one gets bored—one whips oneself up" (D3, Feb.11'28). From Vita
who has left for an extended trip to Germany she asks for a "practical
demonstration in the art of love." Does Vita think Virginia knows her
"intimately"; does she know Virginia feels like a "moth with heavy
scarlet eyes and a soft cape of down, a moth about to settle in a sweet
bush—would it were, ah but that's improper" (L3, Mar.6'28).

Woolf completed *Orlando*, although the book requires revision. She feels "serene, accomplished," the novel a "joke and yet gay and quick reading, a writer's holiday" (D3, Mar.18'28). Rather anxiously, she writes Vita: "Will my feelings for you be changed? I've lived in you all these months. Coming out, what are you really like? Do you exist? Have I made you up?" (L3, Mar.20'28). Vacationing in France, Virginia describes Vita as a "promiscuous brute" who "goes with any girl from an Inn" (L3, Apr.17'28). During this time, she receives the Prix Femina Vie Heureuse for *To the Lighthouse*.

Back in England, feeling abandoned by Vanessa's excessively prolonged stay in France, Woolf is frantic, writes Vanessa that Angelica is "essential" to her, and "an awful spurious maternal feeling" has overcome her. Rather insensitively she tells Vanessa, a doting mother, not to permit her son, Julian, to become like his father, in his (Clive's) "twitching persistent uneasiness—he takes his poems a little too much to heart as Clive does his derision, at the hands of the great Stephen family." Her incestuous strivings intact, Woolf tells Vanessa to kiss Duncan for her, adding "I often wonder how we should have done married" (L3, Apr.29'28).

Fame she finds "vulgar and a nuisance. It means nothing and yet takes one's time" (D3, May 4'28). Thanking Vanessa for the photographs of Angelica who posed for portraits of Sasha, sweetheart of Orlando, Woolf suggests Angelica looks too young; then she indicates she will ask Vita who does not want to be "accused of raping the underaged" to look at them, inappropriately adding, she too "shall rape Angelica one of these days" (L3, May12'28). Some weeks later, she writes Vanessa she feels "barren and dry"; when Vanessa is away for too long, Woolf goes "gadding wherever she is asked" and ends in a "rage of misery against my kind" (L3, May25'28).

Considering *Orlando* unequal, brilliant now and then, Woolf feels Leonard regards it more seriously than she expected. He perceives *Orlando* as in some sense better than *To the Lighthouse*, concerned with more interesting matters; feels it is generally more life-oriented, covers a larger canvas, and, in addition, thinks it highly original. Apparently Woolf began it as a "joke," then found herself going on with it "seriously" (D3, May31'28).

Rather unconscious of her hostility, she writes Vita: "what a bore Orlando is—I'm so tired of him" (L3, Jun.17'28). Perhaps she is weary of Vita and her flamboyant personality, although this may not as yet have entered awareness; the unconscious purpose of writing a novel about someone she thought she was in love with was in effect to quell the passion.

In her diary she writes she is "so sick of Orlando," she can neither read nor write. She hates her own volubility, her inability to act: why be "always spouting words?" Is she also saying the writing of *Orlando* was merely an intellectual exercise and she no closer to Vita: "This is the worst time of all. It makes me suicidal. Nothing seems left to do. All seems insipid and worthless." Not in black despair or literally suicidal, Woolf's emotionally charged project is finished and she at loose ends. She needs refueling and feels ready to go adventuring on the "stream of other people's lives" (D3, Jun.20'28).

Coming to her rescue, as it were, her sister is back: "My earth is watered again. I go back to the words of one syllable; feel come over me the feathery change; as if my physical body put on some sort of comfortable skin." Vanessa is a "necessity: I run to her as the wallaby runs to the old kangaroo" (D3, Jun.20'28).

Regarding her relationship with Vita, a hiatus has taken place, the "gnawing down of strata in a friendship" wherein "one passes unconsciously to different terms" (D3, Jul.7'28). A month later she feels the deceives herself in thinking she matters to other people; she no longer wants children since "ideas possess" her. She cannot tolerate interruptions or the "slow heaviness of physical life," and she is not fond of "people's bodies." As she grows older, she seeks the "marrow, the essence" (D3, Aug.8'28).

Is Woolf's repugnance regarding the physical realm due to diminution of her erotic relationship with Vita; is she turning towards a more spiritualized or intellectualized level of experience? Publication of *Orlando* was accompanied by considerable relief that Vita was not hurt or angry (L3, Oct.12'28).

II

Lytton's suggestion that Woolf write "something wilder and more fantastic," a framework that might be suggestive of *Tristam Shandy*, perhaps proved the intellectual impetus for the book. The notion of Vita's husband, Harold Nicolson, a biographer, that the "biographic form will be given to fiction, the fictional form to biography" concurred with Woolf's predilection at this time. Woolf regarded *Orlando: A Biography* a gigantic spoof, jest, fantasy, lark. Despite its apparent lightness of tone, the novel is concerned with the creative process, the experience of psychological time, issues of personal and sexual identity, and sexual inequality.

Though Woolf considered life for both sexes "arduous; a perpetual struggle' demanding "gigantic courage, strength and confidence in oneself", she in asking how one acquired this "invaluable" quality, responds; "by thinking that people are inferior to oneself . . . by thinking one has some innate superiority" (*Room*, 35). Debunking the usual distinctions between masculinity and femininity in *Orlando*, Woolf sought to rescue women from anonymity, obscurity, discrimination. Two papers on "Women and Fiction"[3] delivered at Cambridge October 11 and October 20, 1928, at the time of *Orlando*'s publication, expanded and published one year later as *A Room of One's Own* (D3, Oct.24'29), suggest the artist must transcend the meaninglessness of sexual classification, which stereotype men as aggressive, rational, tough-minded; women as passive, intuitive, sympathetic. Synchronizing masculine and feminine, the mind is "fully fertilized, uses all its faculties, is resonant and porous, transmits emotions without impediment, is naturally creative, incandescent and undivided" (*Room*, 102). Woolf hoped her novel would express this androgynous vision.

On Woolf's obtaining Vita's approval for *Orlando*, considerable contact, numerous visits, interviews, photographs followed. Woolf worried lest Vita recoil from their friendship, though Vita reassured her she was infinitely flattered. Though narcissistically gratifying to both, the enormous intellectual and emotional enterprise of producing the novel gradually modulated their intimacy at this point. The portrait of Orlando is, of course, permeated with satiric thrusts at Vita, for example, the humorous enumeration of endless lists of his possessions, and in doing so, caricaturing the seamlessness of Vita's writings, the style of her pastoral poem "The Land" and its sententious evocations of nature— barbs which Vita could hardly fail to notice.

Embracing Vita's personal experiences, her gypsy and Sackville-West backgrounds, *Orlando* begins in the sixteenth century when the hero is an aspiring poet of sixteen. In the eighteenth century, he experiences a change of sex from masculine to feminine at age 30. Finally, the novel extends to the author's and Vita's "present time," Orlando a famous writer at this point.

The love affair between Woolf and Vita proved the personal springboard for Orlando. Woolf was mesmerized by Vita's personality, adventures, lesbianism, transvestism, sexual appetite. She embarked on the book to revive the relationship with Vita, more specifically to aggressively wrest her from her new lovers.

Imaginative, picaresque in style and audacious in its use of time, the novel is underlyingly a reflection and re-examination of the author's sexual ambivalence, the shifting roles she assumed in the relationship with Vita.

Orlando is named Treasurer and Steward during Queen Elizabeth's visit to Knole.[4] More than in any of Woolf's novels, the lovemaking between Orlando and Sasha,[5] a Russian princess, is described in sensuous detail. Orlando was ultimately betrayed by Sasha and subsequently exiled by the Court.

Entering a period of solitude, then of prolonged sleep, a state not unlike amnesia, Orlando became melancholic, preoccupied with death. Still unable to relinquish Sasha, a passion for literature and fame seized Orlando and he wrote prodigiously. Then, disillusioned with poets, love, ambition, literature, he burnt all his writings except for "The Oak Tree." Eventually, he was appointed England's ambassador to Turkey.

Spending the night with a gypsy woman after a day of rioting at the Embassy, he was found next day with a deed of marriage to Rosina Pepita,[6] a dancer. Following seven days of "trance" Orlando finds he is female[7] except that he "remained precisely as he had been" (138). Wearing Turkish coat and trousers, Orlando maintained the desired sexual ambiguity, vacillated between man and woman, decided to repudiate "martial ambition, love of power" as well as "all the other manly desires" so she can enjoy "contemplation, solitude, love" (160).

Literally throwing herself at Orlando, the Archduchess Harriet is also revealed as male. Throughout, sexual identity defies appearance.

Now a woman, "it was still a woman she [Orlando] loved" (161), which quickened and deepened the emotions she had as a man, "for now a thousand hints and mysteries became plain to her, that were then dark", namely, the "obscurity which divides the sexes and lets linger innumerable impurities in its gloom" (161). Orlando's predilection for sexual disguises, her walks through London in male garb, seemed stimulated by Vita's experience, perhaps reflected Woolf's own sexual uncertainties and yearnings.

Dwelling on the similarities of male and female and their intermixture, noting that vacillation from one sex to the other occurs in each individual, the author underscores the deception of clothing that reflects "male or female-likeness . . . , while underneath, the sex is the very opposite of what it is above" (189).

Woolf seems confused, oblivious to the mysteries "underneath," denying or negating sexual and genital distinctions. Though masculine-feminine are psychologically ambiguous concepts, the male penetrates in the heterosexual situation. However active the woman, he has the thrusting, inseminating organ. Gender is crucial. Woolf tells us archly, however, that blending of male and female, "one being uppermost and then the other'', lent Orlando's "conduct an unexpected turn. Whether then Orlando was man or woman, it is difficult to say and cannot now be decided'' (190).

Turning to "men of genius,'' Orlando discovered they were much like other people (208). She enjoyed the company of her own sex, yet continued to change from female to male clothing, manifesting little difficulty in sustaining the different roles. Rather, the pleasures of life were thereby increased and experiences multiplied.

With the demise of the eighteenth century, Orlando rediscovered her poem "The Oak Tree,'' begun two centuries earlier. Perceiving how little she had changed, she longed to finish the poem but found she could not, so obsessed was she with the desire to find a husband. Ultimately she met and married Marmaduke Bonthrop Shelmerdine in order to comply with the "spirit of the age'', that is, the custom of the Victorian period, which required that she as a woman must marry and raise a family (252). She now felt free to write, which she did, torrentially. Wishing to communicate with others, above all, to be published, she recognized that poetry is a "voice answering a voice.''

Thinking her husband chivalrous, passionate, and melancholy, she also admired the determination accompanying his "wild, dark-plumed name,'' a name which had in her mind, the "steel blue gleam of rooks' wings'' (251). Both recognized in the other aspects of the opposite sex and felt considerable rapport. Marmaduke was pleased Orlando could be as "tolerant and freespoken'' (258) as a man. Orlando was surprised that Marmaduke's life was predominantly spent in voyaging around Cape Horn in the "teeth of a gale'' (252), he sometimes the sole survivor, the theme of mariner evocative of Mr. Ramsay in *To the Lighthouse*.

Orlando mockingly asked "when one's husband was always sailing around Cape Horn, was it marriage? If one liked him, was it marriage? If one liked other people, was it marriage? And if one still wished more than anything in the world to write poetry, was it marriage? (264).

Orlando felt she neither had to oppose the "spirit of the age'' or give obeisance to it, but rather was part of it, could remain "herself'' (266). Here the author engages in a mock, philosophical-poetical recitation concerning the meaning of life:

One's mind begins tossing up a question or two. Life, life what art thou? Let us go then exploring when all are adoring the plum blossom and the bee. What's life we ask . . . ; Life, Life, Life[8] cries the bird as though he had heard and knew precisely what we meant by this bothering, prying habit of ours of asking questions. (270)

The author ends her exuberant quest by deciding "we don't know" life's meaning (271).

In search of human companionship, Orlando journeys to London and there meets Nick Greene,[9] an old friend from Elizabethan days, now the most prestigious literary critic of the Victorian period. Greene regaled her with mundane gossip concerning the literary great, whereas Orlando regarded literature as something "wild as the wind, hot as fire, swift as lightning; something errant, incalculable, abrupt" (280).

Not articles by Greene on John Donne assume importance, thought Orlando, but something "useless, sudden, violent; something that costs a life; red, blue, purple; a spirit; a splash; like those hyacinths; free from taint, dependence, soilure of humanity or care for one's kind; something rash, ridiculous," perhaps her husband (287). Not long after, Orlando had a son.

It is now the "present moment," October 11, 1928. Shopping at a department store, Orlando encounters an obese, blowsy Sasha. We are regaled with: "Nothing is any longer one thing. Some of us are not yet born though they go through the forms of life; others are hundreds of years old though they call themselves 36" (305). Nor could anything be "seen whole or read from beginning to end" (307).

This leads to the discourse on our multiple selves, "those selves of which we are built up, one on top of another, as plates are piled on a waiter's hand, have attachments elsewhere, sympathies, little constitutions and rights of their own" (308). Each multiplies from his own experience the "different terms which his different selves have made." Orlando too had an infinite variety of selves (many thousands) to embrace: the young man who fell in love with Sasha, the soldier, the ambassador, the courtier, the gypsy, the girl in love with life, the patroness of letters—all were different and Orlando could "call upon" any of them (309).

Frequently, the multiplicity of selves simply refers to profusion of traits, interests, preferences, likes, dislikes, attitudes, levels of thinking and feeling. Linking the selves via threads of memory, sensory stimuli, or association, lending unity to their seeming diversity, the "Captain self," "key self," or true self proved the one Orlando was seeking (310).

Orlando's search for an artistic ideal is noted in his pursuit of the "wild goose,"[10] but the goose is elusive: "always I fling after it words like nets which shrivel and sometimes there's an inch of silver—six words— in the bottom of the net but never the great fish that lives in the coral groves" (313).[11] Losing consciousness of self, Orlando hoped to achieve a complete self:

The whole of her darkened and settled as when some foil whose addition makes the round and solidity of a surface, is added to it, and the shallow becomes deep and the near distant; and all is contained as water is contained by the sides of a well. So she was now darkened, stilled and become, with the addition of this Orlando, what is called rightly or wrongly a single self, a real self. . . . Her mind had become a fluid that flowed round things and enclosed them completely (314).

As with Lily Briscoe, the creative process is again best fertilized in a fluid medium.

Orlando entering 1928 finds herself near the site of the oak tree of 1588, with her poem "The Oak Tree." Though there were seven reprintings of the poem, she scorned fame, this "chatter and praise and blame and meeting people who admired one and did not admire one." Miraculously coming to meet her, emerging from his airplane, was Marmaduke; as he leaped to the ground the "wild goose" formed over his head.

III

In her preoccupation with multiplicity of self in *Orlando*, Woolf sought to come to terms with the ambiguities of her sexual identity. She turned to Vita romantically and for maternal protection, perhaps as Lily sought to embrace Mrs. Ramsay whose life seemed to Lily a work of art. But Vita appeared a poor choice.[12] As Woolf herself noted, Vita was a cold mother to her sons, yet she responded to Vita's overtures and for the rest of her life was self-hurtfully addicted to someone who was exotic and glittering but not consistently caring or predictable. In Vita's view, she was protecting Virginia, fearful of "arousing physical feelings in her because of the madness" (Nicolson, 228). Occasionally nurturing and attentive, more often in Woolf's eyes unfaithful or absconding, Vita seemed an embodiment of Woolf's internalized image of an emotionally unavailable mother. Of course, on her part, Vita could not fulfill Woolf's insatiable needs nor could Woolf fulfill Vita's.

Although Woolf was correct in noting psychological similarities between traits of maleness and femaleness in Orlando and claimed to favor the feminine, she was not deeply attuned to a feminine persona at least at this time.[13] Writing *Orlando*, Woolf satisfied her desire to know what it felt like to be a man. However, Orlando becoming a woman, except for taking time out to have a child, was almost like remaining a man in terms of her activities and predilections.

Discovering he is female, "Orlando stood stark naked. No human being since the world began ever looked more ravishing. His form combined in one the strength of a man and a woman's grace. Orlando had become a woman" but otherwise remained the "same." Orlando's change of sex though it "altered their future, did nothing whatever to alter their identity" (138). Archly implied in remaining the "same" is that though Orlando can have babies, she still has a penis.

When, at the sight of Orlando's ankles, a sailor lost his footing on the mast and was almost killed, Orlando thought "what fools they make of us, what fools we are," censuring both sexes equally as though she belonged to neither. She fluctuated between man and woman, "knew the secrets, shared the weaknesses of each. It was a most bewildering and whirligig state of mind to be in" (158). Kubie considers that in Orlando's "fantastic marriage to herself-himself, she achieves the transmutation so often sought, with tragic futility, in sex and marriage" (193).

After her sex transformation, Orlando proceeded to place several pistols in her belt, adorned herself with numerous strands of emeralds and pearls, gave one "low whistle," then left Constantinople, riding a donkey and accompanied by a gypsy (140). Now female, Orlando ostensibly formed a low opinion of the other sex, yet frequently reverts to maleness.

Though Woolf denies basic differences between male and female, she was a good deal preoccupied with sexual distinctions and in *Orlando* noted there was no evidence of "that vast erection which she had thought everlasting; top hats, widows' weeds, trumpets, telescopes, wreaths, all had vanished and left not a stain, not a puddle even on the pavement" (297). Was the "vast erection" the life of Woolf's past, particularly its challenging masculine components? It is not at all clear that Woolf was cognizant here of her capacity for punning or double entendres.

Was Woolf homosexual? bisexual? intermittently heterosexual? Certainly she was indeterminate in her self-definition and she manifested considerable sexual ambivalence. Not a fixed entity, sexual identity for Woolf shows variations throughout the different developmental phases in her life. Sharply vacillating towards her father, she alternately felt "passionate affection" and "passionate hatred" towards him. Not on as conscious a level, she showed similar alternations of feeling towards mother and mother-figures. Woolf showed constant oscillation between attraction for father and reseeking of mother for much of her life. She perceived her parents as both weak and dominant or phallic, and as noted, there was to some extent a subtle reversal of roles between her parents.

Psychoanalytic studies concerning the creatively gifted mesh with Woolf's pattern of development and with her conflicted identification process. Kubie refers to the "drive to become both sexes" in *Orlando*; this he finds "self-destroying." Here he points to the "frequent struggles to achieve mutually irreconcilable and consequently unattainable identities" (194). One of the "deepest drives in human nature" is, in his view, the need to identify with and to become both parents (211).

Greenacre (1957) finds diminution of sexual polarity in the artist, higher capacity for bisexuality, greater fluidity amongst the various maturational phases. The creative product, she suggests, may replace personal relationships (493), although other investigators attest to the artist's increased sexuality in creative surges. All agree that a blurring of early developmental phases occurs so that oedipal and preoedipal phases interpenetrate, and greater openness to multiple levels of experience is found.

In the "classic" Freudian oedipal pattern, the little girl presumably disappointed in mother because of insufficient suckling experience or birth of new siblings is further disillusioned, in effect feels castrated when she learns her mother does not possess a penis, and has not endowed her with one. She replaces the wish for a penis with the desire to have a baby with father. Should the attachment to father "come to grief", the girl may remain asexual or instead identifies with father and returns to her earlier "masculinity complex." Freud also points to women whose lives show masculinity or femininity as alternately ascendant (Freud, 1925, 1931, 1933). Later investigators, Jones (1935), Klein (1928), Horney, Chassageut-Smirgel, Parens, and others, in contrast to Freud, believe the preoedipal girls' wish for a baby precedes penis envy and is an expression of an identification with mother; the girl turns to father not because of her "castration complex" but as a result of her feminine strivings

Female psychology is no longer the "dark continent" of Freud's early observations. Mothers are envisaged as primary, powerful identification figures and fathers affirm their daughters in other than sexual modes. Turning to father is not replacement for the girl's attachment to mother; nor does she relinquish her internalization of mother, inherent to her earlier development. Rather, the girl sees both parents as "love objects and rivals" throughout the oedipal period. Heterosexuality emerges from the relationship to both mother and father (Chodorow, 151). Both parents reinforce the girl's positive feminine identity, body image and ego ideal (Blum, 1976, 173). Less rigid and punitive, female values are different from the male, but not inferior (Schafer, 468).

Of course, gender roles that evolve in the framework of maturation and learning, influenced by family and culture evidence a unique developmental elaboration in each individual. In Woolf's situation, she envied men the power they generated, wished above all to gain her mother's love which seemed most bountifully bestowed on her younger brother, who possessed the "treasure" she thought her mother so valued. Brought up between two male siblings accorded more observable privileges than she, Woolf decidedly felt rivalrous towards both brothers, especially the younger, Adrian. As we know, her mother for whatever reason wanted a boy before Woolf was born. Sensing this, the knowledge deeply affected Woolf's self-image. In Woolf's last novel, her preoccupation with the word "abortive" signifies she felt she should not have been born, or was not wanted, or should have been someone other than the person she was.

Toward Vanessa, Woolf felt a keen, largely benign and vitalizing rivalry, in terms of winning Thoby's love, almost as though Vanessa and Thoby were surrogate mother and father; this was in tandem with a persistent, romantic attachment towards her much admired older sister, and after Thoby died, was repeated in varying triangular patterns as Vanessa acquired different partners. Woolf continually sought not only the male in Vanessa's life but Vanessa as well.

This triangular situation was superimposed on the earlier one with mother and father. As a child, Virginia felt close to father as though to a mother-surrogate. He mirrored her achievements, delighted in her story telling and affection for him while she in turn felt nourished by his admiration, inventiveness in play and investment in her future. Her perception of him also encompassed an oedipal image of a powerful, attractive, impetuous and occasionally sadistic parent; thus her memory of "being thrown as a child naked by father into the sea."[14] Julia Stephen's postpartum illness or depression following Virginia's birth, Virginia's early weaning, Virginia's sibling envy of Adrian who mother demonstrably preferred, resulted in recurrent fear of abandonment, this in turn affecting Virginia's sense of body and ego integrity. As she painfully wrote: "Take away my affections and I should be like seaweed out of water, like the shell of a crab, like a husk. All my entrails, marrow, juice, pulp would be gone. I should be thrown into the first puddle and drown" (L4, Aug.19'30).

Her mother's unavailability became the substrate of Woolf's deep seated vulnerability, did not create propitious conditions for Woolf's identification process, so that her fragility of self and identity confusion persisted. Though she witnessed her father display the outer pyrotechnics of authority, though he controlled the exchequer, Woolf frequently felt him a weak and castrated figure. Despite seeming submission, her mother appeared the more powerful parent. In effect, Woolf identified with her mother's depression, preoccupation with death and condescension towards Leslie; she also identified with her disparaged and castoff father and thought of herself in similar terms. Of course she identified with positive aspects of both parents, her mother's sociality and father's passion for literature.

Her father's assumption of both maternal and paternal roles further confounded Woolf's identification process. Despite her love for father she undoubtedly felt his early interest in her over-conspicuous, likely to evoke her mother's competitiveness.[15] This at times interfered with her positive relationship with mother and impeded full acceptance of her femininity. Virginia was not conscious of any rivalry with her mother and did not see herself as challenging her mother's superior status. Her mother's death, for which she blamed her father, decelerated the course of Woolf's feminine development. Guilt, idealization and dissociation of anger regarding mother made for an attenuated mourning process; Woolf sought involvement in what proved to be unrewarding maternal relationships, some homoerotic, affording intermittent intimacy, but, for the most part, she typically tended to feel excluded or unpreferred.

As adolescent and young adult, she thought her father discouraged normal developmental experiences otherwise open to her. She felt profoundly bitter that his interest in her now seemed predominantly intellectual; that he found Stella more feminine and attractive; and, that he turned to Stella with an almost conjugal possessiveness so soon after Julia's death. Stella's death three months after marriage and the confusion regarding the cause of death coalesced for Virginia the morbid connection of sexuality and pregnancy with injury or death. Woolf's anxieties might also have meshed with childhood misinterpretations or distortions of anatomical functions and sexual role. Children frequently view parental intercourse as a battle or as dangerous—the male, assaultive; the female, victim. From age 6 when Virginia was sexually molested by Gerald and from ages 13 to 22 when George made sexual overtures to her, her relationship with her half-brothers apparently acquired incestuous overtones that made for bruised, retaliative feelings of sexual violation and sexual abuse; this she concealed and therefore never resolved, which added to her fear of femininity.

Emulating Vanessa's rebellious feelings towards father, Virginia at 15 must have been at the same time keenly aware she emotionally now had father to herself. Intertwined with father, her profoundest identity was that of student, scholar and incipient writer. Enraged with him whenever he and Vanessa clashed over monetary matters, Virginia remained in a childlike bind in relation to warring parents, as it were. Devotedly nursing her father for an extended period, Virginia at 22 was plunged into an acute identity crisis upon his death after a prolonged illness.

Had Thoby lived, Woolf might have found him a better model of masculinity than her father and half-brothers; at times, she compared him to a "Greek god." Yet her portrait of him in *Jacob's Room* suggests he lacked firm identity patterns. As it was, Vanessa's marriage provided an opportunity to absorb or identify with aspects of Vanessa's feminine role and became the fulcrum of Woolf's life. Woolf wished in her flirtation with Clive Bell to take Vanessa's place, re-evoking the earlier enmeshment with her parents, and the childhood rivalry with Vanessa for Thoby's attention. She also wished to take Clive's place with Vanessa, have Vanessa to herself, she in father's role wooing mother.[16]

Fearful of Clive's availability after the breakup of the Bell marriage, Woolf distanced herself from him, though she had been titillated and in some degree was for the first time deeply involved as a woman with him; this was incorporated in *The Voyage Out* in the lively but dissonant relationship between Terence and Rachel that goes nowhere however, and in the immense attraction between Clarissa and Peter in *Mrs. Dalloway*, also unfulfilled. To some degree, Virginia's wavering between male and female identities during the marriage of Vanessa and Clive seems so much role-playing; basically, Virginia desired to be Vanessa's suckling infant.

Marriage to Leonard led to Virginia's sense of sexual ineptness and abnormality, to what she felt was rejection of her femininity by her husband, and to collapse of her expectations of having children. This occurred with the collusion of Vanessa, Virginia's ego ideal and maternal model. Virginia's third breakdown and almost successful suicide attempt followed. Leonard withholding *The Voyage Out*, depicting Virginia unfavorably in *The Wise Virgins*, precipitated her massive anger, channelled in manic attacks against Leonard and men in general. Virginia later referred to this phase of her marriage as that "strange prelude" when her "brains went up in a shower of fireworks".

Woolf, after recovery from her breakdown, became even more deeply involved in Vanessa's life and tried to place herself in her sister's skin, as it were, envying her her maternal role, as well as her relationship with Duncan. Of course, Woolf knew Duncan was predominantly homosexual, pursued or lived with other men; knew that Vanessa's suffering in this masochistic arrangement in which she was mother to Duncan as she had been to Thoby, was considerable, actually making it difficult to identify with her, despite the pretense of doing so. Perhaps in her constant communication to Vanessa of her own availability, she was telling her sister she would be better for her than Duncan.

Although Woolf felt she had resolved her ambivalent mourning process for mother by writing *To the Lighthouse*, this was not borne out.

Rather, responding to Vita's pursuit, she turned to Vita for feminine modelling. Predominantly, Virginia was the admiring child; Vita a dazzling, intermittently nurturant, androgynous mother. Vita became Woolf's lover, though for the most part feelings of insecurity and abandonment accompanied the affair throughout.

Marriage with Leonard worked in a formal sense—he became devoted caretaker and she the sick one. Up to this point, Leonard extravagently praised then published the novels Virginia spawned, and she basked in his admiration of her "fertility". Althogh she was encased in a network which consisted of friends, literary world, printing press, Vanessa, Vanessa's children, and most vitally, her own work, Woolf keenly felt the anomalousness and childlessness of her marriage, felt hers in many ways an unlived life, externalized in her next novel, *The Waves.*

XII "I ride rough waters and shall sink with no one to save me— more cruel than the old torturers, you will let me fall"—*The Waves*

I

Although *To the Lighthouse* is, via critical acclaim, Woolf's most harmonious novel and in it she hoped to divest herself of the constant preoccupation with her parents whose "invisible presences" so obsessed her, *The Waves*, which revives unresolved conflicts and themes central to earlier novels and to her life, is perhaps her most ambitious endeavor, more skeletal and brutally direct in its summing up of unlived lives. Shortly before finishing, *To the Lighhouse*, Woolf alluded to the "mystical side" of her solitude: "how it is not oneself but something in the universe that one's left with. It is this that is frightening and exciting in the midst of my profound gloom, depression, bordom. One sees a fin passing far out. What image can I reach and convey what I mean" (D3, Sept.30'26). Her mood proved catalyst for *The Waves* which she wrote three years hence, following *Orlando*, though she thought about it intermittently

Vanessa writing Virginia a letter on May 3, 1927, describing moths flying "madly in circles" around her, especially a huge one which clung to the window though she sought to etherize then chloroform it without effect, until finally it succumbed (Bell, v.2, 126), propelled her sister's novel, *The Waves*, initially called *The Moths*. Virginia responded: "Your story of the moths fascinates me so that I'm going to write a story about it. I could think of nothing else but you and the moths for hours after. Perhaps you stimulate the literary sense in me as you say I do your painting sense" (L3, May8'27). Vanessa also wrote that her "maternal instinct" which Virginia deplored so much, did not permit her to leave the moth. Most likely, Virginia imagined she was the moth hovering about Vanessa's flame or rather, her illuminated window in Cassis. Identified with this moving, disquieting, desperate image, Virginia herself seems to be frantically seeking warmth, a hearth, in short wants to be be taken in. Had she not referred to herself as Vanessa's "first born?"

Woolf wrote an essay at this time which she refers to as "The Death of the Moth":

> It was as if someone had taken a tiny bead of pure life and decked it as lightly as possible with down and feathers, had set it dancing and zigzagging to show us the true nature of life . . . . But the insignificant little creature now knew death. As I looked at the dead moth, this minute wayside triumph of so great a force over so mean an antagonist, filled me with wonder. The moth having righted itself now lay most decently and uncomplainingly composed. Oh yes, he seemed to say, death is stronger than I am. (*DM*, 16).

The story of Vanessa's moth would be background for Woolf's idea of a "play-poem . . . , some continuous stream, not solely of human thought but of the ship, the night, all flowing together; all intersected by the arrival of the bright moths" (D3, Jun.18'27). Woolf's intention, after the sprawling, self-revealing looseness of *Orlando*, was to emphasize form, abstraction, and in so doing, to woo Vanessa; that is, to accomplish in writing what her sister and Duncan were attempting in painting;[1] to visualize her novel as "spatial form which unites disparate ideas and emotions . . . in an instant of time" (Frank, 381). Wishing to avoid the "incessant, remorseless analysis of falling into love and falling out," Woolf longed for a "more impersonal relationship . . . , for ideas, for dreams, for imagination, for poetry."[2]

Could another stimulus for Woolf's "play-poem" have been competition with the award given Vita for "The Land", accorded considerable attention in the press, which Woolf scorned however, as distinctly lightweight?

Germinating for two years, *The Moths* hover at the back of her brain as she practices an ever greater visual acuity. She seeks to "make more and more vivid the roughness of the air current and the tremor of the rook's wing . . . , as if the air were full of ridges and ripples and roughnesses." Only a small amount of what she sees so vividly or feels in some "nervous fiber or fan-like membrane" in her spine can actually be captured in writing. Describing herself as "under orders," she marches on a "definite stage with each book," though it is one she arranges herself (D3, Aug.12'28).

Noting that several friends were unusually warm, taking "pleasure in intimacy as if the sun were sinking," she feels her own "physical state colder now, the sun just off one," alluding to her "change of life," the irrevocable loss of her reproductive powers (D3, Sept.10'28). Comparing herself to the students at Girtin College where she lectured on the women's movement, she felt "elderly and mature."

To Woolf, inordinately preoccupied with her "fertility," gestating a novel might approximate childbirth. Envying Vanessa's maternal role, Woolf bemoaned her childlessness, then discountenanced having children.

Now, holding onto her fantasies of pregnancy, she indicates she will refrain from writing until she has her next work "impending in me; grown heavy in my mind like a ripe pear; pendant, gravid, asking to be cut or it will fall." Thinking of *The Moths*, she desires to ". . . eliminate all waste, deadness, superfluity; to give the moment whole" (D3, (Nov.28'28).

Writing to Vita, off on another trip, this time to Germany to join her husband who was Counsellor to the British Embassy there, Woolf puns about requiring more paper to continue her letter: "but this'll need a new sheet and they're double bed sheets, fit for Long Barn on a summer's night" (L3, Dec.29'28).

As usual, the new year brings a summing up and comparison of herself with Vanessa: "so I have something instead of children, and fall comparing our lives. I note my own withdrawal from those desires." She is absorbed in what she calls her "vision" (D3, Jan.4'29)

Sparked by Vita's presence in Germany, the Woolfs travelled to Berlin and were joined by Vanessa, Quentin, and Duncan. The trip proved a series of disastrous frustrations and antagonisms, especially between Vanessa and Vita.

Given a sedative by Vanessa for the North Sea crossing back to England, Woolf was not easily roused afterward, fell into a temporary coma, and remained in bed for approximately a month, with the usual headache and heart dysrhythmia; she referred to this as nervous exhaustion. Nor was she "permitted" to work for another three weeks though she carried on a lively correspondence with Vita, still in Berlin. Writing Vita that she suffered a combination of flu, headache, and after-effects of the drug somnifene, Virginia conveyed she does not read "anything with interest" except for Vita's letter (L4, Jan.29'29).

Leonard wrote Vanessa, who returned earlier, that when he tried to awaken Virginia en route to London she was in a "drugged" state though she had only taken 20 drops of somnifene,[3] and was in bed with an "old-fashioned" headache ever since. His theory was that Virginia overextended herself with late nights in Berlin and that she was "on the point of breakdown" when she took the drug.

Here "breakdown" seems misleading, suggesting mental disorder as it does, when a simpler explanation seems the more expedient. Virginia merely chose to be a good deal alone with Vita who whisked her about in her car while Leonard was quite content to spend his time meeting socialists and politicals. Intensely disliking Germany and Vita, Vanessa however, was in a state of "profound irritability" most of the time according to her son's recollections: "The Nicolsons seems such an unnecessary importation into our society . . . ," Vanessa wrote Roger Fry (Jan.19'29; Bell v.2, 141–142). An enraged Vanessa could be formidable; hence, Woolf's recourse to illness.

Interestingly enough, the drug Woolf took for seasickness was identical to veronal. As recalled, she almost succeeded in taking her life with an overdose of that drug in 1913. The possibilty that a gigantic cover-up was taking place and that Woolf had attempted suicide emerges, although the data is inconclusive.

Reconciled with Vanessa, she notes her sister's departure to France for four months and expects a fairly lonely and painful time but hopes to work on *The Moths*. She suspects this "sudden fertility which may be mere fluency." Now her mind is so "impatient, so quick, in some ways so desperate." Perceiving this "impetuous torrent" in herself neutralizes her sense of unattractiveness and aging; she feels full of "shape and color . . . , bolder as a writer . . . , on the verge of some strenuous adventure" (D3, Mar.28'29).

Woolf writes Vita, in an amusing vein, of speaking to Vanessa in a chemist's shop of "our passion." Vanessa asked whether Virginia "really liked going to bed with women . . . and how d'you do it?" talking "loud as a parrot" (L4, Apr.5'29). After a weekend with Vita, Woolf writes her: "You make me feel like a baby having drunk sweet milk" (L4, Apr.18'29).

Now in southern France with her sister, Woolf mused about Vanessa's "odd, intimate, yet edgy, happy, free, yet somehow restrained intercourse" with Duncan, felt Vanessa's "overpowering supremacy" (D3, Jun.15'29). Referring to Vanessa's "boasting" concerning her older son, Woolf childishly counterposes the 2,000 pounds earned by writing *Orlando*, enabling her to travel and possibly buy a house close by. To this Vanessa responded that she, Vanessa, felt she was a failure as a painter.

On Woolf's return, a sense of "nothingness rolls about the house," a comparison between the sociality and family life she has left and the emptiness at home. She feels better as she critically tosses aside Lytton's new book *Elizabeth and Essex* (D3, Jun.15'29), no longer thinks of him as a more successful writer than she. Calling herself a "born melancholic," she thinks only by writing can she function: "directly I stop working I sink down, down, down." But should she sink further she will reach "the truth," realize there is "nothing, nothing for any of us. Work, reading, writing are all disguises; and relations with people. Yes, even having children would be useless". With this gloomy forecast, Woolf is prompted to pierce her vagueness concerning *The Moths*, hopes to begin with "dawn, shells on a beach," introduce the "voices of cock and nightingale" as well as "children at a long table" performing lessons; in childhood one finds "things oddly proportioned" and encounters "unreality." The "beautiful, single moth" must appear and the waves heard throughout. Everything becomes "green and vivified" when she thinks of her work and she thoroughly enjoys entering into the lives of others (D3, Jun.23'29).

Feeling betrayed by Vita, who on return from Germany, announced she was again going abroad, this time on a walking holiday with a new friend, Woolf mocked Vita's "passion for the earnest middle class intellectual, however drab and dreary." Seeking to finish the many articles she is working on and pursue her novel, Woolf hopes to go "down step by step into that queer region" (D3, Aug.5'29), referring to the unconscious.

Remembering Angelica was at school and that this would "end Vanessa's 21 years" of child-rearing, Virginia imagines "all the private scenes, the quarrels, the happinesses, the moments of excitement and change as they grew up" (D3, Sept.21'29).

Neglecting her book for the moment, Woolf wishes to be embroiled in living; a new oil stove excites her, the possiblity of exotic meals with "dashes of wine," on which Leonard puts a damper, so she must restrain herself (D3, Sept.25'29). Writing to Gerald Brenan[4] she laments: "What do all the books I have written avail me; one never knows all these years how to end, how to go on; one never knows more than a page ahead; why then does one make any pretensions to be a writer?" (L4, Oct.4'29).

Grappling with her "vague yet elaborate design," some inner loneliness permeates her: "no one knows how I suffer walking up this street engaged with my anguish as I was after Thoby[5] died—fighting something alone. But then I had the devil to fight and now nothing." Despite her success and that of Hogarth Press, Virginia notes there is "vacancy and silence somewhere in the machine," then realizes how much she misses Clive. Switching to thoughts of Vanessa and Julian visiting Angelica at school, Virginia vicariously imagines the visit: "Nessa will hold her very tight to get the sensation of her child's body again." Virginia decides Vanessa is a "jealous woman", not wishing Virginia to "know" her sons (D3, Oct.11'29).

Worried about her possible shrillness in *A Room of One's Own*, she suspects her intimates will dislike it, predicts she will get no criticism except of a teasing sort from Lytton, Roger, and Morgan; the press will be kind and talk of her "charm" though she will be attacked for a "feminist and hinted at for a sapphist." She doubts the book will be taken seriously, again, alludes to her childlessness, a repetetive theme during the writing of *The Waves* (D3, Oct.23'29).

Dreaming she had a heart ailment that would kill her in six months, she felt "relief, well I've done with life anyhow; then horror; desire to live; fear of insanity;" regret concerning her incompleted book; and a "luxurious dwelling" upon her friends' sorrow. She told Leonard he must remarry. On awakening she felt groggy, and "odd feeling of life and death mingling" (D3, Nov.2'29). Here, one gleans a sense of martyrdom, a desire for the sympathy of others. The heaviness she describes seems similar to her post-Germany affliction which afforded her considerable attention. These moods are probably not lost on Leonard. Does she obtain his sympathy or his form of punitive caretaking? Or, is she expressing anger at his original decision to not have children?

Woolf and Vita are separated by the illness of one or the other; now it is Woolf's turn to console Vita, in bed with flu (L4, Nov.13'29). Verbally flogging Vita's friend Hilda Matheson, Talks Director at the British Broadcasting Company, for ruining her (Woolf's) article, programmed for a talk on Beau Brummell, Woolf expostulates: "She [Hilda] affects me like a strong purge, as a hair shirt, as a foggy day, as a cold in the head" (L4, Nov.19'29). She hated the "secondrateness" of Vita's friends, more likely inveighing against Vita's growing intimacy with Hilda (D3, Nov.25'29).

Launched on the second part of *The Waves*, she feels she is merely accumulating notes for a book (D3, Nov.30'29). Recipient of Lytton's negative reaction to *A Room of One's Own*, Virginia is glad they did not marry, else she could not have written at all: "He checks and inhibits me in the most curious way. Leonard may be severe but he stimulates. Anything is possible with him" (D3, Dec.14'29).

Recurrent illness is considered "partly mystical: something happens in my mind; it shuts itself up. It becomes chrysalis. I lie quite torpid, often with acute physical pain." Quite unexpectedly "something springs."[6] Seeing Vita, Woolf experiences a "tremendous sense of life beginning"—perhaps for Vita, not for herself: "Vita's life so full and flush and all the doors opening." Back to the metaphor of the moths, she writes: "this is I believe the moth shaking its wings in me. I then begin to make up my story whatever it is." Ideas accost her even before she can "control" her "mind or pen" (D4, Feb.16'30), suggesting she has been inundated by her associations regarding the book and will soon sort it out.

After a day of "intoxication" with her writing, the competition with Vanessa surfaces: "Children are nothing compared to this. When I sat surveying the whole book complete, I find it the most difficult and complex of all my books . . . " (D4, Mar.28'30). The first version of her novel is finally completed on April 29, 1930, representing the "greatest stretch of mind" she ever knew. Although she feels the last part solid and substantial the entire book will require much "rebuilding, remodeling." She is also worried about her next work which must emerge swiftly else she will become "pecking and wretched" (D3, May18'30).

Hoping to make Vita jealous by informing her that her time is now monopolized by a new friend, Ethel Smyth[7] (L4, Jun.12'30), Virginia is delving into her past to accommodate Ethel's unending questions. For Ethel, Virginia reviews her relationship with Leonard, telling her that after they met in 1904, Leonard seemed infatuated with both Stephen sisters. Also the "stories" concerning Leonard intrigued Virginia: "how his hand trembled and he bit his thumb through in a rage." According to Lytton, Leonard "like Swift would murder his wife"; from another source Virginia heard Leonard "had married a black woman." Virginia added that her "terror of real life" kept her in a "nunnery." Remembering her "madness" in 1913, the six months in bed under doctors' discipline—"you shant read this, you shant write a word, you shall lie still and drink milk"—taught her about "what is called oneself," though she was almost "crippled" in the process (L4, Jul.22'30).

Continuing to respond to Ethel's unabashed prodding, reassuring her she is "diverse enough to want Vita and Ethel and Leonard and Vanessa", Woolf claims that in relation to men she feels spiritual or intellectual, that she felt physical attraction for a man only two or three times in her life; however, the male in question was so uncomprehending or ineffective that not much happened. Clive and Vita both call her "fish," yet what she wants (this "while holding their hands and getting exquisite pleasure from contact with either the male or female body") is "illusion—to make the world dance." She cannot write unless "perpetually stimulated" (L4, Aug.14'30), a far cry from the state of unconsciousness she usually claims is imperative.

Reassuring Ethel she had not, on a recent occasion, meant to say she was unaffectionate, she touchingly makes amends: "Take away my love for my friends and my burning and pressing sense of the importance and lovability and curiosity of human life, and I should be nothing." Telling Ethel "what a crazy piece of work" she (Woolf) is, she compares herself to a "cracked looking glass in a fair." Led on the by the beauty of a pharase, she is in actuality "so simple, just give her things to play with, like a child" (L4, Aug.19'30).

After a weekend with Vita, Woolf feels she is not "consistently anything;" She is revising *The Waves*, now a series of dramatic soliloquies,
moving homogeneously in and out, following the rhythm of the waves.
The book is the "greatest opportunity" she has ever given herself;
though she anticipates "complete failure", she "respects" herself for
writing it (D3, Aug.20'30).

Exclaiming over the "pressure like a wire cage of sound round her
head", thinking she was "diseased" or would surely die, Woolf fainted
while walking with a friend. There was the "drumming" of her heart, "the
pain, the effort got violent at the doorstep; overcame me; like gas; I was
unconscious" (D3, Sept.2'30). Then she came back to life. Aside from
"heat prostration," could this fainting episode of August 30, be connected with Vita's visit the day before? Or with Leonard's impatience?
Virginia histrionically preferred to consider this another brush with
death, a rather persistent preoccupation.

Convinced nothing can be "destructive" of the relationship between
Vanessa and Duncan because it is based on "Bohemianism," Woolf's
predilection is in that direction as well. Experiencing a period of
"obscurity" she writes: "I am not a writer. I am nothing but I am quite
content." Attracted to spontaneity and "looseness," she is writing *The
Waves* to a "rhythm, not to a plot," synchronous with what the painters
are doing though completely opposed to the tradition of fiction (D3,
Sept.2'30). Despite her illnesses, she considers this one of her "happiest
summers" at Monk's House, is at ease with the pattern of "silence,
brooding," and writing a good deal more than she uses. She finds this
"fertilizing," although she would like to have another life lived "in action" (D3, Sept.8'30).

Thinking it hopeless to see Vita apart from Hilda, Woolf wrote Ethel
about the "uselessness" of her life—"what are the arguments against
suicide?" (L4, Oct.30'30). Hoping to integrate *The Waves* she desires to
make the "blood run like a torrent from end to end," dispensing with
chapters. When she is working well, the "whole world falls into shape; it
is this writing that gives me my proportions" (D3, Dec.30'30).

Woolf now records finishing *The Waves* in a "state of glory and calm
and some tears, thinking of Thoby"; conveys "how physical" is her
"sense of triumph and relief." Her book, "good or bad," is completed
and she likes the result, feels she has "netted that fin in the waters which
appeared to me over the marshes of my window at Rodmell when I was
coming to an end of *To the Lighthouse*" (D4, Feb.7'31).

Compared to her contemporaries, Woolf feels "unsuccessful: how
little I've seen, done, lived, felt, thought." Adding to her malaise, she
feels Vanessa "does not want" her: "My ship has sailed on. I toss among

empty bottles and bits of toilet paper." Here Woolf's lamentations sound like T.S. Eliot's sense of alienation. Actually, all she cares for is her "capacity for feeling. If I weren't so miserable I could not be happy" (D4, Feb.17'31).

Leonard thought *The Waves* a "masterpiece"; the best of her books (D4, Jul.19'31). Feedback regarding *The Waves* now appeared. John Lehmann, general manager of Hogarth Press, told Virginia he "truly loved" *The Waves* and was "deeply impressed and amazed by its achievement in an entirely new method." He thought she maintained the "speed of prose and the intensity of poetry"; Virginia was tremendously moved and touched, her brain "flushed and flooded" (D4, Sept.16'31).

Indicating her gratefulness, especially since she was convinced *The Waves* was a failure and would not properly convey her meaning, she wrote John that he had gone deeper and further in understanding her drift than she thought possible.[8] In *The Waves*, she had hoped to:

> eliminate all detail; all fact; and analysis; and my self; and yet not be frigid and rhetorical; and not monotonous (which I am) and to keep the swiftness of prose, and yet strike one or two sparks and not write poetical but purebred prose and keep the elements of character and yet that there should be many characters, and only one; and also an infinity, a background behind. (L4, Sept.17'31).

Thinking Lehmann's suggestion that she define her views about modern poetry, "brilliant", she is "seething" with "wild" ideas concerning prose, poetry, contemporary writers and the general state of literature.

What she wants most of all is to be told *The Waves* is "solid and means something; what it means I myself shan't know till I write another book" (D4, Sept.22'31). Her novel was published on October 8, 1931.

II

Though preoccupied with aging, suicide, and death, Woolf claims that by writing, she feels "feminine" and harmonious: "I was in a queer mood thinking myself very old; but now I am a woman again as I always am when I write" (D3, May31'29). Identifying with Vanessa's sense of maternal fulfillment, Woolf at times also wished herself part of her sister's brood: Vita was an imperfect and fleeting mother, frequently abandoning her, perhaps like Virginia's own. Hoping her book would please Vanessa and Duncan, her adoptive family as it were, she wrote *The Waves* in consonance with the painters' vision.

In writing *The Waves*, Virginia intermittently and insistently compared herself with her sister; she felt "ugly, in every way inferior" to Vanessa, envied Vanessa's maternal role and her relationship with Duncan. Critical of the poetry of her nephew Julian, Woolf seemed unaware competing with him could alienate her sister.

Though fantasies of fertilization and pregnancy accompanied her writing, there is at this time the persistent need to negate, to deny the meaningfulness of the maternal experience, as she asserts having children cannot compare to the exhilaration of writing. Preoccupied with change of life she felt too "old" to be sexually attractive to Vita. Jealous of Vita's popular success, Woolf scorned Vita's poetry, which in part propelled *The Waves*.

Woolf turned to Ethel who was vociferously, enthusiastically in love with her. Though she refers to her relationship with Ethel, aged 70, as that "curious unnatural friendship" where all seems "incongruous," she respected the "old crag" that has been "beaten on by the waves: the humane, battered face that makes one respect human nature; or rather feel that it is indomitable and persistent." She feels Ethel "startlingly quick" with a "lightning speed of perception" (D3, Aug.25'30).

The Waves gave Woolf her "proportions," enabling her to write the "memoirs of one's own times." Contemplated as interior monologues of six friends, who have known each other from childhood, Woolf hoped to convey the subjective, inarticulate, or subliminal. Writing *The Waves* also seemed a means of gathering friends and family ("us four") around her, resurrecting her brother Thoby in guise of Percival, a shadowy, athletic hero who dies young, and who assumes an integrative function in the novel, bringing the friends together. Reflected only in the minds of the others, Percival is depicted as an instinctive, "natural" man, a great "master of the art of living," around whom everyone is poised.

If any of those closest to Virginia—Lytton, Nessa, Duncan, Leonard, Clive, Morgan—die, her life would not be worth living, she asserted. In her novel, she projects another group of six, similar in age, who grow up together, differentiate as they leave for school, come together from time to time, sharing crucial experiences. Bernard, the central character, feels intertwined with the others as though one: "It is not one life I look back upon. I do not know altogether who I am: Jinny, Susan, Neville, Rhoda or Louis, or how to distinguish my life from theirs" (368). Although Virginia felt her temperament or fantasy life encompassed all six, she is chiefly, emotionally identified with Bernard and Rhoda.

In this novel of immense poetic grandeur and intensity, the metamorphosis of each individual leads inexorably to a tragic sense of life, its disillusionments, sense of human separateness and inner isolation, a view of human life as an inexorable shrinking of possibilities: "we could have been anything. We have chosen now or . . . , it seems a choice was made for us—a pair of tongs pinched us between the shoulders" (324).

Jinny, a sensuously oriented individual, feels herself constantly in transit, flitting from one relationship to another, involving physical intimacy but little else. She feels no certainty about anything but wishes to be special, to be "summoned . . . , called away" by one person who comes to find her, who cannot keep himself from her (206): "My body goes before me like a lantern down a dark lane. I dazzle you; I make you believe that this is all" (264). Living dangerously, she compares herself to a "mountain goat leaping from crag to crag," not settling anywhere for long, not attaching herself to a particular individual. If she simply "raises her arm," she is confident someone will respond (296). She wishes to be part of the heterogeneous crowd, though she expects to be "buffeted, flung up and down" (298). Her body, her "companion", always sends signals, rejecting or beckoning in "rapid, running arrows of sensation" (298). Never alone, she compares herself to a "little dog that trots down the road after the regimental band, stops to sniff some brown stain . . . ," then unexpectedly runs across the street after some stray dog (329). Jinny is the sexually oriented woman Woolf may secretly wish to imitate but fears to do so.

Susan, based on Vanessa, is attracted to the concrete and immediate. Differentiating herself from Jinny, she disclaims feminine wiles, desires only to be in the country where "all the world is breeding" (214). By cooking and baking she hopes to emulate her mother. She wishes to merge with the seasons, become involved with fertility, nature's and her own, describes herself as a "field bearing crops in rotation." Her children will perpetuate her, "carry her on; their teething, crying, going to school and coming back will be like the waves of the sea" (266). "Glutted with natural happiness" (295), she feels "debased and hidebound by the bestial and beautiful passions of maternity: I shall push the fortunes of my children unscrupulously." In her adult relationships, she is "torn with jealousy," loves with "ferocity," and feels devastated should there be any disruption of her world (267). Despite the peaceful, productive years, she feels fenced in, "planted here like one of my trees." She still "gapes like a young bird, unsatisfied," for something that might have eluded her (338).

Louis' earliest memory, "a great beast's foot is chained" and "stamps" over and over, (180) together with his self-image of "caged tiger" (264), suggest his sense of imprisonment and point to the turbulent emotions he much check. He feels one with the stalk in the garden; his roots go down to the "depths of the world." He feels fibrous, shaken by "tremors," the "weight of the earth" pressed to his body; feels he has lived many lives (182), has been born out of hatred and discord (201). Perhaps more brilliant than the others, he is fearful of showing his intellectual prowess, surreptitiously studies the Greeks at night. Aware of the bullying and sadism of the athletic heroes at school, he at the same time admires one of them, namely Percival, who "inspires poetry." Louis is ashamed of his origins, and feels he is an outsider, shunned, inferior, attributing this to his Australian accent. When his friends follow more traditional paths, he enters his father's business world, but at the same time deplores his fate. He is conscious of "flux, disorder, annihilation and despair" (239). We see him in maturity, still the intellectual, now a prestigious businessman wielding power (291), acquiring monumental responsibilities (293). Louis is frequently linked with Leonard.

Neville knows great minds, great poets, but he cannot cope with typically masculine pursuits and feels despised for his inability to enter athletic contests; he harbors a "mystic sense of adoration" for Percival, and with this feels a "completeness that triumphed over chaos," a need to surrender or offer his being to one "god" (210). At college, the "bells that ring for life" reinforce his conviction that he is a good poet, perhaps a great one, yet inevitably Neville feels some "flaw" in himself, a "fatal hesitancy" (232). He is particularly concerned lest he is "doomed always to cause repulsion" in those he loves (235). Mourning Percival's accidental death, Neville feels at one with him, sacrificially wishing to share his pain. Frequently thereafter, he changes lovers, feels it is his fate to excite pity in others, not love. He requires strong sensations, tumult, to feel anything. Yet he desires a fairly domesticated relationship, and he is no longer inclined to cavort "half naked like cabin boys on the deck of a ship squirting each other with pipes" (312). Neville conjurs up Lytton and, in his creative proclivities, Virginia.

In childhood, Rhoda who represents Virginia in her extreme states of anxiety, is withdrawn, fragile, oversensitive, finds refuge in her fantasy world. At school, ordinary lessons terrify her. Alone, she is free of "hard contacts and collisions," but then she cannot always control her dreams of sinking and falling. In one dream she tries to escape her aunt, but almost drowns and is tossed by "these long waves, these endless paths, with people pursuing, pursuing."⁹ Her dream becomes a nightmare as the water or waves which she controlled in her daytime fantasies as commander of ships, inundate her, and in her dream life she feels endangered and persecuted. In her dream she cries "let me pull myself out of these waters. They sweep me between their great shoulders" (193).

Similar to her progenitor, Rhoda is phobic concerning her "looking-glass" face and feels she has no persona but shifts and changes. She must observe what others do before she acts:

> They know what to say if spoken to. They laugh really; they get angry really while I have to look first and do what other people do. They have friends to sit by. They have things to say privately in corners. But I attach myself only to names and faces; and hoard them like amulets against disaster (204).

Inarticulate when face to face with anyone outside her circle, the intensity of her emotions rock her from "side to side." Imagining others are critically observing her, she "dies pierced with arrows" to elicit their tears (204).

When alone, she might "fall off the edge of the world into nothingness," and must experience pain to feel in touch with her body (204). Rhoda feels we are bound to life as "bodies to wild horses," encountering "intermittent shocks sudden as the springs of a tiger" (219). As we know, despite their hurtful implications, shocks in Virginia's view are welcome catalysts to the creative process.

At 21, Rhoda feels on the edge of experience: "the door opens" but "terror rushes in" (247). She refrains from socialization yet cannot avoid seeing others engaged in relationships. If a male approaches her, she finds him "indifferent," "cruel." Since she cannot relate, she feels "thrust back to stand burning in this clumsy, ill-fitting body, to receive the shafts of his . . . scorn." Envying Jinny and Susan their social assurance, she feels "broken into separate pieces . . . , no longer one" (248), feels all her life she will be ridiculed.

At the farewell dinner for Percival she is further alienated, fearing others will taunt her. Bleakly she sees herself "flap like paper against endless corridors . . . ," follows the others to "light my fire at the general blaze of you who live wholly in the moment . . . " (265–266). After Percival's death, she feels the rush of that "great grindstone within an inch of my head," and she is ever more "alone in a hostile world" (286).

By his death, Percival has given her this "present: there is a square; there is an oblong. The players take the square and place it on the oblong . . . , make a perfect dwelling place" (288). Square and oblong are obviously linked to death. However, the author has not clarified Rhoda's drift toward death, merely describes her terror of ordinary life, her quivering sensibilities, reflecting Woolf's disinclination or inability to delve deeply into the areas of her own or Rhoda's subjective disturbance.

With the advent of middle age, Rhoda reiterates her dread of human-
kind, feeling the "dissolution" of her soul necessary to get through one
day, what with "lies, bowings, scrapings, fluency and servility." Rhoda
and Louis now become lovers, then separate. Rhoda is the one to leave,
fearing Louis's dominance, his "embraces."[10] At the last, Rhoda will as-
cend a Spanish mountain and expects at the pinnacle to see Africa; a
mule's back will be her bed. She plans then to leap to her death, thinking only a "thin sheet" will be between her and the "infinite depths"
(319).

At the reunion in Hampton Court she is aware she hates, loves, and
envies the others and cannot be truly free with anyone (330). After all,
they are part of the social stream of things; children, authority, fame, or
love are intrinsic to their lives, whereas she feels she has no roots. After a
momentary response to the talk of children, poems, or ailments, she expects to "fall alone into gulfs of fire" and no one will help: "more cruel
than the old torturers you will let me fall" (331). She trusts only solitude
and the "violence of death", feels hopelessly divided from the others.
Despite Rhoda's almost unmitigated suspiciousness and distrust, relent-
less pursuit of death, attraction to violence and deformity, she longs to
be rescued, to be understood, but she is unable to communicate this to
others. Instead of believing her friends might regret their unrespon-
siveness to her plight or think of her lovingly, she expects after her death,
they will "devour" her: "you will tear me to pieces when I am fallen"
(331).

As with Virginia, Bernard was an early storyteller. As a child, he
shares with Susan his fantasy of Elvedon, they the discoverers of a secret
territory. Here Woolf faithfully reproduces the world as seen through the
eyes of children. Bernard describes his delight in the others as they as-
cend the stairs like ponies, "stamping, clattering, one behind another,"
to participate in sensuous bath rituals: "pouring down the walls of my
mind, running together, the day falls copious, resplendent. I lie under
this thin sheet, afloat in the shallow light which is like a film of water
drawn over my eyes by a wave" (192–193).

Attending school, Bernard is easily distracted, unless with others. He
mocks himself: "the lake of my mind . . . heaves placidly and soon sinks
into an oily somnolence" (199). Hoping to put phrases like this in a notebook when he is older, perhaps write a novel, he tells stories he sometimes cannot finish; a match is "set to fire; something burns." His book
will fill volumes, including many permutations of the human condition.
Open to all things human, he feels he has no aptitude for reflection, is

highly concrete. Neville finds him amusing but as prone to seeing everyone with "blurred edges" (221).

At Cambridge, Bernard is intoxicated with the infinite possibilities of personality. In public he effervesces, in private, he is reflective, often indeterminate, clearly "not one and simple but complex and many" (227). Variously, he is Hamlet, Shelley, Dostoevski, Tolstoy, Napoleon, Meredith and is generally more comfortable feeling part of other people's lives. In his search for self-definition he must effect numerous "transitions," covering the "entrances and exits of several different men who alternately act their parts as Bernard"; this seems a form of role-playing.

Seemingly dispersed, Bernard feels connected underneath: "You, my self, who always comes at a call . . . ; you understand that I am only superficially respresented by what I was saying tonight." Possessing the "double capacity to feel, to reason," he is like Neville, "complex . . . , in my case something remains floating, unattached" (228). Looking at Byron's tree at Cambridge which he describes as: "lachrymose, down-showering, lamenting," he feels similar to Byron though Neville chides him, telling Bernard he is "merely himself" (236). Alone, Bernard ceases to invent or is accosted by self-doubting: "which of these people am I? It depends so much upon the room" (230).

He seduces Neville with the charm and flow of his language: "more and more hobbles into my mind as I talk, images and images." Yet Bernard cannot finish a letter he is writing. Feeling "potency, the sense of what is to come" (232), Bernard is devastated by Neville's disapproval concerning his (Bernard's) "Byronic untidiness" (237). Intimidated by Neville's orderliness, he is moved by his friend's confidences, his personal defeats. Containing more "selves" than Neville thinks, Bernard repeats: "We are not simple as our friends would have us to meet their needs" (236).

Travelling on the train to attend Percival's farewell dinner, Bernard on arriving is ready to "sink deep into this omnipresent . . . life". He feels no ambition, will let himself be carried on the "general impulse," merely reflecting the passing throng. The sounds of traffic and stream of undefined faces "drug him into dreams" (253). Thinking our bodies are "in truth naked," that buried underneath the city are "shells, bones and silence," Bernard wishes to go under, visit the "profound depths," explore, embrace the wide world with "arms of understanding." Engaged to be married, he hopes to have children and "cast a fling of seed" for future generations, enhancing his confidence, his "central stability" (254).

Feeling he has been travelling too long in the "sunless territory of non-identity" (255). Bernard is drawn back by curiosity, greed, desire to be himself; he requires his friends to rescue him from "darkness" (256). Claiming there is no stability in the world, he questioned the validity of his experiences; all seems flux and change. Unable to stand on his own, his personality completely depends on the stimulus others provide. He feels he is "made and remade continually", that different people elicit different words from him (268).

Middle-aged, Bernard mourns the loss of his youth. Satisfaction occurs when his "facets are exposed to many people." Otherwise he feels "full of holes," shrivels into insignificance, "dwindling like burnt paper" (304). Formerly embracing home and children, lulling himself into thinking life was complete, he no longer harbors such illusions. Thousands of stories he has written, filled a multitude of notebooks, but has not yet integrated these into a meaningful work (305).

Meeting his friends at the Hampton Court reunion, Bernard notes the diminution of freedom and adventure in their lives, the stultifying effect of repetition, domesticity; he too feels "wedged" into place. However, he is still "wrapped round with phrases": unless words coil like "rings of smoke" round him he is "nothing." Yet he feels open, impressionable, no longer has any conviction of permanence: "our lives too stream away" (334). For him, "marriage, death, travel, friendship, town, country, children" constitute a "many-faceted flower. Let it blaze against the yew trees. One life. It is over. Gone out" (335).

Again, Bernard tries to explore the meaning of his life: "I was the inheritor; I the continuer . . . , the one chosen to carry on" (352). He feels below the surface of polite formalities lies a "rushing stream of broken dreams, nursery rhymes, street cries, half-finished sentences and sights—elm trees, willow trees, gardeners sweeping, women writing— that rise and sink" (354). Referring here to early memories and unconscious processes, Bernard retrieves these from formlessness with words.

He reiterates his enmeshment with friends: "I am not one person but many . . . " (368). Always he has felt "leap up that old impulse to be thrown up and down on the roar of other people's voices, singing the same song . . . " (370), engaged in meaningless revelry. Reiterating that he did not always know whether he was man or woman, Bernard, Neville, Louis, Susan, Jinny, or Rhoda, the "rhythm stopped, the rhymes and the hummings, the nonsense and the poetry" (373); he saw the deleterious effects of habit, regretted his lack of accomplishment.

Bernard addressed that self accompanying him on so many passionate adventures (373),[11] the man who felt mobilized in situations of

emergency, "banged his spoon on the table saying 'I will not consent,'"
but that self made no answer and he felt complete desertion: "No fin
breaks the waste of this immeasurable sea" (374) he thought, repeating
Woolf's image. He now assumes Woolf's point of view, adopts the prose
of the authorial passages, shows an expansion of consciousness. In
thinking of the "story of his life," he recalls "shadows of people" or
"unborn selves" (377) he might have been, for example, the "old brute,
the savage, the hairy man" who "gobbles and belches"; who "shows
half-idiot gestures of greed and covetousness." But all of this is finished
(378).

Bernard now feels on his own in a "new world, never trodden," a
"man without a self" (376). Here Woolf refers to Bernard's loss of
egotism, Bernard viewing his aging process and the world in general with
greater truth and objectivity: "all this little affair of being is over" (376).
He can confront the "central shadow,"[12] that is, tolerate uncertainty and
ambiguity. He now feels "immeasurably receptive, holding everything,
trembling with fullness" (378-379). No longer consumed by curiosity or
"desire," the man he called Bernard is "dead" (379).

He requires a new language, a child's tongue speaking to his mother,
"a howl, a cry" (381). Aware of the day breaking, the "eternal renewal,
the incessant rise and fall and fall and rise again," in Bernard, too, is the
feeling of a wave rising, swelling, arching its back. He is aware of a "new
desire . . . rising beneath him like the proud horse whose rider first
spurs and then pulls him back." The enemy he now perceives is death
and it is death against whom he rides with "spear couched and . . . hair
flying back like a young man's, like Percival's when he galloped in
India." Against death he flings himself "unvanquished and unyielding"
(383).

In the fusion of horse and rider with the overriding symbol of the
waves, wherein the wave "arches its back" like a horse and the "rider's
hair flies back like a wave's crest," both hurling themselves against
death, like waves breaking on the shore—the waves' destructive elements
are channelled into an image of the "human soul riding heroically into
life and death" (Fleishman, 171).

III

The Waves does not convey in its characterizations the celebration of
self delineated in *Orlando*, but rather a sense of confusion and disparate-
ness of self. The novel records the rise and fall of the waves and passage
of the sun as metaphor for the course of the individual life, from child-

hood through maturity and decline. Italicized passages delivered by an impersonal, authorial consciousness alternate with nine scenes or soliloquies as lived by minds speaking in condensed, symbolic, rhythmic prose, expressing their inner experiences in the presence of others but not involving direct response.

Woolf's poetic rendering of nature and her sensory elaborations fulfill her aim of seeking in prose, images that can be verbalized only with enormous difficulty. Each introductory section is a presentiment of central themes in the lives of the soliloquists: the "birds had fear in their song and apprehension of pain, and joy to be snatched quickly at this instant (225). Now and then they plunged the tips of their beaks savagely into the sticky mixture" (226). Waves "drummed on the shore like turbaned warriors with poisoned assegais who whirling their arms on high, advance upon the feeding flocks, the white sheep" (227).

Blunt and jarring, Woolf's metaphoric conception of the human condition is personified in Rhoda's projection of human malevolence: "Throwing faint smiles to mask their cruelty, their indifference, they seize me." The "scorn and ridicule" of others pierce her. "I am pinned down here, exposed. The tiger leaps. Tongues with their whips are upon me. Hide me, I cry, protect me for I am the youngest, the most naked of you all" (247–248). At social functions, the "flickering tongues cut [her] like knives" (249). Frequently, Rhoda requires pain to optimally define he boundaries.

Woolf endows all of her dramatis personae with surges of intense feeling, a good deal of it sadomasochistic, in the interplay of aggressive and self-punishing imagery. Jinny's imagining a "beast" in the forest "hunting, rearing high, plunging down among the thorns, piercing" her or "driven deep" within her (298), suggests sexual fantasies involving injury or pain. Feeling debased by the "bestial" passions of motherhood, Susan or Woolf may refer to fear of the physiological processes of pregnancy and childbirth. Of course, there is no gainsaying that biological phases of human reproduction are part of the animal kingdom, but Woolf uses the word "bestial" pejoratively, or she may be prodding Vanessa's intense involvement with her children. Feeling "stigmas burnt in his quivering flesh" (241), Louis evokes Leonard's sense of inferiority in being Jewish. Neville asks for pain to "pierce his flesh with its fangs, to tear him asunder" (281); this together with Neville's other fantasies suggest his linking of pain and pleasure.

As in *To the Lighthouse*, the overarching, dominant metaphor of *The Waves* is sea, water, waves. Waves are equivalent to the rhythmic aspect of life, the ineluctable cycle of building up and destroying, the fluid universe of which Woolf has always felt a part. In a letter to Vita, she refers to the creative process as follows: "This is very profound what rhythm is and goes far deeper than words. A sight, an emotion, created this wave in the mind," before words can be found. In writing she seeks to rediscover this. (L3, Mar.16'26).

To her self-image of a girl with "pen in hand," Woolf associates someone fishing at the edge of a deep lake dreamily holding a rod over the water, letting her "imagination sweep unchecked round every nook and cranny, lying submerged in the depths of her unconscious being,"[13] lending herself to the fluidity of existence.

Or, she describes to Ethel the "fertile hour after tea for hatching, planning," when she hoped the waves would form could she but let her mind "lie asleep like a tideless sea." Imagining she can surmount all obstacles regarding *The Waves*, Woolf would "take her writing board and let herself down like a diver very cautiously into the last sentence." She sees " a light in the depths of the sea and stealthily approaches" for one's sentences are an approximation, a "net one flings over some sea pearls which may vanish" (L4, Sept.28'30).

Near Susan's home the waves are miles long. On winter nights she hears them "booming; the previous Christmas a man was drowned sitting alone in his cart." Susan felt the waves of her life "tossed broken round me who am rooted"; she sees the lives of others "eddying like straws round the piers of a bridge," while she pushes her needle in and out (205).

Jinny thinks of being adrift on the tide, the "brisk waves slap her ribs rocking gently, her heart riding at anchor like a sailing ship whose sails slide slowly down onto the white dock."

Louis hears the "sullen thud of the waves and the chained beast stamps on the beach" (215).

Neville associates words that have "lain dormant and now lift, now toss their crests and fall and rise, and fall and rise again" (231).

Incessantly preoccupied with taking or losing her life, Rhoda almost drowns even in her dreams. Planning her suicide, Rhoda riding up the mountain on her mule sees "rippling small, rippling grey, innumerable waves spread beneath: "We may sink and settle on the waves. The sea will drum in my ears. Rolling me over, the waves will shoulder me under. Everything falls in a tremendous shower, dissolving me" (319).

Contrary to Gordon's notion that death for Rhoda is not the "enemy" but a "natural return to the immortal seas from which she has never strayed" (Gordon 217), Rhoda expects to "fall alone into gulfs of fire," rides "rough waters and shall sink with no one to save" her (286), suggesting she wants to be saved. She seeks "publicity and violence and to be dashed like a stone on the rocks" (286), expects others to gloat after her death. Evident here is hatred and vindictive triumph.

Aside from its much touted and innovative form, its "abstract, eyeless, mystical qualities," the novel in its psychological substrate revives conflicts and themes inherent in Woolf's earlier works and in her life, apparently still unresolved. Underneath her storminess and rage, Rhoda feels empty, insignificant, self-hating, nonhuman, compares herself to a "ribbon or weed flung far every time the door opens." When the wave breaks she is the "foam that sweeps and fills the uttermost rims of the rocks with whiteness" (249). Her self-immolation is similar to Woolf's, who wrote Ethel that without friendship she feels like a "membrane, a fibre, uncolored, lifeless, to be thrown away like any other excreta" (L4, Aug.19'30). Rhoda's nightmare describing a severe, unyielding mother-image with "eyes hard like glazed marble," is culled from Woolf's repository of depriving maternal introjects.

Woolf shows oneness with Bernard who "drops off satisfied like a child from the breast" (253) or with Neville's comment: "We are in that passive and exhausted frame of mind when we only wish to rejoin the body of our mother from whom we have been severed" (338). Writing her novel in hope of greater closeness with her sister, Woolf frequently fantasized herself Vanessa's child. Louis, who felt like "some vast sucker, some glutinous, some adhesive . . . mouth" (316), synchronizes with Woolf's own omniverous, insatiable need for affection.

In Susan, Woolf reviews somewhat mockingly, defensively and caricaturingly the domain of motherhood, finds it can drain one's resources, reinforcing her current feeling that writing is preferable to childbearing. Woolf feels Jinny's exotic sexual adventures are titillating but mindless and dangerous, exonerating her (Woolf's) asexuality and fear of femininity. Neville's sense of sexual deviance and Louis' social humiliations, Woolf fully shares.

Why in this novel does Woolf reintroduce her grief over her brother's death? To reveal that Percival-Thoby though worshipped, can be sadistic, or that heros can be flawed? Or, perhaps Percival-Thoby's death enables Rhoda-Virginia to face dying with less terror; Percival has given Rhoda this "present." In *The Waves*, Woolf rallied her family of six, real and extended, round her to cushion her bruised feelings regarding Vita, but ultimately, inevitably she felt herself abandoned and unloved.

Both Woolf and Bernard are storytellers; he repeats many of her fantasies, utterances, and anxieties, her feelings of obscurity as a writer; the frequent sense of futility and falling short; the need to fight adversity, to defeat death on one's own terms. Bernard's preoccupation with role-playing reflects Woolf's confusion and diffusion of identity, intensified in the relationship with Vita. Is her self-concept that of child, mother, lover, wife, male, female, husband, or artist?

Like Woolf, Bernard's vulnerability sends him "dashing like a moth from candle to candle" (380). Here Woolf returns to her metaphor of the outsider seeking warmth, shelter, succorance, yet courting danger. Alerted to slights, Rhoda's penchant for suffering, envy, anger, victimization, and self-destructiveness resembles Septimus Smith, that is, Woolf's more fragile self; Rhoda's dysphoric temperament, love of fantasy, quivering sensitivity, sense of exposure and isolation suggest Woolf's everyday persona. Comforted by the control she felt she had over her life or death, Rhoda had her counterpart in Woolf, who had a similar script for much of her life. Rhoda and Bernard are doppelgänger in their acute sensitivities and vulnerabilities, though in this novel, Bernard opts for life.

Exacerbating Woolf's severe anxiety at this point in her life was the knowledge that her mother, prematurely aged, died at 49, Woolf's age when *The Waves* was published.

Bodkin sees concordance between Woolf and Emily Brontë in both writers' passionate love of nature. In *The Waves*, Woolf aspired to more "impersonal" relationships, hoped to find a non-human modality, as she writes in her essay on Emily Brontë. Woolf's impulse to create was similar to that propelling Emily Brontë which was not "her own suffering or her own injuries," but rather, "she looked out upon a world cleft into gigantic disorder and felt within her the power to unite it in a book"[14]. Brontë felt herself a lost, doomed, unwanted, unloved child, a child of the earth; primordial feelings are close to the surface in her work. Her novel *Wuthering Heights* expresses that which is "deepest, most terrible and most beautiful in human life," its passions as "universal as Greek tragedy" (Dooley, 234).

Similar to Woolf, Brontë's early loss of mother and older sister carried a tragic sense of deprivation. Brontë's love of native heath, desire for solitude and liberty emerged from this loss; nature became her mother as nature is mother in dream and myth. Both Brontë and Woolf sought substitutes for sustaining human love in nature.

XIII "There must be another life . . . not in dreams but here and now . . . with living people"—*The Years*

I

Woolf's relationship with Ethel, despite its occasional abrasiveness, became one of the central emotional experiences in her life in the 1920s, as the impact of the bond with Vita decelerated. Regarding Ethel, Woolf frequently became the imploring child "crying for the nurse's hand in the dark" (L4, Apr.1'31); she entreated "let me fasten myself upon you" (L5, Mar.4'32), indicating her persistent desire for maternal nurturance.

Ethel's abiding admiration, the challenge of her insistent though benign probing; her intrusive questions regarding Woolf's marriage, illness, and writing excavated areas of Woolf's life and experience never before explored with anyone. Ethel was a former suffragette, active in the women's movement. Examining Ethel's memoirs and autobiography revived Woolf's interest in feminist issues, in large part inspired her talk concerning the obstacles women face as they enter professions. Woolf's speech at the London National Society for Women's Services on January 21, 1931, incorporated in her article "Professions for Women," catalyzed *The Pargiters*, her novel-essay concerning the sexual life of women, begun in 1932; this evolved because she thought it too propagandistic, into *The Years* and a subsequent, companion volume, *Three Guineas*.

Woolf had for long been interested in equal rights for women; wrote about the history of women; was sympathetic to women's issues in the cooperative, feminist, suffrage, and labor groups she belonged to or supported. Sharing Leonard's interest in the Labor Party and his antifascist position, she felt herself in contrast to him a pacifist concerning the events leading up to World War II.[1] Describing Ethel, Woolf swashbucklingly writes:

> She is one of the race of pioneers . . . , one of the ice-breakers, the gun-runners, the window smashers, the armored tanks who climbed the

207

rough ground, drew the enemy's fire and left behind her a pathway—a
not yet smooth and metalled road . . . , for those who came after her.[2]

Ethel's ability to accept Woolf's irrational moods help modulate
Woolf's oversensitive reactions to the "little things"[3] people say.
Though "nods and hints" disturb her, Woolf confides:

> I look at you and think if Ethel can be so downright and
> plainspoken . . . , I need not fear instant dismemberment by wild
> horses. You do it by being so uninhibited, so magnificently unself-
> conscious. This is what people pay 20 pounds a sitting to get from
> psychoanalysts—liberation from their own egotism (L4, Apr.1'31).

Woolf never lets pass an opportunity to negate psychoanalysis, her
brother Adrian's profession. Occasionally, hostility towards Ethel surfaces, for example dreaming Ethel died; this she notes in a letter to Vita
(L4, Apr.28'31). Is Woolf's intention one of reassuring Vita that she
(Vita) was first in her affections?

Whether Woolf found a release of sorts in the exchanges with Ethel
concerning one's most intimate feelings or wished to be bolder
regarding her sexuality in consonance with the theme of her next
novel, she appeared conspicuously freer and lustier in expressing rather
polymorphously erotic feelings in letters and diary, during the lengthy
period of gestating *The Years*. Dreaming that Vanessa had a child with
Hilton Young, Woolf's former suitor (L4, Apr.24'31), can be interpreted
as Woolf's persistent longing for children, identifying with Vanessa as
earth mother and sexual woman incarnate. Woolf also indicates she and
Clive jest about "going to bed," this in front of Angelica (D4, Jan.1'32).

Obtaining revenge for Woolf's caustic response to her poem, "The
Land," Vita was severely critical of *The Waves*, finding it "boring in the
extreme" (D4, Oct.17'31). Woolf, re-evoking an ancient sense of exclusion, dreamt Vita abandoned her for another woman, with Vanessa exclaiming "she [Vita] is tired of you" (D4, Nov.17'31). It is unlikely Vita
was tired of her but rather this was Woolf's mode of showing contempt
for herself, signifying her sense of aging and unattractiveness, exacerbated by Vita's sexual involvement with other women. Woolf's bruised
feelings led to headache and its appurtenances.

Not long after this, Woolf wrote Lytton Strachey she dreamt she was
at a play and Lytton, sitting in front, turned and looked at her; both
went into gales of laughter (D4, Dec.10'31).[4] Learning of Lytton's illness
in mid-December 1931, Virginia and Leonard felt stricken, remained
closely in touch with him. Woolf never forgot Lytton's emotional sup-

port when her brother died and the fact she and Lytton almost married; they maintained a lively correspondence⁵ in the past, and as we know, she was intensely competitive with him as a writer. She informed Ethel of the ebb and flow of Lytton's health. Answering Ethel's letter which conveyed Woolf cared for "so few," Woolf retorts that Ethel underestimates the "strength" of her feelings. The trouble has been that those closest to her, Nessa, Lytton, Leonard, and Maynard, are all "silent," so she has forced herself into silence, propelled by the "terror" of her "unlimited capacity for feeling" (L4, Dec.29'31).

Lytton's death from cancer on January 21, 1932, marked the first of their circle to die: "Duncan, Nessa and I sobbing together in the studio— a sense of something spent, gone: that is to me so intolerable: the impoverishment: then the sudden vividness" (D4, Jan.22'32).

Despite her grief over Lytton's death, Woolf finished her essay "A Letter To A Young Poet," instigated by and dedicated to John Lehmann. Her essay suggests that the poet instead of delineating a world that exists only for himself, must feel related to other people, must try to "reach unconscious, automated states," should allow the "rhythmical sense to wind in and out among men and women, omnibuses, sparrows—whatever comes along the street—until it has strung them together in one harmonious whole. The poet's task is to find the relation between things that seem incompatible yet have a mysterious affinity" (*DM*, 221).⁶

Woolf's penchant for sexual fantasy undiminished, she dreams about Duncan and writes Vanessa: "Why dream of Duncan? He never dreams of me, nor thinks of me either; nor writes to me" (L5, Apr.19'32).

After a "chaste" night with Ethel, Woolf writes: "Please live 50 years at least; for now I've formed this limpet attachment it can't but be a part of my simple anatomy forever. Wanting Ethel I say live, live, and fill my veins with charity and champagne." She apologizes for her "terrible irregularities," her "spasms of one emotion after another, those spikes she drives into her fingers." She reminds Ethel of the sight of the "woman's face when you vociferated about sitting in the lavatory" (L5, Mar.4'32).

On holiday with Roger and his sister, Margery Fry, Woolf writes Vanessa that her leaning toward "Sapphism" might be revived by the "carts of young, Greek peasant women in lemon red and blue handkerchiefs . . . , and the general fecundity and bareness" (L5, May2'32).

However, on return from Greece, Woolf felt she was an "organ that takes blows," exclaimed about the "inane pointlessness of existence," her hatred of her "brainlessness and indecision," the old "treadmill feeling." Here she referred to her sadness over Lytton's death, her anxiety about her book, worst of all, her "dejected barrenness" (D4, May25'32). Added to this were the difficulties between Leonard and John Lehmann engendered by Lehmann's wish to be made partner and Leonard's reluctance to relinquish power, which made for explosiveness in their ongoing business relationship. Leonard saying "things have gone wrong somehow," when they learned Carrington killed herself, remained in her thoughts. Walking along a street with "scaffolding," she felt the "violence and unreason in the air" (D4, May25'32).[7] Were these not her own and Leonard's feelings she projected? Overtly agreeing with Leonard's complaints regarding John Lehmann, Virginia felt inwardly torn, aware Vanessa and Julian defended John's position and attacked what they felt was Leonard's irascibility.

Virginia's fainting episodes seemed connected with the emotionally loaded Leonard-Lehmann impasse (D4, Jul.8'32), suggesting her conflict about taking sides as well as her tendency to dissociate negative feelings towards Leonard, whom Lehmann accused of authoritarianism and of perpetuating a long series of misfortunes with business managers in the past. In later years, Woolf acknowledged her husband's desire for power and domination; she had already attributed these qualities to Louis in *The Waves*. Declaring herself "immune," she wished to function "apart from rubs, shocks, suffering, to be beyond the range of darts; to have enough to live on without courting flattery, success, to not mind other people being praised," (D4, Jul.14'32).

Describing another fainting episode, Woolf alluded to "galloping hooves" which got "wild" in her head. Her heart "leapt and stopped and leapt again" as she "tasted that queer bitterness at the back of her throat and the pulse leapt" into her head and "beat and beat more savagely, more quickly." She felt "this struggling team galloping, pounding," then thought something would "burst" in her brain, felt "pain as of childbirth;" lying down, she presided "like a flickering light, like a most solicitous mother, over the shattered, splintered fragments" of her body (D4, Aug.17'32). Are these violent images of childbirth related to Woolf's ambitious, iconoclastic conceptions for the new, autobiographical novel she is gestating?

The differences between John Lehmann and Leonard become increasingly contentious. Deciding not to accept Leonard's new business arrangement, which still did not guarantee partnership, Lehmann left on expiration of their old agreement. Virginia deplored his "jealousies, vanities, and ambitions, his weakness and changeableness" (D4, Sept.2'32), but Lehmann felt Virginia was "following suit", that is, imitating Leonard's outrage (Lehmann, 1978, 38).

Now called *The Pargiters*, Woolf's novel-essay would "take in everything, sex, education, life," and "come with the most powerful and agile leaps like a chamois across precipices from 1880" to the present (D4, Nov.2'32).[8] Her concept seemed bold, adventurous, a bit dangerous. She tries to check her vast capacity for fact, avoid sarcasm, maintain the correct degree of "freedom and reserve" (D4, Dec.19'32).

Feeling at the "height of her powers" in reading some 12 to 15 books, she has a "sense as of a Rolls Royce engine purring its 70 miles an hour" in her brain, an extremely powerful, masculine image; she adds a more recognizable feminine one: "I am also encouraged to read by the feeling I am on the flood of creativeness in *The Pargiters*—what a liberation that gives one, as if everything added to that torrent—all books become fluid and swell the stream" (D4, Jan.5'33).

Prompted by the meagerness of her own sexual experience or stimulated by the lives of her fictional characters and by the excitement of writing, Woolf's sexual preoccupations continue. At Vanessa's studio party she describes "large dishes of hot writhing sausages, looking indecent, like black snakes amorously intertwined." Telling Bunny (David Garnett) she dreamt she was in his arms, he thereupon obliged her. Woolf refers to him as "pale phantom of old love—the love of men and women in the pantry" (D4, Jan.19'33).

In *The Pargiters*, Woolf wishes to present society in its entirety, to combine fact and vision, to include "satire, comedy, poetry, narrative"; she aims at "immense breadth and immense intensity," many ideas but "no preaching—history, politics, feminism, art, literature," the totality of her knowledge, a "summing up of all I know, feel, laugh at, despise, like, admire, hate" (D4, Apr.25'33).

Woolf, on vacation, is in a joshing, salacious mood as she sits at a balcony, overlooking the bay in which Shelley drowned. Writing Ethel from "fascist" Italy, she imagines a phallic Ethel is "inducing a large penis into a small hole"; she supposes Ethel is rehearsing "masses and comic operas, tippling, browbeating and leading the forces of womanhood against ignorance and corruption" (L5, May18'33). Previously she had referred to Ethel as "old, castrated tomcat."

Thinking of a young friend, Francis Birrell, who awaited surgery for a brain tumor, Woolf dreamt of sitting next to him on the sofa; they "kissed and kissed as friends" (D4, Aug.30'33).

Woolf's "novel-essay" proves excessively long and unwieldy, and she must rewrite. In her essay "The Novels of Turgenev," she compares her approach with that of this Russian writer who endlessly wrote and rewrote, engaged in a long struggle of elimination, before achieving a "simplicity so complex" (D4, Aug.16'33).

Feeling she must go on "adventuring, changing, refusing to be stamped and stereotyped," Woolf wishes to free her "self, to let it find its dimensions, not be impeded" (D4, Oct.29'33). Indicating she has gotten "rid of vanity, of Virginia" she feels she has "cut the string that ties" her to that "quivering bag of nerves—all its gratifications and acute despair." Resolutions of this sort generally occur as the new year approaches (D4, Nov.29'33).

Another "full flood" of *The Pargiters*, changed to *Here and Now*, occurs; the style of the novel is her "random, rapid letter writing style" (D4, Jan.16'34). Exploring in her novel the unconventional "relation of a woman and a sod" (sodomite),⁹ Woolf asks her nephew Quentin, whether one can write openly on this theme (L5, Jan.24'34).

What with flu, "rigidity and nothingness," Woolf is still making headway with her manuscript, warns herself to go "very slowly, to stop in the middle of the flood; to lie back and let the soft subconscious world become populous; not to be urging foam from my lips"; then, she must "enrich and stabilize" (D4, May22'34).

Nearing completion, she thinks of making a "general statement," perhaps involving a "chorus," wants to make the transition from particular to general (D4, Aug.7'34); feels the lesson of *Here and Now* is that she is free to use a variety of forms in one book (D4, Aug.21'34).

With the death of Roger Fry, a "thin blackish veil" prevailed; she noted the "poverty of life . . . ; the substance had gone out of everything" (D4, Sept.12'34). Yet an exalted sense of being "above time and death" propels her to go on with her novel (D4, Sept.20 34). The "ghost" of Roger continues to haunt her: "such a blank wall. Such a silence. How he reverberated" (D4, Oct.17'34).

After the initial relief of completing her novel, Woolf misses the characters, the ideas, the pressures of the created universe that has permeated her being (D4, Oct.17'34). Confronted with nine volumes (eight holograph notebooks) of *The Pargiters*, to be reread, rewritten, compacted (D4, Nov.15'34), she is in despair over what she considers the "badness" of the book, wonders how she could have written "such stuff" and with "such excitement." Upon reconsidering, she thinks it good again, "advises other Virginias with other books" that "this is the way of the thing: up, down, up, down—and Lord knows the truth" (D4, Nov.17'34).

Considerable tension with Vanessa over the issue of Julian's writing endeavors emerges. Woolf's rivalry with her nephew Julian, completely submerged, her sensitivity to Vanessa's maternal pride nowhere in evidence, she is critical of Vanessa's "maternal partiality," that is, the "hush and mystery of motherhood" (D4, Nov.27'34), referring to

Vanessa's unconditional defense of her son in face of Virginia and Leonard's belief Julian is too young to publish his poetry.

Changing her title once again, this time to *Ordinary People*, Woolf is revising, substituting one sentence for an entire page. Interjecting "ideas" in her fiction is a "sticky" process and interferes with the "creative subconscious faculty." Persistently she has had difficulty with the outspokenness of one of her central characters and is conflicted about fitting her into the "mainstream." Here she refers to Elvira's pacifism and general nonconformity. Yet she feels Elvira is a vital force (D4, Feb.20'35).

Woolf finds her work "jerky," a process of greater integration and condensation necessary (D4, Feb.27'35). She claims however at age 53 she still struggles, feels the "rush and the glory and the agony and never gets used to any of it" (D4, Mar.6'35). Wishing her sentences to "form and curve" under her fingers again, she would like to have done with copying and typing (D4, Mar.11'35).

Visiting Vita, Woolf noted their friendship was at an end, "not with a quarrel, not with a bang but as a ripe fruit falls." There was no "bitterness, no disillusion, only a certain emptiness" created by Vita's "defection," Roger's death, Vanessa's imminent departure for Italy, in addition to the diminution of "letters and fame" (D4, Mar.11'35).

On Clive's telling her that Segonzac, the Fauve artist, considers Vanessa the finest painter in England, surpassing Duncan, Woolf avers she will not be jealous, but thinks it paradoxical Segonzac finds "gifts" in Vanessa since her sister has "everything else" (D4, Jun.15'35).

Writing Vanessa that she twice dreamt of "kissing Angelica passionately across a hedge," deducing that "incest and sapphism embrace in one breast," Virginia seems rather inappropriate in describing her sexual fantasies towards her niece (L5, Jul.17'35).

Deciding that she was assuming too strident a tone in her writing and could not comfortably embrace politics and art, Woolf opted for fiction, and now called her novel *The Years* (D4, Sept.5'35), incorporating her ideological views in a companion book, *Three Guineas* (D4, Oct.15'35). Intended as Woolf's manifesto against war, *Three Guineas* would question the meaning of patriotism and democracy in what she designated as a male-dominated society that subordinated women. To her, the patriarchal state and fascism seemed closely allied.

In neither *The Years* nor *Three Guineas* could she externalize her original aim of more openly discussing women's sexuality. Despite these restrictions she claims to enjoy her writing more fully, looks forward to working on *Three Guineas* and her biography of Roger Fry (D4, Oct.27'35).

Imperative now, she must rewrite her "incredibly tough old serpent, this albatross" she promised to deliver by February 15, 1936 (D4, Dec.10'35); she questions writing a long novel again, one that has to be held in the "brain at full stretch" for almost three years (D4, Dec.28'35). Thinking she has written the last words of *The Years*, she doubts whether it does indeed "hang together."

She must now "subconsciously wean" herself from the novel and "prepare another creative mood," feels her fictional world will "fade away and something else take its place." Her main feeling concerning *The Years* is its "vitality, fruitfulness, energy"; she wrote "with the whole mind in action" (D4, Dec.29'35), never enjoyed writing a book more.

Trying for another "final" revision of *The Years*, Woolf desperately claims that "one false move means racing despair, exaltation and all the rest of that familiar misery; that long scale of unhappiness" (D5, Jan.4'36). Reading over the last part she was convinced it was "feeble twaddle." The next morning *The Years* seemed a "full, bustling live book" (WD, Jan.16'36). Rewriting and compressing since the previous October (D5, Mar.4'36), she decided to print it in galleys before Leonard sees it (D5, Mar.11'36).

Sending the manuscript to the printer before obtaining Leonard's opinion was an unusual procedure for her. Subsequently she showed Leonard the galley proofs, detecting a "certain tepidity in his verdict so far; these are disgusting, racking days." She dreads going through 600 pages of "cold proof" (D5, Apr.9'36).

After two months of headache, of feeling wretched and a failure (D5, Jun.11'36), deeply affected by Leonard's lack of enthusiasm, Woolf resumed her revisions, her first voluntary writing since the previous April. On her doctor's recommendation, she worked one-half hour at a time, feeling "humility, impersonal joy, literary despair" (D5, Jun.21'36).

Her penchant for sexual fantasy still flourishing, she reveals to Vanessa she might in the past have fallen in love with "Tom Eliot" had they been "in the prime and not in the sere." How important is "copulation" to friendship, she asks; and, when does love become "sexual"? (L6, Jul.22'36).

Questioning whether she can still write (D5, Oct.30'36), she felt her manuscript should be destroyed. On reading the revised novel, Leonard conveyed it was as fine as any of the others, indeed was "extraordinarily good" (D5, Nov.3'36). Now that it was necessary to again get to work and correct immediately, can she? (D5, Nov.4'36). She did.

The "miracle" accomplished, Leonard was decidedly for publication, likes *The Years* better than *The Waves*; she was witness to his absorption as he read on and on, "in tears" (D5, Nov.5'36). Still feeling
discouraged, Woolf can only cling to Leonard's "verdict" (D5,
Nov.9'36).

Since Leonard considered the book too long, Woolf once more
drastically revised. She alluded to her book as a "long childbirth" (D5,
Nov.10'36), her maternal preoccupations still in evidence. Almost finished,
she felt exalted, thought the book had "more real life in it—more blood
and bone": she can accept "appalling watery patches" (D5, Nov.30'36).
Containing far less of her antiwar commentary and political asides, *The
Years* finally appeared in page proofs (D5, Dec.30'36). With some final
rewriting, *The Years* was published March 15, 1937. Woolf anticipates
the book will be "damned with faint praise; its failure deliberate,"[10]
she knew she had reached her "point of view as a writer, as being" (D5,
Mar.7'37).

II

The Years[11] consists of time frames[12] from 1880 to 1937, each with a
dominant theme and persistent rhythm in which repetitive patterns involving musical refrains, collective memories, childhood experiences,
street sounds, discrete words, phrases, tones and images, connect past
and present, conveying permanence and change. The novel traces the
destinies of three generations of Pargiters, beginning with Colonel Abel
Pargiter and his brother Digby, their wives, children, grandchildren, and
cousins. For the most part, the focus is on the second generation,
ultimately the third. In her elaboration of theme and character, Woolf
borrows a considerable amount of Stephen family history.

Woolf begins her novel in a dramatic vein, with Colonel Abel
Pargiter and his daughters Delia, Eleanor, Rose and Milly; his sons
Morris, Edward, and Martin, waiting for Rose senior, wife and mother
to die during 1880, again resurrecting Julia Stephen's death in 1895.
Their wish that Mrs. Pargiter not prolong her dying, the paucity of genuine feeling, concern or grief regarding her imminent loss, is startling,
evocative of Vanessa, Thoby, and Adrian wishing their father, lengthily
ill, would die.

Impatient with her mother's prolonged illness, Delia at the mother's
bedside thinks of a large, public meeting in the cause of "Liberty and
Justice," under the mentorship of Parnell, Irish statesman and nationalist

leader with whom she is infatuated. She was angry at what she thought was her father's meaningless display of feeling for her mother, felt her parents' relationship an empty formality.

At the funeral, Delia thinks their mourning a mockery: "none of us feel anything at all, we're all pretending" (*TY*, 87). Actually, at one point during the ceremony, Delia was overcome by some "generalized and solemn" emotion (85). Watching her mother's coffin in the grave, Delia wanted to "feel" something; "it was the last chance that was left her" (87). Life she felt, was peculiarly mixed with death, and in a sense, death became part of life.

Gazing at her father, Delia suppresses a desire to laugh, not unsimilar to Woolf's memory of wishing to do the same, in perceiving what she felt was the nurses' hypocrisy in crying at Julia's deathbed.

Inability to grieve at her mother's death is cited as intrinsic to Woolf's breakdowns, though she describes her reaction to her mother's death as appropriately emotional at the time. For instance, she cried along with her brothers and sister, though it is more likely her preoccupation with her characters' inability to mourn in *Mrs. Dalloway* and *The Years* suggests her response was intrinsically ambivalent, involving dissociation of anger. This is also evidenced in her curiously unfeeling reactions to the deaths of mother-figures she had formerly been close to.

Woolf's inability to resolve or fathom her early feelings of abandonment regarding her mother, or dislodge her deeply buried, internalized image of an unavailable mother, insufficiently worked through in *To the Lighthouse,* creates an aura of collective shallowness and superficiality in *The Years* in the family's desire to be done with the process of dying. We are given no indication of the basis for the Pargiters' indifference nor know the essential nature of Abel's relationship with his wife or the difficulties with his wife leading to his affair with Mira, his mistress. In *The Pargiters,* the relationship with Mira was romantic, her room a refuge from the bleakness of old age, a dying wife, the responsibilities of father and husband. This was replaced by the illicit, somewhat duplicitous liaison, described in *The Years.*

Abel's clutching, invasive, infantilizing, sexualized behavior with each of his daughters is of central interest in the early manuscript. In *The Pargiters* he is imperious, guilt-provoking, authoritative, a benevolent despot, requiring a systematized account of each child's activities and expenditures. The girls must hide their attraction to men, disavow interest in their bodies, must never be caught "looking out the window," presumably to witness "street love, common love and general love, a love different from the other love inside the drawing room" (*TP*, 38). The children cannot marry or enter a profession without his consent. Invited to dinner and asked to bring but one of his daughters, Abel creates consternation, each daughter feeling acutely jealous of the one chosen, though this is unacknowledged.

Formerly an officer, reputedly courageous, Abel lost several fingers in battle; his wound suggests imperfection, impotency, and is evocative of Leslie Stephen's frailties and collapsibility. Possibly because Woolf thought her portrait of Abel too critical, his dominance is considerably modulated in *The Years*. Though he exerts control, he is a somewhat lost, pathetic figure, envious of his brother, Digby's more intact family. When in a serene mood, however, "there was an opulence, an ease and charm about him" (*TY*, 35). He took the children sailing and fishing, ran races, rigged boats, built wigwams, played games, or engaged in family jokes, in which they all revelled. His daughters became "children again," when he was in good temper.

Reverberative, highly symbolic themes and tropes appear throughout *The Years*. One repetitive refrain expresses directionlessness, lack of moorings, imprecise identity formation. At the sickbed of their mother, Delia asks "where am I." As she stared at a white jug, stained pink by the sun, Delia seemed in some "borderland between life and death"; "life" referred to her desire to join forces with Parnell and home rule (*TY*, 25), to escape her chores at home. At times, Eleanor felt overcome with "blankness," also asks "where am I," felt "alone in the midst of nothingness" (*TY*, 43), possibly suggesting her conflict, usually submerged, in shouldering the responsibilities of oldest daughter and mother-surrogate.

Looking at the river, Sara asks whether she is a "weed" buffeted about. Maggie[13] wonders in the early portion of the novel "What's 'I'? Am I that or am I this? Are we one or are we separate" (*TY*, 140). Peggy[14] similarly wonders "where does Eleanor begin and where do I end?" Later in thinking she and Eleanor were two separate bodies driving across London, Peggy asks: "What is this moment and what are we?" (334) North felt he was "no one and nowhere in particular" (311). Kitty asks "where am I? What am I doing? Where am I going? (267).

Generally these states of confusion or meditation occur during moments of transition or reverie, or follow dreams. They express frustrated ambitions, missed opportunities, wasted youth and occasionally, they are followed by insight, personal revelation or sharper self-definition.

Woolf is immensely preoccupied with her own dreams at this time, which present her with what she considers the "essence of a relationship" that may not find "expression in real life." Dissociating her hostility, she dreams of Ethel or Angelica dying. Or, unable to nuance her resurgance of sexual feelings, she dreams of making love with Francis Birrell, David Garnett, or Duncan, rather obvious wish-fulfillments.

Though Woolf is emotionally invested in all her characters, the portrayals of Eleanor, Rose, Sara-Elvira, North, and Peggy more clearly emerge as self-representations, espouse her social outlook, are evocative of autobiographical vignettes pertaining to childhood as well as later developmental periods.

Focusing on Eleanor, whose problems seem synchronous with her own inner conflicts, Woolf hones in on Eleanor's dreams and her frequently altered state of consciousness on awakening, her optimism and exaltation regarding the future. Eleanor is impressed with Nicholas'[15] dictum in 1917 that we must be more in touch with ourselves, "ordinary people" (281), before we can make suitable laws and religions for others. Glad she is alive after the air raid, stimulated by Nicholas' idealistic hopes for humanity, his theory of the "soul wishing to expand and form new combinations" (296), Eleanor wished to learn how to live more naturally, adventurously, not like "cripples in a cave" (297). She felt something unknown within her, optimistically thought "we shall be free."

At Delia's party, Eleanor in response to Sara's wish to hear more about her life, thought ruminatively: "My life? I haven't got one. Oughtn't a life to be something you could handle and produce. I've only the present moment. How did they compose what people called a life?" (366). Clenching her hand she felt the "hard little coins" she was holding. Is there "I" at the middle, she asks, a "knot, a center" (367). She felt there was a "pattern, a theme recurring like music, half remembered, half foreseen, momentarily perceptible". Perhaps "everything comes over again, a little differently?" (369). In the past, Eleanor vicariously lived through or nurtured the lives of others.

With her mother's illness, then death, Eleanor became both surrogate wife and mother. Emulating her mother, carrying her accounts to her father's study, (91) Eleanor achieves the status of "housekeeper" (92). Father and daughter are exceedingly compatible, like "brother and sister" or husband and wife for that matter. Designating her young cousin Maggie, "niece," Eleanor's slip of the tongue betrays overeagerness to take her mother's place. Apparently she is unaware of her father's extramarital involvement, while he in turn resents Eleanor's outside interests.[16]

Neither Eleanor nor Abel have the emotional awareness their domestic arrangement might be crippling for her. In actuality, Eleanor appears to enjoy the rituals of taking care of their home, yet glimpses expanded possibilities for herself could she but relinquish the insulated enclave of her family. Philanthropic work with the poor absorbs her as she hopes to ameliorate their lot by destroying their tenements (97).

In his 70s, her father has a stroke, becomes inert, ponderous. Eleanor at 51 is empathic, similarly feels heavy, dull, old. With the diminution of her father's strength and authority, life was in effect over for her, too. Her siblings became dispersed upon their father's death and Eleanor feels without central attachment, gives up the family house, travels, assumes she will be labelled an old maid who watches birds though feels "not in the least like that" (203). On meeting a former friend at her brother Morris' home, she reveals a glimmer of interest in an old, lost love, sacrificed in her need to be totally available and obeisant to her father (199).[17]

For the first time in her life, Eleanor is aware of sexual attraction, namely for Renny, Maggie's husband, 20 years younger than she; a man similar to him she might have married had they met earlies (*TY*, 299). Eleanor's sexual awakening is suggested in the description of her travels in which she tells Peggy: "the natives are so beautiful, half-naked, going down to the river in the moonlight." Forming a friendship with Nicholas, a homosexual with a philosophical bent, also appears to have broken through her more characteristic reserve.

In her effort to condense the novel, Woolf deleted "two enormous chunks," sections preceding and following the "1917" chapter, both concerning Eleanor. The earlier, pre-1917 portion, depicts Eleanor reacting with anger, guilt and terror when she learns of the death during the war of a young man she met at her brother's home. Cynical about her solitary efforts concerning the solution of social problems, Eleanor assumes more human proportions, wonders whether helping others has principally served her own needs, a theme evoking Mrs. Ramsay questioning her good deeds.

In the second, post-1917 "chunk," Eleanor muses that people are afraid of one another; she finds it difficult to articulate what she feels, let alone know others. Fearful while walking alone in the city, it seemed to Eleanor there was something "violent and crazy" in the world. Perhaps some scaffolding was falling, "pitching forward to disaster." She felt "no order, no purpose in the world, all was tumbling to ruin" (Radin, 87–88).

In the "Present Day" chapter, Eleanor on awakening from a dream, felt extraordinarily happy," thought "life was a perpetual discovery . . . , a miracle" (383). Asking her niece Peggy for the meaning of dreams, Peggy, a doctor, self-deprecatingly denied special knowledge: "Doctors know very little about the body; absolutely nothing about the mind" (385). Representing an epiphanic experience wherein Eleanor reaches self-awareness and feels she can now embrace the world, Eleanor's dream which she feels is prophetic, mitigates her sense of nonfulfillment.

Awakening from yet another dream, Eleanor, as though "standing on the edge of a precipice," felt "there must be another life . . . , not in dreams but here and now, in this room, with living people". Thinking "we know nothing, even about ourselves. We're only beginning to understand", she felt life too short, too fragmented. She wanted to "enclose the present moment; to make it stay, to fill it with the past, the present and the future until it shone, whole, bright, deep with understanding." Then skepticism took over. For Eleanor there would be the "endless night, the endless dark. She looked ahead of her as though she saw opening in front of her a very long, dark tunnel" (427–428). Here Woolf links the "endless night" of Catullus with the "long dark tunnel" of Sophocles' Antigone (Leaska, 1977a).[18]

Eleanor's preoccupation with life and death is interrupted by a curious episode which occurs at this juncture. Fetched from the basement, the caretaker's children stared at the monied guests. Given some cake and questioned about themselves, they did not wish to speak but instead burst into a shrill, inchoate song.[19] Completely obscure to everyone, Eleanor thought "there was something horrible in the noise they made . . . so shrill, discordant, meaningless" (430); she considered the song primitive, dissonant, fiercely intoned, in a sense beautiful. Possibly Woolf points to the shriek and anger of childhood, wishing she as a child, could have thusly voiced her rage and fury. Here Woolf might have been making a pointed statement about the more naked emotions of the lower classes.

With the advent of dawn, it was time for everyone to leave; the room looked "prosaic but unreal; cadaverous but brilliant." Near the window the Pargiters were "gathered in a group, the old brothers and sisters", as though "carved in stone"; soon everybody began to disperse (432).

Eleanor watched a taxi that stopped nearby; a young man emerged followed by a girl; as the man opened the door to his house, Eleanor turned round and said to Morris, "and now," holding out her hands to him. Then the sun rose and the sky above the houses "wore an air of extraordinary beauty, simplicity and peace." With random occurrences such as the repetition of the childhood refrain of the pigeons' chant "take two coos taffy," and the return of the couple across the way, life apparently resumes (433–434).

Though Woolf mocked, disclaimed, debunked psychoanalysis, she explores some of its basic tenets in *The Years*, such as the importance of oedipal attachments, dream states, and childhood experiences. Indicating that the impressions of childhood are those that "last longest and cut deepest," she added in her essay "Lewis Carroll," that "wisps of childhood persist" when the child is grown: these memories return "sometimes by day, more often by night": "To become a child is to be very literal; to find everything so strange that nothing is surprising; to be heartless yet so passionate that a snub or a shadow drapes the world in gloom." (*TM*, 82).

Children led wretched lives, the "awful" details of which must be concealed, Rose Pargiter as an adult frequently thought. Here she refers to her childhood encounter with male perversion and to slashing her wrist after she was unjustly accused[20] of breaking a microscope, though her brother Martin's friend was the real culprit (157). At strategic moments when she finds herself reminiscing, longing to revive or communicate these early experiences that seem in retrospect so damaging, Rose is inhibited and ashamed. Always she sees herself as living simultaneously on two levels, childhood and present: "What is the use of trying to tell people about one's past? What is one's past?" (167). Formerly close as children, Rose tells Martin, when they are adults, of her early suicide attempt.

It is of interest Rose can share her suicidal episode with her brother but cannot divulge witnessing a male exhibitionist, which may be a cover for her conception of male sexuality in general. Attempting to take one's life is depicted in *The Years*, as it was in *Mrs. Dalloway*, as though it were an inevitable, retaliative response to frustration.

Rose has not "worked through" her sense of sexual abuse or the more profound basis of her anxieties, the lack of central authority in her childhood; feels insufficiently protected and unable to confide in anyone. Is Rose's isolation due to her mother's death or were there earlier schisms in that relationship? Woolf does not make altogether explicit the connection or continuity between childhood and adulthood, tends rather to stress only the highly dramatic, links Rose's childhood sexual trauma with the fact she does not marry.

Rose's early defiance of authority is later channelled into militance regarding the women's movement. Considerably identified with her father, Rose appears uncomfortable with her feminine role, is lesbian in *The Partigers*, Woolf's earlier manuscript. Her military game of brandishing her toy pistol at the "enemy," her rescue mission as "Pargiter of Pargiter's Horse" (*TY*, 27), her need to acquire as bathtub toy a red "squirt" (16), her "head thrown back" as though she were a "military man" (358) or holding her knife "erect" (416), all suggest a masculine model, a need for phallic extension. Morbidly fascinated by her father's "smooth knobs of mutilated fingers" (51), Rose worshipped her father like a "savage for the God of Sun and Thunder" (*TP*, 35), thought him infallible and omnipotent, though it is a castrated image she admires.

Ethel proved to some extent prototype for Rose, was similarly imprisoned for suffragette activites. Woolf saw Ethel predominantly as an accepting, admiring mother-image, as an enveloping, masculine, at times unpredictable or abrasive mother as well. Once when Ethel violently rejected Woolf's arm and almost threw her "to the ground" with her fist, Woolf remonstrated: "How did you brew this violence?" (L5, Jun.18'32). On the way to a suffragette meeting, during a political discussion, Rose knocked Sara violently against a wall, calling her a "damned liar" (*TY*, 187).

Essentially however, Ethel is a "majestic, sea-going, white-spread, dolphin-encircled ship forging on and on," Woolf a "little, tossing tugboat that whips and tumbles" in Ethel's "foam" (L6, Mar.1'37).

Intrigued with variations on the themes of deviance, Woolf imaginatively uses metaphor and symbol in delineating Sara, formerly Elvira, variously depicted as "angular," "sallow," "cadaverous"; as looking like a "bird at the zoo awkwardly hopping swiftly across the grass"; "a great ape crouching"; "a disheveled fowl"; or, as "folding herself like a grasshopper". These images suggest grotesqueness, body distortion, a sense of crippledness. Overtones of early parental neglect also appear: "dropped" when she was a baby, one of Sara's shoulders was "slightly higher than the other" (*TY*, 122).

Along with her poetic sensibility, Sara, with whom Woolf is saliently identified, is the most outspoken, unconventional, rebellious and anarchistic of Woolf's female dramatis personae, more so than Rose who, despite her activities for the women's movement, upholds the basic tenets of the government she fought, supports the war effort in 1914. Sara is totally opposed to war. Frequently contradictory, she inveighs against poverty, yet does nothing to alleviate her impoverished status or that of others, accepts her state of privation and loneliness in preference to conformity with societal verities.

Sara's pacifism notwithstanding, her imagery and body language is often unconsciously martial, for example her caricature of her father "pirouetting with a sword between his legs" and a similar, mocking image of her cousin, North as a soldier with a "switch between his legs." Or, she holds her knife and fork as though they were "weapons" (285).

At one point Sara's lip "raised itself like that of a horse going to bite" (134). During the writing of *The Years*, Woolf's identification with horses became a reverberative mataphor. Once she gets "into the canter over *Three Guineas*", she shall "see only the flash of the white rails and pound along to the goal" (D5, Feb.24'37). Her father at this juncture reminded her of a "racehorse." These are images of power and straining for mastery.

Exuberant, expressive, a wild creature dancing around the bonfire as a child, Sara feels imprisoned as a young woman when she cannot go to parties because of her spinal disorder. Alone in her bedroom while her parents and sister are at a dinner party, Sara overhears fragments of conversation, emanating from a gathering across the way of song lyrics such as "broken heart, love is best, it is all we have, imperfect though it may be" (134). These appear to imply lack of personal fulfillment, longing for love.

In an early diary, Woolf, alone in her room, the same age as Sara, 21, similarly seemed lonely and forlorn as she heard revelrous sounds issuing from a party nearby.[21]

Enveloped in the sharp, white folds of her sheet, Sara looks like a "chrysalis" (144)[22] suggesting she is potential, unformed, her life ahead of her. Yet one wonders about Sara's future, accosted as we are by the author's sinister prognostications of doom and stunted growth when Sara compares herself to a "dead black" tree (133), feels the sun does not nurture or "shine" on her. Expected to lie straight and still because of her "condition," burrowing under sheet and blanket, she identifies with Antigone, about whose fate she is currently reading. She imagines the danger of being "buried alive" (136), is attuned to that aspect of Antigone which is rebellious and challenging of authority.

Sara hates her father, mocks the symbols of his masculinity, suspects her mother of infidelities. An outburst of joyousness is evidenced in childhood in the beautiful scene where Eugenie, Sara's mother, dances for her children. Here the mother's submerged sexuality, the suggestion of subterranean passions and family disharmony are evoked.

When her parents die, Sara lives with Maggie, her sister, with whom she has an exceedingly close relationship. With Maggie's marriage to Renny, Sara lives alone, forms an attachment to Nicholas. She and Nicholas clearly love each other, but we are told Nicholas is homosexual. Was the obscurity in describing their relationship an aspect of Woolf's fear of censure, her fear of personal disclosure?

During Sara's encounter with her young cousin, North, with whom she corresponded when he was in the army in World War I and later when he raised sheep in Africa, they reminisce at length about their respective letters to one another. These letters were frequently poetic, occasionally angry and chiding on Sara's part. North comments on their foolishness when "young," writing "purple passages." Here Sara peels a banana as if "unsheathing some soft glove . . . , the banana skin like the finger of a glove that had been ripped open," while the "curl of apple skin lay on North's plate coiled up like a snake's skin" (322). These are clearly rather suggestive sexual images.

Though their conversation is core to core and their feelings full of warmth, North sensitive to Sara's idiosyncracies, she to his loneliness, there is no indication they could be lovers. Most probably Woolf is making a comment about the deep affection between an older woman and younger man, or illustrating her theory of love without sex.

An episode which does not ingratiate Sara to the reader involves an anti-Semitic comment about a Jew taking a bath in their common bathroom, inconsiderably leaving a "line of grease round the tub." (339) Toward the Jew, Sara feels disgust and repulsion, engages in an attack on the "polluted city"; must she work, join the "conspiracy" and "serve a master because of a Jew?"[23] (340–341). Sara's repudiation of society and condemnation of the "servile, innumerable army of workers" (341) seem related to her need to deny she is herself "poor" and must earn her living.

III

Woolf felt she and Sara were kindred spirits. Writing was a form of "mediumship" where she "becomes the person." Both she and Sara blamed the masculine ethos for the recurrence of war, though in *Three Guineas*, Woolf hoped the liberation of women would also help men actualize themselves. In avoiding university honors and awards of "all kinds for writers," Woolf refusing the "Doctor of Letters" at Manchester University, felt "real life" provided her with the situation she was indeed writing about, namely Elvira refusing the bribes of society: "I hardly know which I am, Virginia or Elvira—in the Pargiters or out" (D4, Mar.25'33).

In *The Pargiters*, Elvira-Sara was depicted as a critic and essayist who tries to validate her feelings and very existence in writing. Distrusting appurtenances of organized power and money, Elvira-Sara relied only on her own emotional reaction: "It is an utterly corrupt society and I will take nothing it can give me" (D5, Mar.25'33) she insisted. Woolf feared Elvira might become too "dominant," but basically she was concerned that Elvira's deviance might assume autobiographical dimensions.

Though she claimed to eschew fame, Woolf was sensitive to attack by Wyndham Lewis who had accused her of being a "fundamental prude" (D5, Oct.14'34); she felt "queer, disreputable pleasure in being abused, in being a martyr" (D4, Oct.11'34). Feeling "hated, despised, and ridiculed" by the critics Swinnerton and Mirsky, Woolf must continue to "expose" her mind, "opened and intensified as it is by the heat of creation, to the blasts of the outer world" (D4, Mar.18'35).

Confronted with the dilemma of appearing too strident, Woolf found Huxley's novel "Point Counter-point," published at this time and similar in theme to *The Years*, "raw, uncooked, protesting" (D4, Jan.23'35). Still viewing Elvira-Sara's abrasiveness her chief difficulty in writing *The Years*, Woolf felt her solution was to minimize the propagandistic, remain with the "creative, subconscious faculty" (D4, Feb.20'35).

Sara and her sister Maggie have been referred to by critics as Antigone and Ismene, Sara the rebel and nonconformist. Maggie though sympathetic to her sister, did not sever her ties to society. Despite the tawdriness of the flat they shared, though the night was full of "roaring, cursing, unrest, and outside there were nasty little creatures driven by uncontrollable lusts," Maggie because of her capacity for deep feeling, saw the night as full of beauty: the large factory windows opposite were illuminated and looked she thought, like a "palace of glass with thin black bars across it," which, ironically, seems a reflection of their imprisonment. Maggie married Renny with whom she has a close and solid relationship and with whom she has children.[24] Secure in his masculine role, Renny shares in household routines and child rearing.

During 1917, the Pargiters gather in Renny's and Maggie's home, sit through a harrowing air raid in their cellar. Maggie brings them together, feeds them, her home a haven of warmth and strength.

Maggie's visual acuteness is in evidence as she fetches Sara and North to bring them to Delia's party in 1937. As they rose to go, Maggie looked at the cheap lodging-house room and noted the dish of fruit on the table, the "heavy sensual apples" next to the "yellow spotted bananas," an "odd combination, the round and the tapering, the rose and the yellow." Switching off the light, the room was in darkness, except for a "watery pattern" flickering on the ceiling. In this "phantom evanescent light, only the outlines showed; ghostly bananas, and the specter of a chair. Color was slowly returning as her eyes grew used to the darkness, and substance . . . " (*TY*, 350). Maggie's perception of the fruit reinforces the previous suggestion of muted sexuality between older woman (Sara) and younger cousin.[25]

In the general conviviality of the final chapter, Maggie is asked at one point to make a speech but refused, "throwing her head back as if . . . possessed by some genial spirit outside herself, that made her bend and rise, as a tree is tossed and bent by the wind." She intoned "no idols, no idols, no idols," (425). Maggie is of course richly evocative of Vanessa.

At Delia's party during 1937, Peggy, Morris' daughter, a doctor, and third generation Pargiter, bitter that one of her brothers was killed in World War I, is relieved her brother, North, back from Africa and protesting that the others talk only of money and politics, is alive. Perceiving people talked too loudly or were "making believe," she thought of "other worlds, indifferent to this one, people toiling, grinding in the heart of darkness."[26] She questioned the state of happiness in a world replete with misery and suffering. On every placard at street corners, one read of "death . . . , tyranny, brutality; torture; the fall of civilization; the end of freedom" (388). Clearly Peggy projects Woolf's social outlook at this time. Peggy was convinced everyone was merely "sheltering under a leaf which will be destroyed" (388). Meaning to be affiliative towards North, Peggy blundered, apparently offended her brother by telling him he was merely interested in marriage, money and writing "little books" (396): "If one meant to help, one hurt" (397).

North was bruised by her derogatory comments, yet he felt they still had something profound in common. At odds with his cousins at Delia's, North thought their desire to reform the world should "begin there, at the center, with themselves" (405). North too felt he was in the "middle of a jungle in the heart of darkness." Groping his way towards the light, he was provided only with "broken sentences, single words with which to break through the briarbush of human bodies, wills and voices that bent over him, binding him, blinding him" (411). They were all afraid of each other, of criticism, of laughter, of people who think differently.

Asked to make a toast, Nicholas proclaimed "humanity which is now in its infancy, may it grow to maturity! Ladies and gentlemen! I drink to that!"

Considerable attention has been accorded the name of the upper middle class, Victorian family that Woolf fictionalized, Pargiter,[27] which is derived from the word "parget," originally found in Joseph Wright's *English Dialect Dictionary*. There it is defined as "plastering or whitewashing with cement, made of cow dung."

Alluding to her room and the cellar they gather in during an air raid, as caves made of "mud and dung," Sara unconsciously suggests that being a Pargiter dooms one from the start, equated as it is with dirt or contamination; or she strongly states that inherently a Pargiter is basely constituted, lowly, or smelly. Having been born a Stephen might also lead to disease, stunted growth, or entombment.

Woolf was intrigued with the author of the *English Dialect Dictionary*, Joseph Wright, who was raised in a workhouse. His mother, a charwoman, provided him with a proper education, propelled his subsequent achievement as a writer of dialect dictionaries. To honor or repay his mother, Wright in turn sought to improve the education of working women. Woolf respected the marriage of Joseph and his wife, Lizzie, thought their relationship truly equalitarian, felt them kindred spirits. They proved prototype for the Robsons in *The Years*, an unpretentious family where everyone shares the work, and with whom Kitty,[28] a cousin of the Pargiters, closely identifies as a young woman, feeling limited by the constraints of her father's academic circle and by her father's derogation of her intellectual abilities.

Several critics cite the overdetermined family name Pargiter, as a central metaphor in the novel, suggesting that it represented the older generation's attempt to cover up their hypocrisies and mendacities, transmitting hushed, enigmatic family secrets to their children. In Leaska's view, Woolf herself was a "pargeter" in extirpating massive portions of her narrative, "smoothing over" emotionally loaded areas dealing with sex and ideology out of consideration for Victorian decorum and fear of disclosure concerning her own class, family and personal relationships.[29] In particular he cites the need to submerge her intense ambivalence regarding her father, the need to bestow blame on him for the wrongs endured in childhood, the need to avoid awareness of the strong sexual component in her attachment to him (Leaska, 1977a, 198).

Suggesting that use of Pargiter as a surname indicated "moral and physical ambivalence in a novel about the patriarchal family, perhaps a combination of whitewash and filth, a true 'whited sepulchre,' outwardly beautiful but full of dead men's bones within," Marcus (1977a) feels the characters are all "pargeters" plastering over the flaws in British society. The artist, Marcus suggests is a "master-plasterer; his materials whitewash and dung, vision and reality. We are made to see the truth of our wretched lives, but to keep on going forward despite it" (Marcus, 301).

Based on Woolf's conception of her father's marital and paternal roles and his youngest daughter's entanglements in them, Abel latches onto all of his daughtes in an intrusive, dictatorial way, hindering their pursuit of a more suitable heterosexual destiny. He seemed more emotionally available to them when they were children.

There is the suggestion Woolf might have found her parents' previous marriages hard to assimilate and fathom, especially her mother's first marriage, surrounded as it was with halo and myth. Perhaps Woolf faulted her mother for endowing her with full-blown half-brothers who sexually molested her. In the novel, the incestuous theme most clearly encompasses the relationship between Eleanor and father.

It is also hinted Abel and his sister-in-law Eugenie have had an affair and spawned Sara and/or Maggie, so that the Pargiter cousins might be siblings. In life, Woolf felt incestuously linked with her half-brothers

and father; she later saw father as "promiscuously" transferring his affections to Stella when their mother died, despite Woolf's prior claims.

Projected in *The Years* are conflicting images of family life, one
reflecting Martin's notion that it is an "abominable system . . . , con-
sisting of "people boxed up together telling lies" (223), another, Sara's,
that the family assumes the inexorableness of a caravan crossing the
desert, its members cleaving together in face of the depredations of the
outside world. Despite the painful self-revelations of her characters,
Woolf suggests, though guardedly, that they might be capable of a more
harmonious existence.

Of central interest in *The Years* is Woolf's incisive portrayal of the
lives, interactions and family relationships of the Pargiter children and
cousins. Informing the novel are repeated metaphors communicating
lack of clarity concerning individual worth, inability to feel, the notion
that pain must outweigh pleasure in human relationships; recurrent images of despair and alienation such as "cripples in a cave" or "caves
scooped out of mud and dung." Metaphors such as these correspond to
the sense of unlived life, of not progressing, of entrapment, a feeling of
meaninglessness pertaining to the human condition. The author's concern with the passing of time, Peggy's and North's allusions to Conrad's "heart of darkness," Eleanor's preoccupation with the "endless
dark," references made to the cadaverous and crypt-like, the deaths of
king, parents, and others—point to Woolf's central theme, the transitor-
iness and insubstantiality of life, the fleeting conditions of mortality.

These themes alternate with insights and epiphanic awarenesses suggesting an embrace of life, of the sentient moment, the importance of
connection. After Eleanor's meditation on life and death, she, carried
along by the lives of others, turns to the pale light of dawn, North to
seminal images of renewal. For him there was "another life; not halls
and reverberating megaphones, not marching in step after leaders, in
herds, groups, caparisoned; not black shirts, green shirts, red shirts." He
hoped to keep the "emblems of North Pargiter . . . but at the same time,
spread out, make a new ripple in human consciousness, be the bubble
and the stream," (*TY*, 410) he and the world as one.

When Edward Pargiter, "masked-like" and "locked up," is unable
to answer North's question about a passage in *Antigone* which Edward
himself, an Oxford scholar, has translated, North thinks Edward overly
fearful of ridicule and that fear keeps people separate one from another.
Actually, the avoided reference is Creon's statement "A foe is never a
friend not even in death" and Antigone's reply "it is not my nature to
join in hating but in loving" (Fleishman, 198). This seems in consonance

with Woolf's expressed desire to overcome the divisions she finds
permeating modern life.

The *Years* received laudatory reviews and became a popular success.
E.M. Forster thought the book "dead and disappointing," yet Woolf as
always, felt stimulated by his comments (D5, Apr.2'37). Contempo-
rarily, *The Years* has abeen resuscitated by some as the most politically
and socially sophisticated of Woolf's novels. Marcus (1977b) considers
The Years the "female epic," in effect "Woolf's answer to *The Waste-
land* and *Ulysses* . . . , bursting with the 'content'" that Joyce omitted.
The Years is a "communal and antiheroic odyssey with Nausicaa as its
heroine," continues Marcus, with Eleanor as "that militant but non-
violent maiden" who "washes away the sins of a war-torn world, bringing fresh air, light and water out of the Victorian gloom" (Marcus, 435).
Eleanor as "militant" projects considerable idealization.

Summarizing her intention in writing *The Years*, Woolf conveys to
Stephen Spender that she meant to give a "picture of society as a whole,
give characters from every side; turn them towards society not private
life, exhibit the effect of ceremonies; keep one's toes on the ground at the
end." Seeking to shift from present to future, "show the old fabric in-
sensibly changing without death or violence, into the future," she suggested a "recurrence of some pattern; of which we actors are ignorant.
And the future was gradually to dawn" (L6, Apr.7'37).

Was Woolf nearer a "complete breakdown" with *The Years* in 1936
than she had been since 1913, as Leonard attests (3LW154). Leonard
based his pronouncement on his wife's allusion to her "dismal . . . ,
almost catastrophic illness" wherein she had "never been so near the
precipice to my own feeling since 1913." But then with her usual recoverability, did she not state: "I am again on top. I have to rewrite and rub
out most of *The Years* in proof" (D5, Jun.11'36). This was her first
voluntary writing since April 9 when she indicated Leonard's "verdict"
or response to *The Years* was not favorable. In this context, "verdict"
suggests a sentencing.

Due at the printer's February, 1937, Virginia was no doubt panicky
about her manuscript. Most likely she felt artistically and personally rejected by Leonard's coolness regarding the novel. Her tendency to avoid
discussion of her completed manuscript with anyone but Leonard was
potentially risky, placing her in a helpless, suppliant position.

Actually, despite headache, she only temporarily ceased working on
her novel. In June, she felt sufficiently recovered to start revising once
again; feelings of failure alternated with relief, respite, hope. For her at

this time, reading Flaubert's letters which communicated the ex-
cruciating difficulties of writing, were "consoling, admonishing" (D5,
Jun.21'36).

The Woolfs decided to remain at Rodmell where Virginia could pursue a more sedentary regime. Leonard indicates she was unable to write
or check her proofs, yet he told her publisher, Donald Brace, that she
worked on the first batch, revising them to a considerable extent (Radin,
114). This is also noted in Woolf's later diary entry (D5, Nov.10'36) where
she alludes to working that summer despite morning headaches, indicating a more sustained effort than Leonard describes.

Was her anxiety and Leonard's "tepidity" about the novel due to
their unspoken but separate awareness of the anti-Semitic passages? It is
not at all clear why Woolf chose to create and elaborate the unsavory
character she pointedly identified as a Jew who, after his bath, left the
common tub in a grimy and sorry state, to the scorn and contempt of
Sara, his lodging-house neighbor.

Echoing Virginia's views and countering Leonard's, Sara was
ideologically a vociferous pacifist. When Hitler occupied the Rhineland
in 1936, Leonard no doubt felt annoyance concerning his wife's antiwar
position which at this time directly countered his beliefs.

Possibly the relationship between the asexual, iconoclastic, unregen-
erative Sara, undisguisedly Woolf, and Nicholas, a robust, likeable
homosexual, also proved threatening to Leonard, not terribly secure concerning his sexual belongingness.

Leonard eventually told Virginia her book was "most remarkable"
(D5, Nov.5'36). Actually, he felt both disappointed and relieved in
reading it, considered it a failure, neither as valuable as her other novels,
nor as appallingly bad as she would have it. He chose to hedge, since the
truth, he felt, would kill her (Bell, n.2, 196). This is puzzling inasmuch as
her publisher Donald Brace, in New York City, was highly enthusiastic
regarding *The Years*.

Noting in her diary (D4, Mar.11'35) that the romantic bond with Vita
was at an end, with nothing to take its place, Woolf indicated Vita had
grown "fat," was the "indolent country lady, run to seed," no longer interested in books or writing poetry, giving herself over merely to dogs,
flowers, new buildings and to working on her Sissinghurst garden. Is it
possible that because of her hurt and anger towards Vita, Woolf killed
off Mrs. Pargiter with such lack of feeling?

XIV "Oh that our human pain could here have ending" — *Between the Acts*

I

On July 18, 1937, Woolf heard the staggering news of her nephew, Julian's death, at 29, at Villanueva de la Canada in the Battle of Brunete in Spain where he had been an ambulance driver for over a month, volunteering for Spanish Medical Aid, fighting on the side of the Loyalist forces in the Spanish Civil War. In a reversal of roles, Woolf now ministered to her sister in her grief. She writes Vita: "Nessa likes to have me and I'm round there most of the time. It is very terrible" (L6, Jul.21'37). To a friend she writes that her sister's children are as though her own, explains that Julian found it "necessary" to go to Spain, and "there is a kind of grandeur in that, which now and then consoles one" (L6, Jul.26'37).

Ruthlessly probing her feelings for Julian in a memoir written July 30, Virginia acknoweldged her coolness regarding Julian's writing, as well as her envy of Vanessa's maternal role. To Leonard, who frequently accused her of greater involvement with her sister's family than with his own, she attributed an enormous penchant for criticizing Vanessa's children. Actually, Virginia thought Julian "careless, not an artist, too personal in what he wrote and all over the place." Deeply regretting she did not encourage Julian more as a writer, however, she avers "that's my character and I'm always forced in spite of my jealousy to be honest in the end"[1] (Bell, v.2., 255). Woolf had for long been jealous of Julian usurping Vanessa's attention, almost as though he were a younger sibling.

Vanessa faulted the Woolf's tough stance in feeling Julian should not publish so young, citing Hogarth Press' rejection of her son's "letter" concerning Roger Fry.

Writing to Julian the year before his death, Virginia conveys that his "Roger Fry letter" was too "long, discursive and loosely knit." Essentially, she and Leonard could not accept his work because their "letter series" had ceased. Julian had been hurt and Woolf angry with herself for thus bruising him. After Julian's death, the Woolf's stated his "letter" was too "full of himself". At first T.S. Eliot considered publishing

231

Julian's selected essays, including the Fry "letter," although ultimately Julian's essays, personal letters and portions of his poems, edited by his brother, Quentin Bell, were posthumously published by Hogarth Press in November 1938 (L6, n.1. 155).

Further personal eruptions occur between Woolf and her sister. Threatened when Helen Anrep, Roger's mistress, visited Vanessa, Woolf wondered whether Vanessa preferred Helen to her: "the green goddess jealousy lit on my pillow and shot this bitter shaft through my heart". Woolf furthermore deplores Vanessa's "deficiency of taste" (L6, Aug.31'37).

Unable to express appreciation for Virginia's emotional support which sustained her, following Julian's death, Vanessa asked Vita to tell Virginia of her feelings. Thanking Vita for her letter, Woolf commented on the decided oddness of Vanessa's inability to be more direct (L6, Oct.1'37).

Woolf writes her sister that when she, Vanessa is not there "I merely exist dry and dusty" (L6, Oct.2'37). Despite the greater rapport between the sisters and Woolf's genuine grief regarding Julian, Vanessa could not forgive her for holding back publication of Julian's writings when he was alive.

Meanwhile, *Three Guineas*, Woolf's personal attack on war, masculine values and prerogatives, "pressed and spurted" out of her . . . "like a physical volcano," almost as though a bodily "expulsion"[2] (D5, Oct.12'37). Expecting a "chill bath of disillusionment" from Leonard regarding *Three Guineas*, she reiterates how imperatively, she needed to write this book, has now recovered her equanimity, has had her "say." Others can "take it or leave it" (D5, Apr.12'38).

For her next novel, *Pointz Hall*, Woolf thinks "we" shall replace "I", "we" representing "all life, all art, all waifs and strays, a rambling, capacious, unified whole." Feeling "entirely free, afraid of nothing, no longer on a pedestal," on her own "forever," she is imbued with a sense of expansiveness and liberation (D5, Apr.26'38).

Thinking the whole of Europe may soon be in flames, Woolf regards *Three Guineas* as a "moth dancing over a bonfire" (D5, May24'38). Uneasy at "autobiography" in public, she feels relief and closure in finishing *Three Guineas*, though an uncustomary sense of hostility and victimization follow: "Now I am quit of that poison and excitement. Having spat it out, my mind is made up. I am an outsider; the pack may howl but it shall never catch me" (D5, May20'38). Combining *The Years* and *Three Guineas*, she envisages the end of six years of "floundering, striving, much agony, some ecstasy" (D5, Jun.3'38). *Three*

Guineas is the "mildest childbirth" she has ever known, she claims, still preoccupied with her fertility (D5, Jun.5'38).

Should war come, Woolf is fearful not only of Quentin's conscription but of the "complete ruin of civilization" in Europe (D5, Aug.17'38). Leonard is worried inasmuch as Hitler's forces are poised for war which would bring barbarism,[3] "conceivably death" of friends and relatives. Since they are all "equally in the dark" they cannot "cluster and group" (D5, Sept.5'38).

Though Woolf feels inundated by "facts" in beginning her biography of Roger Fry, Roger now "surrounds" her; she "blesses" him for giving her "himself". He is a support in this "welter of unreality" (D5, Sept.10'38). Roger's "persuasiveness, eagerness, absorption, stir," urging others to agree with his prejudices, create a "vibration like a hawk-moth round him" (D5, Sept.20'38). Woolf further extols him to Vanessa: "Roger is so magnificent—I'm so in love with him" (L6, Oct.8'38).

Is Woolf in scrutinizing the correspondence between Vanessa and Roger now "in love" with him because she is plunged into Vanessa's past affair with him? Of course, Woolf has always been titillated by Vanessa's lovers or husbands, and now feels "pulverized" without Vanessa, who is in southern France (L6, Nov.2'38).

Evaluating her public reputation at this point, Woolf reflects on her past fame, in strong language states she felt "decapitated" by Wyndham Lewis and Gertrude Stein. Currently, she feels outmoded, doubts she can "write anything good again." She feels she is "second rate," bound to be "discarded altogether." Of course she never considered herself famous; basically she is an "outsider," does her best "back to the wall." Yet she feels "odd . . . , writing against the current" (D5, Nov.22'38). Significantly, she is revising "Lappin and Lapinova,"[4] a short story written in 1918 about a couple who encourage each others' imaginative flights. At the last, the husband rejects his wife's proneness for fantasy and she dies (D5, Dec.19'38).

While Leonard "gallops" through his books, Virginia writes Ethel she is "toiling, revising" and rewriting *Roger Fry* (L6, Apr.14'39), finding painful the "severance" war brings. Life loses meaning, nothing can be planned. She muses on the "community feelings: all England thinking the same thing, this horror of war—at the same moment" (D5, Apr.15'39).

Reading Pascal evokes Lytton: "my dear old serpent . . . ; that he should be dead and I reading him." She tries to fathom Lytton's and her own possible impact on the world, occasionally feels life an "illusion—gone so fast; lived so quickly." Nothing remains except "these little books" (D5, Jun.29'39).

Somewhat suspiciously, Woolf now finds "all books surrounded by a circle of invisible censors. Hence their self-consciousness, their restlessness." Rather grimly she describes the advent of age, the gradual coming of death, perhaps as others refer to love; she wishes to "detect every one of the gradual stages toward death which is a tremendous experience, and not as unconscious, at least in its approaches, as birth is" (D5, Aug.7'39).

Seeking to revive her relationship with Vita, hoping to be back amongst the annointed, Woolf submissively tells her friend: "whatever rung I'm on, the ladder is a comfort in this kind of intolerable suspension of all reality—something real" (L6, Aug.29'39).

With Hitler invading Poland on September 1, 1939, England declared war the next day. The Woolf's first air raid warning sounded several days later. Woolf bemoans their isolation; their world is now "empty, meaningless." She expects she is a physical coward, feels "all the blood has been let out of common life." There are no movies, theater, or mail; friends neither write nor telephone. She envisages a "long sea voyage with strangers making conversation and lots of small bothers and arrangements . . . , all creative power cut off" (D5, Sept.6'39).

Calling her home a "refuge haunt" with clerks from Hogarth, other "fugitives" and neighbors descending on them, Woolf's day is fragmented she tells Ethel, except that she manages to write mornings. Leonard, released to work on his many projects since John Lehmann became partner of Hogarth Press, published his second volume of *After the Deluge: A Study of Communal Psychology*, which Virginia thought a "masterly work" (L6, Sept.26'39). Most likely, Virginia is threatened by Leonard's surge of writing activity since a pervasive uncertainty about her own abilities prevailed at this time.

Continuing to revise *Roger Fry*, which must be "compacted, vitalized," her hand is "tremulous as an aspen" (D5, Oct.6'39), a frequently repeated, doom-laden lament from this point forward.

Still immersed in her personal friendships, jealous of Ethel's "two new loves" (L6, n.2, 359), Woolf claims to have nothing with which to lure her back. Working furiously, she is "damp and dull," but "there's a peace in the country" that surrounds her as a "mouse is surrounded with cheese" (L6, Oct.9'39). Evocative of Sara's expostulations in *The Years*, she writes Angelica that "rats in caves live as we do" (L6, Oct.16'39).

Admiring Gide's frankness in journal and novels regarding his homosexuality, Woolf wonders why, in view of this, she cannot externalize in her biography, *Roger Fry*, the "comparatively modest truth about Roger and his affairs" (L6, Nov.5'39), alluding to his bisexuality.

Jostled both by *The Times Literary Supplement*'s criticism of her pamphlet "Reviewing"[5] and a similarly attacking letter in *The New Statesman* (WD, Nov.9'39), Woolf feels her essay writing evokes more anger than constructive comment (L6, Nov.16'39). No doubt this contributes to her "jaded, tired, depressed, cross" feelings, and she finds *Roger Fry* is dragging (D5, Nov.30'39). To "enlarge the circumference," ignore the "shrinkage of age," she reads Freud for the first time (D5, Dec.2'39).

Referring to an article she is writing[6] that focuses on "pooling men's and women's work, removing men's disabilities," Woolf's hostility towards male aggression is ill-concealed as she asks: "How can we alter the crest and spur of the fighting cock?" Hoping war will debunk the unreality of "glory", and "white feathers," she wishes for "natural happiness" (L6, Jan.22'40).

Woolf finds her London home a "bright cave," the city "silent: a great dumb ox lying couchant" (D5, Feb.18'40). Finishing *Roger Fry*, she must send the manuscript to his sister Margery Fry for approval, and she feels like a "small boy" preparing an exercise (L6, Feb.20'40).

Also given the manuscript of *Roger Fry* to evaluate, Vanessa wrote: "Since Julian died I haven't been able to think of Roger. Now you have brought him back to me" (Mar.13'40; Bell, v.2, 214). This in turn prompted Woolf to write that she was concerned Vanessa would not approve her efforts: "I never wrote a word without thinking of you and Julian and have longed to do something that you'd both like. As for thanking me, well, when you've given me Julian and Quentin and Angelica . . . " (L6, Mar.15'40).

Yet Leonard did not feel positively regarding her biography. Virginia felt his disapproval and anger regarding *Roger Fry* exaggerated. He "lectured" her on the first half:

> It was like being pecked by a very hard strong beak. The more he pecked, the deeper. At last he was almost angry that I'd chosen what seemed to him the wrong method, merely analysis not history. Austere repression. In fact dull to the outsider. All those dead quotations. His theme was that you can't treat a life like that; must be seen from the writer's angle D5, Mar.20'40).

Perceiving this a "curious example" of Leonard at his "most rational and impersonal," she felt convinced of "failure," except for the conviction that Leonard's critique might have been personally motivated. As they talked and the "beak struck deeper," she felt this "completely detached interest in Leonard's character" (D5, Mar.20'40). It is unlikely she felt "detached" but detected Leonard's anger was exaggerated and he jealous of Roger. Margery Fry gave "unbounded admiration" for the book.

An active member of the Rodmell Women's Institute, Virginia is asked to write and produce a play[7] for the community; she disparages Rodmell as "full of doings villages are, of violent quarrels and incessant intrigues." She and Leonard are considered "red hot revolutionaries" simply because the Labor Party meets at their home (L6, Apr.6'40).

In Prime Minister Churchill's asking everyone to contribute to the war effort, all else shrinks in importance.[8] Leonard tells Virginia there is "petrol" in the garage for committing suicide if Hitler wins. Despite the tumult of war, Woolf's feelings for Roger are so strong she cannot get the "odd incongruity of feeling intensely, and at the same time knowing there is no importance in that feeling. Or is there more importance than ever?" she asks (D5, May13'40).

A note of both normativeness and anxiety is present in Woolf's next letter to Ethel in which she affirms the importance of having "books to believe in" as well as "drudgeries" such as ordering food and rehearsing her village play. Then she thinks of Montaigne's phrase "let death find me planting cabbages" (L6, May17'40).

War is "like a desperate illness" as Woolf endures the worst week so far (D5, May20'40). The Nazis broke through, took Amiens and Arras, are now at Boulogne. The Allies were outwitted. Rodmell is agog with rumors that they might be bombed and evacuated (D5, May25'40).

In a chatty, gossipy letter to her niece, Judith Stephen, Virginia describes Leonard organizing Fabians in London and finishing *The War for Peace*; Duncan painting battleships in Plymouth, Quentin in the country ploughing; Virginia herself in charge of village plays written by the gardener's wife and the chauffeur's wife and acted by the other villagers. Persisting in her morbid preoccupation with the aging process, she refers to T.S. Eliot as "old" Tom Eliot though he was 52, six years younger than she. She concludes her letter "Your 'old' aunt," which is in keeping with the depiction of her female characters in *The Years* as "ravaged," "worn," perhaps emotionally burnt out though middle-aged (L6, May29'40).

Despite the "desperate battle" going on, hope revives as the Allies are in a holding position. Woolf saw a hospital train, "grieving, tender, heavy laden and private—bringing our wounded back carefully through the greenfields" (D5, May30'40).

Harcourt Brace in New York accepts *Roger Fry* and Woolf seriously grapples with *Pointz Hall*. She is "bubbling" over with her "scraps, orts

and fragments," a phrase also appearing in *Pointz Hall* (D5, May31'40).
At the same time the pivotal battle deciding their "life or death" continues (D5, Jun.7'40), and there is an anxious note: "I will continue
but can I? The pressure of this battle wipes out London. Should they lose
the war Jews must surrender, go to concentration camps: "So to our
garage." Woolf is here referring to a suicide pact with Leonard should
the Nazis succeed (D5, Jun.9'40).

To Ethel she writes: "I read myself into a state of immunity." (L6,
Jun.9'40). She makes up scraps of poetry, in part for her book, some
"desperate," some "hopeful." Sending off the page proofs of *Roger
Fry*, she is convinced it is a failure, suggested by Leonard's "coolness"
and John Lehmann's "silence" (D5, Jun.10'40).

Her anxiety unresolved, Woolf is irritated, cannot stick to reading
one book, and feels she should at least complete *Pointz Hall*: "oughtn't I to
finish something by way of an end? The end gives its vividness, even its
gaiety and recklessness to the random daily life"; she thought she might
be taking her "last walk." Delight in rereading Coleridge and Shelley
catalyzes the wish to make "swifter," "lighter," more "intense" and
"fluid" the writing of her essays. The problem is to "keep the flight of
the mind, yet be exact. All the difference between the sketch and the
finished work" (D5, Jun.22'40).

Woolf complains her hand has staggered into the "stages of illegi-
bility." Derogating herself, she does not know why Ethel cares for her:
"How when she's picked every plum off the tree, can she have fingered
my crude little unripe apple?" Reading Ethel's new book[9] Woolf is impressed with its "ripeness;" she prefers Ethel's "humility" to her
"brilliancy." Ethel acknowledges "openly" what Woolf hides so
scrupulously, namely her homosexual orientation. Self-deprecatingly,
Woolf compared her "tethered and literal rubbish heap grubbing in
Roger Fry," with Ethel's "complete, free-handed and profound revelation," then sounded a warning note: "I'm writing against time" (L6,
Jul.9'40).

Indicating her belief that every book is only a fragment, that one may
be brighter or bigger but to complete the whole one must read them all,
she begs Ethel to continue writing because "you do continue, being,
thank God, not a finished precious vase,[10] but a porous receptacle that
sags slightly, swells slightly, but goes on soaking up the dew, the rain, the
shine" and all else populating the earth: "Isn't that the point of being
Ethel Smyth" (L6, Jul.24'40).

The day before publication of *Roger Fry*, Woolf dreaded the reviews.
She claims "all the protecting and reflecting walls, wear so thin in this
war. There's no standard to write for: no public to echo back; hence a

certain energy and recklessness" (D5, Jul.24'40). With *Roger Fry* launched, the "main people" affirm her effort. Woolf muses on her "curious relation" with Roger: "I who gave him a kind of shape after his death." She wondered whether he resembled her portrait, felt "very much in his presence," as though she were "intimately connected with him, as if we together had given birth to this vision of him, a child born of us" (D5, Jul.25'40). Previously, Virginia felt she and Leonard together gave birth to her books.

With the *Times* benignant regarding *Roger Fry*, Woolf is "aware of something permanent and real" in her life, "proud" of achieving a "solid work" (D5, Jul.26'40). Desmond MacCarthy writes a laudatory review; friends, among them the younger generation, think *Roger Fry* "important," affording her a "calm rewarded feeling." She produced what was asked of her, presented her friends with what they "wanted" (D5, Aug.4'40).

Clive approves, thinks it the "best biography" in years. Now that Clive gives his accolade, she does not care a "snap" what anyone says. She is "confirmed" in what she felt when she took "that beak-pecking" walk with Leonard in March "with a temperature of 101" (D5, Aug.6'40). Her great difficulty with the book, she tells Clive, was to avoid personal intrusions yet not be overly factual; never has she attempted anything so strenuous (L6, Aug.6'40). Morgan and Vita are not particularly laudatory (D5, Aug.10'40).

Ethel immediately grasped Woolf's intention in the writing of *Roger Fry*, recognized the book required modulation of Woolf's personal impressions and proved a "gamble" in a sense on Roger's capacity to project himself. To Woolf, he was "so rich, alive, various and masterly" that she knew he would "shine by his own light better than through any painted shade of mine" (L6, Aug.16'40).

Pointz Hall is a current challenge. Bombs come close; she and Leonard lay down under the tree, flat on their faces, hands behind heads, not pressing their teeth together. Bombs shook the windows of Virginia's lodge; she and Leonard might be "broken together" (D5, Aug.16'40).

Then *Roger Fry* "flops"—is it due to the air raids on London (D5, Aug.23'40)?

After a period of quiescence, Woolf is free to write *Pointz Hall* "poetry." Invasion is expected in three weeks but it is still highly uncertain. Watching a wounded German plane swooping over them, they might easily have been "popped off on the terrace playing bowls" (D5, Aug.28'40).

Renewing her friendship with Vita, Woolf writes after Vita's visit to Monk's House that she has arranged flowers in Vita's room and thinks of her friends sitting in her own home with bombs falling round her; "What can I say except that I love you and I've got to live through this strange quiet evening thinking of you sitting there alone. Dearest let me have a line." As an afterthought, Woolf as though summing up, alarmingly writes: "You have given me much happiness" (L6, Aug.30'40).[11]

The bombings in central London seemed preparatory to invasion. Thus far the Woolf's London home in Mecklenburgh Square was spared, Hogarth Press moved their offices to Letchworth. To Ethel, Woolf describes the difficulty of writing in a "vacuum," feels no one will read her work: "the audience has gone." Yet she must continue (L6, Sept.11'40). What moved her most was the grimy old woman at the lodging house at the back, all dirty after the raid, preparing to sit out another" (L6, Sept.12'40).

She and Leonard are now alone in their "ship"; Mabel, their maid of five years, has left and Virginia looks forward to "merry kitchen harum scarum ways" (D5, Sep.16'40). They have a need of all their courage: the bomb at Mecklenburgh Square finally exploded, destroying china and glass; the ceilings are down, windows smashed, though there is actually less damage than expected (D5, Sept.18'40).

Personal irritations abound in Woolf's exchanges with Vanessa concerning Helen Anrep, Roger's former mistress who wishes to rent a cottage in Rodmell. Woolf was relieved in learning the Anreps would stay but one week. Vanessa thought her sister "unnecessarily angry" about the situation (L6, Sept.24'40), unaware she was jealous of the closeness between her and Helen. Confiding to Ethel her present "grumble" is that friends she dislikes are "refuging" in the village, Woolf asks: "Why does this annoy me more than the war?" She considers this an "ignoble fret" (L6, Sept.25'40).

Her admiration for "chars, shopkeepers, even politicians," for "tweed-wearing, sterling, dull women with their grim good sense," Virginia considers a side effect of the war (L6, Sept.25'40). Bombs drop so close she thought it was Leonard slamming the window. "Marooned" in their home, their life at times is "happy," "free," "disengaged" (D5, Sept.29'40).

The "cadaverous" twanging in the sky now begins; the planes are on their way to London. Virginia told Leonard she doesn't wish to die quite yet, wants ten more years, tries to imagine death via a bomb:

> The scrunching and scrambling, the crushing of my bone shade in on my very active eye and brain; the process of putting out the light— painful? Yes. Terrifying . . . . Then a swoon, a drain, two or three gulps attempting consciousness—and then dot dot dot (D5, Oct.2'40).

Temporarily contented with the routines of breakfast, writing, walking, tea, bowls, reading, sweets, bed, Woolf is fearful of "passive acquiescence," and she must live in "intensity." All their friends are
"isolated over winter fires." Facing the grisly thought of "who'll be killed tonight," each day is seen in terms of possible body risk (D5,
Oct.12'40). Then, too, there is the exhilaration of losing one's belongings, perhaps starting life "in peace, almost bare—free to go anywhere"
(D5, Oct.20'40).

Unexpectedly bursting its banks, the Ouse River comes down in a
cascade and Woolf is lyrical: "the sea is unfathomable, the haystack in
the floods" (D5, Nov.3'40), this at the bottom of their field. She sees the
marsh water "of such incredible beauty, in the sun deep blue," along
with "gulls, yellow island, leafless trees, red cottage roofs." She hoped
the flood would never subside. A sexually suggestive image, the flood
reminded her of a "virgin lip: as it was in the beginning." In addition,
she feels "fertile," enthused about *Pointz Hall* (D5, Nov.5'40).

Describing her "inland sea" to Ethel, as "always changing, day and
night, sun and rain," she is mesmerized by it, fell into a six foot hole,
and emerged dripping wet afterward. Enamored of this "savage
medieval water moved, all floating tree trunks and flocks of birds and a
man in an old punt," she sees herself as "eliminated of human feature,"
as a "stake walking" (L6, Nov.14'40).

Woolf has now finished *Pointz Hall* begun in early 1938, and thinks
of her next book, *Anon*, a "common history book." An attempt at a
new method, *Pointz Hall* is more "quintessential" than the others. Written during the "drudgery" of *Roger Fry*, she found it enjoyable
throughout (D5, Nov.24'40).

Sarcastically thanking Vita for her goodies—a large "pat" of butter
scarce in wartime, a broken "po" (chamber pot), some wool—Woolf
writes: "I wish I were Queen Victoria, then I could thank you from the
depths of my Broken Widowed heart. Never, never, Never have we had
such a rapturous, astounding, glorious . . ." (L6, Nov.29'40). Idiosyncratic and exaggerated in style, her letter mocks Vita, points to considerable unconscious hostility regarding Leonard as well as a sense of abandonment by him.

Because of the imminence of death, hope of reconciliation with her
parents seemed particularly strong: "How beautiful they were, those old
people. How simple, how clear, how untroubled. He loved her, and was
so candid and reasonable and transparent." Their life seemed "serene
and gay; no mud; no whirlpools. And so human with the children and
the little hum and song of the nursery" (D5, Dec.22'40). An overideali-
zation of her parents who were not "simple, clear, untroubled" is

evidenced. As for "no mud, no whirlpools" in their lives: as in whose? Vita's?

Continuously preoccupied with her "trembling paw," a recurrent refrain, Woolf attributed this to the cold, to the strenuous work of arranging books and possessions transported from London. She writes Ethel: "my hand trembles . . . ; my mind is churned and frothed; and to write one must be a clear vessel." Commending Ethel as not only the first woman to write an opera but also the first to tell the truth about herself, she quips: "I should like an analysis of your sex life" (L6, Dec.24'40).

Woolf detests the "hardness of old age—I feel it. I rasp. I'm taut." Aware the reason she dislikes and likes so many things "idiosyncratically" is her "growing detachment from the hierarchy, the patriarchy," she reiterates "I am I; and must follow that furrow, not copy another. That is the only justification for my writing, living" (D5, Dec.29'40).

Reflecting an unaccustomed religious preoccupation, Woolf looking at Asheham down, with the cross so "melodramatically against it," thinks of the phrase "look your last on all things lovely." In the same diary entry, her thinking seems bizarre: "Yesterday Mrs. Dedham was buried upside down. A mishap. Such a heavy woman . . . feasting spontaneously upon the grave." Woolf follows this with the threatening comment that "all life is so fair" at her [Woolf's] age, but, "without much more of it . . . to follow" (D5, Jan.9'41).

She plans to walk to her old haunts in London, "that great city representing Chaucer, Shakespeare, Dickens," her only "patriotism." Feeling humble, unable to "believe in being anyone," she says with "amazement: Yet Ethel wants to see me! We shall meet one of these days" (L6, Jan.12'41).

Writing Vita "it was a joke—our drifting apart," Woolf masochistically recalls Vita's lovers, remembers that Violet Trefusius was "like a fox cub, all scent and seduction." Rather pathetically Woolf confides: "I rather think I've a new lover, a doctor, a Wilberforce,[12] a cousin—ah! does that make you twitch? Am I still on the third rung from the top" (L6, Jan.19'41)?

Woolf is now distinctly upset concerning a letter from Harpers Bazaar rejecting her short story (L6, Jan.23'41). According to Leonard, Virginia's "trough of despair," the first indication of "serious mental illness," occurred January 25, 1941, lasting 10 to 12 days, without the usual prelude of headache, sleeplessness, or inability to concentrate.

Linking her depression to Harpers' rejection of her short story,[13] Woolf described her effort to combat it by housecleaning, memoir writing, and revising *Pointz Hall*. She needed action, the "old spurt." They "live without a future. That's what's queer: with our noses pressed to a closed door" (D5, Jan.26'41).

In a transparent effort to make Ethel jealous, as she had attempted with Vita, Woolf tells Ethel that she has a "faraway lover to match your translator, a doctor, a cousin, a Wilberforce." She asks Ethel to send her "lighthouse beam over this dark spot"; tells her she is reading the whole of English literature and by the time she reaches Shakespeare, the bombs will annihilate them. Somewhat suicidally she has "arranged a very nice last scene, reading Shakespeare; having forgotten her gas mask, she shall fade far away." Confessing she has rarely indulged in food to such an extent while alone,[14] she ends her letter, painfully asking Ethel "do you still love me? Do love me" (L6, Feb.1'41).

Contributing to her depression is Woolf's conflicted relationship with Vita. Feeling unattractive, old, not enticing enough, she decided to give Vita a "treat," invited Enid Bagnold, Vita's ex-lover to the luncheon originally planned for herself and Vita, to follow Vita's lecture at Rodmell on February 18,1941 (L6, Feb.2'41).[15]

Meanwhile, the cold has "reduced her hand to such a frozen claw" she writes Desmond (L6, Feb.2'41), continuing the theme of emotional and physical paralysis regarding her writing.

Vita is an "overflowing Cornucopia, pampers and spoils" Woolf with gifts of butter. Out of Vita's wool Woolf has made a thick jersey which "saved" her life. In short, Vita bestows blessings, yet Woolf looks forward to Vita's visit on February 18 with trepidation (L6, Feb.4'41). Her depression subsiding, she is revising *Pointz Hall* with some "glow" (D5, Feb.7'41), then writes that her hand is like the "cramped claw[16] of an aged fowl" (L6, Feb.10'41), finally notes the completion of *Pointz Hall*, now called *Between the Acts* (D5, Feb.26'41).

To Ethel, still her principal confidante she describes an article she is trying to write for a new *Common Reader*. "Stuck" in reading Elizabethan plays, she feels as though "glued on flypaper." They are in the worst stage of the war, have no "future." Catastrophe mobilized Leonard, but Virginia, plagued with "suspense," is chafing from the irritations of village life (L6, Mar.1'41).

Her letter to Vita gives warning: "I suppose your orchard is beginning to dapple as it did the day I came there. One of the sights I shall see on my death bed. Oh to think I shall never sit in the cold again. Ain't this a pretty pattern for a letter?" (L6, Mar.4'41). Writing in the margins of her note paper shows a decided departure from her usual form.

Practically amphibious, Woolf writes T.S. Eliot: "so much water has flowed under the bridge that I feel at sea" (L6, Mar.8'41). Regarding her last diary entry on the same day, she tells herself "observe perpetually.

Observe the oncome of age. Observe greed. Observe my own despondency. I insist upon spending this time to the best advantage. I will go down with my colors flying. Occupation is essential."

Her oral preoccupation is marked: "I think it is true that one gains a certain hold on sausage and haddock by writing them down" (D5, Mar.8'41).

II

Between the Acts contrapuntally presents a village pageant dramatizing successive periods of English history, and projects the emotionally charged, subterranean tensions and marital dissonances of Isa and Giles Oliver, whose home is borrowed for the occasion of the festival. The couple live with the elderly, rational Bart, Giles' father and Bart's mystical, religiously oriented sister, Lucy; Lucy belongs to the "unifiers," Bart, to the "separatists" (118). Arriving unexpectedly on the day of the play, Mrs. Manresa, a rather florid, sensual, brash woman, clearly an embodiment of Vita, remains as guest to witness the play, together with her homosexual companion, William Dodge. Miss LaTrobe, unconventional author and director of the play, mourning the breakup of her lesbian relationship, is Woolf's artistic alter-ego though Woolf is also clearly identified with Isa's conjugal unhappiness and sense of victimization.

Essentially we are offered glimpses of Woolf's fictional characters via their inner musings, ruminations, and monlogues, interspersed with authorial comments regarding landscape, the outer pageant, and occasionally the personalities of her protagonists. The setting is semirural, as Woolf highlights the patterns made by trees, and makes much of the abundant cacophonous animal life, the cows and birds in the surroundings. The larger, outer world embraces embattled, contemporary Europe of World War II.

Rhythmic, poetic, and repetitive, the depressive substrate of the novel as established by Isa, informs us pungently and sharply, in consonance with Woolf's letters and diary, of the serious emotional disturbance of both author and one of her central characters.

On opening, the novel plunges us into a "cesspool," (*BA*.4) the County Council's topic of concern, as some of our cast of characters form on the lawn of Pointz Hall, the night before the pageant. "Cesspool" strikingly reminds one of the animality of the human condition, the levelling, possibly regressive implications of excremental smells, the filth of human drainage and sewage, evocative of the mud and dung of *The Years*.

Conveying disgust and repugnance, Woolf also projects considerable rage as she juxtaposes to cesspool the devouring, biting oral greed of one of the village characters, "a goosefaced woman with eyes protruding as if they saw something to gobble in the gutter" (*BA*, 3). This is in keeping with Woolf's diary entry, describing a villager with a "nose like the Duke of Wellington, with great horse teeth and cold prominent eyes, with knitting (needles) in her hands and an arrow fastening her collar" (D5, Mar.24'41). Sharp, stabbing, biting, staring, these are orally and visually aggressive images.

Fairly swiftly, we glean Isa is unhappily married and finds "mystery and in his silence, passion," in the "ravaged" face of her neighbor, the ephemeral Mr. Haines, a "gentleman farmer." Given to poetizing, Isa imagines herself and Mr. Haines "two swans floating downstream"; however his "snow-white breast was circled with a tangle of dirty duckweed, and she too in her webbed feet was entangled, by her husband, the stockbroker" (5). Obviously "dirty duckweed" and "webbed feet" connect with Woolf's sense of humiliation regarding the early sexual harassment involving Gerald and George Duckworth, and with Isa's guilt concerning her attraction for Haines whose "words lie between them like a wire, tingling, tangling, vibrating" (15).

Isa's inner life impinges via the constant stream of songs, ditties and poems to which she seems addicted, as for example the following verse with its undercurrent of sadness, plaintiveness and unattachedness: "Where we know not, where we go not, neither know nor care; flying, rushing through the ambient, incandescent summer, silent air, there to lose what binds us here" (15).

Most clearly expressing Isa is the world "abortive," states Woolf. Does the author refer here to the fact Isa was born too soon, came to nothing, was arrested in development or unwanted by her mother? Woolf's meaning is none too clear. Rather cryptically we are told Isa "never looked like Sappho or one of the beautiful young men whose photographs adorned the weekly papers" (16). Does this suggest Isa would like to be sapphist, or would have wished to be a man, or, like the author, is confused in sexual identity? Isa is described for us as "thick in waist" and large of limb, and she does not have conventional good looks.

Since Isa is attracted to Haines who is unavailable, does she seek involvement in emotionally unrewarding situations? Certainly she does not particularly enjoy the role of housewife and mother, feels attached to motherhood only as a "captive balloon—by a myriad of hair-thin ties." She "loathed the domestic, the possessive, the maternal" (19).

Scanning her father-in-law's newspaper, Isa reads that a woman has been brutalized by troopers, dragged to a barracks room and thrown upon the bed. Partially stripped of her clothing, the woman screamed and hit the trooper on the face (20). Recurrent allusions to Isa's feelings of sexual victimization are reinforced by Lucy's recollection of a fishing expedition with Bart who "forced" her to remove the fish from a fishing hook, her shock in seeing the gills saturated with blood (21).

After a discourse on the silence and emptiness of the house, the family is invaded by uninvited guests, namely Mrs. Manresa and her young friend William, "an unknown" man with a "twisted" (37) face; they simply barge in, bringing their own lunch. Depicted as vulgar in gesture and demeanor, overdressed and oversexed for a picnic in the country, staking out her claim to be a "wild child" (41) of nature, Mrs. Manresa apparently captivated Bart. Her glamor and exoticism remind us of Vita, capriciously re-entering Woolf's life,[17] creating a temporary flurry or tumult of emotion and pseudo-intimacy, followed by its denouement, a sense of the tawdry surrounding her and entourage.

A go-between in arranging a meeting between Vita who agreed to lecture at the Women's Institute, and her former lover, Enid, Woolf felt furious when Vita and her friend rekindled their old passion. Yet is was Woolf who arranged it, unable to believe she was lovable in her own right.

With the introduction of Mrs. Manresa we are simultaneously told, with unconscious purpose, that the lily pond had collected water to a depth of four to five feet, covering a black layer of mud; that fish swam under the thick plate of green water and in that "deep center, in that black heart" a woman had drowned herself for love (44).

Giles, infusing his masculine vigor and "fierce, untamed presence," now appears, enraged by a Europe on the brink of war, bristling with atrocities, with guns poised. Seeing him, Mrs. Manresa "furbishes up her ancient batteries" (47).

Isa thought of Giles with pride and affection as father of her children; insofar as their marital relationship was concerned she felt both love and hate, but it is the latter that comes through. She felt a bond of sorts with William, the "half-man" (73), who sought to hide the fact he was an artist just as Isa concealed her poetry from Giles.

Isa continues to mutter snatches of poetry: "to what dark antre of the unvisited earth or windbrushed forest, shall we go now? Or spin from star to star and dance in the maze of the moon" (51)? Here a need for shelter and maternal protection is counterposed to a sense of moving in space.

Aware of the sexual current between Giles and Mrs. Manresa, who seemed to charge the atmosphere with her eroticism, Isa is jealous though encourages their liaison by her inaction. Giles in his turn was none too sanguine concerning the rapport between Isa and William, felt "manacled to a rock" watching them. Realizing her husband designated William that "toady lick-spittle," derogating his masculinity,[18] Isa wonders "do we know each other, why judge each other. Surely one sun would shine and all would be clear" (61).

The play is about to begin and we are introduced to the playwright, Miss LaTrobe, past unknown, a stocky figure with whip in hand, puffing away on a cigarette, using "strong language"; it was rumored she formerly lived with an actress but they quarreled (58). LaTrobe was bossy and abrupt in manner, barked rapid decisions in her gutteral accent. Yet "someone must lead . . . ; let them blame her" (63). The villagers quarreled, but she kept out of the fray, pacing back and forth between the birch trees, which looked like "columns in a church" or an "open-air cathedral." Swallows darted about making a "pattern" among the trees, "dancing like the Russians, only not to music but to the unheard rhythm of their own wild hearts" (65).

The author tells us the minds and bodies of the audience were "too close yet not close enough . . . " (65). Is Woolf alluding here to the relationship between Isa and Giles which was not "close enough"? The relationship between herself and Leonard? Giles continued to glare and Isa felt imprisoned: "through the bars of the prison, through the sleep haze that deflected them, blunt arrows bruised her; of love, then of hate" (66).

Still attracted to Haines, Isa thinks of flying away "from night and day and issue where no partings are—but eye meets eye" (83). Every half hour the music wailed "dispersed are we." Isa hums: "All is over. The wave has broken. Left us stranded, high and dry. Single, separate . . . " (96).

Pleased she captured the audience's attention for 25 minutes, Miss La Trobe felt "a vision imparted was relief from agony even for one moment" (98). Glimpsing Giles' displeasure, she suspected her theatrical venture was a failure. On the contrary, Giles was angry about William's homosexuality and conflicted about his own lust for Mrs. Manresa. Seeking some form of action to modulate his tension, he stamped to death a snake that seemed to be choking with a toad in its mouth, unable to swallow it, the toad unable to die. It was "birth the wrong way" round, a "monstrous inversion" (99), in short, a sticky, bloody mess.

"Inversion" may of course be equated with perversion, an expression of Woolf's sense of freakishness and abnormality, of her distortions concerning sexual, anatomic, and birth processes.

In the barn for refreshments, Isa murmurs another ditty: "dispersed are we . . . ; let me turn away from the array of china faces, glazed and hard, till I come to the wishing well . . . ; what wish should I drop into the well? That the waters should cover me" (103). Continuing her morbid, suicidal thoughts, she mused that the dead leaves would fall on the water after her death. Would she mind not seeing the trees, hearing the thrush sing, or the yellow woodpecker "dipping and diving" as though he "skimmed waves in the air" (104)?

Strained relations with her husband and romantic unrequited fantasies concerning Haines, prompt Isa's suicidal wish, alluded to for the second time. Deeper chords of sadness, despair, anger, and frustration propel her desire to take her life but of these we are afforded no elaboration except for the previously mentioned concept, "abortive." Most likely Isa's inner conflicts reflect the emotional turmoil of the author, agitated, desperate, and cut off more than ever at this point in her life, unaware of the intricacies or wellsprings of her depression.

Surely Giles has had other fleeting attractions; this with Mrs. Manresa certainly seems ephemeral, negligible. Then of course Isa rejects his conciliatory efforts when they occur, displaying her masochistic game-playing, her need for punishment or rejection.

Also in the barn, Mrs. Manresa playfully thinks herself "Queen", cleaves to Giles, her "surly knight." Lucy notes the "swallows flitting from rafter to rafter" excited by the company. Year after year they came "across Africa, France, came to nest here" (108). She also thought, in highly sexualized terms, of hummingbirds quivering "at the mouths of scarlet trumpets" in prehistoric times, a possible allusion to sexual occurrences in childhood.

Asked his opinion of the play, Bart did not respond, instead mutters a line from Swinburne: "Swallow my sister, o sister swallow" in which the poet refers to the Greek myth involving Philomela, seduced by Tereus, her sister's husband who removes her tongue to prevent her from externalizing his crime; she subsequently becomes a swallow. Did Woolf in feeling violated by incestuous figures in her life, in some complex fasion feel identified with Philomela? Ashamed and fearful of censure, Woolf did not speak out about her half-brother's sexual harassment until this point, actually, in her memoir *A Sketch of the Past*, and in a letter to Ethel.

Isa thought Giles' infidelity would go unnoticed, she blamed. Avoiding her husband, showing her distaste for his bloody boots, she went off with William, making it easier for Giles to continue his flirtation with Mrs. Manresa (111). Isa's poems remain dysphoric: "Fly away. I grieving stay. Alone I linger, pluck the bitter herb by the ruined wall, the churchyard wall . . . " (112).

Picking up a knife from the plank, she recites: "from her bosom's snowy antre drew the gleaming blade. Plunge blade! she said. And struck. Faithless! she cried. Knife, too! It broke. So too my heart" (113), which is a precis of Isa's tense drama with Giles, turning inward her fury towards him.

She and William talked as though they had been lifelong friends— weren't they conspirators, seekers after "hidden faces?" Perhaps they conversed naturally because they probably would never meet again. The "doom of sudden death" (114) hung over them. There was no "retreating and advancing" for them as well as for the old folk.

Unhappy his son was out of sorts, Bart addressed himself to the end of the day: "And the ice will dart its splinters and the winter will fill the grate with ashes." He and Lucy felt "it's time to go" (118), expressing their closeness to death and the author's preoccupation with dying.

The audience reassembling, Mrs. Manresa, goddess-like, buoyant, abundant, had both Giles and Bart in tow. Scraps of conversation penetrated: "What about the Jews? The refugees . . . , people like ourselves, beginning life again" (121)? Similarly Woolf, who expressed elation in losing her possessions, wishing to start life over again.

Miss LaTrobe despaired of resuming her play after intermission. The actors procrastinated; the audience "slipped the noose, split up into scraps and fragments" (122) but finally the play got under way. At one point when the action flagged and Miss LaTrobe thought "this is death— illusion has failed," the cows bellowed and the world was filled with "dumb yearning"; the "primeval voice" filled the emptiness (140). We are down to fundamentals.

After seeing her man in gray surrounded, inaccessible, vanished, Isa again expressed herself in doom-ridden terms: "Where do I wander: Down what draughty tunnels? Where the eyeless wind blows? (154) To issue in some harvestless dim field where no evening lets fall her mantle; nor sun rises. Unblowing, ungrowing are the roses there." Feeling burdened with "possessions, memories", she refers to herself as the "last little donkey in the long caravanserai crossing the desert" (155), evoking as did *The Years* the fragility yet indomitableness of the family.

During the next intermission, Giles and William were "damnably unhappy. They were all caught and caged; prisoners; watching a spectacle" (176): "They were neither Victorians nor themselves; they were suspended, without being, in limbo." Isa murmured "four and twenty blackbirds strung upon a string, down came an ostrich, an eagle, an executioner" (178). The theme of murder, of death, is now obsessive.

Wishing to present the last act, "Present time: Ourselves," (178), Miss Latrobe found the audience had dispersed; here she was rescued by the natural occurrence of a downpour as though "all the people in the world were weeping." Rain poured down Isa's cheeks as though tears, she murmuring "O that our human pain could here have ending" (180).

Miss LaTrobe used reflecting surfaces to snap them as they were, before they could collect themselves (184). All evaded or shaded themselves except Mrs. Manresa. Unashamed, she alone maintained her identity. The mirror bearers were "malicious, observant, expectant, expository" (186). A megaphonic, anonymous voice boomed: "Liars most of us. Thieves too . . . . Don't hide among rags. Or presume there's innocence in childhood.[19] Consider the gunslayers, bomb droppers. They do openly what we do slyly" (187).

Summing up, the reverend tells the audience: "We are members one of another. Each is part of the whole . . . . We act different parts but are the same. Nature definitely takes a part. Dare we limit life to ourselves" (192). Again the gramophone sounded: "Dispersed are we, who have come together. But let us retain whatever made that harmony" (196). The "old cronies" suggest: "What we need is a center, something to bring us together" (198), Someone said "we all act, but whose play" (199), and "If we're left asking questions, isn't it a failure as a play?" (200).

As Mrs. Manresa left, "like a goddess, buoyant and abundant, with flower-chained captives" following in her wake, Bart felt a sag at his heart, "the ash grown cold and no glow on the log," but then he thought: "on with the hobble, on with the limp, since the dance was over" (202). It occurred to Bart that LaTrobe did not care for their thanks but rather like that "carp moving in the water" wanted "darkness in the mud," a whiskey and soda at the pub and "coarse words descending like maggots through the waters" (203).

Then one of the actors: "The play's over, the actors have departed" (207). At the last, Miss LaTrobe thought "it was in the giving that the triumph was" (209). Her gift was negated since the meaning was obscure to the audience, the actors not in good touch with their parts. She felt her play a failure.

As though to deny this thought, a group of starlings attacked the tree behind which she had hidden. The entire tree vibrated as though each bird "plucked a wire." The tree "became a rhapsody, a quivering cacophony, a whizz and vibrant rapture, branches, leaves, birds, sylla-

bling discordantly, life, life, life without measure, without stop, devouring the tree" (209). Concerning Woolf's passionate, affirmative statement, Hillis Miller suggests:

> for her there is a creative power in the mind which thrusts itself forward,
> in spite of obstacles and hesitation. This energy pushes out to fill in
> gaps and pauses, to weave a web which ties this to that, one thing to
> another, in the assertion of a continuous power of production
> (213–214).[20]

Feeling she had "suffered triumph, humiliation, ecstasy, despair, for
nothing" (210), Miss LaTrobe since the quarrel with her lover, felt
permeated with the "horror and terror of being alone", felt "nature had
set her apart from her kind" (211). Yet she felt enslaved by her audience;
approval and applause were imperative to her. Irrepressibly, she thought
of her next play: there would be two "scarcely perceptible figures" and
the "high ground at midnight. She heard the first words" (212).
    At the corner bar there would be "shelter," "voices," "oblivion"
(211). She was in a semitrance as she drank, and "words of one syllable
sank down into the mud" which then became "fertile. Words rose above
the intolerably laden, dumb oxen plodding through the mud. Words
without meaning, wonderful words" (212). Her creative powers sustained her.
    Now everyone had departed and only the family remained. Giles of-
fered his wife a banana which she refused. He "stubbed his match and
out it went with a little fizz" (213). Does Isa deflate his sexuality? Looking like a "tragic figure from another play" (214), Lucy thought: "What
a small part I've had to play." But LaTrobe has helped her feel she
"could have played . . . . Cleopatra. You've stirred in me my unacted
part (153)"[21]
    When Lucy indicated they made more money regarding this year's
play than last year's, Isa murmured "this year, last year, next year,
never . . ." (214), again teasing us with her (and the author's) suicidal intention. In answer to Lucy's question about the meaning of the play, Isa
answered perfunctorily "yes, no, yes," meaning "yes, the tide rushed
out embracing, no it contracted, death again beckoning" (215).
    Isa thought Giles, father of her children, extremely handsome; loving
and hating him "tore her asunder."[22] She needed a "new plot invented."
Isa remembered the newspaper story of the girl who had been violated,
noted the flowers had faded (215).
    Shadows "crept" over Bart who looked "leafless, spectral . . . ; as a
dog shudders its skin, his skin shuddered . . . " (218). Lucy is still

reading her book about England during the time it was a swamp; thick forests covered the land and prehistoric man, half-human, half-ape roused himself from a semicrouching position. The old people then retired for the night.

Alone for the first time Giles and Isa argued, then made up. From their "embrace another life might be born," states the author, but "first they must fight as the dog fox fights with the vixen, in the heart of darkness,²³ in the fields of night." The house had lost its shelter. The night seemed as though primeval: "dwellers in caves had watched from some high place among rocks. Then the curtain rose. They spoke" (219).

Is Woolf suggesting an aggressive, primitive, divisive exchange as prelude to a sexual turn-on? It is highly unlikely she is here describing a lusty or close relationships. Isa has been preoccupied with sexual victimization; sex is linked with pain and suffering. She rebuffs her husband's overtures during the pageant yet proclaims she "loves" him as father of her children; then she turns to William, a homosexual, whose gender might simply be a disguise. Constantly Isa thinks of death as surcease. Is Woolf telling us Isa is suicidal because of her disowned homosexuality? Or is Woolf taking a sideswipe at sex and procreation, suggesting that children stemming from unions such as this grow up and make war on a larger scale? Ultimately, Isa turns to her husband.

Woolf ends her book affirming Miss LaTrobe's creative thrust as she also affirms the continuity of human life.

In Miss LaTrobe, Woolf presents us with a complex portrayal of a lesbian playwright, erstwhile actress, former tea-house proprietor. Hints of sapphism and homosexuality abound in most of Woolf's novels; these emerge with more rounded lineaments after the writing of *Orlando*, although Woolf's sexually ambivalent fictional characters are generally in some sense damaged, except for Nicholas Pomjalovsky in *The Years*. Miss LaTrobe is a writer who, like Woolf, always gestates another work after the one she has just written. She is involved in directing a village play, has recently emerged from an unhappy love affair with an actress. We are given no other details concerning her sexual leanings. There are no male exhibitionists in her childhood creating a turn-off to men, as with Rose Pargiter, in *The Years*.

As we are introduced to Miss LaTrobe we learn she is "not altogether a lady," and has a "passion for getting things up," (58) which comments are charged with innuendo. Dominating, staccato in manner, she makes swift decisions, barks her instructions in accented voice. Swarthy, overweight, she is of Russian origin, has square jaw, "thick ankles", wears

"sturdy shoes" (63) and a smock, is given to gnashing her teeth and cursing when necessary. Obviously, there is nothing conventional about Miss
LaTrobe. Woolf suggests she looks like a "Commander," or an "Ad-
miral" pacing the deck. Generally, she is smoking a cigarette and carries
a whip.

Here Woolf is allowing herself to create a fairly uncamouflaged,
masculine woman, who would have preferred to be a man. This is unlike
the veiled references regarding Woolf's other fictional women.

Most likely, Miss LaTrobe's play or pageant, with townspeople as
performers, embodies Woolf's experience during 1940 at Rodmell
Women's Institute where she directed a play with members of her community as actors.

For Woolf, this represented a reaching out, an extending of herself;
she wished to be part of the collective or community feelings uniting
England at this point in history. In a moment of asperity however, Woolf
writes that her contribution to the war effort is a "sacrifice of pleasure."
She is "bored" and

> appalled by the ready-made commonplaces of the plays which they can't
> act unless we help. I mean the minds so cheap, compared with ours, like
> a bad novel—that's my contribution—to have my mind smeared by the
> village and the WEA[24] mind and to endure it and the simper. What's
> wrong is the conventionality not the coarseness (D5, May29'40).

So much for Woolf's working-class allegiances!

In letters to friends there are references to Woolf's role in the community production, but no further mention of the outcome of the play.
One might interpolate from her diary entry and from the vicissitudes of
the play within the novel, that there were difficulties, disillusionments,
frustrations, a sense of alienation towards those who collaborated with
her.

Though Miss LaTrobe felt considerable excitement regarding her
production she felt no one understood her meaning which was contained
in her parting message: "Let's talk in words of one syllable without lard-
ing, stuffing, or cant. Let's break the rhythm and foget the rhyme. And
calmly consider ourselves. Some bony. Some fat. The poor are as bad as
the rich are. Perhaps worse. Don't hide among rags. Or let our cloth or
book learning protect us." LaTrobe considers a "tyrant half a slave,"
marvels that the "great wall we call civilization" has been built by "orts,
scraps and fragments like ourselves" (*BA* 187–188), levelling everyone.

With the play over, the actors and audience dispersed, the brashness, defiance, and assurance we have become accustomed to are no longer in evidence. The illusion of unity over, Miss LaTrobe now feels an "outcast," isolated from society, no longer the center from which all radiates. Recovering temporarily, she, indomitably, is spawning a new play. There is no certainty about her future since she felt that from the earth which was indeed fertile and produced "words," "green water" also "seemed to rise over her." (210). Preoccupation with violence, death and suicide is striking throughout the novel.

In noting the "emptiness at the center of the pageant, which itself lies between the acts of ongoing life," Fleishman suggests there is similarly a "state of negativity at the core of human affairs." Yet the need for action, for making a "fuss about nothing" brings renewed life to both the theatrical situation and the human condition. Death ensues "when illusion fails." Propelling the quest for illusion is "natural desire," which "fills the nothingness, brings art and history into being, gives form to inchoate matter" (Fleishman, 214).

III

Holding Virginia's completion of *The Voyage Out* responsible for her third breakdown and suicide attempt in 1913 when problems in consolidating their marriage proved the more crucial issue, Leonard similarly implied that the completion of *Between the Acts*, the pressures and strains of revising—decisively contributed to her final breakdown and suicide in 1941. He referred to "black clouds which gathered and spread over her mind whenever a book finished, she had to face the shock of severing the mental umbilical cord and send it to the printer, reviewer and public" (5LW79).

Contrary to the official view that finishing her novel led to breakdown or suicidal behavior, Woolf displayed a sense of competence and accomplishment on completion of *Night and Day, Jacob's Room, Mrs. Dalloway*, and *Orlando*. Physical illness and depression accompanying or following the writing of *The Voyage Out, To the Lighthouse, The Waves, The Years*, or her last novel were concomitant to oscillations of self-esteem in context of her emotional difficulties or conflicted personal relationships at the time.

Though Leonard thought her oversensitive to adverse criticism, Virginia seemed eager for feedback as are most writers, had been realistic and cynical[25] regarding the inevitable fluctuations of opinion issuing from friends and critics; in 1938 she for the first time sounded an alarming note in referring to the "pack—reviewers, friends, enemies" who "pay her no attention and sneer." At the same time, she asserted her freedom and immunity.

Woolf sent her manuscript, *Between the Acts*, to John Lehmann for his "casting vote"[26] (L6, Mar.20'41). He praised the novel, yet she indicated she would not publish it in its present form, felt it too "silly and trivial," accused herself of writing it while working on *Roger Fry*, her "brain half asleep"; she would revise by the fall (L6, Mar.27'41).

Is she fearful lest the fictional relationship between Giles and Isa, their mutual hostilities, are overly autobiographical? That Isa's ruminations are too flagrantly suicidal? Isa seems intent on death in an aggressive, knife-wielding vein (*BA*, 113). Her rage turned inward, Isa feels "prisoned," or hopes death will overtake her, passively waits for the sea to "cover" her. This, Woolf's last novel, is replete with tumultous, subterranean emotions of love, hate, and self-destruction.

With the correction and return of the galleys of her manuscripts, Woolf found it necessary to wrench herself from the finished work before turning to another, creative mood. In effect, there is no definitive termination of the artistic project. An artist finds connection, empathic involvement, reunion, separation, loss, desire for repair; may experience birth or rebirth via his or her work. Needless to say, writing for Virginia was an emotionally intense, total experience. On completion of a novel, she frequently experienced the "lust of creation" or a "long childbirth," embracing the "offspring" she did not have in reality.

Actually, the crucial issue at this critical time in her life though she experienced feelings of barrenness and feared diminution of her sense of "fertility," was the shrinking of social and professional supports. She felt her writing "I" had "vanished: No audience. That's part of one's death" (D5, Jun.4'40). The war removed her "outer wall of security. No echo comes back. I have no surroundings. These standards which have for so many years given back an echo and so thickened my identity are all wide and wild as the desert. We pour to the edge of a precipice . . ." (D5, Jun.22'40).[27]

Though the sense of abandonment in her personal relationships seemed externally due to the unavailability of friends and family, concomitant to the impingements and primacy of problems of sheer survival engendered by the war, Woolf's tendency to masochistically revive unrewarding or rejecting relationships, the supplicating, subordinate role she allotted herself in the resumed relationship with Vita were more central issues. Setting up a luncheon appointment with Vita and procuring Vita's former lover for the occasion, obviously thinking she, Virginia, not enticing enough, led to feelings of humiliation and defeat.

Writing Ethel about the meeting with Vita and Enid, Woolf described the charged atmosphere as "sordid and squalid. There I was; the cat scratched a hole in the chair cover, and a visiting dog lifted his leg against the table . . . " (L6, Mar.1'41). Underneath her ostensible surface gratitude, Woolf bitterly took issue with Vita's gifts of butter, connected as this was with the meaningless rest-cure regimen of the past. Her last letter to Vita, sent March 4, 1941, was replete with suicidal innuendo and ill-concealed accusation.

With Ethel who was more available, Woolf conducted a most prolific and intimate correspondence, although did not otherwise respond to her overtures of intimacy, later became jealous of Ethel's revived love life. Woolf admired Ethel's productivity, cruelly depreciated her own achievement as compared to Ethel's.

Communicating an on-going series of emotionally charged warnings, and signals in diary, memoir, and letters at this time, Woolf conveys her desperate sense of deprivation and emotional isolation. For example she writes Ethel: "I can't make a warm hollow for myself—never mind, you don't care much" (L6, Dec.24'40). Several weeks before her death she writes Ethel: "I can't move back or forwards." She feels "we have no future" (L6, Mar.1'41).

In her last letter to Ethel she expresses her loneliness, deplores their separations: "When you're back, let's try to bridge this solitude". She alludes to Ethel's involvement with new friends and a former lover, then added she was writing to "belatedly wave a hand of thanks" (L6, Mar.10'41). Is she saying her good-byes?

The rift between Woolf and Vanessa was quite serious, more hurtful because of the contrast with their closeness when Julian died and Woolf took care of her sister. Vanessa was angry and unforgiving regarding Woolf's seeming rivalry with Julian, her slowness or disinclination to publish Julian's posthumous works, implicating both Virginia and Leonard for not encouraging Julian more when he was alive.

Personal animosities were additionally aroused by Vanessa's desire to help Roger's mistress Helen Anrep find a cottage in Rodmell, which threatened Woolf inordinately and engendered considerable rivalry with Helen.

When Vanessa was physically or emotionally not there, the "color goes out of my life as water from a sponge" (L6, Oct.2'37), writes Woolf. She is desolate without Vanessa who is the "breath of life" (L6, Nov.2'38). The metaphors concerning her attachment to Vanessa are not as erotic or playful as formerly but rather seem more evocative of survival, of life or death issues.

In the past, Woolf's means of experiencing heterosexual love had been vicarious, consonant with her identification with Vanessa. Via her biography, *Roger Fry*, Woolf felt extreme closeness with Roger, creating an imaginary triangle as of old, reviving her enmeshment with Vanessa.

Woolf's elemental need for protection and shelter, generated at this time, is further evidenced in the idealization of her parents, particularly mother; and in her longing for maternal love, manifested in the revival of early memories of sitting on her mother's lap, or of hearing the waves and feeling the "purest" ecstasy while lying in the children's nursery (*SOTP*, 65–66).

Though exalting her mother, Woolf also notes her unavailability: "Of course she [mother] was central," but Virginia never achieved sufficient objectivity to see her as a person; her mother was a "general presence" rather than a particular person to Virginia as a child of seven or eight (*SOTP*, 83).

The symbolic tone of Virginia's early memories, the womblike impressions, the sense of premature expulsion from the maternal orbit, must be evaluated in light of their documentation during 1939 and 1940, one of the most difficult phases of her life, when an acute sense of abandonment in her personal relationships emerged.

With the deceleration of Leonard's awed worship of Virginia's work, his initial coolness regarding *The Years*, his dislike of *Three Guineas,* and unaccustomed anger concerning her biography, *Roger Fry*, that "odd posthumous attachment for Roger"—Virginia felt an as yet imperceptible dissolution of the symbiotic-like relationship with her husband, especially concerning her writing and the implicit fantasy she and Leonard could together produce a "child" via Virginia's creative process. Leonard up until this time participated in the "childbirth" initially exalting, then personally publishing her books. Possibly Virginia threatened Leonard in feeling close to Roger, since in her fantasy she and Roger had together given "birth" to her book *Roger Fry*, and she referred to her biography as the "child born of us." Of course feeling "so in love" with Roger betokened closeness with Vanessa, formerly his lover.

Woolf's enigmatic phrase "their minds and bodies were too close yet not close enough" (*BA*, 65) suggests both the symbiotic nature of her relationship with Leonard as well as their distance; points to her sense of failure in marriage. Her diminished self-esteem is manifested with pathetic clarity, as she refers to herself as "such a new moon slip of a life" compared to Ethel's "full, orange harvest glow" (L6, Jul.9'40). She asks, "What do you call a voracious cheese mite which has gnawed its way into a vast Stilton and is intoxicated with eating" (L6, Nov.14'40)? Here her identification with an infinitesimally small, orally aggressive, parisitic creature, is a far cry from "racehorse," the more powerful, dynamic image propelling her writing of *The Years*.

Strikingly, as Leonard relinquished his tremorousness, Virginia's hand began to tremble. Her fear of not controlling the writing process now incessantly plagued her. She complained the cold immobilized her hand, or considered her hand disfigured, caricaturing herself an elderly "fowl." It is not clear whether she was describing an arthritic ailment or a psychosomatic symptom but certainly an exchange of roles seemed evidenced insofar as Leonard was the more productive and mobilized, and Virginia now feared the loss of her writing powers. She wrote Ethel: "It's difficult I find, to write. No audience. No private stimulus, only this outer roar" (L6, Mar.13'41).

With cascades of water roaring over the marshes, creating an island of Rodmell, Woolf saw herself as an elemental force of nature as though losing her human identity. Her "inland sea" evoked Cornwall, the exalted island of her childhood. Formerly used references concerning the sea returned: she looked forward to seeing Vita as a "drowning sailor[28] to Spice Islands," or felt in the "wild gray water" after a period of turmoil, she wrote Ethel.

The dual occurrences of a cosmic, capricious overflowing of nature and the unleashing of man's destructive forces in the war might have created an exultation in the tumult, absurdity and levelling effects of human and natural devastation. "Alone in their ship" Virginia and Leonard felt as though on a "desert island" (D5, Sept.17'40).

Still amphibious, Woolf in her memoir writes that people are "sealed vessels afloat on what it is convenient to call reality; that is, those scenes that survive undamaged year after year." Seeing herself as a "fish in a stream; deflected; held in place," she cannot describe the stream. Then, with horrifying prescience, she relates that the past returns when the "present runs so smoothly it is like the sliding surface of a deep river. Let me like a child advancing with bare feet into a cold river descend again into that stream" (*SOTP*, 98).

Although Leonard thought Virginia calmer and more serene during the latter part of 1940 (5LW69), Virginia's diaries, letters, and novel attest to her morbid obsession with death, to her need for succorance and rescue. These were related to her sense of acute helplessness, deepened sense of personal deviance, occasional thought distortion, and masked rage.

She is obsessed with "vampires," feels "sucked by leeches" (D5, Nov.29'40). Could this be related to her jealousy over Vanessa's dedicated interest in Helen Anrep? Woolf was enjoined against her will to find a home in Brighton for Helen at this time, and she felt exploited and manipulated, reviving, since Vanessa was mother-image incarnate, ancient rivalries with her sister.

Angry while in a woman's lavatory in a Brighton restaurant, with "common little tarts powdering and painting," Woolf's thinking is disturbed and orally obsessive as she observes an obese woman with a white "muffin" face "consuming rich cakes," her companion "grilled," or sees a "van unloading biscuits." She asks: "Where does the money come from to feed these fat white slugs. Brighton a love corner for slugs. The powdered, the pampered, the mildly improper . . . ; Helen [Anrep] has fallen through. I mean the house I got her with Enid the day Enid lunched here with Vita and I felt untidy yet cool; and she edgy and brittle" (D5, Feb.26'41).

Here Woolf is lambasting Vita's sensuality, maliciously sees Enid as part of Vita's entourage. Linking Helen with Enid, Woolf sees them as devouring, she, Woolf, unattractive, cast off and orally deprived. At the same time, she is full of rage and exploitative victimization, shows a swing towards bulimia,[29] a sense of oral omnivorousness prevailing, perhaps in denial of her underlying depression and in contrast to her usual anorectic disposition when under severe emotional stress. Now Woolf's oral envy is more overt and encompassing, not camouflaged by aesthetic transformation and is therefore out of control, toxic.

Enraged cocerning soldier's protestations that women were taking their jobs, Woolf's antipathy towards men was additionally evidenced in the depicted sexual violence in *Between the Acts*, wherein a young woman, as described in a newspaper article, is sexually abused by policemen. In a concurrent letter to Ethel, Woolf records the sexual intrusiveness of Gerald Duckworth when she was six (L6, Jan.12'41); and in the memoir written at this time, *A Sketch of the Past*, the ongoing sexual harassment by George following her mother's death. In contemporary psychological parlance, sexual interference by parents, their surrogates or other adults is considered sexual abuse; this the child, generally compliant, confused or terrified, fearing loss of love, does not reveal, which was the case with Woolf.

Referring to the ruins of her old squares "gashed, dismantled, the old red bricks all white powder, all that completeness ravished and demolished" (D5, Jan.15'41), Woolf's personalized description of her former home also points to a sense of profound violation of her inner being and personal identity. "Ravished" evokes rape, seizure, carrying away forcibly. Her anger, sense of body insult and damage to the self, largely repressed, could never be "worked through."

What about Woolf's "faraway lover," Dr. Octavia Wilberforce, a physician and distant cousin living in nearby Brighton, who was Woolf's medical consultant in Rodmell? Dr. Wilberforce, alerted by Leonard concerning his wife's depression, provided milk and cream from her farm. Overeating of rich food, inflicted on Woolf during her past bouts of neurasthenia, was anathema to her, although considered of central importance in the Weir Mitchell rest-cure.

In response to Dr. Wilberforce's suggestion that Woolf try to complete her manuscript, *Pointz Hall*, in exchange for milk and cream provided by the doctor's farm, Woolf angrily wrote: "I've lost all power over words and can't do a thing with them. I can't as you see make my hand cease to tremble. Now as a doctor your hand is firm. So you can write" (L6, Dec.31'40).

Dr. Wilberforce, in a highly inappropriate response, indicated she was pleased Woolf "lost all power over words,"[30] ignoring her patient's profound involvement in the writing process, her sense of hopelessness in feeling blocked in her work, her underlying despair and retaliatory rage.

Accusingly, Woolf answered: "Nothing we both ever to the end write can outweigh your milk and cream at this bitter and barren moment. This hand doesn't shake from book-lugging but from rage" (L6, Jan.9'41). Several weeks later she wrote: "If I can't write I can eat. As for writing it's a washout" (L6, Jan.25'41).

Reacting to her physician's lack of insight into her (Woolf's) emotional state of sterility and depression, Woolf shifted to Dr. Wilberforce her submerged, cumulative rage regarding all ineffectual, dictatorial, disillusioning caretakers in her life, bitterly accosted her: "You've reduced me not to silence but to a kind of sputter.[31] I mean the cream, the cheese, the milk. You don't come here so I could speak by way of mouth. I'm dumb" (L6, Feb.23'41).

Leonard consulted Dr. Wilberforce professionally during the early months of 1941. Conflicted about taking "drastic" steps, that is, having Virginia remain in bed, eat rich foods, they felt should Virginia take these "necessary" measures, her resistance would increase, her depression worsen. Dr. Wilberforce, without sophistication in matters psychiatric, seemed a poor choice, simply went along with Leonard who decided to do nothing. In addition, she was Woolf's cousin and in Woolf's fantasies, her "newfound lover."

Assuming Virginia's emotional crisis was related to finishing her book, Leonard showed little comprehension of possible psychological motivation. In his autobiography he cited "ominous," unpublished diary excerpts, indulged in a fairly irrelevant, extended discussion of Dr. Wilberforce's gentrified background and her attachment to Elizabeth Robins, a former actress and friend of Julia Stephen (5LW80–86).

In Leonard's diary for March 18, 1941, he did not rule out that earlier in the week Virginia unsuccessfully attempted to commit suicide.[32] Trying to overtake Virginia who was walking in the water meadows on this extremely rainy day, Leonard saw her "soaking wet, looking ill and shaken. She said she had slipped and fallen into one of the dykes. At the time I did not suspect anything though I had an automatic feeling of desperate uneasiness" (5LW90).

Leonard told Dr. Wilberforce who visited the Woolfs on March 21, 1941, that his wife was on the verge of "danger"; Virginia was depressed and her "thoughts raced beyond control" (5LW91). By March 24, she seemed slightly better but by March 26, Leonard felt Virginia might at any moment kill herself.

He saw "desperate depression" claiming her, and she, "terrified of madness." He felt the "only chance was for her to give in and admit she was ill but this she would not do" (5LW91). At her husband's instigation Virginia, insisting she had no "mental problem," agreed to consult Dr. Wilberforce as both physician and friend.

Acquiescent regarding the physical examination suggested by Dr. Wilberforce on March 27, Virginia seemed "like a child being sent up to bed," confessed "some part of her fears . . . that the past would come back, that she would be unable to write again" (Bell, v.2, 225). Dr. Wilberforce found Virginia "detachedly pleased" at her wish to help. The doctor did not as yet approach her patient with the desirability of a more protective environment; she was undecided about recommending complete rest for fear of challenging Virginia's denial of illness, felt a wrong word might impel her towards suicide.

Dr. Wilberforce pondered the advisability of a trained nurse. When she telephoned the next day, as planned, to check on her patient's condition, it proved too late.[33] Leonard felt he had been mistaken in not forcing the issue, one involving constant surveillance (5LW42). One derives a sense of diminished personal vigilance on his part, especially the avoidance of emergency measures following his wife's suicide attempt during the week of March 18.

Nicolson and Trautman state there were definitely two suicide notes by Virginia to Leonard, written March 18 and March 28, 1941, respectively (L6, n489), though both Leonard and Quentin Bell were convinced the letters were written at the same time, at the end, and that Virginia had simply misdated them (L6, 491).

Virginia's first suicide note to Leonard (L6, Mar. 18, 1941) describes her conviction of insanity and "disease," that is, hearing voices and inability to concentrate, with no resources to cope with this onslaught. Yet we know of course she had shown recoverability before. In stating in her first suicide note "I don't think two people could have been happier till this terrible disease came," she is repeating a mythical phrase similar to that uttered by her mother in relation to her perpetually mourned first husband: "No two people have ever been as happy as we have been"; and by the wavering, indecisive hero in *The Voyage Out*, at his fiance's deathbed: "We'd be free together. No happiness would be like ours" (244).

An accusing, sacrificial theme reverberates in Virginia's suicide note to Leonard, the desire to absolve him of guilt: "I know that I am spoiling your life; that without me you could work." Leonard of course had always written; he produced 17 books during their marriage. Yet she suggested taking care of her would interfere with his need to write the many books he planned since leaving Hogarth.

There is the implication she felt she adversely affected his life, that without her to burden him he would function better. Her note flatters: "If anybody could have saved me it would have been you." Apparently no one could proffer that help between March 18 and March 28.

Vanessa had written, admonishingly to Virginia on March 20, "You must be sensible." Admitting she had not seen much of Virginia "lately," she nevertheless thought about her and the fact Virginia "looked very tired." She suggested Virginia allow herself to "collapse and do nothing"; she might then "feel tired" and "rest a little." Virginia was in the state when one does not acknowledge one is troubled, Vanessa wrote. She chided Virginia to "not go and get ill just now. What shall we do when we're invaded if you are a helpless invalid. I shall ring up sometime and find out what is happening" (L6, n.485).

Distant, scolding, and guilt-provoking, Vanessa misjudged her sister's precarious state, one which required more direct support and caretaking.

Virginia's response did not reach Vanessa until after her death:

> You can't think how I loved your letter. But I feel that I have gone too far this time to come back. I am certain now I am going mad again. It is just as it was the first time. I am always hearing voices, and I know I shan't get over it now (L6, Mar.23'41).

Here Virginia reiterated her strong affection for her husband, asking her sister to reassure him of this, indicating he had work to do, which would prosper best without her burdensome presence.

There is little doubt of the failure of the personal relationship between Leonard and Virginia, or that between Virginia and Vanessa for that matter. Leonard could no longer display the authoritative, at times ruthless protectiveness of his previous caretaking, which in the past, despite her protestations, offered Virginia's precarious equilibrium some degree of ballast. Virginia's first suicide note is longer, more hopeful and flowing than the final note of March 28, which though still apotheosizing her husband, seems terse and resigned, without hope of rescue (L6, Mar.28'41).

A vignette written by Louie Mayer, the Woolfs' housekeeper, describes Virginia's last day. Leonard, perhaps insensitively, asked Louis to give his wife a "duster" to keep her occupied the last morning of her life, which might conceivably have appeared humiliating to her. As Louie Mayer stated:

> I gave her a duster but it seemed very strange. I had never known her want to do any housework with me before. After a while Mrs. Woolf put the duster down and went away. I thought that probably she did not like cleaning the study and had decided to do something else. (Noble, 160–161).

Apparently Virginia left the house in the morning after leaving letters for her husband and sister. Her body was found two weeks later. Louie, perhaps the sole, nonintellectualizing voice writing on this lugubrious episode, added bluntly and unencumberedly in her memoir: "There were heavy stones in the pockets of her jacket and she must have put them there, and then walked straight down into the river. And that was terrible. It was the most terrible thing I have known." Here Louie expresses unalloyed horror at both the self-destructiveness, and the retaliative rage evidenced in Virginia Woolf's determined drowning.

XV   Epilogue

I

When Nicolson and Trautman suggest Woolf's suicide was due to her conviction that she had "lost the art" of creating and therefore "her whole purpose in life had gone" (L6, xvi), they disregard more basic, emotionally weighted issues, the diminutiveness of Woolf's self-concept, noted in her ongoing sense of exclusion, deprivation, and loss; the tenuousness of her identity formation; the feeling of abandonment and betrayal in her personal relationships at the time; her sense of victimization and rage.

Woolf's sense of repulsion regarding her "frozen claw," the fear of stasis concerning her writing process, the fear her last novel was lightweight, contributed to her feelings of severe inadequacy, although *Between the Acts* is considered by many critics one of her finest novels. Actually she never stopped writing, and she had begun another book. She found it difficult, nevertheless, to write: professional, literary, and social networks, feedback concerning her writing, necessary for her identity as writer and her personal identity, were obliterated by the exigencies of war.

Agreeing with Hillis Miller that the writer's creativity is an "extension of the creativity of nature, takes what it is given, the orts and fragments of reality, fills the spaces between them with the intrinsic rhythmical order of the mind" (214), it is clear that Woolf's writing capacities were not actually foundering or declining at this time, but rather she experienced an acute, immobilizing sense of emotional impoverishment and unlovability. Her self-regard considerably diminished, she could not so easily as was her wont for most of her life, feel as nourished or restored by her writing.

Identifying with her sister, Woolf's creative powers during her lifetime frequently meshed with metaphors of sexuality, fertility, childbirth, maternality, orality. She claimed to feel most "feminine" when writing. She wrote Vanessa: "I have imagined what it is like to have a child. I understand as in a revelation, the precise nature of the pain. Now, if I could only see my novel like that" (L1, Aug.10'08). Here she refers to the writer's psychic pain but emphasizes the physical aspects of writing which she often equates with rhythmic patterns. Competing

263

with her nephew, she tells her sister she (Woolf) writes as Julian "sucks his bottle" (L1, Aug.11'08), which is in keeping with the psychoanalytic notion that writing or creating words is a device so to speak, for autonomously producing mother's milk (Kris, 1952, 20, n.11).

Completing *To the Lighthouse* is like some "prolonged, rather painful, yet exciting process of nature which one desires inexpressibly to have over" (D3, Sept.13'26), perhaps analogous to pregnancy. Afterward, Woolf's mind is "virgin" of books (D3, Sept.30'26). Obsessed with images of fertility in writing *The Waves*, Woolf asserts that a novel might best be written in "breathless anguish" so that for "nine months one is in despair," a fairly obvious equation of writing with childbirth. Now she has reached the stage of "hatching, the portal, the opening through which I shall go upon this experience" (D3, Mar.28'29).

Concerned about "change of life," Woolf asserts that during "difficult and dangerous times" she is most "fruitful artistically" and sometimes does her best work. Her mind becomes "chrysalis," so that lying "quite torpid, possibly with acute pain, suddenly something springs," and she feels "a tremendous sense of life beginning," makes up her story (D3, Feb.16'30).

Still competing with Vanessa, Woolf suggests having children cannot compare to the "pressure of the form, the splendor, the greatness," again referring to *The Waves*, the most recondite of her books (D3, Mar.28'30). Yes, not wishing to miss any of Vanessa's procreative experiences, Woolf vicariously identifies with Vanessa's miscarriage, compares the writing process to living in a "protected shell: the membrane breaks and the fluid escapes" (L4, Jul.6'30).

After the pressure and urgency of writing *Three Guineas*, Woolf highly satisfied with her effort, experienced the "mildest childbirth" she ever had (D5, Oct.12'37).

Embracing what to her mind was both the pain and excitement of childbirth, Woolf identified, in her writing and was thereby enlivened and enriched by, Vanessa's motherhood. Occasionally, Woolf engaged in a curious process of denial, stating motherhood was destructive or limiting, though alternately, she would boast she was as "spotted with the maternal taint" as Vanessa.

Deeply enmeshed with her sister, Woolf's creative process was also a means of wooing Vanessa, of winning or regaining her attention and affection during the oscillations of their relationship. Many of Woolf's books, those incorporating aspects of her sister's personality and ambience, in particular *Night and Day, To the Lighthouse, The Waves,* and *The Years,* suggest as does the writing of *Orlando* and *Roger Fry* with reference to Vita and Roger, that these are "love gifts" presented as consummate expressions of her art, as "near perfection as possible"; offered to the recipient with "pride and misgiving," (Greenacre, 490), with pleasure and sense of exposure at the same time.

Of course, the creative process is more complex than correlative fantansies of pregnancy and childbirth would have it. For Woolf, writing recaptures the past, encapsulates memory, represents reunion with mother and brother who died before their time, ensures the immortality of all those she resurrected in her fiction. Inasmuch as Virginia and Leonard had no children, the desire for personal immortality[1] is great, as is the fantasy of starting life over. Writing makes for greater coherence and integration of self, helps to anchor oneself in the present. When "backed by the past, the present is a thousand times deeper than the present when it presses you so close you can feel nothing else."

II

Spelled out in "Professions for Women," Woolf asserts a novel should be as "unconscious as possible, induce a perpetual lethargy so that nothing disturbs these mysterious nosings about, feelings round, darts, dashes, and sudden discoveries of that elusive spirit, the imagination" (*DM*, 240). In "The Leaning Tower" Woolf also claims that in permitting a free play of associations which the novelist shapes or restructures as he or she chooses, the "uppermind drowses" while the "undermind[2] works at top speed"; when the "veil lifts," one's story emerges, "simplified, composed" (*TM*, 134).

Counterposed to a style that is "loose-knit, yet not slovenly, so elastic it will embrace anything solemn, slight or beautiful," Woolf frequently sounds an aggressive note. She "must make the most direct and instant shots at the object, lay hands on words and shoot them with no more pause than is needed to put my pen in the ink" (D1, Apr.20'19). This was written when Woolf felt threatened by the advent of Vanessa's third child, Angelica. Woolf is now "fifth on the list," following Duncan, Quentin, Julian, and Angelica in Vanessa's affections. Maliciously, Virginia suggested Vanessa name her baby Moll Flanders, after Defoe's incestuous and wayward heroine. However, she had just written *Night and Day* and can now compete by way of the pen.

On completing *Mrs. Dalloway*, Woolf claims to make a quick and flourishing "attack" on *To the Lighthouse* (D2, Sept.5'25). Regarding the complicated emotions sought in *Mrs. Dalloway*, her approach synchronized with Dostoevski's, wherein the soul "tumbles upon us, hot, scalding, mixed, marvellous, terrible, oppressive" (*CR* v.1, 243).

In working on *The Pargiters* and *The Years*, Woolf is poised to "shoot forth quite free, straight and undeflected my bolts, wherever they are." Never had she "lived in such a race, such a violent impulsion and compulsion" (D4, Dec.19'32). Her novel will be "venturous, bold, take every possible fence" (D4, May'31'33). She feels she is "racing along, almost in sight of the end" (D4, Aug.7'34), must "break every mold and find a fresh form of being" for all she feels and thinks, though this involves constant effort, anxiety and risk (D4, Jul.28'34).

In writing *The Years*, Woolf was frequently imbued with a sense of immense power, fantasized herself a "race horse," had referred similarly to her father. Permitting herself to be thusly assertive, masculine, or potent in her conception of writing, concerning the material subsumed in her novel, she can apparently more readily accept her sexuality, at least in her fantasy and dream life, which seemed permeated at this time with an infinite variety of erotic themes.

Woolf's imagery is on occasion murderous or self-destructive, which leaps out in her fiction; for example, in *The Voyage Out*, there is a substrate of tension between the lovers, as Terence asserts Rachel could "blow his brains out." Sequentially, this occurs after he has coolly caricatured her appearance. He adds "there are moments when if we stood on a rock together, you'd throw me into the sea." Then they fought for "mastery" (298). At a later time, Rachel imagined a woman "slicing a man's head off with a knife" (339). These metaphors of strife between the lovers seem connected to their mutual indecision, but more likely to Rachel's fury at and capitulation to her aunt's subtle sabotage of Rachel's relationship with her lover.

Woolf and her fictional characters show instances of personal suffering, require pain to define their boundaries, feel hopeless, isolated, assaulted. These emotional states are fueled by prior feelings of worthlessness, self-disparagement, hypersensitivity to felt rejection, massive rage turned inward. Woolf and her characters frequently show a masochistic need for drama or sensation, thereby acquiring an illusory sense of aliveness. Rhoda feels the conversation of others "cuts" her like a knife. In feeling "violently cheated" or "brutally" reminded not to hope for things after Stella's death, Woolf shows a simultaneity of aggression and submission. Unaware of how they contribute to their suffering, they project anger, feel victimized, seek to take their lives, perhaps obeying the hidden dictates of others. Negotiation of differences rarely occurs.

Woolf's creative process brought the "whole universe to order." When working she felt "fully energised, nothing stunted" (D4, Jul.28'34). Yet writing was not the sum total of her life. Personal or emotional problems and dissonances in her relationships with others were clearly the issues that interfered with her work and affected her mood.

III

Phyllis Rose suggests that for Woolf, reworking her suicide note "bespeaks the discipline, rationality, concern for those she is leaving behind, pride in her self as a craftsman. To prevent their loss she killed herself" (Rose, 244). Indicating that for Woolf, as for her fictional character, Septimus Smith, death was an "exciting challenge, another voyage of discovery," Gordon links this to Woolf's notion that our sojourn on earth is momentary, as compared to the "unseen part of us" which permeates the atmosphere formerly inhabited (Gordon, 282).

Pointing to the final section of *Between the Acts* as upbeat, counterindicating suicide, Kenney postulates that the final section of Woolf's earlier typescript, written between May and August of 1940, offers clues concerning Woolf's decision to take her life. Here the typescript communicates human beings are powerless, forced to take parts in a drama they either do not understand or have no control over (Kenney, 281).

Stating that Woolf was not "mad" when she died but her fear of madness justified the coroner's verdict, or that she killed herself while the "balance of her mind was disturbed," Nicolson and Trautman add that she "died courageously on her own terms" (L6 Introduction, xvll). Here they corroborate Kenney's suggestion that Woolf's suicide was her "last desperate act of free will."

True, death arbitrarily claimed many of those closest to Woolf, and, by taking her life, she could feel in control. Romanticizing the suicidal act as an "exciting challenge" or as rational and disciplined however, ignores her fury and rage and overlooks her ongoing need for rescue. In the suicidal gesture, there is in addition to despair and intolerable frustration, hope of eliciting a caring response, of scaring the love object into greater attentiveness, which obscures the more unconscious, manipulative, guilt-provoking and accusing, possibly revengeful and blackmailing communication.

An agitated, impatient feeling that something must be done immediately, the wish to rid oneself of unbearable tension at all costs, often converge as culmination of a detailed, lethal plan. The act of suicide may represent passive surrender, a "tired wish for surcease"[3] with hope of relief or escape from suffering; may indicate a need for sacrifice, atonement or restitution; may point to aggression turned against the self or one's internal objects.

Woolf's diary entries towards the end of her life suggest her preoccupation with "vampires," the feeling she is sucked by "leeches," most likely a projection of her own need to devour, reflecting extreme oral envy. In contrast to her usual anoretic tentativeness about eating, Woolf is at this time enormously preoccupied with food.

Jumping from a window close to the ground, Woolf's first suicide gesture in 1904 though subsuming her terror of life without father, was largely attention-getting and histrionic, addressed to the living. Attempting suicide the second time, one year after marriage, was more lethal in intention, in response to the feeling her feminine self was shunted aside by Leonard, her desire to have a child denied, support of her sister withdrawn, her novel withheld, and her life not particularly valued inasmuch as Leonard left the veronal box unlocked. Quite possibly Leonard's guilt prompted his subsequent role as committed though infantilizing caretaker.

Woolf's final suicide was more complexly motivated, her need to protect loved ones considerable, her ambivalent emotions largely submerged, though cryptic signals and warnings were present for some time. Generally, the suicide "plan," frequently deflected, manifests an inexorable thrust towards completion.

Letters, diary, and novel at this time emphasize Woolf's extraordinarily diminished self-esteem, her lack of central, organized identity, her frustration and masked rage. Perceiving her fictional counterpart, Miss LaTrobe, freakish and abnormal, Woolf too might have felt that "nature set her apart" (*BA*, 211).

Insufficiencies in her personal relationships are striking, in particular Leonard's diminished protectiveness.[4] Possibly Leonard had been threatened by Virginia's proclaimed feeling of closeness to Roger. Or, Leonard was simply no longer interested in a caretaking relationship, was mobilized instead to write his own books, hoping to establish his personal immortality, which is human enough. A fascinating reversal of roles had occurred inasmuch as Virginia's hand became "tremulous," whereas Leonard, tremorous all his life, now goal-directed and productive regarding his political aims and activities, was symptom-free.

Indicating that Leonard and Trekkie Parsons, a neighbor in Rodmell, were close friends during the war, John Lehmann (1978) notes Mrs. Parsons eventually came to stay with Leonard at Monks House, and, following the war, was his travelling companion (148). Lehmann does not clearly state when their friendship began, whether their closer bond preceded or followed Virginia's death.[5] In her novel, *Between the Acts*, Woolf recurrently elaborated the sexual dalliances of her marital couple, Isa and Giles.

Giles, more overt in his indiscretions, is attracted to the sensual and seductive Mrs. Manresa who uninvited, arrives at the pageant with William, her homosexual friend; Giles makes love to her after rebuff by his wife. Isa can confide in William, is attracted to a tenuous "gentleman farmer," but is essentially preoccupied with a newspaper account of rape. Early on, there is the hint Isa may be "sapphist"; Woolf clearly feels at one with Isa's depression and rage.

At the same time, Woolf is identified with Miss LaTrobe, the distinctly masculine, author-director, deeply involved in the creation of a village play, a project Woolf was simultaneously, engaged in, and later bitterly disillusioned with. Emotionally deflated because of the demise of her homosexual friendship and failure of her play, Miss LaTrobe reembraces her artistic role. All three, Isa, LaTrobe, and Woolf share intolerable feelings of aloneness, are not intimate with anyone, are pervasively suicidal in their ideation.

Jolted by her sense of abandonment by Vita, Ethel, Vanessa, and Leonard, as well as by the shrinking of her "collective audience," Woolf felt she was writing in a vacuum, continued to write nevertheless, but was unhappy with her efforts.

Her feelings of estrangement from Vanessa; her feelings of rejection regarding both Vita and Ethel who were pursuing other loves; her disillusionment with her physician, Dr. Wilberforce who was ineffectual, misunderstood Woolf's malady and did not perceive her patient's transferential reaction to her "faraway lover," that is, Wilberforce herself, —exacerbated Woolf's depression and basic fragility of self.[6] Unable to acknowledge her hostility, Woolf became inordinately self-deprecating, tried to wrest sympathy and attention via her symptoms.

Throughout her life, Woolf related to a multiplicity of shifting parent-surrogates. As this point, without close attachments that were palpable, she along with Miss LaTrobe, feared the "horror and terror of being alone" (*BA*, 211), felt she had no vital tie with anyone. Woolf's cryptic assertion in *Between the Acts*: "this is death—illusion has failed" does not imply that diminishment of her creative imagination can only lead to death. Rather, Woolf feels life too is replete with illusion, states: "We are spectators and also passive participants in a pageant."[7] Perhaps she feels in regard to her life as well as her novel, that for her "the play is over, the actors have departed."

Obsessive concern with her "aged claw" suggests Woolf's anger and frustration, identification with her father's sense of failure and diminished capacity towards the end of his life,[8] though he too continued to write.

Her preoccupation with the sea, as she saw herself part of the non-human realm, as a stake in the water when the Ouse River banks burst, her constant allusion to drowning in *Between the Acts*, showed further identification with father, as "castaway," and also seemed a means of rejoining mother.

Woolf's depression and suicide may be perceived in context of Abraham's (1911) and Freud's (1917) brilliant linking of mourning and melancholia. Like the mourner, the depressed individual devalues the self, feels worthless, dejected, self-annihilating, helpless. The mourner feels the world impoverished, the melancholic himself. Predisposed to depression because of her early sense of exclusion, deprivation and bereavement, Woolf's response to loosening of the symbiotic relationship with Leonard was to further extol him, deprecate herself, and deny any difficulties.[9]

Paradoxically, a strong wish not to die may occur along with the wish for suicide. Conflict between the desire to cling to life or destroy oneself may become intense. According to Jensen and Petty (1958) the "fantasy of being rescued from suicide is channelized into a suicide attempt that gives warning and invites the intervention of the rescuer" (327). Although Leonard suspected Virginia made a suicide attempt on March 18th, ten days before her death, he did not properly heed her warning.

Her fictional character, the failed poet Septimus, did not in his last moments wish to die: "Life was good, the sun hot." Yet he felt others "clamored" for him to kill himself (*MD*, 226). Rhoda felt that after her death "they" will "devour" her, "tear her to pieces" (*TW* 331).

Feeling similarly isolated, Woolf wished to avoid lapsing into "private" separation, asserted "we moderns lack love"; she wrote "we need a center, something to bring us all together" (*BA*, 198), although she suspected the "game" was over for her. In her novel, the separation between players and audience, fiction and reality, is obliterated; Woolf's obsessive suicidal ideation parallels Isa's and Miss LaTrobe's. Finally, Woolf would "look her last" on "all things lovely," go down with her "colors flying."

Woolf's agitated depression seemed related to a simultaneous sense of "submission and rebellion," to an "accusatory demonstration of misery[10] in hope of eliciting love, forgiveness and reconciliation. She may have felt in touch with a surge of power and redemption, achieved a "final though fatal victory"[11] in her ultimate suicide.

Notes

Regarding references, the precise information as to the author, publication, and original and copyright dates are in the bibliography. Unless Harvest edition is cited for Harcourt, Brace Jovanovich who have for the most part published Woolf's works, the hardcover issue is indicated. In the text, when alluding to the source of a particular quotation, the author's name and page of article or book quoted is generally given. The date of publication, offered only when more than one book for an author is used, is otherwise available in the bibliography.

Abbreviations of Works by Virginia Woolf

BA	*Between the Acts*
CDB	*The Captain's Death Bed and Other Essays*
CR	*Common Reader*, vols. 1 and 2
CW	*Contemporary Writers*
D	*Diaries of Virginia Woolf*, vols. 1 to 5
DM	*The Death of the Moth and Other Essays*
GR	*Granite and Rainbow Essays*
JR	*Jacob's Room*
L	*Letters of Virginia Woolf*, vols. 1 to 6
MB	*Moments of Being*
MD	*Mrs. Dalloway*
ND	*Night and Day*
O	*Orlando*
PH	*Pointz Hall*
Rem.	*Reminiscences*
RF	*Roger Fry*
Room	*A Room of One's Own*
SOTP	*A Sketch of the Past*
TM	*The Moment and Other Essays*
TP	*The Pargiters*
TVO	*The Voyage Out*
TW	*The Waves*

TY   *The Years*
TTL   *To the Lighthouse*
TG   *Three Guineas*

Other Abbreviations

Maus   *Sir Leslie Stephen's Mausoleum Book*, ed. A. Bell
SP   G. Spater and I. Parsons: *A Marriage of True Minds*
TWV   L. Woolf: *The Wise Virgins*
Berg   Berg Collection: New York Public Library

Chapter I

1. For uniformity's sake, I use Woolf, which allays the objection that employing the first name of female writers is denigrating. Occasinally, when it seems awkward, for example in relation to her childhood, premarital situations, or *vis a vis* Leonard, I call her Virginia.

2. Woolf's *A Sketch of the Past*, written during 1939–1940, was begun at her sister Vanessa's suggestion. An earlier memoir, *Reminiscences*, embarked on during 1907–1908, was ostensibly written for Vanessa's children. Both essays appear in *Moments of Being*, 1976. *A Sketch of the Past* is expanded in the later edition of *Moments of Being*, in 1985. A rich source of Woolf's early memories, family life and inner stirrings, *Moments of Being* is a seminal document.

3. This was held under the auspices of the National Psychological Association for Psychoanalysis in 1980.

4. (3LW79) is shorthand for Leonard Woolf's *Autobiography*, v.3, 1911–1918, *Beginning Again*, 79.

5. Without wishing to appear overly clinical, it seems relevant, since aspects of Woolf's emotional illness assume importance in her life, to clarify these in simplified psychological and psychoanalytic terms. Woolf had four mental breakdowns: the first, which occurred in 1895 concomitant to her mother's death, suggests a severe adolescent crisis at 13 exacerbated by her ambivalent feelings regarding mother; the second breakdown, which involved a suicide attempt, followed her father's death in 1904, when she was 22, and faced with torturous issues regarding her personal and sexual identity; the third breakdown subsumed a depressive phase involving an almost lethal suicide attempt in 1913, and a fairly agitated, manic episode in 1915, both connected to seemingly insoluble impasses in her marital relationship; her final breakdown, which occurred during her depression in the early part of 1941, was linked to the loss of intimacy in her personal relationships and was followed by a determined suicide.

6. (D3, Feb.28'27) is shorthand for *The Diaries of Virginia Woolf*, ed. Anne O. Bell, v.3, 1925–1930, entry of February 28, 1927.

7. Contemporary studies of creativity, synthesize "primary" or preverbal with "secondary" or reasoning processes; primary process is not synonymous with chaos but rather the "basic facts of cognitive development lay the groundwork for primary and secondary processes alike" (Holt, 364).

8. This is in accord with Trilling (1966) stating: "The poet is in command of his fantasy," culled from "Freud and Literature" in *Psychoanalysis and Literature*, ed. H. Ruitenbeck, 260.

9. Dr. Ernest Jones (1920) indicated the dangers of the isolation technique and suggested that the personality of the physician was most central in the efficacy of the Weir Mitchell approach.

10. Virginia Woolf: "On Being Ill," in *The Moment and Other Essays*, 13–14.

11. This quotation is from Virginia Woolf's essay "The Leaning Tower," in *The Moment and Other Essays*, 149. Woolf here refers to British writers of the 1930s such as Auden, Isherwood, Spender, MacNiece, and Day Lewis.

12. In the past, Virginia Woolf was "diagnosed" in absentia as schizophrenic by Dr. Kimaya and manic-depressive by Dr. Frank Fish, both of whom relayed this in correspondence with Leonard Woolf, after her death. Letters from Dr. Fish to Leonard Woolf, dated Feb. 28, 1966, and Oct. 31, 1966, are in Monk's House Papers: University of Sussex Library.

13. Nessa is short for Vanessa Bell, Virginia Woolf's sister, an abstract artist.

14. Quentin is Quentin Bell, distinguished biographer, writer, and artist, Virginia Woolf's nephew, son of Vanessa and Clive Bell.

15. In her diary, Woolf links her anxiety-attack to "time of life" and preoccupation with the critical reaction to *The Years* (D5, Mar.2'37). Her response was also linked to Leonard's lukewarm reaction to *The Years*, to her capitulation to his wish she delete propagandistic passages in her book and to the ensuing, adverse effect on her self-esteem.

16. Using a psychoanalytic approach with an individual manifesting Woolf's symptoms, how proceed? Of primary importance, one must never underestimate suicidal threats since a theatrical or hysterical gesture might prove lethal, especially when anticipated or fantasized rescue is not forthcoming. Suicidal threats might suggest one feels too disoriented, helpless, enraged, or intolerant of frustration to reach out by verbal means. Empathizing with the individual's hopelessness and despair is central and prelude to eliciting feelings of anger and vengefulness, usually submerged but ill-concealed. Deep-seated developmental difficulties are present in personalities such as Woolf whose disillusionment concerning loss of protection or intimacy is continuous with early vulnerability and damage. One must explore and work through the nature of the individual's personal relationships and fragile self-concept, past and present, as well as the intricacies of the current life situation that led to feelings of self-condemnation, depression, preoccupation with taking one's life. Most crucially,

one must perforce, be involved, intuitive, on occasion confronting, provide a lifeline when necessary and feel attuned to one's own emotional responses.

17. Transference refers to the patient's projection in the psychoanalytic encounter with the psychoanalyst, of feelings, frequently distorted or exaggerated, engendered by and belonging to the early relationship with parents.

18. In this context, it is of note that psychoanalytic ego psychology took the leap from sole preoccupation with the artist's [or patient's] unconscious fantasies, to elaboration of multiply determined formations, that is, to character, life history, mother-child attachments, defensive structures, developmental patterns, identity themes, self- and object- representations. Rather mechanical, "object" is an unfortunate term in psychoanalytic terminology though we are stuck with it. The mother-image in the nursing situation is the first "object," her sustained nurturance crucial for the child's maturation and development.

19. In connection with "working through," see the work of Freud, 1914; Kris, 1956a, 1956b; and Greenson.

20. Without gainsaying the possibility of healing oneself via writing or the cathartic, reparative components in art, it is the therapeutic relationship that is crucial and makes for change in the psychoanalytic situation. The therapist, with the patient's collaboration, externalizes and integrates the more disguised, unconscious aspects of the self, shares the momentum for resolving transference emotions, tries to bring the analytic work to completion by providing an empathic "holding" environment.

21. Though Marcus (1981) cites Woolf's line, "thinking back through our mothers" from *A Room of One's Own*, as indicating that Woolf's friendship with women offered her "freedom and protection" and that the "mother will never abandon her daughter," (13) in actuality Woolf frequently depicted both real and fictional mother-figures as unavailable. Having many mothers in her life left Woolf with no single, significant adult to relate to in a meaningful way, when she vitally needed one.

22. Virginia Woolf: "Phases of Fiction," in *Granite and Rainbow*, 141.

23. Experimental observations indicate that the infant responds to both caretaker and environment from early on in a multitude of visual-motor, emotional, and social behaviors and shows decided needs for stimulation, feedback, activity, exploration, and exercise of growing capacities and skills.

24. In the studies of Mahler et al (1975) concerning the behavior of children between 5 months and three years, "separation-individuation" synchronizes two lines of development in context of the relationship with mother. "Separation" refers to the child's gradual "differentiation, disengagement and boundary formation" whereas "individuation" is concerned with the child's evolving "autonomy, perception, memory, cognition and reality testing" (63). Following the upsurge of exuberant, spontaneous exploration upon learning to

walk, the child shows an increased need to again feel part of the mother's orbit. Highly crucial at this time and reflecting her earlier behavior is the mother's sustained emotional acceptance, her sensitivity to the child's struggle between autonomy and clinging. Resolution of these processes which usually occurs by the third year, optimally leads to consolidation of individuality and beginning of "emotional object constancy" (109), that is, the internalized capacity to have available the mother's psychological presence, and subsequently the ability to turn to other relationships.

We do not have details of the way Woolf coped with the impingements of these phases of development but there is the suggestion her mother from early on was inconsistent, frequently absent from home, at times infantilizing, at times available but only briefly except for emergencies, because she was mother to so many and so openly showed her preference for Adrian. Woolf therefore found it difficult to integrate disparate mother images into a unitary whole. When splitting occurs and the maternal image is internalized as an "unassimilated, bad introject," the relationship with the "actual" mother is idealized, "protected from the child's hostility" (McDevitt, 1980, 141). Neither the internalization of mother or thrust towards ego autonomy, self- and object-constancy evolve in any meaningful, predictable sense in the depressive individual, perpetually preoccupied with loss, victimization and rage.

25. Contemporary psychoanalysis does not, as in the past, view sexual ambivalence as disease or pathology. Regarding Woolf's situation, she was obviously deeply conflicted regarding her feminine role. Current psychoanalytic theory no longer views femininity as "primary masculinity, disappointed maleness, masochistic resignation to fantasied inferiority or compensation for fantasied castration" (Blum, 1976, 18). Recent studies concerning female psychology suggest "core gender identity" is most crucially linked to "habitual patterns" of caretaking, that is, to parental attitudes regarding "sex assignment." (Stoller, 77).

26. In *Three Guineas* Woolf expressed her need to reject the usual forms of political organization, proposed as alternative, an "Outsider's Society" for women.

Chapter II

1. These sources are especially culled from the biographies of Quentin Bell, v.1 and 2, Noel Annan and Jean Love; Virginia Woolf's *Moments of Being* 1976, 1985; the unpublished correspondence of Julia and Leslie Stephen, in Berg Collection, New York Public Library.

2. Woolf's play, *Freshwater: A Comedy in Three Acts*, is based on the home life of Julia Cameron (Bell v. 2, 189n). Some of the famous who visited Little Holland House and Freshwater were Robert Browning, George Eliot, William

Thackeray, John Ruskin, Benjamin Disraeli, William Gladstone, Dante Rossetti, Henry James, and Ellen Terry.

3. *Sir Leslie Stephen's Mausoleum Book*, (ed.) A. Bell, 35.

4. Julia's pamphlet, *Notes From Sick Rooms* (1883), is a manual of practical nursing.

5. Virginia Woolf: "Professions for Women" in *The Death of the Moth and Other Essays*, 241.

6. At times the adult Leslie mumbled, chanted, or shouted poems when walking in the park, or climbing his beloved Alps.

7. Woolf too frequently referred to herself as "thin-skinned."

8. Love notes that by 1882, the year Virginia was born, Leslie Stephen's correspondence with his wife regained the tone of "self-pity and complaining," typical of his letters prior to marriage (Love, 104).

9. Vanessa Bell: *Notes on Virginia's Childhood.*

10. In *Night and Day*, Katharine's Hilbery's mother agrees to her daughter's marriage since this will provide Mrs. Hilbery with a son.

11. Although we know nothing regarding Virginia's reactions to the birth or infancy of her brother, child observation studies of youngsters between 16 and 24 months who show cumulative disturbances in the maternal relationship due to the mother's depression or unavailability, point to the occurrence of "moderate to severe castration anxiety reactions" (Galenson and Roiphe, 1976, 33) when children become aware of anatomical differences. In specific, girls show anger, fear of abandonment and increased, hostile dependence concerning the mother at this time. (Roiphe and Galenson, 1981, 2; 19).

12. Julia occasionally took with her those of her children who were age two and one-half years or younger when attending her mother. (Love, 117; 215).

13. Angelica Garnett, daughter of Vanessa Bell and Duncan Grant, states in a recent memoir that her mother experienced episodes of "lethargy" persisting for several years, indicating Vanessa's proneness to "severe depression" (Garnett, 32).

14. Virginia and Vanessa both emulated aspects of their father's interests.

15. Anger at her father in not according her a university education was undoubtedly a precursor of Woolf's feminism.

16. Some of these are "screen" memories; that is, attempts to ward off, deny, or repress painful feelings. *A Sketch of the Past* was written during 1939 to 1940, when Virginia Woolf felt enormous emotional isolation, sought to resurrect her childhood memories, in particular hoped for closeness with a mother-image.

17. In the childhood of the creatively gifted, Greenacre finds marked response to "rhythm and gestalt relationships of form," resulting in a "wide range of awareness" of the child's own body, as well as the outer surround (1957, v.2, 497).

18. This suggests the period of Virginia's adolescence or preadolescence.

19. Here a hysterical reaction rather than temporary depersonalization is suggested, based on an inner conflict immobilizing her voluntary movement at the moment.

20. Wolfenstein (1966) suggests adolescence is a "trial mourning" involving diminution of the attachment to parents and their internal images. Adolescence also offers a "second chance", as it were, to correct the imbalances of childhood (Blos, 1978, 141).

21. Leslie Stephen/Stella Duckworth Correspondence: Berg Collection, New York Public Library. Actually, Woolf read her father's entire correspondence when assisting Frederick Maitland with his biography of her father in 1904.

22. Suggesting that all of Woolf's breakdowns were due to female developmental processes: menstruation, marriage, and menopause, Showalter compares Woolf's symptoms during her first breakdown to "female adolescent shame and anxiety" with regard to the onset of menstruation (268).

23. Rhoda, very much Virginia Woolf's self-portrait, is one of the central characters in *The Waves*.

24. Virginia's fears, as noted in her 1897 diary, concerned accidents she claimed to witness, involving unruly or unpredictable behavior by horses. Perhaps preoccupied with Stella's and Jack's sexuality, she is occasionally fantasy-ridden in describing the tumultuousness of horses, especially observing one horse lying down and another moving friskily above it. Unpublished *1897 Diary:* Berg Collection, New York Public Library.

Chapter III

1. The 1985 edition of *Moments of Being* contains expanded passages from Woolf's unpublished diaries of 1940. This book when referred to will be noted as *A Sense of the Past*, 1985. No date is given when the 1976 edition is quoted.

2. Hyman suggests that Woolf, in describing her father's rage in her 1939–1940 memoir, projects feelings she cannot accept in herself at this time (Hyman, 1982, 20).

3. This becomes "passionate fumbling fellowship" in *A Sense of the Past*, 1985. In the later edition of *A Sense of the Past*, Virginia's portrait of her father expresses greater love and attraction.

4. Janet and she remained friends until Janet's death in 1937. Janet was prototype for a fictional character in *The Pargiters*, a tutor who was underpaid because she was a woman.

5. This manuscript is found in Virginia Stephen: "Friendship Gallery," 1907, an unpublished story: Berg Collection, New York Public Library.

6. Although hallucinatory symptoms such as hearing voices might suggest a schizophrenice process, they may be present in affective disorders as well, perhaps illusions or transformations of actual perceptions related to the prevailing mood of the person (Arieti, 457).

7. Starving herself or anorexia might at this time have been Virginia's defiant reaction to the recommendation of her doctor advising a diet of rich food.

8. As recalled, Thoby tried leaping out the window in 1894.

9. Writing *Mrs. Dalloway* between 1923 and 1924, one of the central characters an insane poet who hears birds singing in Greek, Woolf is here obviously sorting out the meaning to her of her hallucination in 1904 of "birds singing in Greek," most likely related to guilt regarding the "crime" of one's homosexual predilection or the crime of not properly mourning one's parents.

10. The relevance of this myth was brought to my attention by Professor Virginia Hyman.

11. Septimus perceived birds "swooping, swerving, flinging themselves in and out, round and round and yet always with perfect control," something both he and Woolf wished to emulate.

12. Avoiding food can be a means of experimenting with the possibility of death since life might not be worth living with the loss of father (Abraham, 1953, 436–437).

13. Virginia Stephen's unpublished *1903 Diary* is in Berg Collection, New York Public Library.

Chapter IV

1. Bell indicates Adrian at this time is a "tease" and Virginia "eminently teasable"; they apparently argued at great length. Nevertheless, Bell imparts, their feelings for one another were "profound." (Bell, v. 1, 117).

2. The exchange of letters between Virginia Stephen and Clive Bell concerning *Melymbrosia* is found in Bell, v.1, Appendix D: "Clive Bell and the Writing of *The Voyage Out*," 207–212.

3. In later years, Virginia informed Clive he was the first person who ever thought she could write well (L2, Jul.24'17). Clive wrote Leonard Woolf on Aug. 24, 1956, that this was the "finest tribute" he ever had (Bell, v.1, Appendix D, 212.)

4. The "Dreadnought Hoax" refers to the attempts of Virginia and cohorts, dressed as Abyssinians, to deceive the British navy and tour the man o'war, "H.M.S. Dreadnought." They felt the official reaction, one of intense disapproval, showed "brutality and pomposity" (Bell, v.1, 160).

5. Indeed, Virginia was having a fantasied affair with each.

6. Clive's letter of August, 1912, is found in the Clive Bell Correspondence: University of Sussex Library.

Chapter V

1. G. Spater and I. Parsons, *A Marriage of True Minds: An Intimate Portrait of Leonard and Virginia Woolf*, 54.

2. Leonard continues: "It was an intellectual aristocracy of the middle class, the nearest equivalent in other countries being the French eighteenth century noblesse de robe" (3LW186).

3. Rather boastful about her sexuality, Vanessa does not apparently believe in the possibility her sister might change or require considerable encouragement.

4. A mandrill is a large, fierce, strong baboon of western Africa.

5. Dr. Hyslop was proponent of a theory of eugenics, namely, sterilizing the unfit (Trombley).

6. Jean Thomas had a "violent homosexual passion" for Virginia (Bell, v.2, 16n).

7. Using artistic prerogative Woolf in *To the Lighthouse*, arranged for Prue, the Ramsays' daughter, to die during childbirth.

8. Julia, despite her idealization as mother in *To the Lighthouse*, may not in actuality have been in Woolf's eyes a good mother. In *A Sketch of the Past*, Woolf describes a lack of intimacy between herself and mother, felt her mother was basically unavailable.

9. In a letter to Gwen Revarat, Woolf describes her feelings: "You can't think what a raging furnace it still is to me—madness, and doctors are being forced always" (L3, May1'25).

10. Bellak (1958) suggests disagreement between and turnover of doctors are highly disruptive to the emotionally ill (82). Especially upsetting to Virginia at

this time was discarding Dr. Savage, not only because he felt affirmatively about the issue of having children, but because he was for so long the Stephen's family doctor and friend, a familiar figure in their lives, representing continuity with the past.

11. Hyoscyamine might have exacerbated Woolf's symptoms but these were by now her lifelong, reflexive reactions to stress (Trombley, 142).

12. Harry tells Camilla: "There's no life in you. Your women . . . leave one cold. No dark hair, no blood in them" (*The Wise Virgins*, 52).

13. Of relevance is Sidney Waterlow's conception of Virginia and Vanessa: Vanessa is seen as icy and cynical, Virginia as emotional and "interested in life other than beauty" (Bell, v.1, 176). Waterlow was a member of the Cambridge and Bloomsbury circles and one of Woolf's many suitors before her marriage.

14. This passage was pointed out to me by Dr. Benjamin Brody.

15. Leonard was a man who was "self-created" (Ozick, 37). In Virginia he married a "kind of escutcheon" who "represented the finest grain of the finest stratum in England. What he shored up against disintegration was the life he had gained, a birthright he paid for by wheedling porridge between Virginia's resisting lips" (Ozick, 42).

Chapter VI

1. *The Voyage Out* was envisaged by Fleishman in archetypal terms, as a story of "initiation and heroic quest," as a "tragedy of inexperience" and "loss of innocence," wherein "death and initiation are interchangeable" (Fleishman, 3).

2. "Euphrosyne" was the name Vanessa originally suggested for Woolf's heroine; it was also the name of a Cambridge journal and was one of the Graces, whose name is associated with happiness.

3. In *Melymbrosia*, Rachel's aunt thinks "this girl [Rachel] might be a boy" (9).

4. Richard Dalloway reappears in Woolf's later novel, *Mrs. Dalloway*, as husband of one of the central characters, Clarissa Dalloway.

5. Woolf, who might have felt similarly oppressed by her mother's expectation of doom, quotes her: "let us make the most of what we have, since we know nothing of the future. The melancholy echoes answered: What does it matter? Perhaps there is no future" (*Rem*, 36).

6. Prior versions of *The Voyage Out* are an "Earlier Typescript" (undated), "Later Typescript" (undated), and a "Holograph" (1912). Berg Collection: New York Public Library.

7. These lines are from "Comus, A Mask" written in 1634 by John Milton.

8. Rachel at the bottom of the sea, Rachel passively tossed about by the waves, and Sabrina drowning all suggest Woolf's continuous preoccupation with dangerous watery depths.

9. Earlier manuscripts of *The Voyage Out* suggest to DeSalvo (1980) that as Woolf revised the novel's death scene, she herself "went mad and once tried to commit suicide" (x). However, Woolf's emotional disturbance in 1913 was linked to complex enmeshments and conflicts concerning self, husband, sister, and physicians.

10. In Moore's (1981) analysis of *The Voyage Out*, Rachel assumes the role of Persephone to her aunt's Demeter. Rachel-Persephone's "ritual propitiation" to Helen-Demeter is the "inevitable sacrifice to a society still incapable of respecting the spiritual needs of women" according to Moore (101) who thereby exonerates Helen's malevolence.

11. Dr. Savage, though limited, was a friend as well as family physician and, in the past, kept Woolf from the more catastrophic phase her breakdown here assumed.

12. For both Rachel and Woolf, rage was unacceptable and, therefore, must be channeled into physical symptoms, "madness," or suicide.

Chapter VII

1. Ottoline was otherwise hostess and patroness of the arts; her husband, Philip, was a barrister and Liberal member of Parliament between 1908 and 1918. At their homes, Garsington Manor in Oxfordshire and later in Bloomsbury, they were hospitable to artists and writers as well as those opposed to the war: *The Diaries of Virginia Woolf*, v.3, Appendix I, 351. Comment by Anne O. Bell.

2. Did Woolf, commiserating with her father's doubts concerning his literary efforts especially towards the end of his life, deny her own writing aspirations?

3. It is of interest that the previous quotation from *Night and Day* "it's life that matters . . . ", appears in Dostoevski's *The Idiot* (Bazin 232n).

4. Fleishman interprets this passage as the Shakespearian perception of life as an "illusion surrounded by nothingness" and suggests the "imagination that has been found to govern love is now rendered suspect by its connection with the meaningless life of possession and struggle" (Fleishman, 37).

5. This allusion to Katharine whose prototype is in part Vanessa, is precursor to the emotionally laden image of "lighthouse" in *To the Lighthouse*.

6. Mr. Hilbery's aversion to his daughter's relationship with Ralph is similar to Leslie Stephen's disapproval when Stella wished to marry.

Chapter VIII

1. "Luminous halo" evokes William James' writings on the stream of consciousness, his portrayal of the mental image with its "halo of relations," "psychic overtone" or "fringe," related to the "moment of being" in Woolf's novels (Richter 10). "Luminous halo" also evokes Ralph Denham's "little dot with flames round it, that encircling glow or halo softening sharp outlines" (*Night and Day*, 522).

2. *The Diaries of Virginia Woolf*, ed. Anne O. Bell, v.2, 1920–1924, Appendix III, 339–342.

3. We do not know the cause of the flareup, but Thoby might have been jealous over the advent of a younger sister when he was one and one-half years old and as a child resented Virginia.

4. Phyllis Rose considers parts of *Jacob's Room*, in its tone of "fatigue," influenced by Eliot's early poetry (Rose, 105).

5. Dionysus, linked with the Roman god, Bacchus, is associated with wine and revelry.

6. Virginia Woolf: "Reading," in *The Captain's Deathbed and Other Essays*, 165–169.

Chapter IX

1. *Mrs. Dalloway:* "Introduction." Modern Library edition (1928).

2. Wanting so badly evokes an early sense of maternal deprivation, a theme resuscitated in her next novel, *To the Lighthouse*.

3. Septimus is a central character in *Mrs. Dalloway*, his symptoms largely based on Woolf's conception of her behavior during her breakdowns.

4. These notes are found in "Mrs. Dalloway Revisions": *Jacob's Room Notebook* in Berg Collection, New York Public Library.

5. "Fear no more the heat of the sun nor the furious winter's rages" is from *Cymbeline*," by William Shakespeare.

6. According to Naremore (1973, 103), Woolf views the self not merely as an "ego bound by space and time", but embraces the self's relationship with the physical world that survives when life is over.

7. Critics frequently link Peter with Clive Bell.

8. This is Woolf's self-image as well.

9. It is of interest that in the various definitions of "verge" in *Webster's Second International Dictionary*, it is also defined as rod, penis, or encircling line or border, where masculine and feminine seem combined.

10. Since Clarissa is frequently described as frigid, the substitution of cold for heated feelings is of interest, suggesting Clarissa's fear of passion.

11. The name is a give away.

12. Does this refer to his homosexuality?

13. The issue of an unnaturally strong attachment between parent and child, a theme present in all of Woolf's novels thus far, is raised by Leaska (1977a, n.12, 92).

14. Here Woolf's description of Septimus and Evans is similar to the restrained physicality between Jacob and Bonamy in *Jacob's Room*.

15. Zwerdling (1977) empahsizes the demise of the Conservative-Liberal Coalition and rise of Labor in 1923 in British politics. The ruling class represented by the Dalloways were no longer ascendant.

16. Similar fears and distortions were voiced by Woolf during her 1913 breakdown after she was told she could not have children and resorted in her thinking to primitive conceptions of pregnancy and childbirth.

17. Spilka wonders whether Septimus counterposes the "filth" of copulation to the "rough and tumble purity" of homosexual love (Spilka, 63).

18. Unable to accept responsibility for his own feelings, externalizing them instead, Septimus responds as though others accused him of weaknesses he may have avoided confronting in himself.

19. Clarissa, too, felt she was an outsider looking on.

20. Screen suggests barrier.

21. Is this a rhythmic counterpart to his mood?

22. As we know, Woolf also heard "birds singing in Greek" during her 1904 breakdown.

23. Schlack (1979) and Leaska (1977a) suggest Septimus' name is culled from Dante's *Inferno* and refers to the "seventh circle" of punishment, for war, suicide, and perversion.

24. "Drowned sailor" is an ominous theme reverberating in many of Woolf's novels.

25. Perhaps it is Woolf's intention to describe the constriction of severe mental illness.

26. Clarissa and Peter "lived in each other"; Septimus was merged with nature.

27. Possibly Septimus is now repelled by the physical act of sexual intercourse and the intimacy of conceiving a child.

28. For Woolf, the "visible world of light and life is the mirror-image or repetition in reverse of an invisible world of darkness and death" (H. Miller, 198).

29. "If 'twere now to die 'twere now to be most happy" is from *Othello*, by William Shakespeare.

30. Despite Woolf's confusion regarding feminine role, she was propelled by positive feelings toward her maternal ego-ideal, Vanessa, and originally wanted children. In writing that Richard insisted she (Clarissa) must sleep undisturbed (46), we can glean Woolf felt Leonard rejected her sexually.

31. In stating neither Clarissa nor Woolf confront their grief, guilt, or anger regarding their losses and that they appear shallow and undeveloped as a result, Spilka (73) seems judgmental and overlooks the complex nature of human motivation. Emotional conflicts need not necessarily interfere with social or intellectual development.

32. Did Virginia feel Leonard, in leaving the veronal pillbox unlocked in 1913, wished her dead?

Chapter X

1. Middleton Murry, the literary critic, disliked Woolf's lack of interest in plot.

2. Leonard and Virginia via Hogarth Press had just published Vita's novel *Seducers in Ecuador*, which was selling very well.

3. Before his death on March 7, 1925, Jacques Reverat dictated a letter to Woolf concerning his highly favorable impressions of *Mrs. Dalloway*.

4. The last stanza in William Cowper's "The Castaway" is as follows:
No voice divine the storm allayed
No light propitious shone
When snatched from all effectual aid
We perished each alone;
But I beneath a deeper sea
And whelm'd in deeper gulfs than he.
"The Castaway," in *English Literature and its Backgrounds: From the Forerunners of Romanticism to the Present*, ed. B. Grebanier, v.2, 54.

5. Lighthouse is a pervasive, powerful, multi-levelled symbol in *To the Lighthouse*.

6. Convolvulous are trailing, twining, or erect plants with trumpet-shaped flowers.

7. As recalled, Virginia at 16 had an intense crush on Madge. Later, she felt disillusioned with Madge's "commonplace mind."

8. This seems the first glimmering of Woolf's prose-poem, *The Waves*, which concerns "six lives," based on her intimates and herself.

9. Not a breakdown in terms of mental illness, Woolf here refers to physical symptoms and depression, which in the past gained Vanessa's attention.

10. Virginia Woolf's mother used to say: "Oh the torture of never being left alone" (*A Sketch of the Past*, 90).

11. Julia Stephen was also continuously engaged in "doing good" (*A Sketch of the Past*, 90).

12. The fairy tale, concerning the relationship between a fisherman and his wife, bears an interesting counterpoint to the interplay between Mr. and Mrs. Ramsay. When the fisherman declares he did not wish to be king, his wife retorted "If you won't be king, I will" (86).

13. Virginia Woolf notes that her mother "looked very sad when not talking" (*A Sketch of the Past*, 82).

14. Woolf and her fictional women frequently and nostalgically allude to father's feet or shoes, generally considered phallic symbols.

15. Seeing Mr. Ramsay as "King," "leader," "lion," Lily expresses Woolf's admiration of her father when he is mobilized, her awareness that his need for support is not as depleting as she on other occasions implies.

16. Is Woolf attributing her creativity to her mother? Did she feel she learned from her mother's artful handling of many human situations?

17. Could Lily's negation of marriage represent aspects of Woolf, musing about a single life, similar to Lily, or to Mary Datchet in *Night and Day*?

18. The Ramsays make an attempt at confrontation, which did not have its counterpart in the Stephen marriage.

19. Woolf frequently described her writing process as one of placing herself in a "trance."

20. Lily requires the frequent presence or aura of her mother-surrogate, Mrs. Ramsay, to entrench her identity as person and as artist, as though she experienced a defect in mothering, not dissimilar to Woolf who became ill when dissonances in her maternal attachments took place.

21. Leslie Stephen's grandfather was once shipwrecked: "lashing the four survivors together," he climbed a cliff in the stormy night, with others behind him (Annan, 7).

22. Naremore (1973) suggests Woolf's prose is full of "erotic impulses and sexual themes" (242) and that these are major elements in *To the Lighthouse*.

23. According to Auerbach, Woolf's emphasis on the "random occurrence" such as the "measuring of the stocking," viewing it not in the service of a planned continuity of action but "in itself," yields "something new and elemental"; that is, the "wealth of reality and depth of life in every moment to which we surrender ourselves without prejudice" (552).

24. Leaska (1970) points to Woolf's "angle of narration" as requiring "special attention," since the distinction "between narrator and character, between one character and another or between author and narrator, has dissolved" (20-21).

Chapter XI

1. Dora Carrington was a painter who lived with Lytton Strachey, as companion and housekeeper in a ménage à trois with her husband, Ralph Partridge.

2. The name Orlando has the word "land" in it—the name of Vita's prize poem.

3. Virginia Woolf: "Women and Fiction" in *Granite and Rainbow: Essays*, 76-84.

4. Nigel Nicolson suggests *Orlando* restored or forever identified Vita with her ancestral home, Knole, of which Vita's birth as a girl deprived her (231).

5. Sasha was based on Violet Trefusius, Vita's lover.

6. Pepita apparently had an affair with Vita's grandfather who was a descendant of Thomas Sackville, consul to Queen Elizabeth.

7. Orlando's sex change may be seen according to Fleishman, in context of the "rites de passage" observed in all societies, as a "coming out of oneself, a transcending of one's own historically controlled situation and a recovering of an original situation" (Fleishman, 146).

8. "Vita" is Latin for "life."

9. In describing Shakespeare's "extraordinarily gifted sister," Woolf asks "who shall measure the heat and violence of the poet's heart when caught and tangled in a woman's body", suggesting had Shakespeare's sister gone to London to be a poet-playwright, she might have been taken advantage of sexually, found herself "with child" by Nick Greene, and would then have killed herself. (*Room*, 49-50).

10. In Woolf's early manuscript of *Orlando*, the "wild goose" is the "secret of life" (Hoffman, 443). According to Bodkin, "with the type figure of the sea captain perpetually braving the world's storms, we find related through the wild goose symbol, the figure of the poet, master-adventurer, and treasure-seeker in the realms of mind." Bodkin also sees in Orlando a "modern rendering from the woman's standpoint, of the intuition that through the immortal and ever-elusive Image formed in each of the other, man and woman alike find a way of approach to Reality or to the Divine" (Bodkin, 307).

11. Kubie here points to Orlando's sense of "haunting failure" (262), attributing it to penis envy.

12. Moore thought Vita represented the "womanhood Woolf felt she never had" (Moore, 1984, 94). She quotes Woolf as exclaiming about Vita's "capacity to take the floor in any company; to represent her country; to control silver, servants, chow dogs; her motherhood; her being in short what I never have been, a real woman" (D3, Dec.21'25). Woolf's comment however seems a mixture of adolescent crush, snobbery, and ingratiation; she thought Vita an inadequate mother to her sons.

13. As with Lily Briscoe, Woolf required a constant mother-image for emotional nurturance and feminine modelling, generally Vanessa, with whom to complete her ever-elusive identification process.

14. In the recent edition of *Moments of Being*, Virginia's portrait of her father is intensely affectionate. Virginia "loved" her father's idiosyncracies, his "unworldliness, honesty, lovableness, sincerity," even his opinionatedness (*A Sketch of the Past*, 1985, 110–111). Woolf was frequently on father's side even when he was "exploding": she shared his moods, not her mother's. Describing him as a very "striking man" especially when his "hair was curled in a thick bob behind his ears," she claimed he was a "magnificent figure in his Hills Brothers clothes, had a great charm for women, and was himself attractive to the young and lovely" (112–114). She and father had a great deal "in common," obviously a special empathy that was theirs alone. The rest of the discussion in *Moments of Being* concerning her father is as already noted, markedly negative. Virginia had been reading Freud's theory concerning the nature of ambivalence and was possibly analyzing her feelings towards father in this context.

15. Julia's literary efforts - essays and children's stories which are unpublished, "run to formula", though Zwerdling adds she possessed a flair for language and a shrewdly observant eye (Zwerdling, 1986, 190). In reading *Notes From Sickrooms*, Julia's sole published work, one is impressed by its formality, woodenness and forced professionalism. Feeling inferior with "words", Julia was undoubtedly rivalrous with her precocious daughter and her daughter's literary rapport with Leslie.

16. Showalter suggests androgyny was the "myth" that caused Woolf to avoid "confrontation with her own painful femaleness" and that caused her to "choke and repress her anger and ambition" (264). Embracing the experience of

a woman might have led to an "understanding of what it means to be a man. This revelation would . . . result from daring to face and express what is a unique, even if unpleasant, taboo, or destructive in one's own experience, and thus it would speak to the secret heart in all people" (Showalter, 289).

Chapter XII

1. At times the poetry of Woolf's prose reads like an abstract painting:

> The sun laid broad shoulder blades upon the house. The light touched something green in the window corner and made it a lump of emerald, a cave of pure green like stoneless fruit. It sharpened the edges of chairs and tables and stitched white tablecloths with fine gold wires . . . . Everything became softly amorphous as if the china of the plate flowed and the steel of the knife were liquid (*The Waves*, 195).

> The sun fell in sharp wedges . . . ; a plate was like a white lake. A knife looked like a dagger of ice . . . (251).

2. Virginia Woolf: "Narrow Bridge of Art," in: *Granite and Rainbow* (19).

3. Woolf reiterated she took less than the proper dosage and from the same bottle Vanessa used for herself.

4. Brenan was a young writer, living in Spain, with whom Woolf regularly corresponded. They frequently exchanged ideas about writing and literature.

5. In her thoughts at this time, Thoby is pivotal in her novel, embodied in the character of Percival.

6. Woolf frequently equates the creative process with the imagined pain of childbirth.

7. Ethel Smyth, a composer, wrote Woolf, warmly commending *A Room of One's Own*; after several postponements due to Woolf's physical illness at the time, they met on February 20, 1930.

8. Also giving Virginia considerable pleasure was E.M. Forster's positive review of *The Waves*. He felt it an "important" book, experienced the "sort of excitement over it which comes from believing that one's encountered a classic" (D4, Nov.16'31).

9. In an early version of *The Waves*, Woolf saw waves as "many mothers endlessly sinking, falling, and lying prostrate, each holding up, as the wave passed its crest, a child" (Richter, n.91). Richter points to the similarity between Woolf's imagery and DeQuincey's description of ocean waves containing "innumerable faces, imploring, wrathful, despairing."

10. In an early version of *The Waves*, Louis is the "most constantly passionate of us all" (Gordon, 228). Apparently the businessman supercedes the "dark dreamer."

11. Fleishman describes this aspect of Bernard as his "undiscovered self" (Fleishman, 169).

12. "Central shadow" refers to denial of traditional forms of human behavior (Gorsky, 450).

13. Virginia Woolf: "Professions for Women," in *The Death of the Moth and Other Essays*, 240.

14. Virginia Woolf: "*Jane Eyre* and *Wuthering Heights*," in *Common Reader*, v.1, 225

Chapter XIII

1. Woolf considered herself a pacifist during times of war and peace.

2. This excerpt is from "Professions for Women," Typescript, 1, xxvii, Berg Collection, New York Public Library. In Radin, 3.

3. At a party honoring Ethel's musical accomplishments that Woolf felt "dragged to" against her will, she felt humiliated, betrayed to "wolves and vultures," her sensitivity teetering on "madness" (L4, Mar.11'31). With Ethel, Woolf is apparently free to sound like Rhoda of *The Waves*.

4. The context of the dream refers to the period, short-lived, that Lytton proposed marriage and Woolf accepted.

5. *Virginia Woolf/Lytton Strachey Correspondence*, 1906–1931; eds. L. Woolf and J. Strachey.

6. Woolf felt poets of Lehmann's generation published too young, took themselves too seriously, should maintain continuity with the past. When Lehmann replied she overlooked her own, more experimental efforts, which might indeed have diminished, she agreed, apparently shaken by Lehmann's thrust, then expressed dissatisfaction with her essay.

7. Woolf's tension was incorporated in the 1917 chapter of *The Years* and later deleted.

8. The essays encompassed issues involving love, money, politics, and power at given periods of time, while the narrative portions dramatized these aspects of history through character and situation.

9. Woolf here refers to her characters Sara and Nicholas in *The Years*.

10. During the writing process, Woolf thought all her books a failure. The specific reference here is to the modulation of her original all-encompassing plan, muting the topic of pacifism for esthetic purposes and appeasement of Leonard. Middleton (171) suggests the novel shows the "adverse effects of Virginia's constraints upon selfhood and creativity."

11. Occasionally there will be a linking of *The Years* with its earlier version, *The Pargiters*.

12. The sense of passing time is of central importance, evidenced of course in the title.

13. Sara and Maggie are Abel's nieces, children of Digby and Eugenia Pargiter; Sara is called Elvira in *The Pargiters*.

14. Peggy and her brother North are Morris Pargiter's children.

15. Nicholas Pomjalovsky is based on S.S. Koteliansky, who collaborated with Woolf on translations from the Russian in the early 1920s.

16. As with Eleanor, Woolf felt trapped by her father's importunate needs.

17. It is of interest that next to Eleanor's bedside at her brother's home, is the book *Diary of a Nobody* (*The Years*, 211).

18. Leaska suggests Eleanor has been buried by the past, has deserted an earlier love for love of father, similar to Antigone's love for Oedipus in his last years (Leaska, 1977a, 220–221).

19. This song might have been culled from a classic text, synchronizing as it does numerous Greek and Latin syllables (Fleishman, 200).

> Etho passo tanno hai
> Fai donk to tu do
> Mai to, kai to, lai to see
> Toh, dum to tuh do —
> Fanno to par, etto to mar,
> Timin, Tudo, Tido,
> Foll to gar in, mitno to par,
> Eido, tedo, meido —
> Chree to gay ei,
> Geeray didax . . . (*TY*, 429–430)

20. Rose's dilemma may be evocative of Woolf's childhood tantrums where she would become "purple with rage," perhaps leading to self-injuring, attention-getting situations, occurring when she similarly felt overlooked.

21. "A Dance at Queens' Gate": Virginia Stephen's unpublished *1903 Journal*, in Berg. Collection, New York Public Library.

22. After her mother's and Stella's death, Woolf described herself as a "broken chrysalis."

23. Woolf writes Ethel: "How I hated marrying a Jew—how I hated their nasal voices and their oriental jewelry and their noses and their wattles"—then acknowledged she was a "snob" (L4, Aug.2'30). She describes a visit from Leonard's family: "they are dressed like all Jews as if for high tea in a hotel lounge, never mixing with the country, talking incessantly, but requiring at intervals the assurance I think it jolly to have them." She describes the garrulousness of Leonard's mother, her complaints about raising nine sons (L4, Sept.28'30).

24. Renny is the most attractive of Woolf's male fictional characters.

25. In her sexual fantasies, Woolf too seemed turned on to younger men. Bananas are obvious, repetitive, phallic, and sexual symbols in her novels, but these were her preoccupation at the time.

26. "Heart of darkness," a Conradian theme, is present in many of Woolf's novels.

27. Pargeter was the name of a railway worker Virginia and Leonard were acquainted with.

28. Kitty Malone is attracted to Jo Robson who has "wood shavings" in his hair, worked with his hands mending books and hammering hen coops; he reminded her of a farmhand who kissed her under a haystack when she was 15. Longing to be a farmer, she is instead trapped in a loveless marriage with wealthy Lord Lasswade, after rejecting Edward Pargiter's proposal.

29. Radin on the other hand, suggests Woolf's early manuscripts for *The Years* were purposely discursive and experimental, serving as a source book wherein Woolf made detailed notes before incorporating them in her narrative.

Chapter XIV

1. Julian's friend and contemporary John Lehmann thought highly of Julian's early poetry, considered him original and authentic. David Garnett, of the older generation, also acknowledged Julian's poetic gifts, thought him the "best of his generation" (Stansky and Abrahams, 40–41).

2. Quentin Bell thought Woolf's *Three Guineas* a form of argument with Julian's point of view (Bell, v.2, 204); Julian died four months after Woolf began writing it.

3. Anticipation of disaster with the "forces of history completely out of control" made recourse to war in 1939, according to Leonard, vastly different than during World War I. Should Hitler force the issue England would fight and

Leonard, opposed to Hitler's anti-semitism and totalitarianism, would support his country. Virginia's political ideas, as suggested in *Three Guineas* and *The Years*, ran full tilt against Leonard.

4. Virginia Woolf: "Lappin and Lapinova," in *A Haunted House and Other Short Stories*, 68–78.

5. Virginia Woolf: "Reviewing," in *The Captain's Death Bed and Other Essays*, 127–145.

6. Virginia Woolf: "Thoughts on Peace in an Air-raid" in *Death of a Moth and Other Essays*. Her essay states that freeing women from slavery will free men from tyranny; that Hitlers are bred by slaves (*DM*, 247).

7. The village play is a central theme in *Between the Acts*.

8. Admiring Churchill, avidly following the battles fought in World War II, Woolf does not appear indifferent either to England's participation in the war or to defeating Hitler. E.M. Forster thought her diaries made for excellent war reporting.

9. Ethel's book, *What Happened Next*, is last of nine volumes of Ethel's autobiography.

10. In *A Sketch of the Past*, Woolf's mother is compared to a "vase" or "bowl that one fills and fills and fills . . ."

11. This apocryphal phrase is similar to that used in Virginia's suicide notes to Leonard (L6, Mar.18'41, and Mar.28'41).

12. Dr. Octavia Wilberforce was Woolf's physician in Rodmell.

13. The short story, "The Legacy," about a married woman who commits suicide to "rejoin" her dead lover, is in: *The Complete Shorter Fiction of Virginia Woolf*, ed. S. Dick.

14. Indulging in food while alone, a rare occurrence for Woolf who generally ate frugally, suggests a sense of emotional isolation and a need for succorance.

15. Vita did indeed lecture at Rodmell on February 18. Vita, Enid, and Woolf met for lunch, but Enid wanted to be alone with Vita, which deeply wounded Woolf.

16. This image evokes Abel Pargiter's mutilated fingers: "The muscles of his right hand resembled the shriveled claw of an aged bird" (*The Pargiters*, 13), and suggests feelings of castration, loss of creative power.

17. Leaska (1983) suggests Woolf incorporated in her novel a "private code to Vita which carried the message of love, hate, lust, infidelity, fear and death. Only Vita was meant to decipher the message" (Leaska, 12).

18. It is not at all clear why Giles was jealous of and threatened by the tenuous liaison between Isa and William since he perceives William as effeminate. More likely, inasmuch as in this novel all the world is a stage, we are in and out of reality, and sapphism is linked to Isa, William is female.

19. Is Woolf here alluding to sexual victimization of children?

20. Woolf's "creative power" did not sufficiently modulate her drift towards death.

21. Miss LaTrobe reveals the unlived selves all secretly yearn for.

22. In Woolf's earlier manuscript, *Pointz Hall*, Giles and Isa "tore each other asunder" (Leaska, 1983, 188).

23. This Conradian theme, which also appears in *The Voyage Out, Night and Day,* and *The Years,* suggests we are all prone to dark, savage, primitive passions, all "secret sharers" as it were (Meyer, 1967, 158). We differ, of course, in our ability to resist these degradations.

24. During 1940, Leonard gave a series of lectures at the Brighton Workers' Educational Association on "Causes and Issues of the War" (D5, 244, n.2).

25. "It's the curse of writers to want praise so much and be cast down by blame or indifference. The only sensible course is to remember that writing is after all what one does best, that any other work would seem a waste of life, that on the whole I get infinite pleasure from it, that I make 100 pounds a year, and that some people like what I write" (D1, Nov.13'18).

"E.M. Forster says *The Years* is dead and disappointing . . . ; all the lights sank; my reed bent to the ground. So I'm found out and that odious rice pudding of a book is what I thought it, a dank failure. No life in it. Now this pain awoke me at 4 a.m. and I suffered acutely, but the delight of being exploded is quite real. One feels braced for some reason, amused, round, combative, more than by praise" (L5, Apr.2'37).

26. Sending her completed work to Lehmann was an unusual procedure for Woolf since Leonard generally read her manuscript first.

27. Woolf's need to communicate and receive feedback from her "collective audience," of importance to her emotional equilibrium and self-regard, was cut off at this time.

28. In *Mrs. Dalloway* and *To the Lighthouse*, the metaphor of "drowning sailor" is prelude to death.

29. Bulimia is excessive, morbid hunger, leading to gorging of food, an intense craving for love and aggressive need to devour, its unconscious basis (Alexander, 94).

30. Dr. Octavia Wilberforce Correspondence: unpublished letter from Dr. Wilberforce to Virginia Woolf, Jan. 3, 1941. University of Sussex Library.

31. Sputter: "to eject something with a spitting noise or in an explosive way", Webster's *New International Dictionary of the English Language.* These are infantile sounds or expostulations, actually in response to overfeeding or forced feeding.

32. Leonard is indeterminate as to the date. Virginia's first suicide note was written on March 18, 1941.

33. After Woolf's suicide, Dr. Wilberforce wrote Elizabeth Robins: "I so wish now that I'd gone over more often and tried to get hold of her more as a friend. But as you know, I'm shy so I always felt her aloofness and I had a horror of possibly boring that highly intellectual, cultivated mind so I consciously rationed myself of visits." Dr. Octavia Wilberforce Correspondence, unpublished letter from Dr. Wilberforce to Elizabeth Robins, March 28, 1941, University of Sussex Library.

Chapter XV

1. Pollack claims the ultimate aim of art is to conquer death or fear of death, achieve immortality. Gediman suggests the creative process involves mourning former aspects of the self, working through of depressive fantasies, repairing early losses.

2. Woolf's theory of the "undermind" or preconscious, synchronizes with psychoanalytic concepts concerning the creative imagination. Ehrenzweig (1967) suggests all artistic structures employ preconscious "scanning" processes.

3. See Shneidman (1979) who has written at length on suicide: and Litman and Tabachnik.

4. Leonard might not have been able to assume an authoritative role in his wife's present illness because of her violent reaction to him during her manic episode in 1915.

5. It is of interest that Virginia wrote Ethel on January 12, 1941, that Leonard did not wish her to stay overnight at Ethel's, did not care for the separation involved. Yet on March 10, 1941, Virginia wrote Ethel, inviting herself over, "how damnable these separations (referring to herself and Ethel) are. Shall I come down for a night"?—but Ethel was now involved with a new lover.

6. Psychoanalytic writers differ in their conceptions of the dynamics of depression and suicide. Bibring sees a "primary ego state" of helplessness and crisis in self-esteem as central mechanisms in the dynamics of depression; Gaylin feels Bibring is describing the loss of trust in one's own ego, in its ability to meet and solve problems essential to survival; Brenner considers depression a response

to the "unconscious memory of a childhood disaster" and its revival in the present. Individual features of the "disaster" vary considerably and may encompass object loss, narcissistic injury, guilt and despair (32); Asch views depression as a reactive helplessness, an "affective response to unconscious submission to a passive-masochistic role," death as substitute for the ambivalently loved, lost parent (53); oral envy, sharp oscillations in self-esteem, aggression towards and identification with the frustrating parent or partner, are salient characteristics of depression, according to Stone (359).

7. Virginia Woolf: "Summer's Night," in *The Moment and Other Essays*, 4.

8. On March 1, 1941, Woolf revised her short story, "The Symbol," concerning a woman who observed a mountain climbing expedition, then sees the young men, one of whom she vaguely knew, "swallowed by a crevasse." The story evokes the traumatic death of Julian and of course alludes to Woolf's father, an intrepid mountain climber. In this, one of Woolf's last stories, she reintroduces the theme of wishing one's sick parent dead. After her mother's death, the narrator of the story felt only then could she marry. Is Woolf belatedly confessing she wanted her mother to die and wanted her father, whom she devotedly took care of for two years following his abdominal operation, also to die and not interfere with her growth? Or, does she wish to rejoin him in death? One of Woolf's heroines jumped from a mountain to drown in the sea below.

The holograph version of "The Symbol" suggests the desire, should one arrive at the summit of the mountain, to die in the "crater" at the top which apparently resembles a "spot on the moon." Bowl-shaped, "crater" suggests maternal enclosure, but at the mouth of a volcano! To be buried in a "crevasse" or "crater" in the mountain suggests a reunion of sorts with mother and father. "The Symbol": in *The Complete Shorter Fiction of Virginia Woolf*, ed .S. Dick.

9. Loss or diminution of a close personal relationship, evocative of early deprivation, disappointment and trauma, can lead to severe depression, particularly in those who are ambivalent towards the love object. Idealization and inability to perceive the basic personality of the object, viewing him/her as powerful or omnipotent, is frequently concomitant to devaluation of the self.

10. Fenichel, 401.

11. Jacobson (1970), 231.

Bibliography

Abraham, K. (1953). "Notes on the Psychoanalytic Investigation of Manic-depressive Insanity and Allied Conditions" (1911). In: *Selected Papers on Psychoanalysis.* New York: Basic Books.

Abraham, K. (1953). "The Influence of Oral Erotism on Character Formation" (1924). In: *Selected Papers on Psychoanalysis,* New York: Basic Books.

Alexander, F. (1950). Psychosomatic Medicine. New York: W.W. Norton

Alvarez, A. (1972). *The Savage God.* New York: Random House.

Annan, N. (1984). *Leslie Stephen: The Godless Victorian.* New York: Random House.

Arieti, S. (1974). "Affective Disorders: Manic-Depressive Psychosis and Psychotic Depression." In: *American Handbook of Psychiatry,* vol. 3, New York: Basic Books.

Arlow, J. (1979). "Metaphor and the Psychoanalytic Situation." *Psychoanalytic Quarterly,* 48, 363-385.

Asch, S. (1980). "Suicide and the Hidden Executioner." *International Review of Psychoanalysis,* 7, 51-60.

Auerbach, E. (1953). "The Brown Stocking." In: *Mimesis, the Representation of Reality in Western Literature.* Princeton: Princeton University Press.

Baudry, F. (1980). "Examination of Metaphor in Virginia Woolf's *A Sketch of the Past"* (Paper delivered at symposium on "Psychoanalysis and Literature").

Baudry, F. (1984). "An Essay on Method in Applied Psychoanalysis. *Psychoanalytic Quarterly,* 43, 551-581.

Bazin, N. (1973). *Virginia Woolf and the Androgynous Vision.* New Brunswick, New Jersey: Rutgers University Press.

Beja, M. (1970), ed. *Virginia Woolf: To the Lighthouse.* London: MacMillan.

Beja, M. (1965). "Matches struck in the dark: Virginia Woolf's moments of vision." *Critical Quarterly,* 6, 210-230.

Bell, Alan (1977), ed. and Introduction. *Sir Leslie Stephen's Mausoleum Book.* Oxford: Clarendon Press.

Bell, Anne O. (1977–1984), ed., prefaces & commentaries, *The Diaries of Virginia Woolf*, vols. 1–5 (1915–1941). New York and London: Harcourt, Brace, Jovanovich.

Bell, Clive (1957). "Virginia Woolf." In: *Old Friends, Personal Recollections.* New York: Harcourt, Brace, Jovanovich.

Bell, Clive (1972). In: *Recollections of Virginia Woolf.* Joan Noble, ed. New York: William Morrow.

Bell, Quentin (1968). *Bloomsbury.* London: Weidenfeld and Nicolson.

Bell, Quentin (1972). *Virginia Woolf: A Biography*, vols. 1–2. New York: Harcourt, Brace, Jovanovich.

Bell, Quentin (1984). "A Radiant Friendship," *Critical Inquiry*, 10, 557–566.

Bell, Quentin (1985). "Critical Response: Reply to J. Marcus," *Critical Inquiry* 11, 498–501.

Bell, Vanessa (1974). *Notes on Virginia's Childhood*, ed. R.J. Schaubeck. New York: Frank J. Hallman.

Bellak, L. (1958). *Schizophrenia: A Review of the Syndrome.* New York: Logos Press.

Bergler, E. (1954). *The Writer and Psychoanalysis.* New York: Robert Brunner.

Bibring, E. (1953). "The Mechanisms of Depression." In: *Affective Disorders.* P. Greenacre, ed. New York: International Universities Press.

Black, N. (1983) "Virginia Woolf and the Women's Movement." In: *Virginia Woolf: A Feminist Slant*, J. Marcus, ed. Lincoln: University of Nebraska Press.

Bloom, H. (1973). *The Anxiety of Influence.* New York: Oxford University Press.

Blos, Peter (1967). "Second Individuation in Adolescence." *Psychoanalytic Study of the Child*, 22, 162–187. New York: International Universities Press.

Blos, Peter (1979). *The Adolescent Passage: Developmental Issues.* New York: International Universities Press.

Blum, H.P. (1976). "Masochism, the Ego Ideal, and the Psychology of Women," *Journal of the American Psychoanalytic Association*, 24, 157–192.

Blum, H.P. (1980). "The Prototype of Preoedipal Reconstruction." In: *Rapprochement: The Critical Subphase of Separation-Individuation*. R. Lax, S. Bach and J.A. Burland, eds. New York: Jason Aronson.

Bodkin, M. (1963). *Archetypal Patterns in Poetry*. London: Oxford University Press.

Bowlby, J. (1969–1980). *Attachment and Loss*, vols. 1–3. New York: Basic Books.

Brenner, C. (1974). "Depression, Anxiety and Affect Theory," *International Journal of Psychoanalysis*, 55, 25–32.

Bruch, H. (1979). *The Golden Cage; The Enigma of Anorexia Nervosa*. New York: Random House.

Bruch, H. (1973). *Eating Disorders*. New York: Basic Books.

Carroll, B.A. (1978). "To Crush Him in Our Own Country: The Political Thought of Virginia Woolf," *Feminist Studies*, 4, 99–131.

Chassaguet-Smirgel, J. (1964). "Feminine Guilt and the Oedipus Complex." In: *Female Sexuality*, J. Chassaguet-Smirgel, ed., Ann Arbor: University of Michigan Press.

Chodorow, N. (1978). *The Reproduction of Mothering*. Berkeley, Los Angeles and London, University of California Press.

Chrzanowski, G. (1974). "Neurasthenia and Hypochondriasis." In: *American Handbook of Psychiatry*. S. Arieti and E. Brody, eds. New York: Basic Books.

Coen, S. (1982a). "Essay on the relationship of author and reader: transference implications for psychoanalytic literary criticism." *Psychoanalysis and Contemporary Thought*, 5, 3–15.

Coen, S. (1982b). "L.F. Celine's *Castle to Castle*: the author-reader relationship in its narrative style." *American Imago*, 39, 343–368.

Coen, S. (1984). "The author and his audience: Jean Genet's early work." *Psychoanalytic Study of Society*, 10, 301–320.

Cumings, M.F. (1970). "*Night and Day*: Virginia Woolf's Visionary Synthesis of Reality," *Modern Fiction Studies*, 18, 339–349.

DeSalvo, L. (1981). "Shakespeare's Other Sister." In: *New Feminist Essays on Virginia Woolf*, 61–81. Lincoln: University of Nebraska Press.

DeSalvo, L. (1981). *Virginia Woolf's First Voyage: A Novel in the Making*. Totowa, New Jersey: Ronman and Littlefield.

DeSalvo, L. (1982). *Melymbrosia by Virginia Woolf*. New York: New York Public Library.

DeSalvo, L. (1983). "1897: Virginia Woolf at Fifteen." In: *Virginia Woolf: A Feminist Slant*, Jane Marcus, ed. Lincoln: University of Nebraska Press.

DeSalvo, L. and Leaska, M. (1985). eds.: *Letters of Vita Sackville-West to Virginia Woolf*. New York: William Morrow.

Deutsch, H. (1937). "Absence of Grief." In: *Neuroses and Character Types* (1965). New York: International Universities Press.

Deutsch, H. (1944). *The Psychology of Women: A Psychoanalytic Interpretation*, vols. 1-2. New York: Grune and Stratton.

Dick, S. (1985). ed. and Introduction, *The Complete Shorter Fiction of Virginia Woolf*. New York: Harcourt, Brace, Jovanovich.

Dooley, L. (1920). "Psychoanalysis of the Character and Genius of Emily Brontë," *American Journal of Psychology*, 31, 208-239.

Dorpat, T. (1977). "Depressive Affect." In: *Psychoanalytic Study of the Child*, 32, 3-28. New York: International Universities Press.

Edel, L. (1953). *Henry James: The Untried Years*, vol. 1. Philadelphia and New York: Lippincott.

Edel, L. (1955). *The Psychological Novel*. Philadelphia and New York: Lippincott.

Edel, L. (1959). *Literary Biography*. New York: Doubleday.

Edel, L. (1979). *Bloomsbury, A House of Lions*. Philadelphia and New York: Lippincott.

Edel, L. (1982). *Stuff of Sleep and Dreams: Experiments in Literary Psychology*. New York: Harper and Row.

Edel, L. (1984). *Writing Lives: Principia Biographica*. New York: W.W. Norton.

Ehrenzweig, A. (1967). *The Hidden Order of Art*. Berkeley and Los Angeles: University of California Press.

Eisenbud, R.J. (1982). "Early and Later Determinants of Lesbian Choice." *Psychoanalytic Review*, 69, 85-110.

Erikson, E. (1950). *Childhood and Society*. New York: W.W. Norton.

Erikson, E. (1968). *Identity, Youth and Crisis*. New York: W.W. Norton.

Fenichel, C. (1945). *Psychoanalytic Theory of Neurosis*. New York: W.W. Norton.

Fleishman, A. (1975). *Virginia Woolf: A Critical Reading*. Baltimore and London: John Hopkins University Press.

Forster, E.M. (1927). *Aspects of the Novel*. New York: Harcourt, Brace.

Forster, E.M. (1941). *Virginia Woolf*. Cambridge, England: Cambridge University Press.

Frank, J. (1958). "Spatial Form in Modern Fiction." In: *Criticism: The Foundations of Modern Literary Judgement*. M. Schorer, J. Miles, and G. McKenzie, eds. New York: Harcourt, Brace and Company.

Freedman, R. (1980) "The Form of Fact and Fiction: *Jacob's Room* as Paradigm": In: *Virginia Woolf: Revaluation and Continuity*, R. Freedman, ed. Berkeley, Los Angeles and London: University of California Press.

Freud, A. (1958). "Adolescence." *Psychoanalytic Study of the Child*, 13, 255–279. New York: International Universities Press.

Freud, S. (1905). "Three Essays on the Theory of Sexuality." *Standard Edition*, 7, 173–230. London: Hogarth Press.

Freud, S. (1914). "Remembering, Repeating and Working Through," *Standard Edition*, 12, 145–156. London: Hogarth Press.

Freud, S. (1910). "Creative Writers and Daydreaming," *Standard Edition*, 9, 141–154. London: Hogarth Press.

Freud, S. (1910). "Leonardo DaVinci and a Memory of His Childhood." *Standard Edition*, 11, 59–138. London: Hogarth Press.

Freud, S. (1917). "Mourning and Melancholia." *Standard Edition*, 14, 237–260. London: Hogarth Press.

Freud, S. (1920). "The Psychogenesis of a Case of Homosexuality in a Woman." *Standard Edition* (1955), 18, 145–172. London: Hogarth Press.

Freud, S. (1923). "The Ego and the Id". *Standard Edition*, 19, 3–67. London: Hogarth Press.

Freud, S. (1924). "The Economic Problem of Masochism. *Standard Edition*, 19, 157–190. London: Hogarth Press.

Freud, S. (1925). "Some Psychical Consequences of the Anatomical Distinction Between the Sexes." *Standard Edition*, 19, 243–258. London: Hogarth Paress.

Freud, S. (1928). "Doestoevski and Parricide." *Standard Edition*, 21, 177–198. London: Hogarth Press.

Freud, S. (1930). "Civilization and Its Discontents." *Standard Edition*, 21, 59–145. London: Hogarth Press.

Freud, S. (1931). "Female Sexuality." *Standard Edition*, 21, 223–243. London: Hogarth Press.

Freud, S. (1933). "Femininity." *Standard Edition*, 22, 112–135. London: Hogarth Press.

Friedman, N. (1955). "The Waters of Annihilation: Double Vision in *To The Lighthouse.*" *Journal of English Literary History*, 22, 61–79.

Fromm-Reichmann, F. (1949). "An Intensive Study of Twelve Cases of Manic-Depressive Psychoses." In: *Psychoanalysis and Psychotherapy* (1959). Toronto, London and Chicago: University of Chicago Press.

Fry, R. (1920). *Vision and Design*. New York: New American Library.

Fry, R. (1926). *Transformations*. New York: Doubleday Anchor (1956).

Frye, N. (1957). *Anatomy of Criticism*. Princeton: Princeton University Press.

Galenson, E. and Roiphe, H. (1976). "Some Suggested Revisions Concerning Early Female Development." *Journal of the American Psychoanalytic Association*, 24, 29–58.

Galenson, E. (1971). "A Consideration of the Nature of Thought in Childhood Play." In: *Separation-Individuation*. J.B. McDevitt and C.F. Settlage, eds. New York: International Universities Press.

Garnett, A. (1985). *Deceived with Kindness: A Bloomsbury Childhood*. New York: Harcourt, Brace, Jovanovich.

Gaylin, W. (1968). "Psychoanalytic Contributions to the Understanding of Depression": *The Meaning of Despair*. New York: Science House.

Gediman, H.E. (1975). "Reflections on Romanticism, Narcissism, and Creativity." *Journal of the American Psychoanalytic Association*, 23, 407–423.

Gedo, J. (1983). *Portraits of the Artist: Psychoanalysis of Creativity and its Vicissitudes*. New York: Guilford Press.

Gero, G. (1968). "An Equivalent of Depression: Anorexia." In: *Affective Disorders*. New York: International Universities Press.

Gilbert, S.M. and Gubar, S. (1980). *The Madwoman in the Attic*. New Haven and London: Yale University Press.

Gindin, J. (1981). "Method in the Biographical Study of Virginia Woolf." *Biography*, 4, 96–107.

Glendenning, V. (1983). *Vita: A Biography of Vita Sackville-West*. New York: Alfred Knopf.

Goldstein, J. (1975). "The Woolfs' Response to Freud." *Psychoanalytic Quarterly*, 43, 438–476.

Gordon, L. (1984). *Virginia Woolf: A Writer's Life*. New York: W.W. Norton.

Gorsky, S. (1972). "The Central Shadow: Characterization in *The Waves*." *Modern Fiction Studies*, 18, 449–466.

Graham, J. (1949). "Time in the Novels of Virginia Woolf," *University of Toronto Quarterly*, 18, 186–201.

Graham, J. (1970). "Point of View in *The Waves*: Some Services of the Style." *University of Toronto Quarterly*, 39, 193–211.

Greenacre, P. (1957). "The Childhood of the Artist: Libidinal Phase Development and Giftedness." In: *Emotional Growth*, vol. 2, 479-504. New York: International Universities Press (1971).

Greenacre, P. (1958). "The Family Romance of the Artist." In: *Emotional Growth*, vol. 2, 505-532. New York: International Universities Press (1971).

Greenacre, P. (1958). "Woman as Artist." In: *Emotional Growth*, vol. 2, 575-591. New York: International Universities Press (1971).

Greenson, R. (1965). "The Problem of Working Through." In: *Explorations in Psychoanalysis*. New York: International Universities Press (1978)

Griffin, G. (1981). "Braving the Mirror: Virginia Woolf as Autobiographer," *Biography*, 4, 108-118.

Guiguet, J. (1962). *Virginia Woolf and Her Works*. New York and London: Harcourt, Brace, Jovanovich.

Handelman, S. (1980). "Intimate Distance: The Boundary of Life and Art in *To the Lighthouse*." *International Review of Psychoanalysis*, vol. 7, 41-50.

Hartmann, H. (1964). *Essays on Ego Psychology*. New York: International Universities Press.

Hartman, G.H. (1960). "Virginia's Web," *Chicago Review*, 3, 20-32.

Heilbrun, C. (1983). "Virginia Woolf in Her Fifties." In: *Virginia Woolf: A Feminist Slant*, J. Marcus, ed. Lincoln: University of Nebraska Press.

Heilbrun, C. (1973). *Towards a Recognition of Androgyny: Aspects of Male and Female in Literature*. New York: Knopf.

Hendin, H. (1982). *Suicide in America*. New York: W.W. Norton.

Hill, K. (1981). "Virginia Woolf and Leslie Stephen: History and Literary Revolution." *Publication of Modern Language Association*, 97, 351-361.

Hoffman, C. (1968). "From Short Story to Novel: The Manuscript Revisions of *Mrs. Dalloway*." *Modern Fiction Studies*, 16, 171-186.

Hoffman, C.G. (1968). "Fact and Fantasy in *Orlando*: Virginia Woolf's Manuscript Revisions." *Texas Studies in Literature and Language*, 10, 435-444.

Hoffman, C.G. (1969). "Virginia Woolf's Manuscript Revisions of *The Years*." *Publication of the Modern Language Association*, 84, 79-89.

Holland, N. (1968). *The Dynamics of Literary Response*, New York: Oxford University Press.

Holland, N. (1982). "Why this is transference, nor am I out of it." *Psychoanalysis and Contemporary Thought*, 5, 27–33.

Holroyd, M. (1967–1968). *Lytton Strachey: A Critical Biography*, vols. 1–2, New York, Chicago and San Francisco: Holt, Rinehart and Winston.

Holt, R.H. (1967). "The Development of the Primary Process." In: *Motives and Thought*, R.R. Holt, ed. New York: International Universities Press.

Horney, K. (1967). *Feminine Psychology*. H. Kelman, ed. New York: W.W. Norton.

Hulcoop, J. (1971). "Virginia Woolf's Diaries." *Bulletin of the New York Public Library*, 74, 301–310.

Hyman, V. (1980). "Concealment and Disclosure in *Sir Leslie Stephen's Mausoleum Book*." *Biography*, 3, 121–131.

Hyman, V. (1983). "Reflections in the Looking Glass: Leslie Stephen and Virginia Woolf." *Journal of Modern Literature*, 10, 197–216.

Hyman, V. (1983). "The Autobiographical Present in *A Sketch of the Past*. *Psychoanalytic Review*, 70, 24–32.

Jacobson, E. (1951). "Adolescent Moods and the Remodelling of Psychic Structures in Adolescence." *Psychoanalytic Study of the Child*, 16, 164–183. New York: International Universities Press.

Jacobson, E. (1953). "Contribution to the Metaphysychology of Cyclothymic Depression." In: *Affective Disorders*. New York: International Universities Press (1968).

Jacobson, E. (1971). *Depression: Comparative Studies of Normal, Neurotic and Psychotic Conditions*. New York: International Universities Press.

Jensen, V.N. and Petty, T.A. (1958). "The Fantasy of Being Rescued in Suicide." *Psychoanalytic Quarterly*, 27, 327–339.

Johnstone, J.K. (1954). *The Bloomsbury Group*. London: Secker and Warburg.

Jones, E. (1920). *Treatment of the Neuroses: Psychotherapy from Rest-Cure to Psychoanalysis*. New York: Schocken (1963).

Jones, E. (1935). "Early Female Sexuality." *International Journal of Psychoanalysis*, 16, 263–273.

Kenney, S.M. (1975). "Two Endings: Virginia Woolf's Suicide and *Between the Acts*." *University of Toronto Quarterly*, 44, 265–289.

Kenney, S.M. and Kenney, E.J. (1982). "Virginia Woolf and the Art of Madness." *Massachusetts Review*, 23, 161–185.

Kernberg, O. (1975). *Borderline Conditions and Pathological Narcissism.* New York: Jason Aronson.

Kleeman, J. (1976). "Freud's Views on Early Female Sexuality in the Light of Direct Child Observation." *Journal of the American Psychoanalytic Association*, 24, 3–28.

Klein, M. (1928). "Early Stages of the Oedipal Conflict." In: *Psychoanalysis of Children.* New York: Grove (1960), 179–209.

Klein, M. (1934). "Contribution to the Psychogenesis of Manic-Depressive States." In: *Contributions to Psychoanalysis.* (1948). London: Hogarth Press.

Kohut, H. (1971). *The Analysis of the Self.* New York International Universities Press.

Kohut, H. (1975). *The Restoration of the Self.* New York: International Universities Press.

Kohut, H. and Wolf, E. (1978). "The Disorders of the Self and Their Treatment." *International Journal of Psychoanalysis*, 59, 413–427.

Kris, E. (1952). *Psychoanalytic Explorations in Art.* New York: International Universities Press.

Kris, E. (1956a). "On Some Vicissitudes of Insight in Psychoanalysis." *International Journal of Psychoanalysis*, 37, 445–455.

Kris, E. (1956b). "The Recovery of Childhood Memories." *Psychoanalytic Study of the Child*, 11. New York: International Universities Press.

Kubie, L. (1974). "The Drive to Become Both Sexes." *Psychoanalytic Quarterly*, 43, 349–426.

Laing, R. (1965). *The Divided Self.* Baltimore: Penguin Books.

Lampl-DeGroot, J. (1960). "On Adolescence." *Psychoanalytic Study of the Child*, 15, 95–103. New York: International Universities Press.

Laufer, M. (1966). "Object Loss and Mourning During Adolescence." *Psychoanalytic Study of the Child*, 21, 269–293. New York: International Universities Press.

Leaska, M.A. (1970). *Virginia Woolf's Lighthouse: A Study in Critical Method.* New York: Columbia University Press.

Leaska, M.A. (1977a). *The Novels of Virginia Woolf: From Beginning to End.* New York: John Jay Press.

Leaska, M.A. (1977b). *The Pargiters: The Novel-Essay Portion of The Years.* New York: Harcourt, Brace, Jovanovich.

Leaska, M.A. (1977c). "Virginia Woolf, The Pargiter." *Bulletin of the New York Public Library*, 80, 172-210.

Leaska, M.A. (1979). "Holograph and Typescripts of *The Voyage Out.*" In: *Bulletin of Research in the Humanities*, 328-337, New York Public Library, Berg Collection.

Leaska, M.A. (1983). *Virginia Woolf: Pointz Hall*, New York: Universal Publications.

Lehmann, J. (1972). "Essay on Virginia Woolf." In: *Recollections of Virginia Woolf.* J.R. Noble, ed. New York: William Morrow.

Lehmann, J. (1975). *Virginia Woolf and Her World.* New York and London: Harcourt Brace Jovanovich.

Lehmann, J. (1978). *Thrown to the Woolfs.* New York: Holt, Rinehart and Winston.

Lewin, B. (1950). "The Psychoanalysis of Elation." *The Psychoanalytic Quarterly, Inc.* New York.

Lewis, W. (1934). *Men Without Art.* London: Cassell.

Lichtenstein, H. (1961). "Identity and Sexuality," *Journal of the American Psychoanalytic Association*, 5, 179-234.

Lilienfeld, J. (1981). "The Ramsay's Marriage in *To the Lighthouse.*" In: *New Feminist Essays on Virginia Woolf*, ed. J. Marcus, Lincoln: University of Nebraska Press.

Litman, R. and Tabachnick, N.D. (1968). "Psychoanalytic Theories of Suicide." In: *Suicidal Behavior: Diagnosis and Management.* H.L.P. Resnick, ed. Boston: Little Brown and Company.

Love, Jean. (1977). *Virginia Woolf: Sources of Madness and Art.* Berkeley, Los Angeles, and London: University of California Press.

Mahler, M. (1966). "Notes on the Development of Basic Mood. The Depressive Affect." In: *Psychoanalysis: A General Psychology*, ed. R.M. Lowenstein. New York: International Universities Press.

Mahler, M., Pine, F. and Bergman, A. (1975). *The Psychological Birth of the Human Infant.* New York: Basic Books.

Maltsberger, J.T. and Buie, D.H. (1980). "The Devices of Suicide." *International Review of Psychoanalysis*, 7, 61-72.

Marcus, J. (1977a). "*The Years* as Greek Drama, Domestic Novel and Gotterdammerung." *Bulletin of the New York Public Library*, 80, 276-301.

Marcus, J. (1977b). "Pargeting the Pargiters." *Bulletin of the New York Public Library*, 80, 416–435.

Marcus, J. (1977c). "No More Horses." *Women's Studies*, 4, 265–290.

Marcus, J. (1981). "Thinking Back Through Our Mothers." In: *New Feminist Essays on Virginia Woolf*. J. Marcus, ed. Lincoln and London: University of Nebraska Press.

Marcus, J. (1983). ed. and Introduction: "Virginia Woolf Aslant." In: *Virginia Woolf: A Feminist Slant*. Lincoln: University of Nebraska Press.

Marcus, J. (1985). "Quentin's Bogey." In: *Critical Inquiry*, 11, 686–497.

Marder, H. (1968). *Feminism and Art: A Study of Virginia Woolf*. Toronto, Chicago and London: University of Chicago Press.

McClelland, D. (1963). "The Harlequin Complex." In: *The Study of Lives*. R.W. White, ed. New York: Prentice-Hall. ed. Ann Arbor: University

McDevitt, J. (1980). "The Role of Internalization in the Development of Object Relations During the Separation-Individuation Phase." In: *Rapprochement: The Critical Subphase of Separation-Individuation*. 135–150. New York: Jason Aronson.

McDougall, J. (1970). "Homosexuality in Women." In: *Female Sexuality: New Psychoanalytic Views*, J. Chasseguet-Smirgel, ed. Ann Arbor: University of Michigan Press.

McDougall, J. (1980). *Plea for a Measure of Abnormality*. New York: International Universities Press.

McLaughlin, A.L. "An Uneasy Sisterhood: Virginia Woolf and Katherine Mansfield." In: *Virginia Woolf: A Feminist Slant*, J. Marcus, ed. Lincoln: University of Nebraska Press.

McLaurin, A. (1973). *Virginia Woolf: The Echoes Enslaved*. Cambridge, England: Cambridge University Press.

Meyer, B. (1979). Book Review: *Virginia Woolf's Source of Madness*, by J. Love. In: *Contemporary Psychology*, 24, 124–126.

Meyer, B. (1967). *Joseph Conrad: A Psychoanalytic Biography*. Princeton: Princeton University Press.

Middleton, V. (1977). "*The Years*: A Deliberate Failure," *Bulletin of the New York Public Library*, 80, 158–171.

Miller, A. (1984). *Thou Shalt Not Be Aware: Society's Betrayal of the Child*. New York: Farrar, Strous, Giroux.

Miller, H. (1982). *Fiction and Repetition*, Cambridge, Massachusetts: Harvard University Press.

Miller, J.B.M. (1971). "Children's Reactions to the Death of a Parent: A Review of the Psychoanalytic Literature." *Journal of the American Psychoanalytic Association*, 19, 697–719.

Moore, G.E. (1903). *Principia Ethica*. Cambridge, England: Cambridge University Press.

Moore, M. (1981). "Some Female Versions of the Pastoral: *The Voyage Out* and Matriarchal Mythology." *New Feminist Essays on Virginia Woolf*, J. Marcus, ed. Lincoln: University of Nebraska Press.

Moore, M. (1984). *The Short Season Between Two Silences: The Mystical and the Political in the Novels of Virginia Woolf*. Boston and London: George Allena and Unwin.

Moulton, R. (1966). "Multiple Factors in Frigidity." In: *Sexuality of Women*. New York: Grune and Stratton.

Nacht, S. and Racamier, P.C. (1960). "Symposium on Depressive Illness. II. Depressive States." *International Journal of Psychoanalysis*, 41, 481–496.

Naremore, J. (1973). *The World Without a Self*. New Haven, Connecticut and London: Yale University Press.

Naremore, J. (1980). "Nature and History in *The Years*." In: *Virginia Woolf: Revaluation and Continuity*. R. Freedman, ed. London, Berkeley, Los Angeles: University of California Press.

Nicolson, N. (1973). *Portrait of a Marriage*. New York: Atheneum.

Nicolson, N. and Trautman, J., (1882–1941). eds., prefaces and commentaries. *The Letters of Virginia Woolf* (1975–1980) vols. 1–6. New York: Harcourt Brace Jovanovich.

Noy, P. (1978). "Insight and Creativity." *Journal of the American Psychoanalytic Association*, 26, 717–748.

Ozick, C. (1973). "Mrs. Virginia Woolf." *Commentary*, 56, 33–44.

Panel on Creativity (1972). (From 27th International Psychoanalytic Congress, Vienna, 1971). Reported by C. Kligerman, *International Journal of Psychoanalysis*, 53, 21–30.

Panken, S. (1973). *Joy of Suffering: Psychoanalytic Theory and Therapy of Masochism*. New York: Jason Aronson.

Panken, S. (1974–1975). "Some Psychodynamics in *Sons and Lovers*: A New Look at the Oedipal Theme," *Psychoanalytic Review* 61, 571–589.

Panken, S. (1983). "Working Through and the Novel," *Psychoanalytic Review*. 70, 4–23.

Parens, H., Pollack, L., Stern, J. and Kramer, S. (1976). "On the Girl's Entry Into the Oedipus Complex.'' *Journal of American Psychoanalytic Association.* 20 (suppl.), 79–108.

Patrick, C. (1937). "Creative Thought in Artists." *Journal of Psychology.* 4, 35–73.

Piaget, J. (1951). *Play, Dreams and Imitation in Childhood.* New York: W.W. Norton (1961).

Pippett, A. (1955). *The Moth and the Star: A Biography of Virginia Woolf.* Boston and Toronto: Little Brown.

Pollack, G. (1975). "On Mourning, Immortality and Utopia," *Journal of the American Psychoanalytic Association.* 23, 334–362.

Poole, R. (1978). *The Unknown Virginia Woolf,* Cambridge, England: Cambridge University Press.

Radin, G. (1981). *Virginia Woolf's The Years,* Knoxville: University of Tennessee Press.

Rantavaara, I. (1953). *Virginia Woolf and Bloomsbury.* Helsinki: Annales Academiae Scieniarum Fennicae.

Reed, G. (1984). ''Psychoanalysis, Psychoanalysis Appropriated and Applied.'' (American Psychoanalytic Association Mid-winter Conference.)

Richter, H. (1970). *The Inward Voyage.* Princeton: Princeton University Press.

Roiphe, H. and Galenson, E. (1981). *Infantile Origins of Sexual Identity.* New York: International Universities Press.

Roland, A., ed. (1978). *Psychoanalysis, Creativity and Literature: Towards a Reorientation of Psychoanalytic Literary Criticism.* New York: Columbia University Press.

Rose, Gilbert (1980). *The Power of Form: A Psychoanalytic Approach to Aesthetic Form.* New York: International Universities Press.

Rose, Phyllis (1978). *Woman of Letters: A Life of Virginia Woolf.* New York: Oxford University Press.

Rosenbaum, S.P. (1971). "The Philosophical Realism of Virginia Woolf." In: *English Literature and British Philosophy.* S.P. Rosenbaum, ed. Toronto, Chicago and London: University of Chicago Press.

Rosenthal, M. (1979). *Virginia Woolf.* New York: Columbia University Press.

Rothenberg, A. (1972). ''Poetic Process and Psychoanalysis.'' *Psychiatry,* 35, 238–254.

Ruddick, S. (1981). "Private Brother, Public World." In: *New Feminist Essays on Virginia Woolf,* J. Marcus, ed. Lincoln: University of Nebraska.

Salzman, L. (1970). "Depression: A Clinical Review." In: B. Masserman, *Depression: Theories and Therapies.* New York: Grune & Stratton.

Schafer, R. (1980). "Narration in the Psychoanalytic Dialogue," *Critical Inquiry,* 29–53.

Schlack, B.A. (1983). "Fathers in General: The Patriachy in Virginia Woolf's Fiction." In: *Virginia Woolf: A Feminist Slant.* J. Marcus, ed. Lincoln: University of Nebraska Press.

Schwartz, M. (1982). "The Literary Use of Transference," *Psychoanalysis and Contemporary Thought,* 5, 34–44.

Searles, H. (1960). *The Non-Human Environment.* New York: International University Press.

Shneidman, E.S., Farberow, N.L., Litman, R.E. (1970). *The Psychology of Suicide.* New York: Science House.

Shneidman, E.S. (1966). "Orientations Towards Death: A Vital Aspect of the Study of Lives." *International Journal of Psychiatry,* 2, 167–200.

Shneidman, E.S. and Farberow, N.L. (1961). *The Cry for Help.* New York: McGraw-Hill.

Showalter, E. (1977). "Virginia Woolf and the Flight into Androgyny." In: *A Literature of Their Own.* Princeton: Princeton University Press.

Silver, B. (1983). *Virginia Woolf's Reading Notebooks.* Princeton: Princeton University Press.

Silver, B. (1983). "*Three Guineas* Before and After." In: *Virginia Woolf: A Feminist Slant.* J. Marcus, ed. Lincoln: University of Nebraska Press.

Skura, M. (1982). *The Literary Use of the Psychoanalytic Process.* New Haven, Connecticut and London: Yale University Press.

Socarides, C. (1963). "The Historical Development of Theoretical and Clinical Concepts of Overt Female Homosexuality." *Journal of the American Psychoanalytic Association,* 11, 386–414.

Socarides, C. (1978). *Homosexuality.* New York: Jason Aronson.

Sophocles. "Antigone" and "Electra." D. Fitts and R. Fitzgerald, transl. In: *Greek Plays in Modern Translation.* D. Fitts, ed. New York: Dial Press (1947).

Sours, J.A. (1980). *Starving to Death in a Sea of Objects.* New York: Jason Aronson.

Spalding, F. (1983). *Vanessa Bell*. London: Weidenfeld and Nicolson.

Spater, G. and Parsons, I. (1977). *A Marriage of True Minds: An Intimate Portrait of Leonard and Virginia Woolf*. New York and London: Harcourt Brace Jovanovich.

Sperling, M. (1983). "A Revaluation of Classification, Concepts and Treatment of Anorexia Nervosa." In: *Fear of Being Fat: The Treatment of Anorexia Nervosa and Bulimia*. C.P. Wilson, ed. New York: Jasaon Aronson.

Spilka, M. (1980). *Virginia Woolf's Quarrel with Grieving*. Lincoln: University of Nebraska Press.

Spitz, R. (1965). *The First Year of Life: A Psychoanalytic Study of Normal and Deviant Development of Object Relations*. New York: International Universities Press.

Spitzer, R.L., Williams, J.B.W., Skodol, A.E. (1983). *International Perspectives on DSM-III.*, Washington, DC: American Psychiatric Press.

Sprague, C. (1971). Editor and Introduction: *Virginia Woolf: A Collection of Critical Essays*. Englewood-Cliffs, N.J.: Prentive Hall.

Squier, S. (1981). "The Politics of City Space in *The Years*." In: *New Feminist Essays on Virginia Woolf*. Lincoln: University of Nebraska Press.

Squier, S. (1983). *Virginia Woolf and London: The Sexual Politics of the City*. Chapel Hill and London: University of North Carolina Press.

Stansky, P. and Abrahams, W. (1966). *Journey to the Frontier*. Boston, and Toronto: Little Brown and Company.

Stephen, Julia (1883). *Notes from Sickrooms*. Orono, Maine: Puckerbrush Press (1980).

Stephen, L. *Selected Writings in British Intellectual History*. N. Annan, ed. Chicago and London: University of Chicago Press (1979).

Stephen, L. (1895). *Sir Leslie Stephen's Mausoleum Book*. A. Bell, ed. Oxford: Clarendon Press.

Stern, D. (1985). *The Interpersonal World of the Infant*. New York: Basic Books.

Stewart, W. and Grossman, W. (1976). "Penis Envy: From Childhood Wish to Developmental Metaphor." *Journal American Psychoanalytic Association*, 24, 193, 212.

Stoller, R. (1975). "Primary Femininity." *Journal of the American Psychoanalytic Association*, 24, 59–78.

Stone, L. (1986). "Psychoanalytic Observations on the Pathology of Depressive Illness." *Journal American Psychoanalytic Association*, 34, 329–362.

Strouse, L.W. (1981). "Virginia Woolf and Her "Voyage Out." *American Imago*, 38, 185-202.

Swinburne, A.C. (1949). "Itylus" (1886). In: *English Literature and its Background*, vol. 2, B.D. Grebanier, ed. New York: Dryden Press.

Sypher, W. (1962). *Loss of the Self in Modern Literature and Art*. New York: Random House.

Trilling, L. (1963). "Art and Neurosis." In: *Art and Psychoanalysis*. W. Phillips, ed. Cleveland, Ohio and New York: Meridian Books.

Trilling, L. (1966). "Freud and Literature." In: *Psychoanalysis and Literature*. H. Ruitenback, ed. New York: E.P. Dutton and Co.

Trombley, S. (1981). *All That Summer She Was Mad: Virginia Woolf and Her Doctors*. London: Junction Books.
VanBuren Kelley, A. (1971). *The Novels of Virginia Woolf: Fact and Vision*. Toronto, London and Chicago: University of Chicago Press.

Voth, H.M. (1970). "The Analysis of Metaphor." *Journal of the American Psychoanalytic Association*, 18, 599-621.

Waelder, R. (1936). "The Principle of Multiple Function." *Psychoanalytic Quarterly*, 15, 45-62.

Wilson, D. *Leonard Woolf: A Political Biography*. New York: St. Martin's Press.

Wilson, E. (1929). "Philoctetes: The Wound and the Bow." In: *The Wound and the Bow*. New York: Oxford University Press.

Wolf, E. and Wolf, I. (1979). "We Perished Each Alone: A Psychoanalytic Commentary on *To the Lighthouse*." *International Review of Psychoanalysis*, 6, 37-48.

Wolfenstein, M. (1966). "How is Mourning Possible?" *Psychoanalytic Study of the Child*, 21, 93-123. New York: International Universities Press.

Wolfenstein, M. (1969). "Loss, Rage and Repetition." *Psychoanalytic Study of the Child*, 24, 432-460. New York: International Universities Press.

Wolfenstein, M. (1973). "The Image of the Lost Parent." *Psychoanalytic Study of the Child*, 28, 433-456. New York: International Universities Press.

Woolf, L. and Strachey, J., eds. (1956). *Virginia Woolf/Lytton Strachey Letters* (1906-1931). New York: Harcourt, Brace and Company.

Woolf, L. (1914). *The Wise Virgins*. New York and London: Harcourt Brace Jovanovich (1979).

Woolf, L. (1911–1969). *Autobiography*, vols. 1–5. New York and London: Harcourt Brace Jovanovich.
vol. 1, 1960. *Sowing* 1880–1904 (Harvest).
vol. 2, 1961. *Growing*. 1904–1911 (Harvest).
vol. 3, 1963. *Beginning Again*. 1911–1918 (Harvest).
vol. 4, 1967. *Downhill All the Way*. 1919–1939 (Harvest).
vol. 5, 1967. *The Journey Not the Arrival Matters*, 1939–1969 (Harvest).

Woolf, V. (1915). *The Voyage Out*. New York: Harcourt Brace and World (1948). (Harvest).

Woolf, V. (1919). *Night and Day*. London: Hogarth Press.

Woolf, V. (1923). *Jacob's Room*. New York: Harcourt, Brace and World (1959). (Harvest.)

Woolf, V. (1925). *Mrs. Dalloway*. New York: Harcourt, Brace and World (1953). (Harvest.)

Woolf, V. (1927). *To the Lighthouse*. New York: Harcourt, Brace and World (1955). (Harvest.)

Woolf, V. (1928). *Orlando: A Biography*. New York: Harcourt Brace Jovanovich (1956). (Harvest.)

Wolf, V. (1931). *The Waves*. New York: Harcourt Brace and World (1959). (Harvest.)

Woolf, V. (1937). *The Years*. New York: Harcourt Brace Jovanovich (1965). (Harvest.)

Woolf, V. (1941). *Between the Acts*. New York: Harcourt Brace Jovanovich (1969). (Harvest.)

Woolf, V. (1954). *A Writer's Diary*. ed. L. Woolf, New York: Harcourt, Brace and Company.

Woolf, V. (1915–1941). *The Diaries of Virginia Woolf*, vols. 1–5, 1977–1984, Anne O. Bell, ed. New York: Harcourt Brace Jovanovich.
vol. 1. 1915–1919, (1977).
vol. 2. 1920–1924, (1978).
vol. 3. 1925–1930, (1980).
vol. 4. 1931–1935, (1982).
vol. 5. 1936–1941, (1984).

Woolf, V. (1882–1941). *The Letters of Virginia Woolf* (1975–1980). vols. 1–6, N. Nicolson and J. Trautman, eds. New York: Harcourt, Brace, Jovanovich.

vol. 1. 1888–1912 (1975) (Harvest.)
vol. 2. 1912–1922 (1976) (Harvest.)
vol. 3. 1923–1928 (1977) (Harvest.)
vol. 4. 1929–1931 (1978).
vol. 5. 1932–1935 (1979).
vol. 6. 1936–1941 (1980).

Woolf, V. (1929). *A Room of One's Own.* New York: Harcourt Brace and World (1957). (Harvest.)

Woolf, V. (1938). *Three Guineas.* New York: Harcourt, Brace, Jovanovich (1965). (Harvest.)

Woolf, V. (1932). *The Pargiters: A Novel-Essay.* M.A. Leaska, ed. New York: Harcourt, Brace, Jovanovich (1972). (Harvest.)

Woolf, V. (1942). *The Death of the Moth and Other Essays.* New York: Harcourt, Brace, Jovanovich (1972). (Harvest.)

Woolf, V. (1948). *The Moment and Other Essays.* New York: Harcourt, Brace, Jovanovich (1974). (Harvest.)

Woolf, V. (1950). *The Captain's Death Bed and Other Essays.* New York: Harcourt Brace Jovanovich. (Harvest.)

Woolf, V. (1958). *Granite and Rainbow: Essays.* New York: Harcourt Brace Jovanovich (1975). (Harvest.)

Woolf, V. (1979). *Women and Writing.* M. Barrett, ed. New York: Harcourt Brace Jovanovich. (Harvest.)

Wolf, V. (1965). *Contemporary Writers.* New York: Harcourt Brace Jovano vich. (Harvest.)

Woolf, V. (1976). *Moments of Being.* J. Schulkind, ed. New York: Harcourt Brace Jovanovich (1978). (Harvest.)

Woolf, V. (1985). *Moments of Being.* J. Schulkind, ed. New York: Harcourt Brace Jovanovich. (Harvest.)

Woolf, V. (1933). *Flush, A Biography.* New York: Harcourt Brace Jovanovich (1976). (Harvest.)

Woolf, V. (1944). *Mrs. Dalloway's Party.* S. McNichol, ed. New York: Harcourt Brace Jovanovich (1972). (Harvest.)

Woolf, V. (1921). *A Haunted House and Other Short Stories.* New York: Harcourt Brace Jovanovich (1972). (Harvest.)

Woolf, V. (1940). *Roger Fry.* New York: Harcourt Brace Jovanovich (1976). (Harvest.)

Woolf, V. (1948). *The Common Reader: First and Second Series.* New York: Harourt, Brace and Company.

Woolf, V. (1956). *Virginia Woolf/Lytton Strachey Letters.* Eds. L. Woolf and J.J. Strachey. New York: Harcourt, Brace and Company.

Woolf, V. *The Complete Shorter Fiction of Virginia Woolf,* (1985). S. Dick, ed. New York: Harcourt, Brace, Jovanovich.

Zwerdling, A. (1981). *"Jacob's Room*: Woolf's Satiric Elegy." *Modern Fiction,* 48, 894–913.

Zwerdling, A. (1977). *"Mrs. Dalloway* and the Social System." *Publication Language Association,* 92, 69–82.

Zwerdling, A. (1986). *Virginia Woolf and the Real World.* Berkeley, Los Angeles and London: University of California Press.

Unpublished references

Clive Bell Correspondence:
Letters from Clive Bell to Virginia Stephen, University of Sussex Library by Permission of Backsettown Trust.

Dr. Octavia Wilberforce Correspondence:
Letters from Dr. Octavia Wilberforce to Virginia Woolf, University of Sussex Library.

Letters from Dr. Octavia Wilberforce to Elizabeth Robins, University of Sussex Library by permission of Backsettown Trust.

Letters from Virginia Woolf to Julian Bell, University of Sussex Library.

Monk's House Papers, University of Sussex Library.

Letters from Ethel Smyth to Vanessa Bell, Kings College Library, Cambridge.

Virginia Woolf's early typescripts and holographs of *The Voyage Out, Jacob's Room, Mrs. Dalloway, To the Lighthouse, The Waves.* Berg Collection, New York Public Library.

Virginia Woolf: Autobiographical Fragment: 1940. Berg Collection, New York Public Library.

Virginia Woolf's unpublished diaries: 1897; 1903. Berg Collection, New York Public Library.

Leslie Stephen/Julia Stephen Correspondence. Berg Collection, New York
    Public Library.

Leslie Stephen/Stella Duckworth Correspondence. Berg Collection, New York
    Public Library.

Virginia Woolf: British Broadcasting Company Tape, London.

Index

Abraham, Karl, 270, 278
Affective disorder, 6, 85
Aggression: as writer, 103, 211, 232; personal expressions of, 39, 42, 44, 72, 252; in fiction, 80, 97, 134, 136, 202, 221-24, 244. *See also* Rage
Alter-ego, 37, 143, 243
Ambivalence: toward mother, 13, 16, 36, 178, 216; toward father, 42-44, 49, 180-81, 287n.14; in fiction, 263-65, 287-88
Androgyny, 173, 183, 488-89n.16
Annan, Noel: Leslie's father, 22; Leslie and Julia, 24; Leslie's accomplishments, 25; Leslie's instability, 29-30
Anon, 240
Anorexia: spurious identity, 50-51; control struggles, 68-69
Anrep, Helen: jealousy of Vanessa's friendship with, 232, 239, 255, 257-58
Antigone: alludes to in essay, 49; reads, 54; in fiction, 15, 220, 223, 228
Antisemitism: toward Leonard, 63, 291n.23; in fiction, 224, 230
Anxiety states: Woolf's proneness to, 5, 205, 273n.15
Archetype: Mrs. Ramsay as mythical mother, 1, 163

Arieti, Sylvano, 85, 278
Aristocracy: mother's connection to, 19; Violet Dickinson's friends, 45; meeting Vita Sackville-West, 116, 118
Arlow, Jacob: on metaphor, 17
Artist: openness, 3; making shape out of chaos, 3; art and personality, 6, 12; artistic conscience, 12; trembles as she writes, 58; "queer" individuality, 104; lonely and separated, 105; adventuring, 212. *See also* Creative process
Asheham House, 241
Aspasia, 63
Athenaeum, The, 91
Auerbach, Erich: random occurrence, 162, 286n.23

Baudry, Francis: text as modified free association, 8; Woolf's conception of reality, 11; on metaphor, 16
Bell, Angelica: *See* Garnett, Angelica
Bell, Clive: Thoby's Cambridge friend, 54; marriage to Vanessa, 55; flirtation with Virginia 56-58; reads *Melymbrosia* 58, 77; breakup of marriage, 60; reaction to Virginia's marriage, 60, 89; conscientious objector, 90; Vita and Clive, 144, 191; one of Virginia's six intimates, 194; prototype for